Feelings and Work in Modern History

History of Emotions

Series Editors: Peter N. Stearns, University Professor in the Department of History at George Mason University, USA, and Susan J. Matt, Presidential Distinguished Professor of History at Weber State University, USA.

Editorial Board: Rob Boddice, Senior Research Fellow, Academy of Finland Centre of Excellence in the History of Experiences, Tampere University, Finland

Charles Zika, University of Melbourne & Chief Investigator for the Australian Research Council's Centre for the History of Emotions, Australia
Pia Campeggiani, University of Bologna, Italy
Angelika Messner, Kiel University, Germany
Javier Moscoso, Centro de Ciencias Humanas y Sociales, Madrid, Spain

The history of emotions offers a new and vital approach to the study of the past. The field is predicated on the idea that human feelings change over time and they are the product of culture as well as of biology. Bloomsbury's History of Emotions series seeks to publish state-of-the-art scholarship on the history of human feelings and emotional experience from antiquity to the present day and across all seven continents. With a commitment to a greater thematic, geographical and chronological breadth, and a deep commitment to interdisciplinary approaches, it will offer new and innovative titles which convey the rich diversity of emotional cultures.

Published:
Fear in the German Speaking World, 1600–2000, edited by Thomas Kehoe and Michael Pickering (2020)

Forthcoming:
Emotions in the Ottoman Empire, by Nil Tekgül
Feeling Dis-Ease in Modern History, edited by Rob Boddice and Bettina Hitzer
The Business of Emotion in Modern History, edited by Andrew Popp and Mandy Cooper
The Renaissance of Feeling, by Kirk Essary

Feelings and Work in Modern History

Emotional Labour and Emotions about Labour

Edited by
Agnes Arnold-Forster and Alison Moulds

BLOOMSBURY ACADEMIC
LONDON • NEW YORK • OXFORD • NEW DELHI • SYDNEY

BLOOMSBURY ACADEMIC
Bloomsbury Publishing Plc
50 Bedford Square, London, WC1B 3DP, UK
1385 Broadway, New York, NY 10018, USA
29 Earlsfort Terrace, Dublin 2, Ireland

BLOOMSBURY, BLOOMSBURY ACADEMIC and the Diana logo are trademarks of
Bloomsbury Publishing Plc

First published in Great Britain 2022
This paperback edition published 2023

Copyright © Agnes Arnold-Forster and Alison Moulds, 2022

Agnes Arnold-Forster and Alison Moulds have asserted their right under the Copyright, Designs and Patents Act, 1988, to be identified as Editors of this work.

For legal purposes the Acknowledgements on pp. xi–xii constitute an extension of this copyright page.

Cover design: Terry Woodley
Cover image © John Drysdale/Keystone Features/Getty Images

All rights reserved. No part of this publication may be reproduced or transmitted in any form or by any means, electronic or mechanical, including photocopying, recording, or any information storage or retrieval system, without prior permission in writing from the publishers.

Bloomsbury Publishing Plc does not have any control over, or responsibility for, any third-party websites referred to or in this book. All internet addresses given in this book were correct at the time of going to press. The author and publisher regret any inconvenience caused if addresses have changed or sites have ceased to exist, but can accept no responsibility for any such changes.

A catalogue record for this book is available from the British Library.

Library of Congress Cataloging-in-Publication Data
Names: Arnold-Forster, Agnes, editor. | Moulds, Alison, editor.
Title: Feelings and work in modern history : emotional labour and emotions about labour / edited by Agnes Arnold-Forster and Alison Moulds.
Description: 1 Edition. | New York, NY : Bloomsbury Academic, 2022. | Series: History of emotions | Includes bibliographical references and index.
Identifiers: LCCN 2021031641 (print) | LCCN 2021031642 (ebook) | ISBN 9781350197183 (hardback) | ISBN 9781350197190 (pdf) | ISBN 9781350197206 (ebook)
Subjects: LCSH: Work–Psychological aspects. | Work environment–Psychological aspects. | Emotions. | Work-life balance.
Classification: LCC BF481 .F434 2022 (print) | LCC BF481 (ebook) | DDC 158.7–dc23
LC record available at https://lccn.loc.gov/2021031641
LC ebook record available at https://lccn.loc.gov/2021031642

ISBN: HB: 978-1-3501-9718-3
PB: 978-1-3501-9751-0
ePDF: 978-1-3501-9719-0
eBook: 978-1-3501-9720-6

Series: History of Emotions

Typeset by Deanta Global Publishing Services, Chennai, India

To find out more about our authors and books visit www.bloomsbury.com and sign up for our newsletters.

Contents

List of Figures   vii
List of Contributors   viii
Acknowledgements   xi

1   Introduction   *Agnes Arnold-Forster and Alison Moulds*   1

Part I   Spaces of labour

2   Emotions and sexuality at work: Lyons Corner Houses, c. 1920–50   *Grace Whorrall-Campbell*   19

3   Shop assistants, 'living-in' and emotional health, 1880s–1930s   *Alison Moulds*   37

4   The emotional landscape of the hospital residence in post-war Britain   *Agnes Arnold-Forster*   58

5   Negotiating deindustrialization: Emotions and Ahmedabad's textile workers   *Rukmini Barua*   76

Part II   Professional and personal identities

6   Education, work and self-worth in women's letters to Soviet authorities, 1924–32   *Hannah Parker*   99

7   Money, emotions and domestic service in Buenos Aires, 1950–70   *Inés Pérez*   117

8   Managing feeling in the academic workplace: Gender, emotion and knowledge production in a Cambridge science department, 1950–80   *Sally Horrocks and Paul Merchant*   133

9   Control your feelings and be a leader: Representations of women, emotions and career in Brazilian media   *Tatiane Leal*   151

Part III Emotions, politics and power

10 'Violent emotions': Canine suffering, emotional communities and the emotionally charged work of (anti)vivisection in London, New York and Paris *Chris Pearson* 173

11 Whistleblowing, guilt and liberal democracy *James Brown* 194

12 The 'system' of service: Emotional labour and the theatrical metaphor *Jaswinder Blackwell-Pal* 215

13 Emotional labour and the childcare crisis in neoliberal Britain *Claire English* 234

Afterword *Claire Langhamer* 255

Index 263

Figures

2.1 'The Perfect Nippy': Illustration depicting a Lyons waitress along with instructions on correct dress and posture, *c.* 1930s 24
2.2 Publicity photograph showing the new self-service layout of the Lower Regent Street Lyons Corner House, 29 March 1951 28

Contributors

Agnes Arnold-Forster is a postdoctoral researcher in the Social Studies of Medicine Department at McGill University, Canada. She is a writer and historian of health care, work and the emotions. She completed her PhD at King's College London, UK, in 2017, before working at the University of Roehampton, Queen Mary, University of London and the University of Bristol. Her first monograph *The Cancer Problem: Malignancy in Nineteenth-Century Britain* was published by Oxford University Press in 2021.

Rukmini Barua is a postdoctoral researcher at the Max Planck Institute for Human Development, Berlin, Germany. Her research interests coalesce around questions of labour, urbanism and emotions in modern and contemporary India. She has published on urban housing and politics, gender relations and intimacy with a focus on the Indian working classes.

Jaswinder Blackwell-Pal is an associate lecturer in the School of Arts at Birkbeck, University of London, UK. Her research interests focus on theatre and labour, performance at work and the politics of authenticity. Her most recent article is 'Producing "The Joy of Pret": Theatres of (Emotional) Labour in the Service Industry' (2020).

James Brown is an associate research fellow in the Department of Politics at Birkbeck, University of London, UK. With Samantha Ashenden, he coordinates an interdisciplinary research group devoted to guilt. He also teaches film, theatre and literature. Recent publications include essays for a special issue of *Economy and Society* about guilt, which he co-edited. He has also written about Romanticism, film and literature and political theory.

Claire English is a lecturer in Management and Organisation at the University of the West of Scotland. Claire's research is situated within the sociology of work and draws from feminist and postcolonial organisation studies. Her work explores the ways mothers and carers use the term 'emotional labour' to describe the exhaustion associated with their socially reproductive tasks, against previous usage of this term in a workplace context. She has recently published an article with Rosa Campbell titled 'Striking from the "second shift": Lessons from the "My Mum Is on Strike" events on International Women's Day 2019'.

Sally Horrocks is Associate Professor in Contemporary British History at the University of Leicester, UK, and Senior Academic Advisor to National Life Stories. Her recent publications are concerned with the history of scientific careers and responses to change in the scientific workplace. She has a long-standing interest in gender and science.

Claire Langhamer is Director of the Institute of Historical Research, University of London, UK. She is particularly interested in feeling, experience and ordinariness and has published on children's writing, courtship, happiness, 'home', emotional politics and women's leisure. Her most recent books are *Class of 37* with Hester Barron (2021); *Total War: An Emotional History* edited with Lucy Noakes and Claudia Siebrecht (2020); and *The English in Love: The Intimate Story of an Emotional Revolution* (2013). She is currently writing a book called *Feelings at Work in Modern Britain* for OUP and is a trustee of the Mass Observation Archive.

Tatiane Leal is a postdoctoral researcher at the National Institute of Public Communication of Science and Technology (INCT-CPCT), based at Oswaldo Cruz Foundation (Fiocruz), Brazil. She has a fellowship awarded by the Carlos Chagas Filho Research Support Foundation (FAPERJ). Her research interests focus on gender and media representations, feminist theory, media and sociocultural mediations and emotions. She is also vice-coordinator of the Media, Emotions and Sociability Research Group (NEMES), based at Federal University of Rio de Janeiro (UFRJ), Brazil.

Paul Merchant is an oral historian and researcher at National Life Stories, The British Library, UK. His publications are concerned with the production and use of scientific knowledge, especially in the earth and environmental sciences. He is currently working on life story oral histories of farming, land management and conservation in post-war Britain.

Alison Moulds is an independent scholar and a policy manager at a healthcare organization in the UK. After completing her DPhil at the University of Oxford (UK) she held postdoctoral roles at the Universities of Oxford and Roehampton (UK), working on research and public engagement. Her research interests include Victorian literature and cultural history. Her first monograph, *Medical Identities and Print Culture, 1830s–1910s*, was published by Palgrave in 2021.

Hannah Parker is a visiting fellow at the Aleksanteri Institute, University of Helsinki, Finland. Her current research interests focus on gender, emotion, work and selfhood, as well as letter-writing and materiality, in the early Soviet Union. She is currently examining manifestations of loyalty and gratitude in women's letters to Soviet authorities during the Terror, and is co-editing a special issue on early career research in the field of public history, to be published in *History* in spring 2022.

Chris Pearson is Senior Lecturer in Twentieth-Century History at the University of Liverpool, UK. His research interests focus on environmental and animal history. He is the author of *Dogopolis: How Dogs and Humans Made Modern London, New York, and Paris* (2021).

Inés Pérez is associate researcher at the Argentinean National Council for Scientific and Technical Research (CONICET) and teaches at the Universidad Nacional de Mar del Plata in the Department of Sociology. Her research interests focus on the history of paid and unpaid household and care work, consumption and gender in Argentina. Her most recent books are *El hogar tecnificado. Familias género y vida cotidiana, 1940–1970* (2012) and *Senderos que se bifurcan. Servicio doméstico y derechos laborales en la Argentina del siglo XX* (2018), co-authored with Romina Cutuli and Débora Garazi.

Grace Whorrall-Campbell is a PhD student at the University of Cambridge, UK. Her doctoral project examines the impact of the psychological sciences on workplace emotional cultures in mid-twentieth-century Britain. Grace's research interests include the histories of emotion, labour, gender and mental health.

Acknowledgements

This book would not have been possible without the encouragement of generous academic colleagues. We would like to thank Professor Thomas Dixon for supporting the initial workshop on Emotions and Work in 2019 and for employing us both on the Wellcome Trust-funded 'Living with Feeling' project at Queen Mary, University of London. Similarly, we are indebted to Dr Michael Brown, who gave us both our first jobs post-PhD on the Wellcome Trust Investigator Award, 'Surgery & Emotion', at the University of Roehampton. We met on this project, and it is to his credit that it proved the starting point of an enduring professional collaboration and friendship. We are grateful to the Wellcome Trust, who provided funding for the initial workshop and paid our respective salaries for several years. We would also like to thank the Royal Historical Society that awarded us a conference organization grant.

* * *

Agnes Arnold-Forster. I began researching the emotional landscape of the modern British hospital while working on the 'Surgery & Emotion' project, and I am grateful to Dr Brown for providing me with the intellectual guidance, flexibility and independence required to shape my own research agenda. I would also like to thank Dr Victoria Bates and Professor Claire Langhamer, who both offered me plenty of great advice and insight while I developed my project, 'Working and Feeling in the Modern British Hospital'. Finally, I am endlessly grateful to my partner, Ben, who has put his own life on hold to travel half-way across the world with me, during a pandemic, so that I can continue to do the job that I love.

* * *

Alison Moulds. My research interests in literature and the history of health care flourished while I worked on two projects under Professor Sally Shuttleworth at the University of Oxford. I was a DPhil Candidate on Constructing Scientific Communities (AHRC-funded) and later a Postdoctoral Researcher on Diseases of Modern Life (ERC-funded), where I worked on print culture and medicine and later the cultural history of retail work. Like Agnes, my interest in the history of emotions was nourished during my time working with Dr Brown and Professor Dixon at Roehampton and Queen Mary, respectively. I am grateful to colleagues at all of these institutions for inspiring and honing my research interests and outputs.

Now working outside of academia, I am especially thankful to all those who have enabled me to continue researching and writing in my 'free time' (an interesting concept when it comes to editing a volume on feelings and work). I have enjoyed immensely the support and encouragement from the Academia on the Side network I set up, which to date comprises almost sixty members. Of course, producing an edited collection in my leisure time would not have been possible without an incredible personal support network, including my family, friends and partner Azeez who has kept me going throughout the Covid-19 pandemic.

* * *

We would both like to thank our contributing authors who have produced outstanding scholarship under the impossible circumstances posed by the pandemic. They have been patient, flexible, efficient and engaged, and we must recognize the unusual pressures these past two years have posed. Thanks also to the editorial and production teams at Bloomsbury – as well as the series editors and anonymous peer reviewers – for their support for the project, which has been invaluable.

Finally, we would also like to thank each other. Academic scholarship is not just an individual but also a collaborative endeavour, even if that fact is not always publicly acknowledged.

1

Introduction

Agnes Arnold-Forster and Alison Moulds

This collection was, in part, inspired by our own postdoctoral experiences. The juncture or gulf between attaining a PhD and permanent academic employment – familiar to so many early career researchers in early-twenty-first-century Britain and beyond – is characterized by emotional vicissitudes. There is the excitement of new research ideas and prospective collaborations, the pleasures of first publications coming to fruition, mingled with the disappointments and frustrations of endless job applications and rejections. Professional identities formed during the doctoral years seem to both flourish and be thwarted, while early career scholars question how far their occupational aspirations are compatible with the aims and expectations of their personal lives.

It was in this emotional crucible that we came together to reflect on the relationship between feelings and work. How did we, as precariously employed researchers, feel about our academic labours? This self-questioning was also shaped by our historical and literary research interests. When we began collaborating on this project, Agnes Arnold-Forster was researching the emotional landscape of contemporary healthcare practice, while Alison Moulds was looking into the affective lives of retail workers in the late nineteenth and early twentieth centuries. We were both drawn to questions concerning the emotional regimes and communities that underpinned these different types of work, the entanglement between occupational and personal identities and the spaces of labour and leisure available to these divergent groups.

With these shared interests in mind, we formulated a plan for an interdisciplinary workshop on Emotions and Work, which took place on 1 November 2019 at the Art Workers' Guild in central London.[1] The workshop brought together many of the contributors featured here and sparked a longer-term collaboration between ourselves which led to us co-editing this collection. In turn, our plans for this volume also attracted new collaborators. What underlay both the conference and this collection was an urge to (re)appraise the concept of 'emotional labour', which was becoming so ubiquitous in modern parlance.[2] We wanted to interrogate and move beyond this foundational concept to think more broadly about the complex relationship between feelings and work. Our efforts resulted in this critically and politically engaged collection of essays, which invites readers to think capaciously about the spectrum of emotions which underpins different forms of work across cultural contexts in different countries and at different moments in time.

The history of emotions

Often described as an emerging field of study, the history of emotions has now cohered as a well-regarded and widely investigated subject, appealing to scholars across (and beyond) humanities disciplines. Few historians would now disagree that 'human emotions have contours that vary with time and place' and have played 'a significant role' in historical social change.[3] And yet, what precisely historians of emotions study varies from scholar to scholar. Some are interested in the shifting ways that passions, feelings and emotions have been thought about, studied or conceptualized.[4] Who were the natural historians or scientists of emotions and what methods did they employ to better understand the internal lives of the people around them or their experimental subjects, for instance? Others take specific feelings or emotions and track their histories through time.[5] The most sophisticated of these studies remain attuned to the fact that the manifestation, representation and experience of different feelings alter according to social, cultural, linguistic and historical context. Some historians are compelled by what people in the past felt and experienced, how they articulated those feelings and how those senses and emotions drove them to think, act or behave in certain ways.[6] Others are interested in how people have sought to manage, manipulate or ameliorate people's emotional states.[7]

This edited collection attends to a lacuna within history of emotions scholarship, one which has begun to attract academic attention. In a 2016 article, Claire Langhamer observed that 'while historians have developed new concepts for understanding emotions in the past [. . .] there has been little attempt, as yet, to use emotion as a category of analysis within the history of work'.[8] Traditionally, histories of work and labour have focused on, for example, attempts by legislation to regulate working conditions or the development of trade union movements. Social historians have illuminated the lived experience of different forms of work, while historians of gender have delineated the interrelationship between labour practices and ideas about femininity and masculinity. This volume explores, as Langhamer suggests, feelings 'about' work, the 'impact of work' on emotional health and well-being and the 'management of feelings' in the workplace.[9] Work – whether paid or unpaid – is an almost ubiquitous human experience and it provokes a range of strong and often contradictory feelings. The history of work and the history of emotions have, therefore, obvious points of intersection, and questions pertaining to feelings and work are politically timely and theoretically pressing.

The purpose of this volume is not to create a new subfield within the history of emotions but to use this as a methodological framework or lens through which to rethink histories of work and labour and of wider social and cultural life. This reflects the aspirations of leading scholars within the discipline. In their interviews with Jan Plamper, when asked about future directions for scholarship, Barbara Rosenwein declared that '[t]he ideal history [. . .] will not be a history of the emotions but rather an integration of the history of emotions into "regular" history', while Peter Stearns spoke of the need for more 'comparative' approaches and for 'build[ing] interdisciplinary bridges'.[10] This volume seeks to further those ambitions, by scrutinizing the interrelated histories of emotions and work through an interdisciplinary and comparative lens.

Emotional labour

When confronted with the terms 'feelings' and 'work', many of us would immediately think of 'emotional labour', a term coined by sociologist Arlie Hochschild in her 1983 book *The Managed Heart*.[11] Emotional labour, as she conceived it, referred to the work of managing one's own emotions required by certain occupations. History of emotions scholarship has highlighted similar themes. Through William Reddy's concept of 'emotional regimes', for instance, the spaces of work can be understood as sites which require or promote certain emotional expressions and experiences while suppressing others.[12] In a framework reminiscent of Hochschild's, Reddy contends that the lack of 'emotional liberty' under such regimes causes 'emotional suffering' for those who do not 'respond well to the normative emotions'.[13]

The popularity of the term 'emotional labour' has mushroomed in recent years; Google searches have increased,[14] and the concept has gained currency (perhaps ubiquity) in academic and public discourse. In a 2017 article for *Harper's Bazaar* magazine, journalist Gemma Hartley used the term to describe the household management and life admin undertaken largely by women, which she argued reflected and perpetuated gender inequalities. She defined emotional labour as being the 'manager of the household'.[15] Hartley was not being called upon to do the work of managing her own emotions; she was protesting being made to do the work of managing her home. In an interview published in *The Atlantic* in 2018, Hochschild lamented the 'concept creep' of emotional labour. The journalist Julie Beck summarized these concerns as follows: '[T]he umbrella of emotional labor has grown so large that it's starting to cover things that make no sense at all, such as regular household chores, which are not emotional so much as they are labor, full stop.'[16]

This volume is bookended by chapters which offer a critical reappraisal of 'emotional labour', illuminating this 'concept creep'. Opening the collection, Grace Whorrall-Campbell looks at waitresses at Lyons Corner Houses in the early and mid-twentieth century. Challenging assumptions that the emotional labour of service workers is necessarily a negative or alienating experience, Whorrall-Campbell instead highlights how this group of workers, nicknamed 'Nippies', derived meaning and identity from the (gendered, classed and sexualized) emotional performance expected of them. At the collection's close, Jaswinder Blackwell-Pal revisits Hochschild directly, highlighting her (mis)use of the theatrical metaphor in crafting ideas about 'deep' and 'surface' acting. Misinterpretations about the practices of Russian theatre director Constantin Stanislavski led Hochschild to overlook the role of actors as workers, to neglect how ideas of authentic emotion are constructed, and to foreground individual rather than collective processes of performance and emotional management, Blackwell-Pal argues. Meanwhile, in the volume's final chapter, Claire English similarly reappraises individualistic and collectivist approaches to emotional labour but with a focus on contemporary childcare. English contends that 'feeling alone' is part of the tapestry of British neoliberalism and calls for a different frame of reference to bring together parents, carers, nursery workers and nannies in response to the current crisis of expensive but underpaid childcare. In doing so, she powerfully conveys how emotional labour bridges the political, the personal and the professional.

Management of feelings

Following Hochschild's cue, employers, academics, activists and policymakers have increasingly turned their attention to the harmful effects work can have on people's emotional and mental health.[17] Many of us, to a lesser or greater extent, feel the tensions associated with vocation, professionalism and working conditions and rights, experiences which are shaped by wider structural privileges and inequalities. Should we 'live to work' or 'work to live'? And all of us in paid and voluntary employment must navigate the social lives, unspoken codes of conduct, the emotional regimes and the built environments of our jobs. The deleterious effects labour can have on workers' autonomy, sense of self and emotional well-being are illuminated by a number of chapters in this volume, including Moulds and Arnold-Forster's analyses of practices whereby certain employees (shop assistants and doctors, respectively) were expected to live 'on site' where they worked.

These chapters also elucidate the long cultural history of notions of 'work–life balance' and workplace well-being. The period of history this edited collection covers witnessed workplaces increasingly assuming responsibility for the emotional health of staff and saw an expansion of government policies designed to manage and ameliorate well-being at work. Occupational health, once primarily preoccupied with the threats to physical health posed by certain jobs, acquired a new remit: the mental and emotional health of employees.[18] This responsibility was expressed and enacted in a range of different ways. Some places fundamentally altered working conditions (reducing working hours, for instance) and others offered dedicated mental health support and in-house counselling services. As the twentieth century drew to a close, however, 'well-being' or 'wellness' became an increasingly powerful industry in its own right, with services designed to improve workers' emotional health outsourced to external organizations.[19] Well-being has also increasingly become the responsibility of individual workers who are expected to practise 'self-care' or cultivate their own 'resilience',[20] notions which are critiqued most especially in English's closing chapter.

Feelings about work

Emotional labour is, of course, not the only conjunction between feelings and work, as we have intimated. People can feel all sorts of things about their paid and unpaid work. It can be a source of joy, pleasure, meaning, frustration, boredom, misery, fury and disillusionment. Emotions about labour can range from the intense to the indifferent and can vary according to the day, week or task undertaken. Unlike emotional labour specifically, the literature on the feelings prompted by work is relatively scant. The historiography of certain jobs – such as medicine, nursing, education or law – deals with the positive or pleasurable emotions associated with work, vocation or professional identity.[21] As the Acknowledgements in the book attest, our collaboration began while working on the Surgery & Emotion project at the University of Roehampton – led by Michael Brown – which sought to interrogate the rich emotional landscape of surgical practice, both past and present.[22]

More broadly, the history of emotions and work has been stymied by something that beleaguers the history of emotions more generally. That is, an overwhelming focus on extreme or intense feelings at the expense of the everyday, the mild or the mundane. Not that intense emotions are not worthy of study or do not require careful analysis; quite the opposite, and many of the chapters here deal with extreme emotions experienced by workers with great care. Looking at women's letters to the Soviet authorities in the 1920s and 1930s, Hannah Parker analyses what this correspondence reveals about the place of emotions in socialist mobilization and how this influenced gendered feelings of self-worth (or lack thereof). Meanwhile, Chris Pearson investigates the 'violent emotions' underpinning vivisection and anti-vivisection debates in late-nineteenth- and early-twentieth-century London, New York and Paris. Towards the close of this volume, James Brown draws on the case study of a present-day surgeon to delineate the emotional contours of whistleblowing in the National Health Service (NHS). These encompass guilt and suffering on behalf of the employee and retaliation on behalf of the employer, a context in which – Brown argues – regulatory intervention struggles to function.

The way people feel about their work is not, of course, static or universal. Across the volume, contributors shed light on how work is spatially and temporally understood. It may cohere around very specific sites and places of labour or be interwoven in the tapestries of wider locales and regions. In looking at waitressing, for instance, Whorrall-Campbell shows how occupational identities and experiences were formed in relation to the design and organization of Lyons' tea rooms, spaces which held connotations of both glamour and affordability. At the same time, she reveals how working in the tea rooms was understood more capaciously as a forerunner or training for married, domestic life. This shift from work to married life illuminates how labour is understood in relation to different aspects of time or life stage.

Work can occupy very different amounts of time in a person's day, week and life. It may be part or full time. It may be casual, precarious and short term or more formalized and permanent (situations both defined in contracts and felt as lived experiences). For many, it feels immediate, the day-to-day grind or pleasurable rhythms through which life is lived. For others, it may seem a distant prospect, either due to periods of unemployment or after retirement has begun. A lapse in time can foster old resentments or produce a nostalgic, rose-tinted view. In her essay, Moulds considers how an older H. G. Wells recollected his adolescent apprenticeship to a draper with feelings of indignation and how Margaret Bondfield turned from shop labour to political activism, highlighting the injustices of retail work. Rukmini Barua movingly shows how mill workers in mid-twentieth-century Ahmedabad, India, sustained emotional attachments to their former places of work after deindustrialization, keeping and treasuring mementoes from their past period of employment. In this way, contributors here shed light on how even the more everyday or 'mundane' experiences of work can elicit unexpectedly strong and long-lasting affective responses.

Feelings about work might initially seem like an abstract concern, but the material and embodied aspects of labour loom large throughout this collection. Whether it's the borderline respectable/fetishistic costumes worn by Nippy waitresses (as Whorrall-Campbell reveals) or the way in which letters forged 'tangible emotional connection[s]' between citizens and the state in the Soviet Union (as Parker suggests), authors interrogate how objects mediated feelings about work. Pearson, meanwhile, shows how animals such as dogs became the epicentre of emotion work – experimental medicine and animal activism. The chapters likewise illuminate the physicality of work, how feelings are sparked in relation to bodily toil and corporeal pleasures. Certain affective responses can prompt workers to reflect upon the mental and embodied aspects of their labour in different ways – both Whorrall-Campbell and Barua consider, for example, the power of nostalgia.

One of the prevailing themes of the volume is working relationships, ranging from those underpinned by friendship and romance to those underscored by bitter rivalry and even hatred. Inés Pérez's chapter looks at how familial relationships and economic exchanges were entangled and negotiated within the context of domestic service in Buenos Aires in the mid-twentieth century. In particular, she scrutinizes the emotional meanings assigned to remuneration and lack of payment, drawing on cases filed at the Domestic Labor Tribunal, which grant access to the voices of workers as well as employers. Meanwhile, Sally Horrocks and Paul Merchant draw on oral history interviews to examine closely the texture of relationships that unfolded within a single academic department at the University of Cambridge in the mid-twentieth century. Horrocks and Merchant interrogate feelings of insecurity and self-worth (like

Parker), and they follow Pérez in considering how far work is understood in relation to remuneration and/or social ties. Thinking about interpersonal relationships more broadly, Moulds explores how the relative merits of sociability and seclusion were understood in public discourse about shop assistants in the late nineteenth and early twentieth century, while Barua considers how current political and religious divisions in Ahmedabad are mediated through a nostalgic lens, with past work practices seen as having encouraged greater social cohesion. This volume's focus on workplace relationships builds on Barbara Rosenwein's foundational concept of 'emotional communities' and is a fitting theme for a collection which represents both individual and collective endeavour, the product of personal research pursuits, collaborative interests and friendship.[23]

Work in the twentieth century

The history of emotions offers a critical intervention into the history of work and equips us to reappraise some fundamental shifts that have taken place over the past century or so. In this period, the composition of the global workforce changed dramatically, and working conditions, places of work and the nature of labour were transformed.[24] In the United States, for instance, the size of the nation's workforce increased approximately sixfold between 1900 and 2000.[25] While the century saw plenty of geographical variation, broadly speaking, the make-up of the labour force shifted from industries dominated by primary production occupations, such as agriculture, to those comprising professional, technical and service workers. Service industries as a sector expanded massively and the proportion of the population working in fields like mining, manufacturing and construction decreased.[26]

While the most dramatic changes took place in the Global North (with obvious exceptions such as China), many countries in the Global South have also witnessed significant changes in the way that labour is distributed and therefore felt. These developments do not, of course, follow a simple linear trajectory. Against the backdrop of deindustrialization, Barua focuses on how the meanings attached to labour in the textile mills continued to shape attitudes towards and experiences of the city of Ahmedabad, emotional geographies engendered not only through ideas about the relationship between work and home but also wider social and political changes. Pérez, meanwhile, shows how while domestic service in Argentina underwent a process of commercialization in the early twentieth century, domestic work was performed within 'a variety of relationships that were hard to define' and thus difficult to contain within legal systems.

The nature of work has changed and so has the demographic make-up of the workforce. Over the course of the last century, female participation in the labour market grew substantially. In Britain in 1921, just over 32 per cent of women were economically active. In 2016, that figure had risen to 57.97 per cent.[27] In the United States, 19 per cent of working-age women participated in the labour force in 1900, rising to 60 per cent by 1999.[28] The type of work undertaken by women also shifted. In 1911, about 28 per cent of all women in England and Wales worked in domestic service.[29] Over time, they were more and more likely to occupy traditionally male roles such as lawyers, doctors and politicians. In the second half of the twentieth century, married women began entering the workforce in greater quantities. However, these statistics belie the complex, contested and emotionally fraught experience of the women who undertook paid employment in the twentieth century.[30]

Unsurprisingly, therefore, gender is a key theme in this edited collection and many of the chapters address the representations and experiences of female workers and the affective relationships they formed in and with their jobs. Tatiane Leal's chapter examines portrayals of 'career women' in contemporary Brazilian magazines, attending to the tensions between individualistic and structural approaches to emotional labour, as with many contributions in this volume. Leal shows how journalistic discourse repeatedly neglects systemic inequalities, instead prioritizing the personal qualities and characteristics seen to propel certain women to success in the world of business, namely the ability to manage appropriately their feelings and affective lives. Parker and Horrocks and Merchant's chapters interrogate feelings of insecurity and self-worth, illustrating how these were experienced and understood in gendered ways.

How people have felt about work, and how work organizes and manages their feelings, is determined by a number of factors. As this collection illustrates, professional and occupational identities were and continue to be shaped in relation to other aspects of identity, including those relating to age, gender, class, region, race, ethnicity, religion, caste and sexuality. While Whorrall-Campbell considers how images and experiences of waitressing were understood in relation to heteronormative ideas of domesticity and sex appeal, Arnold-Forster illustrates how medical and surgical workplace identities were formed around ideas of masculine sociability. Meanwhile, Pérez's and English's chapters consider how poorer, racialized women in domestic service and childcare have been represented and/or marginalized in labour disputes and debates about workers' rights.

Hourly pay and salaries have increased for some – often at the expense of other, more disadvantaged, groups. As we have suggested, over the course of the twentieth century, most countries introduced legislation to protect the rights of workers, improve their working conditions and ameliorate their occupational health. However, not all of the changes to the workforce and to working life have been positive and certainly not evenly distributed. As historians and sociologists of work have shown, there have been profound labour market transformations over the past half-century. Paid, permanent employment is becoming increasingly precarious and difficult to find, and workplace cultures are trading in new vernaculars and cultivating altered personal and professional identities.[31] None of this is successfully alleviated by the emerging (and increasingly pervasive) rhetoric of entrepreneurial, resilient individualism or notions about 'self-help', as identified above. As sociologist Richard Sennett reflects in *The Corrosion of Character*, 'uncertainty is woven into the everyday practices of a vigorous capitalism. Instability is meant to be normal'.[32] These themes are threaded through many of the chapters in this collection but appear most explicitly in English's contribution.

Scope and parameters

The purpose of this collection is to interrogate the vexed relationship between emotions and work across multiple different sites and from a range of disciplinary perspectives. It traces the various ways that work made people feel in different spaces, settings and nation states. It investigates the policies and practices institutions and individuals implemented to shape the habits and emotional health of workers and explores the role that feelings played in the reform of different workplaces. It also engages with the theories and experiences of emotional labour and examines how these intersected with gender, race, age and parenthood.

These expansive questions require a varied approach. We, as editors, are from two different disciplinary backgrounds. We have worked together for four years now (first as postdocs employed on the same project and then on this edited collection) and have experienced, first hand, the value of cross-disciplinary collaboration. As a result, this volume features contributions from theatre studies and literature scholars, historians, social scientists and activists and examines the work undertaken and performed in a range of different settings: from shops to hospitals; from university departments to the home.

The intersections between work and emotions are multiple and this edited collection necessarily offers only a selection of contexts and time periods. It takes as its focus modern history, broadly defined, and spans the late nineteenth century to the present day. The collection is predominantly (but not exclusively) concerned with paid work and the concept of remuneration for labour is tackled in a number of chapters, from Pérez's consideration of domestic services in mid-twentieth-century Buenos Aires to English's examination of paid and unpaid caring responsibilities in the present-day United Kingdom.

In developing this collection, we sought contributions that attended to emotions and work in different geographic spaces. The chapters here cover Argentina, India, Brazil, the Soviet Union, France, the United States and the United Kingdom, with attention to both specific political and socio-economic geographic contexts and common themes that traverse different countries. Chapter 10 by Pearson in particular considers the formation and function of transnational emotional communities, looking at the pro- and anti-vivisection groups that developed across the United Kingdom, France and the United States. While seeking to encourage global perspectives, the volume has a predominantly British focus, reflecting our own research subjects and the locus of our professional and academic networks within the history of emotions. Greater concentration on emotions and labour in the Global South would help to expand and diversify current perspectives, which have largely coalesced around the Global North.

Diverse in content and scope, but with myriad points of intersection and common thematic interests, the chapters within this volume could have been organized in any number of ways. We have opted to structure it thematically, dividing the chapters into three sections: 'spaces of labour', 'professional and personal identities' and 'emotions, politics and power'. These groupings highlight some of the most dominant themes that emerge in the collection. First, it is apparent not only that places of work structure and organize the feelings of their employees and local communities but also that sites of labour become infused and even saturated with emotion which, in turn, reshapes how those spaces are used and understood. Second, the elision between professional or occupational and personal identities will come as no surprise to many readers, for whom discussions of 'work–life balance' are likely to be all too familiar. This theme in particular invites readers to pay attention to issues of domesticity and family life, and how work is mapped across different identities and subjectivities. Finally, the last section foregrounds ideological conceptions of emotion work and emotional labour, scrutinizing individual and collective activism, both past and present.

Feelings and Work is best understood not only as a collection of methodologically and thematically complementary chapters but also as the product of a scholarly and emotional community developing around this nascent but flourishing field of enquiry. As with any edited collection it has entailed its fair share of anxieties and frustrations but also excitement and pleasures. Editing this volume has inspired us to think not only about emotions and work as a subject of research but also about how scholarship is an emotionally invested and sometimes emotionally fraught form of labour.

Notes

1. Parker, 'Emotions and Work'.
2. Hochschild, *The Managed Heart*.
3. Sobe, 'Researching Emotion', 690. There are now textbooks, accessible overviews and methodological guides for students in the history of the emotions. See, for example, Barclay, *The History of Emotions*; Boddice, *The History of Emotions*.
4. See, for example, Dixon, *From Passions to Emotions*.
5. Rosenwein, *Anger: The Conflicted History*; McCann and McKechnie-Mason, *Fear in the Medical and Literary Imagination*.
6. Boddice and Smith, *Emotion, Sense, Experience*.
7. Reddy, *The Navigation of Feeling*.
8. Langhamer, 'Feelings, Women and Work', 79.
9. Langhamer, 'Feelings, Women and Work', 77.
10. Quoted in Plamper, 'The History of Emotions', 260, 264–5.
11. Hochschild, *The Managed Heart*.
12. Reddy, *The Navigation of Feeling*; Plamper, 'The History of Emotions', 242.
13. Reddy, *The Navigation of Feeling*, 126; Plamper, 'The History of Emotions', 244–5, 240–1.
14. Google Trends.
15. Hartley, 'Women Aren't Nags'.
16. Beck, 'The Concept Creep'.
17. Elliott and Lawrence, 'The Emotional Economy'; Jackson, *The Age of Stress*; Kirby, *Feeling the Strain*; Palmer, *Who Cared for the Carers*.
18. See, for example, Bonea et al., *Anxious Times*; Long, *The Rise and Fall of the Healthy Factory*.
19. Kirkman, 'The Big, Booming Business'; Wieczner, 'Your Company Wants'.
20. Arnold-Forster, 'Resilience in Surgery'.
21. Dawson, 'A History of Vocation'.

22 Brown, *Emotions and Surgery*.
23 Rosenwein, *Emotional Communities*.
24 Kirk and Wall, *Work and Identity*; McIvor, *Working Lives*; Pahl, *On Work*.
25 Fisk, 'American Labor'.
26 Fisk, 'American Labor'; Saunders, *Assembling Cultures*.
27 See Ortiz-Ospina et al., 'Women's Employment', particularly its data visualizations based on: Long, *The Labor Force*; Heckman and Killingsworth, 'Female Labor Supply' and OECD.stat (2017).
28 Fisk, 'American Labor'.
29 Office for National Statistics, 'Long-term trends'.
30 See: Delap, *Knowing Their Place*; McCarthy, *Double Lives*; Moss, *Women, Workplace Protest and Political Identity*; Mullin, *Working Girls*; Pringle, *Secretaries Talk*; Sharpe, *Double Identity*.
31 Cooper and Lousada, *Borderline Welfare*.
32 Sennett, *The Corrosion of Character*, 31.

Bibliography

Arnold-Forster, Agnes. 'Resilience in Surgery'. *British Journal of Surgery* 107, no. 4 (2020): 332–3.

Barclay, Katie. *The History of Emotions: A Student Guide to Methods and Sources*. Basingstoke: Palgrave Macmillan, 2020.

Beck, Julie. 'The Concept Creep of "Emotional Labor"'. *The Atlantic* (26 November 2018) https://www.theatlantic.com/family/archive/2018/11/arlie-hochschild-housework-isnt-emotional-labor/576637/ (accessed 25 April 2021).

Boddice, Rob. *The History of Emotions*. Manchester: Manchester University Press, 2018.

Boddice, Rob, and Mark Smith. *Emotion, Sense, Experience*. Cambridge: Cambridge University Press, 2020.

Bonea, Amelia, Melissa Dickson, Sally Shuttleworth, and Jennifer Wallis, eds. *Anxious Times: Medicine and Modernity in Nineteenth-Century Britain*. Pittsburgh, PA: University of Pittsburgh Press, 2019.

Brown, Michael. *Emotions and Surgery in Britain, 1790–1900*. Cambridge: Cambridge University Press, forthcoming.

Cooper, Andrew, and Julian Lousada. *Borderline Welfare: Feeling and Fear of Feeling in Modern Welfare*. Abingdon: Routledge, 2019.

Dawson, Jane. 'A History of Vocation: Tracing a Keyword of Work, Meaning, and Moral Purpose'. *Adult Education Quarterly* 55, no. 3 (2005): 220–31.

Delap, Lucy. *Knowing Their Place: Domestic Service in Twentieth-Century Britain*. Oxford: Oxford University Press, 2011.

Dixon, Thomas. *From Passions to Emotions: The Creation of a Secular Psychological Category*. Cambridge: Cambridge University Press, 2003.

Elliott, Jane, and Jon Lawrence. 'The Emotional Economy of Unemployment: A Re-analysis of Testimony from a Sheppey Family, 1978–1983'. *Sage Open* 6 (2016): 1–11.
Fisk, Donald M. 'American Labor in the Twentieth Century'. United States Bureau of Labor Statistics (January 2003).
Google Trends. https://trends.google.com/trends/explore?date=all&geo=US&q=%22emotional%20labor%22 (accessed 29 April 2021).
Hartley, Gemma. 'Women Aren't Nags – We're Just Fed Up'. *Harper's Bazaar* (September 2017) https://www.harpersbazaar.com/culture/features/a12063822/emotional-labor-gender-equality/ (accessed 25 April 2021).
Heckman, James, and Mark Killingsworth. 'Female Labor Supply: A Survey'. In *Handbook of Labor Economics, Volume I*, edited by Orley Ashenfelter and Richard Layard, 103–204. Amsterdam: North-Holland, 1986.
Hochschild, Arlie Russell. *The Managed Heart: Commercialization of Human Feeling*. Updated edition. Berkeley: University of California Press, 2012.
Jackson, Mark. *The Age of Stress: Science and the Search for Stability*. Oxford: Oxford University Press, 2013.
Kirby, Jill. *Feeling the Strain: A Cultural History of Stress in Twentieth-Century Britain*. Manchester: Manchester University Press, 2019.
Kirk, John, and Christine Wall. *Work and Identity: Historical and Cultural Contexts*. Basingstoke: Palgrave Macmillan, 2011.
Kirkman, Alexandra. 'The Big, Booming Business of Wellness'. *Self* (4 August 2017) https://www.self.com/story/the-big-booming-business-of-wellness (accessed 25 April 2021).
Langhamer, Claire. 'Feelings, Women and Work in the Long 1950s'. *Women's History Review* 26, no. 1 (2017): 77–92.
Long, Clarence D. *The Labor Force under Changing Income and Employment*. Princeton: Princeton University Press, 1958.
Long, Vicky. *The Rise and Fall of the Healthy Factory: The Politics of Industrial Health in Britain, 1914-1960*. Basingstoke: Palgrave Macmillan, 2011.
McCann, Daniel, and Claire McKechnie-Mason, eds. *Fear in the Medical and Literary Imagination, Medieval to Modern: Dreadful Passions*. London: Palgrave Macmillan, 2018.
McCarthy, Helen. *Double Lives: A History of Working Motherhood*. London: Bloomsbury, 2020.
McIvor, Arthur. *Working Lives: Work in Britain since 1945*. Basingstoke: Palgrave Macmillan, 2013.
Moss, Jonathan. *Women, Workplace Protest and Political Identity in England, 1968–1985*. Manchester: Manchester University Press, 2019.
Mullin, Katherine. *Working Girls: Fiction, Sexuality, and Modernity*. Oxford: Oxford University Press, 2016.
OECD.stat (2017). http://stats.oecd.org/ [Used for data visualization by Ortiz-Ospina et al – see below].

Office for National Statistics. 'Long-term trends in UK employment: 1861 to 2018'. https://www.ons.gov.uk/economy/nationalaccounts/uksectoraccounts/compendium/economicreview/april2019/longtermtrendsinukemployment1861to2018#womens-labour-market-participation (accessed 29 April 2021).

Ortiz-Ospina, Esteban, Sandra Tzvetkova, and Max Roser. 'Women's Employment'. OurWorldInData.org. https://ourworldindata.org/female-labor-supply (accessed 28 April 2021).

Pahl, Raymond Edward, ed. *On Work. Historical, Comparative and Theoretical Approaches*. New York, NY: Basil Blackwell, 1988.

Palmer, Deborah. *Who Cared for the Carers?: A History of the Occupational Health of Nurses, 1880–1948*. Manchester: Manchester University Press, 2014.

Parker, Hannah. 'Emotions and Work: An Interview with Agnes Arnold-Forster and Alison Moulds'. *History Journal* (27 April 2020) https://historyjournal.org.uk/2020/04/27/emotions-and-work-an-interview-with-agnes-arnold-forster-and-alison-moulds/ (accessed 26 April 2021).

Plamper, Jan. 'The History of Emotions: An Interview with William Reddy, Barbara Rosenwein, and Peter Stearns'. *History and Theory* 49, no. 2 (2010): 237–65.

Pringle, Rosemary. *Secretaries Talk: Sexuality, Power and Work*. London: Verso, 1988.

Reddy, William. *The Navigation of Feeling: A Framework for the History of Emotions*. Cambridge: Cambridge University Press, 2001.

Rosenwein, Barbara H. *Anger: The Conflicted History of an Emotion*. New Haven, CT: Yale University Press, 2020.

Rosenwein, Barbara H. *Emotional Communities in the Early Middle Ages*. Ithaca: Cornell University Press, 2006.

Saunders, Jack. *Assembling Cultures: Workplace Activism, Labour Militancy and Cultural Change in Britain's Car Factories, 1945–82*. Manchester: Manchester University Press, 2019.

Sennett, Richard. *The Corrosion of Character: The Personal Consequences of Work in the New Capitalism*. London and New York: W. W. Norton & Company, 1998.

Sharpe, Sue. *Double Identity: The Lives of Working Mothers*. London: Penguin Books, 1984.

Sobe, Noah W. 'Researching Emotion and Affect in the History of Education'. *History of Education* 41 (2012): 689–95.

Wieczner, Jen. 'Your Company Wants to Make you Healthy'. *The Wall Street Journal* (8 April 2013) http://www.wsj.com/articles/SB10001424127887323393304578360252284151378 (accessed 25 April 2021).

Part I

Spaces of labour

2

Emotions and sexuality at work
Lyons Corner Houses, c. 1920–50

Grace Whorrall-Campbell[1]

Josephine Heslit was one of many former Lyons waitresses, known as 'Nippies', who responded to the company's request for their memories of working in the famous Corner Houses and Teashops. In her letter, she proudly declared: 'I am 73 years but I'm still nipping around' and signed off as 'just another nippy'.[2] Josephine's fondness for her former occupation complicates Arlie Hochschild's assertion that emotional labour had psychologically damaging effects.[3] Hochschild's influential concept has proved a rich source for many other contributions to this volume, including Blackwell-Pal's, English's and Merchant and Horrocks's. She argued that the 'management of feeling' in the course of the job takes a negative psychological toll on service workers, estranging them from their emotions and their capacity to relate to themselves and to others.[4] In this chapter, however, I argue that the performance of emotional labour by Lyons waitresses was a complex experience. Maintaining a smiling, polite façade was hard work, especially so in the face of difficult or threatening customers. However, excelling at this performance of cheery and courteous femininity had the potential to reward workers with the promise of economic, social and emotional security in marriage.

Despite Hochschild's identification of emotional labour nearly forty years ago, historical interest in the emotions involved in work has been stymied by a more general neglect of the service sector. Pamela Cox notes that the rise of a consumer society in late-nineteenth- and early-twentieth-century Britain called for novel forms of gendered emotional, aesthetic and sexualized labour as a response to new expectations of customer service. However, she argues that due to the service sector's feminized labour force, such developments have not traditionally been of interest to labour historians.[5] Significant contributions have instead been made by literary scholars Lise Shapiro Sanders and Katherine Mullin, both of whom illuminated the anxieties embedded in literary and popular representations of these new, eroticized service workers.[6] This chapter is informed by Claire Langhamer's recent use of emotion as a category of analysis within the history of post-war women's work.[7] In particular, her discussion of Benno Gammerl's concept of place-specific emotional styles has influenced my thinking of Corner Houses and Teashops as sites which demanded a particular emotional repertoire.[8]

The workplace is also usefully understood through William Reddy's concept of 'emotional regimes', as a site that sanctions certain emotional expressions and experiences while censuring others. Reddy, in a similar vein to Hochschild, suggests that the lack of 'emotional liberty' under such regimes causes 'emotional suffering' as a result of the suppression of individuals' true feelings.[9] However, as my chapter seeks to demonstrate, adherence to emotional norms did not always lead to emotional suffering but rather could be reflected on with pride and satisfaction.

Furthermore, Lyons Corner Houses, as industrial 'pleasure zones', provide an entry point to think about how sexuality was made present in the workplace.[10] In this I follow Emma Vickers's and Helen Smith's investigations into workplace cultures of homosexuality, as they demonstrate how certain occupational conditions facilitated queer sexual encounters.[11] However, this chapter attends to workplace *hetero*sexuality in an attempt to expose the history and workings of a category often placed 'beyond and outside history'.[12] As Jonathan Ned Katz asserts, both heterosexuality and homosexuality describe historically specific ways of naming and organizing sexual desires.[13] However, because of its normative status, heterosexuality is omnipresent yet often goes unobserved; in Laura Doan's words, it 'lurk[s] obliquely' as an 'absent presence'.[14] In this chapter, I query the operation of heterosexuality in a certain time and place. My approach follows Zoe Strimpel and Hannah Charnock's examinations of heterosexuality's construction and operation as a category in social life. The erotically charged Lyons Corner Houses attest to the role of labour and commerce in beating the bounds between normal and deviant sexuality.[15]

Despite this chapter's focus on the construction of a heterosexual workplace culture, I will necessarily be observant of the queer possibility inherent in the eateries and their staff. Urban space has often been associated with queerness, and sites of mass consumerist leisure provided locations where wider urban sociability intersected with non-normative sexual subcultures.[16] Walkowitz notes that the West End Corner Houses were 'a magnet for men looking for homosex', especially those who 'adopted a look of highly sexualised femininity'.[17] These individuals were drawn to Lyons not just because of its affordability but also because they perceived it as a site of glamour, escapism and gender play.

J. Lyons and the Nippy

J. Lyons and Co. opened their first Teashop in Piccadilly in 1894, ten years after they were founded as a catering company by Joseph Lyons and his brothers-in-law Isidore and Montague Gluckstein. From 1909 Lyons developed the business into a chain of Corner Houses in London and 250 Teashops in provincial towns and cities. The large London Corner Houses were spectacular palaces of industrial leisure: following the building's expansion in 1922, the Coventry Street Corner House could accommodate 3,000 people for twenty-four-hour service.[18] Lyons prided themselves on providing the grandeur and personal service of continental restaurants combined with the affordability of Americanized mass eateries, drawing an eclectic crowd of Soho-ites and suburban day trippers through their doors with the promise of cheap food in a fantastical setting.

These spaces were staffed by an array of serving staff and shop assistants but none more famous than the Nippy. Dressed in their iconic black-and-white uniforms, these servers cut a modern, invigorating figure as they bustled through the palatial establishments. The archetypal Lyons' waitress was young, unmarried and working to lower middle class. However, it pays to be cautious when accepting this youthful image as reality: to do so would say far more about the power of Lyons' brand-building than it would about the waiting staff themselves. Sanders and Mullin demonstrate that the figure of the working girl was culturally overdetermined, her representations colouring and obscuring the experience of these workers.[19] Despite Nippies' construction as youthful 'girls', teashop staff actually included even younger members. The youngest, in their early teens, were known as Service Maids: when they reached their late teens, they became 'Trippies', who were tasked with trolley service, before finally getting to don the fashionable Nippy uniform.[20]

In 1925, the demure dresses, prim aprons and starched caps worn by Edwardian waitresses were brought up to date with a design that spoke of modern womanhood.[21] The skirt was shortened to fall just below the knee, a dropped waist created the modish androgynous silhouette and a wide scooped neckline replaced the high collar. The redesign distanced the Nippy uniform from those worn by domestic servants. The apron shrunk to become small, neatly pleated and hung from the waist and the white coronet that wrapped around the waitresses' bobbed hair now bore the Lyons logo.[22]

The staff attired in these smart uniforms were required to manipulate their own emotions to create a pleasant affective experience for the customer. A cheerful demeanour was crucial: a Lyons handbook entitled 'Hints to waiters and waitresses' put 'Cheerfulness' fourth on its list of 'Golden Rules'. It declared: 'A smile costs nothing and cheerfulness in business is a great asset.' The handbook went on to acknowledge the difficulty of this, 'especially when you have your own private worries and troubles', but advised workers 'the best thing to do is to try to forget them during business hours by giving undivided attention to your work'.[23] The handbook's advice corresponds with Hochschild's assertion that emotional labourers were expected to 'suppress or induce feelings' – summoning up genuine happiness rather than plastering on a fake smile.[24] As Jaswinder Blackwell-Pal's later chapter in this volume reminds us, this performance of authentic emotion relies on a historically specific model of the self.

In the 1930s, a silver shield was awarded annually to the best Teashop, decorated with a 'winged Nippy, à la Mercury' along with the inscription 'Courtesy and Efficiency'.[25] Efficiency was vital for Corner Houses, which relied on a high turnover of covers to offset the low prices paid by the customer. Even the 'Nippy' label, devised in 1925, reflected the waitresses' prompt service.[26] *Lyons Mail*, the firm's staff magazine, boasted that the epithet was chosen 'to typify the smartness, alacrity and alertness of the Lyons teashop waitress' and had quickly become synonymous with 'dignified service'.[27]

Many customers did remember Nippies in the way Lyons hoped they would, as 'very efficient and composed'.[28] However, the expectation of courteous service did not always match reality. Phyllis Frankwell, who worked as a Nippy in Romford in the 1930s, recalled an 'incident' between a Nippy and a customer. Rather than waiting to be shown to a table, the customer demanded his coffee directly upon entrance, calling 'to the waitress at the top of his voice'. Frankwell reported with some glee and a fair amount of scandal the waitress's response: 'I can see her face even now[. S]he just turned round and said[, "]introduce your backside to the seat [and] I will be along there shortly."' Despite the customer's own discourtesy, Frankwell was still shocked by her colleague's rejoinder – as she explained, 'in those days the customer was always right.'[29]

Frankwell's memory disrupts the carefully constructed image of the Corner House as a sophisticated establishment. However, in her telling of the story, Frankwell sought to limit its disorderly implications. The former Nippy narrated the incident as a humorous anecdote, gliding over any negative emotions involved in this fraught exchange. Furthermore, Frankwell made recourse to the offending Nippy's working-class origins, explaining her rudeness through a stereotypical image of the mouthy 'East Ender' whose father was a barrow boy.[30] Nevertheless, Frankwell's memory exposed, even while attempting to contain, the constant tension between 'rough' and 'respectable' that underpinned the charged atmosphere of Corner Houses.

That the Nippy's rudeness was explained through her father's occupation is revealing; waitresses' refined femininity distinguished them from working men. While an article published in *The Evening News* in 1929 praised the Nippy by comparing her to postmen, policemen and porters, the author claimed that feminine grace set her apart. Customers would 'never see *her* blow her hands . . . limp . . . or hear her grumble . . . because she does not ram home any of the disadvantages of her job'.[31] The waitress's supposedly natural pleasantness and eagerness to please discouraged her from giving any visible signs of discomfort, despite the hard physical work.[32] Moreover, this comparison was quickly reneged upon. The article declared that 'she earns her wages by the constant patter of her little feet', infantilizing the waitress, emphasizing her delicacy and ultimately trivializing the work's physicality.[33] Media representations of Nippies as youthful and feminine were echoed and amplified by Lyons; it is telling that this article was republished in *The Lyons Mail*. A number of scholars have noted that the gendered character of service work, despite recourse to assumed emotional and biological differences between men and women, required constant reinforcement through workplace practices.[34] Lyons constructed waitressing as a youthful feminine occupation not only through the gendered division of labour but also through grooming standards and uniforms that enforced feminine presentation, as well as describing Nippies as 'girls' in the staff magazine.[35]

The article also overlooked the considerable emotional labour done on the job. Emotional management was naturalized through association with feminized qualities, such as patience, sympathy, attentiveness and tact, and therefore was not easily understood within the framework of work.[36] Thus Nippies' labour, both emotional and physical, was poorly remunerated. Waitresses took home 25 shillings a week. Former Nippies remembered their tips as a lifeline, as they had to pay for their uniform, which cost the significant sum of £2 12s., out of their meagre wages.[37] By imagining Nippies as youthful and feminine, and thus naturally sprightly and kindly, Lyons justified the small wages. These small wages motivated effusiveness towards tipping customers: the risks and opportunities this created will be discussed in the next section.[38]

Glamour, sex and seediness

Not only were Lyons waitresses expected to be cheerful, polite and efficient, they were also expected to be glamorous. Lyons relied extensively on images of elegant women workers in their marketing campaigns of the mid-1920s and 1930s. The firm paid renowned cartoonists Arthur Ferrier and Gilbert Wilkinson to depict their iconic waitresses as slim women with bobbed hair and dark lips, balancing their heavy trays with poise as they glided along.[39] Realizing this ideal required extensive effort and discomfort for the real Nippies[40] (Figure 2.1). Former waitresses recalled daily dress inspections: hands had to be spotless, all sixty buttons down the bodice present, hair neatly rolled and apron

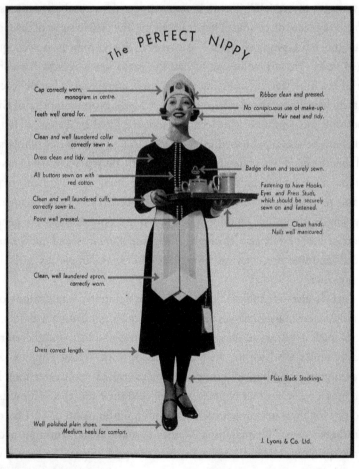

Figure 2.1 'The Perfect Nippy': Illustration depicting a Lyons waitress along with instructions on correct dress and posture, c. 1930s. © London Metropolitan Archives.

and cuffs white and gleaming.[41] Workers who did not fit this glamorous image were concealed from customers. One man who courted a Lyons waitress in the early 1930s remembered feeling sorry for '[his] Nippy' Florence Overton as her slim and less buxom figure earned her 'one of the worst stations on the floor'.[42] Undertaking service work was an embodied performance that relied as much on attractiveness as cheerfulness to convey the impression of good service.

Peter Bailey has argued that glamour operated as the visual code for parasexuality, the 'everything but' – the desire that comes from being able to look but not touch.[43] Parasexuality has proved influential in making sense of feminized embodied labour in the service sector.[44] As discussed below, Lyons controlled waitresses' appearance in ways that can be illuminated through parasexuality's 'managed arousal'.[45] However, the concept has significant limits.[46] Nippies, who darted between tables, were not sheltered from customers' amorous intentions. Furthermore, the distanced desire described by parasexuality does not capture the real and imagined association between service work and sex work.[47] The shop assistant corrupted into sex work was a notable feature of fictional depictions of retail work, as demonstrated by Alison Moulds in Chapter 3 of this volume. Delap notes that Nippies socialized outside of work with customers, receiving presents in return, suggesting that, for some, this practice existed on the fringes of the sexual economy.[48] At least one Nippy recalled sex workers using the cafés for rest, recuperation and solicitation. As Julia Laite notes, the increasing criminalization of street prostitution in the early twentieth century forced many sex workers to take their business indoors, utilizing the proliferating sites of commercialized leisure such as cafés, bars and nightclubs.[49] Moreover, both waitressing at Lyons and sex work required a similar competence in emotional management, and both involved selling an embodied fantasy of feminine sex appeal that sometimes verged on concrete sexual encounters. Workers did not always have the power, or the desire, to maintain the distance of 'everything but', and they negotiated a complex balance between their own wants, those of the customer and the company's instructions.

Lyons consciously reinforced the romantic and sexual promise of Nippies, even while they aimed to contain this desire within the frameworks of heterosexual courtship and marriage. The company enthusiastically promoted marriages between waitresses and customers, claiming that the marriage rate for Nippies was higher than in any other occupation.[50] This assertion further indulged customers' fantasies about the sexual and romantic availability of waitresses. Not only was this canny marketing, it was also a savvy recruitment strategy: Lyons recognized that in the absence of generous wages, the opportunities for courtship made the job attractive, particularly when compared with the limited romantic options associated with domestic service.[51]

Lyons also attempted to contain customers' sexual desire by strictly managing waitresses' self-presentation. There was a tension between the lipsticked Nippies in Lyons adverts and the stringent regulations for the flesh-and-blood waitresses, who were required to keep the use of cosmetics 'to a minimum', avoid 'startlingly extravagant' hairstyles and refrain from an 'exaggerated or gaudy' appearance.[52] One respondent recounted her mother's memory of being made to stand on a wooden box while the manager shone a torch through the hem of her uniform to make sure the petticoat properly obscured what was underneath.[53] Another former Nippy, Kathleen Pittman, saw these 'unbelievable' rules and regulations as the mark of a more respectable bygone age. However, she exhibited a complex reckoning with the dissonance between respectability and sexuality, proudly comparing her occupation to being a Bluebell Girl, a member of the risqué cabaret troupe founded in Paris in the early 1930s.[54] Pittman therefore saw herself as occupying both the respectable femininity of a pre-permissive era and an erotically charged glamour. These opposing gender norms claimed by Pittman echoed the sexual double standard promoted by Lyons, which advertised their waitressing staff as sexually available but not sexually active.

Nippies' glamorous reputation was undoubtedly something many waitresses found enjoyable. One server recalled her excitement when, in the late 1930s, they were allowed to swap their sensible black stockings and shoes for silk hosiery and court shoes, saying 'it was a highlight to make one feel more glamorous'.[55] However, embodying a fantasy was not always pleasurable, and women did not always appreciate sexually charged encounters. Even many years later, these women found it difficult to express their feelings towards what we might understand today as sexual harassment. Gladys Foster recalled a letter from a soldier addressed to her and another Nippy. The letter instructed them to look under the stamp: after steaming it from the envelope, they found he had written 'Im [sic] hard to get of [sic]' underneath. Whether the two waitresses interpreted it as a playful prank or a lewd suggestion Gladys does not say.[56] Gladys's compulsion to relate this memory, combined with her inability to find the words to describe the feelings connected with it, suggests emotional confusion.[57] Her confusion regarding whether to be flattered or threatened by the attention echoed the tension between licit and illicit sexuality held within the space of the Corner Houses.

Nippies' disciplined body and emotion work was crucial not only to maintain order between respectable and racy modes of female presentation but also to stabilize hierarchies of ethnicity and sexual deviance.[58] Not only was J. Lyons & Co. a Jewish-owned company, their London Corner Houses were popular with Jewish Soho-ites who worked in the fur and cloth trades in the area. Lyons' association with Jewishness posed a problem for the caterers during the rising anti-Semitism of the late 1930s.[59] Waitresses' strict dress codes and restrictions on cosmetic use should therefore be seen in the context of anti-Semitic prejudice towards Jewish women who were deemed to be overly sensual.[60] Nippies' polite, efficient and restrained self-presentation referenced an ideal of white English femininity, disavowing both the Jewish origins and the Jewish patrons to appeal to suburban day trippers looking for inexpensive and 'respectable' refreshment.

The chic atmosphere and cheap menu made these establishments popular sites of queer sociability. Quentin Crisp, having moved to London and scraping by with what money he made from sex work, remembered the 'chain teashops' as his and his friends' 'great money-saving device'.[61] Utilizing the bustle of peak hours to their advantage, they would sneak out one by one after eating without paying, even going up to the cashier to ask for change for the telephone in order to look like they were settling up. This, Crisp recalled, was almost foolproof: 'In six months, we nearly always ate one or two free meals a day.'[62] Queer customers flaunted norms of respectability not only in their impunity towards paying the bill but also in their behaviour and appearance. The flamboyant figure of the 'quean', who cultivated a feminine personage consistent with their sense of sexual selfhood, was an iconic member of the West End queer scene.[63] Decked out in colourful, feminine clothing and cosmetics, and adopting a camp manner, queans' embodiment of highly sexualized femininity provided the unruly mirror image to the heterosexual, restrained attractiveness demanded from Nippies.

Hanging up the uniform

The post-war years marked the slow end of the particular emotional culture and affective experience that had existed in Teashops and Corner Houses in the first half of the twentieth century. Many of Lyons' city-centre eateries had suffered bomb damage as a result of the Blitz. When Lyons refurbished the buildings, they kitted them out for self-service. One such Teashop opened on 15 March 1951: the publicity material celebrated its 'luxury self-service "salon" design' (Figure 2.2).[64] Waitresses no longer nipped between tables. Instead, servers in sparkling white uniforms doled out meals from behind the polished granite and stainless-steel counter. Labour shortages meant that Teashops' labour-intensive service

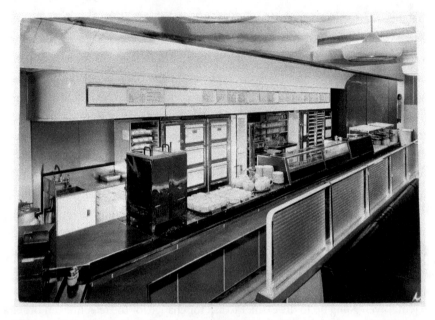

Figure 2.2 Publicity photograph showing the new self-service layout of the Lower Regent Street Lyons Corner House, 29 March 1951. © London Metropolitan Archives.

style was no longer possible, and rising real wages destroyed a business model underpinned by cheap female labour.[65] Although the iconic Lyons waitress did not completely disappear, she continued as a shadow of her former self, used only for special occasions and outside catering. Despite a modernized uniform which swapped out the pre-war column silhouette for an A-line skirt and broader, fashionable shoulders, the Nippy was fast becoming a relic of a bygone age.[66]

Working as a Nippy required significant feeling management skills as well as physical and emotional energy to deal with long shifts and difficult customers. The emotional experience of work could be boring, frustrating, humiliating and even degrading. However, being one of the chosen few was also a source of pride for many workers. Lyons presented the job as every girl's dream; *Lyons Mail* frequently sported photographs of young girls dressed up in the iconic uniform. Adults, too, were not immune from the fantasy of the glamorous waitress: in 1935, the magazine boasted they had loaned 581 Nippy costumes between May and December the previous year.[67] It is tempting to speculate on the various unruly uses these costumes were put to, given that Nippies were not only an object for aspiration and identification among young women and others who cultivated a feminine, glamorous presentation but also a focus for heterosexual desire.[68]

The uniform certainly retained a talismanic quality for some former Nippies. Mrs Butters, who began work as a Nippy in 1942, confided in her letter that she had kept the identifying number sewn onto her uniform 'for very sentimental Nippy reasons'.[69] Former waitresses' fond memories of and continued emotional investment in their previous occupation suggest that the emotional management and body work required by the job were understood as sources of pride and satisfaction. It is necessary to ask why a job that involved considerable emotional labour, long hours and poor pay was remembered so positively. This change in attitude was partly the influence of a retrospective view, as frustrating experience passed into nostalgic memory. It was also partially conditioned by the context in which the letters emerged. The company's request for former Nippies to share their memories might have stimulated feelings of pride from the letter writers, as it indicated that their work as waitresses was worthy to enter the historical record. Although the appeal for reminiscences might have called forth such emotions, there were a number of ways in which the Nippy experience could have been interpreted. Respondents were not shy in describing the pressures, strains and injustices of the job, but those memories were overwhelmed by feelings of pride in their work and in their smart and glamorous appearance.[70]

Former Nippies were able to reinterpret their emotional and aesthetic labour as meaningful, despite feminized service work's low status. Indeed, for them, it was the gendered nature of the work that made it so valuable. Many reflected proudly upon how the skills they first cultivated at work had served them well in their domestic duties. Mrs Camac, a Nippy from 1949 to 1954, wrote:

> What an eye opener it was for me and a great influence on the rest of my life, it was to me like a finishing school for a working class girl ... I'm still at the age of sixty one being complemented for the lovely table I lay and the ease at which I serve my guests and that was what the great J. Lyons taught me.[71]

Mrs Camac found that the gendered performance involved in service work could be repurposed to suit the social script later in life, when she undertook social reproductive labour within the household as a wife and hostess.

Langhamer too has noted how easily such gender performances were transferred between the domestic setting and workplace. She argues that in the post-war workplace, the identities of wife, mother and worker blurred, as women in clerical and secretarial posts were expected to provide the same duty of care to their bosses as to their husbands.[72] Chapters 8 and 9 in this volume, by Horrocks and Merchant and Leal, also demonstrate similar configurations of gendered emotion work in different temporal and professional contexts. Indeed, the fact that many Nippies met their husbands at work, as both the letters and announcements in *Lyons Mail* attest, would have served to further vindicate the transition between waged and domestic work. For many of these women, not only did the company give them valuable domestic skills, in the vein of a 'finishing school' according to Mrs Camac, it also introduced them to the men they would perform these skills for in the domestic environment. Former Nippies appreciated that their emotional and embodied labour was a valuable commodity in married life and thus were grateful to Lyons for the training which they could convert into the social stability and economic security of marriage.[73] Furthermore, the discipline they were expected to show over their body and manners, so as to embody an ideal of glamorous yet respectable femininity, could be reframed as labour that benefitted them both socially and materially.[74]

Lyons Corner Houses were aptly named, sitting as they did at a number of conceptual junctions. These establishments were chic yet cheap; glamorous, but with a seedy underbelly; they offered a reassuring, replicable atmosphere for suburban customers while also catering to a cosmopolitan clientele. The iconic waitresses were the fulcrum around which these oxymorons balanced. Nippies' capacity for physical and emotional labour was corralled into stabilizing the unruly, dynamic atmosphere customers found so alluring. Despite the humiliation, frustration and exhaustion this work engendered, later in life former Nippies were able to reframe their labour as a source of pride and satisfaction.

Historians have often noted how spaces of commercialized leisure toyed with the desires and fantasies of the consumer.[75] However, as this chapter has demonstrated, the manipulation of desire also implicated the bodies and hearts of those who laboured there. When Josephine Heslit signed herself off as 'just another Nippy', Lyons had lodged itself deep in her heart. She did not experience the alienation from her work that Hochschild identified. Rather, she had transformed the gendered and sexualized performance which had made value for Lyons into an identity which she herself found valuable.

Notes

1 This research is funded by the Arts and Humanities Research Council's Open-Oxford-Cambridge Doctoral Training Partnership.
2 Josephine Heslit, 12 January 1990, ACC/3257/235.
3 Hochschild, *The Managed Heart*.
4 Hochschild, *The Managed Heart*, 7, 18–19.

5 Cox, 'Shop Girls, Social History and Social Theory'; historians have begun to address this lacuna, see Schwartz, *Feminism and the Servant Problem*.
6 Sanders, *Consuming Fantasies*; Mullin, *Working Girls*.
7 Langhamer, 'Feelings, Women and Work in the Long 1950s'.
8 Gammerl, 'Emotional Styles'.
9 Reddy, *The Navigation of Feeling*.
10 Walkowitz, *Nights Out*, 10.
11 Vickers, *Queen and Country*; Smith, *Masculinity, Class and Same-Sex Desire*.
12 Doan, 'A Peculiarly Obscure Subject', 88.
13 Ned Katz, *The Invention of Heterosexuality*.
14 Doan, 'A Peculiarly Obscure Subject', 88.
15 Charnock, 'Teenage Girls'; Strimpel, *Seeking Love in Modern Britain*.
16 Houlbrook, *Queer London*.
17 Walkowitz, *Nights Out*, 203; Houlbrook, 'The Man with the Powder Puff'.
18 Walkowitz, *Nights Out*, 195, 198.
19 Sanders, *Consuming Fantasies*; Mullin, *Working Girls*.
20 'Dreams in a Teashop!', *Lyons Mail*, Vol XXIII No 7, 1938, ACC/3527/288, 133; 'Nippy Barnett', n.d., and Beatrice F. Morgans, 20 January 1990, ACC/3257/235.
21 Zweiniger-Bargielowska, 'The Making of a Modern Female Body'.
22 'A Jubilee Contrast', 1934, ACC/3257/624, J. Lyons and 'A Jubilee Contrast', 1934, ACC/3257/624; also see Walkowitz, *Nights Out*, 204.
23 'Hints to waiters and waitresses', c. 1930–50, ACC/3257/200, 5. In Chapter 3 of this volume, Alison Moulds describes a similar emotional regime of politeness and cheerfulness among turn-of-the-century retail workers.
24 Hochschild, *The Managed Heart*, 7; Scheer, 'Are Emotions a Kind of Practice?'; Addison, 'Overcoming Arlie Hochschild's Concepts'.
25 'Courteous and Efficient', *Lyons Mail*, Vol XX No 2, 1935, ACC/3527/285, 33. On the concept of 'efficiency' in late-nineteenth- and early-twentieth-century psychology and business, see Rabinbach, *The Human Motor*; Thomson, *Psychological Subjects*.
26 Previously the waitresses had been known as 'Gladys': a name that also demonstrated the qualities expected of these affable, feminine figures. *Lyons Mail*, July–August 1992, ACC/3527/565.
27 *Lyons Mail*, February 1929, Vol XIII No 10, ACC/3527/279, 228. The association between Nippies and efficiency was powerful, remaining in the memories of customers decades later: *The Times*, 2 May 1995, ACC/3527/565.
28 Terry Monaghan, 8 January 1990, and S. Morgan, 9 January 1990, ACC/3257/235.
29 Phyllis Frankwell, 27 January 1990, ACC/3257/235.
30 Phyllis Frankwell, 27 January 1990, ACC/3257/235. On rudeness and respectability see Skeggs, *Formations of Class and Gender*; Thom, *Nice Girls*.
31 'The Waitress', *Lyons Mail*, Vol XIII No 11, March 1929, ACC/3527/279, 269.

32 Nippy Alice Brown remembered waitressing as 'really hard work, hard on one's feet' and being so exhausted at the end of the day that 'it was an effort to keep awake going home on the train'. Nevertheless, she said 'life was enjoyable'. Alice Brown, 21 January 1990, ACC/3257/235.

33 'The Waitress', *Lyons Mail*, Vol XIII No 11, March 1929, ACC/3527/279, 269. Moulds, in Chapter 3 in this volume, also discusses how the living-in system common in the retail sector at the turn of the twentieth century infantilized shop assistants.

34 de Groot and Schrover, *Women Workers and Technological Change*; McDowell, *Working Bodies*; Hicks, *Programmed Inequality*.

35 'Lyons Loveliest Girl', *Lyons Mail*, Vol XXIV No 2, June 1939, ACC/3527/288, 30-31; photos of 'Miss Lyons' winner, 1950s, ACC/3527/511. After the Nippy name fell out of use, waitresses were known as 'Teashop Girls', *Lyons Mail*, August 1950, ACC/3527/293, 6.

36 Hochschild, *The Managed Heart*, 163-4.

37 'Story of a Nippy's day', *Picture Post*, 4 March 1939, ACC/3257/234. However, one customer remembered being told that Nippies were not allowed to accept tips. Ivy Hudson, 1 March 1990, and S. Morgan, 9 January 1990, ACC/3257/235.

38 Edwardian social reformers worried that low wages drove shop girls and barmaids to court male attention, facilitating moral corruption. Mullin, *Working Girls*, 115-17.

39 Illustrations of Nippies, c. 1920-30s, ACC/3527/565.

40 McDowell, *Working Bodies*, 8, 50; Pamela Cox calls this 'aesthetic labour', Cox, 'Shop Girls'.

41 Margaret Sheppard, 22 January 1990; Ivy Hudson, 1 March 1990; A. McGaffrey, 9 January 1990; Rosemary Laird, 10 January 1990, ACC/3257/235.

42 John Dixon, c. 1990, ACC/3257/235.

43 Bailey, 'Parasexuality and Glamour'; Dyhouse, *Glamour*.

44 Reekie, 'Decently Dressed?'; Gagné, 'Romance and Sexuality'; Mears and Connell, 'The Paradoxical Value'; 'parasexuality' has also been usefully applied to histories of pornography and print culture; see Cocks, 'The Social Picture'.

45 Bailey, 'Parasexuality and Glamour', 152.

46 These limits have also been identified by Mullin, *Working Girls*, 7, 8, 171.

47 Mort, *Capital Affairs*, 305.

48 Delap, *Knowing Their Place*, 183; for an unsettling depiction of a teashop waitress who slides into sex work after an affair with a customer, see Maugham, *Of Human Bondage*.

49 Laite, *Common Prostitutes*, 134.

50 'Story of a Nippy's day', *Picture Post*, 4 March 1939, ACC/3257/234. The *Lyons Mail* regularly published lists of Nippy marriages; they did not do the same with their other employees. 'Nippy Weddings', *Lyons Mail*, Vol XIX No 9, 1935,

ACC/3527/285, 173; 'Nippy Weddings', *Lyons Mail,* Vol XXIII No 5, 1938, ACC/3527/288, 95.
51 Gillis, 'Servants, Sexual Relations'.
52 'Hints to waiters and waitresses', *c.* 1930s–50s, ACC/3257/200, 7. 'The Perfect Nippy', 1930s, ACC/3527/201/A. Conway finds a similar discrepancy between the heavily made-up young women observed by contemporaries such as J. B. Priestley and photographs of beauty contest entrants that indicate limited use of cosmetics. Conway, 'Making the Mill Girl Modern?'
53 Goodwin, 14 January 1990, ACC/3257/235.
54 Kathleen Pittman, 10 February 1990, ACC/3257/235.
55 P. Hughes, 7 January 1990, ACC/3257/235.
56 Gladys Foster, n.d., ACC/3257/235.
57 Stanley, 'We Were Skivvies'; Koven, *The Match Girl and the Heiress*; Jackson, 'Not Seeking Certain Proof'.
58 McDowell defines body work as 'the production of an embodied performance by workers and the labour involved in the care of others' bodies'. McDowell, *Working Bodies*, 50; Wolkowitz, *Bodies at Work*; Cox, 'Shop Girls'.
59 Walkowitz, *Nights Out*, 202, 207.
60 Valman, *The Jewess*; Valman, 'Bad Jew/Good Jewess'.
61 Crisp, *The Naked Civil Servant*, 43.
62 Crisp, *The Naked Civil Servant*, 43–4.
63 Houlbrook, *Queer London*.
64 Photograph of Lower Regent Street Teashop, 29 March 1951, ACC/3527/580.
65 In post-war Britain, it was migrant women who were concentrated in low-paid and low-status service jobs. See Webster, *Imagining Home*; McDowell, *Working Lives*.
66 'Nippy is Snappier Now!', January 1947, ACC/3527/565.
67 'I Want to be "Nippy"', *Lyons Mail,* Vol XIV No 4, August 1929, ACC/3527/279, 91; *Lyons Mail,* Vol XIX No 10, February 1935, ACC/3527/285, 201.
68 For a discussion of interwar sexuality, including kinks and fetishes surrounding uniforms and 'crossdressing', see Sigel, *Making Modern Love*.
69 Mrs Butters, 9 March 1990, ACC/3257/235.
70 Edith Walker, 18 December 1989; Amelia Flanders Attenborough, 8 January 1990; A. McGaffrey, 9 January 1990; M. Shuman, n.d.; Alice Brown, 21 January 1990, ACC/3257/235.
71 M. Camac, 14 January 1990, ACC/3257/235. Delap finds a similar attitude among some former domestic servants; Delap, *Knowing Their Place*, 28.
72 Langhamer, 'Feelings, Women and Work', 86–7.
73 Skeggs, 'Uneasy Alignments'.
74 On pragmatism in courtship and marriage in this period, see Giles, 'You Met 'Em and That's It'; Szreter and Fisher, *Sex before the Sexual Revolution*.

75 Nava, 'Modernity's Disavowal'; Rappaport, *Shopping for Pleasure*.

Bibliography

Addison, Michelle. 'Overcoming Arlie Hochschild's Concepts of the "Real" and "False" Self by Drawing on Pierre Bourdieu's Concept of Habitus'. *Emotion, Space and Society* 23 (May 2017): 9–15. https://doi.org/10.1016/j.emospa.2017.01.003.

Bailey, Peter. 'Parasexuality and Glamour: The Victorian Barmaid as Cultural Prototype'. *Gender & History* 2, no. 2 (1990): 148–72. https://doi.org/10.1111/j.1468-0424.1990.tb00091.x.

Charnock, Hannah. 'Teenage Girls, Female Friendship and the Making of the Sexual Revolution in England, 1950–1980'. *The Historical Journal* (2019): 1–22. https://doi.org/10.1017/S0018246X19000396.

Cocks, Harry. '"The Social Picture of Our Own Times": Reading Obscene Magazines in Mid-Twentieth-Century Britain'. *Twentieth Century British History* 27, no. 2 (2016): 171–94.

Conway, Rebecca. 'Making the Mill Girl Modern?: Beauty, Industry, and the Popular Newspaper in 1930s' England'. *Twentieth Century British History* 24, no. 4 (2013): 518–41. https://doi.org/10.1093/tcbh/hwt004.

Cox, Pamela. 'Shop Girls, Social History and Social Theory'. *Revista Brasileira de História* 37, no. 75 (16 August 2017): 243–71. https://doi.org/10.1590/1806-934720 17v37n75-11.

Crisp, Quentin. *The Naked Civil Servant*. London: Flamingo, 1985.

Delap, Lucy. *Knowing Their Place: Domestic Service in Twentieth-Century Britain*. Oxford: Oxford University Press, 2011.

Doan, Laura. '"A Peculiarly Obscure Subject": The Missing "case" of the Heterosexual'. In *British Queer History: New Approaches and Perspectives*, edited by Brian Lewis, 87–108. Manchester: Manchester University Press, 2013.

Dyhouse, Carol. *Glamour: Women, History, Feminism*. London: Zed Books, 2010.

Gagné, Nana Okura. 'Romance and Sexuality in Japanese Latin Dance Clubs'. *Ethnography* 15, no. 4 (2014): 446–68.

Gammerl, Benno. 'Emotional Styles – Concepts and Challenges'. *Rethinking History* 16, no. 2 (June 2012): 161–75. https://doi.org/10.1080/13642529.2012.681189.

Giles, Judy. '"You Met 'Em and That's It": Working Class Women's Refusal of Romance between the Wars in Britain'. In *Romance Revisited*, edited by Lynne Pearce and Jackie Stacey, 279–92. London: Lawrence and Wishart, 1995.

Gillis, John R. 'Servants, Sexual Relations, and the Risks of Illegitimacy in London, 1801–1900'. *Feminist Studies* 5, no. 1 (1979): 142–73.

Groot, Gertjan de, and Marlou Schrover. *Women Workers and Technological Change in Europe in the Nineteenth and Twentieth Centuries*. London: Taylor and Francis, 1995.

Hicks, Mar. *Programmed Inequality: How Britain Discarded Women Technologists and Lost Its Edge in Computing*. London: The MIT Press, 2017.

Hochschild, Arlie Russell. *The Managed Heart: Commercialization of Human Feeling*. Updated edition. Berkeley: University of California Press, 2012.

Houlbrook, Matt. 'The Man with the Powder Puff in Interwar London'. *The Historical Journal* 50, no. 1 (2007): 145–71.

Houlbrook, Matt. *Queer London: Perils and Pleasures in the Sexual Metropolis, 1918–1957*. Chicago: University of Chicago Press, 2005.

Jackson, Will. 'Not Seeking Certain Proof: Interracial Sex and Archival Haze in High-Imperial Natal'. In *Subverting Empire: Deviance and Disorder in the British Colonial World*, edited by Will Jackson and Emily J. Manktelow, 185–204. Hampshire: Palgrave Macmillan, 2015.

Koven, Seth. *The Match Girl and the Heiress*. Princeton: Princeton University Press, 2014.

Laite, Julia. *Common Prostitutes and Ordinary Citizens: Commercial Sex in London, 1885–1960*. Hampshire: Palgrave Macmillan, 2012.

Langhamer, Claire. 'Feelings, Women and Work in the Long 1950s'. *Women's History Review* 26, no. 1 (2017): 77–92. https://doi.org/10.1080/09612025.2015.1123025.

Maugham, W. Somerset. *Of Human Bondage*. Newburyport: Open Road Media, 2017.

McDowell, Linda. *Working Bodies: Interactive Service Employment and Workplace Identities*. Oxford: Wiley-Blackwell, 2009.

McDowell, Linda. *Working Lives: Gender, Migration and Employment in Britain, 1945–2007*. Sussex: Wiley-Blackwell, 2013.

Mears, Ashley, and Catherine Connell. 'The Paradoxical Value of Deviant Cases: Towards a Gendered Theory of Display Work'. *Signs: Journal of Women in Culture and Society* 41, no. 2 (2016): 333–59.

Mort, Frank. *Capital Affairs: London and the Making of the Permissive Society*. New Haven: Yale University Press, 2010.

Mullin, Katherine. *Working Girls: Fiction, Sexuality, and Modernity*. Oxford: Oxford University Press, 2016.

Nava, Mica. 'Modernity's Disavowal: Women, the City and the Department Store'. In *Modern Times: Reflections on a Century of Modernity*, edited by Mica Nava and Alan O'Shea, 38–76. London: Routledge, 1996.

Ned Katz, Jonathan. *The Invention of Heterosexuality*. Chicago: University of Chicago Press, 2007.

Rabinbach, Anson. *The Human Motor: Energy, Fatigue and the Origins of Modernity*. Berkeley: University of California Press, 1992.

Rappaport, Erika Diane. *Shopping for Pleasure: Women in the Making of London's West End*. Princeton: Princeton University Press, 2000.

Reddy, William M. *The Navigation of Feeling: A Framework for the History of Emotions*. Cambridge: Cambridge University Press, 2001.

Reekie, Gail. 'Decently Dressed? Sexualised Consumerism and the Working Woman's Wardrobe 1918–1923'. *Labour History* 61 (November 1991): 42–56.

Sanders, Lise Shapiro. *Consuming Fantasies: Labor, Leisure and the London Shopgirl, 1880–1920*. Columbus: Ohio State University Press, 2006.

Scheer, Monique. 'Are Emotions a Kind of Practice (and Is That What Makes Them Have a History)? A Bourdieuian Approach to Understanding Emotion'. *History and Theory* 51, no. 2 (May 2012): 193–220. https://doi.org/10.1111/j.1468-2303.2012.00621.x.

Schwartz, Laura. *Feminism and the Servant Problem: Class and Domestic Labour in the Women's Suffrage Movement*. Cambridge: Cambridge University Press, 2019.

Sigel, Lisa Z. *Making Modern Love: Sexual Narratives and Identities in Interwar Britain*. Philadelphia: Temple University Press, 2012.

Skeggs, Beverley. *Formations of Class and Gender: Becoming Respectable*. London: Sage Publishing, 1997.

Skeggs, Beverley. 'Uneasy Alignments, Resourcing Respectable Subjectivity'. *GLQ: A Journal of Lesbian and Gay Studies* 10, no. 2 (2004): 291–98.

Smith, Helen. *Masculinity, Class and Same-Sex Desire in Industrial England, 1895–1957*. Hampshire: Palgrave Macmillan, 2015.

Stanley, Jo. '"We Were Skivvies/We Had a Ball": Shame and Interwar Ships'. *Oral History* 38, no. 2 (2010): 64–74.

Strimpel, Zoe. *Seeking Love in Modern Britain: Gender, Dating and the Rise of 'the Single'*. London: Bloomsbury Academic, 2020.

Szreter, Simon, and Kate Fisher. *Sex before the Sexual Revolution: Intimate Life in England 1918–1963*. Cambridge: Cambridge University Press, 2015.

Thom, Deborah. *Nice Girls and Rude Girls: Women Workers in World War I*. London: I. B. Tauris, 1998.

Thomson, Mathew. *Psychological Subjects: Identity, Culture and Health in Twentieth-Century Britain*. Oxford: Oxford University Press, 2006.

Valman, Nadia. 'Bad Jew/Good Jewess: Gender and Semitic Discourse in Nineteenth-Century England'. In *Philosemitism in History*, edited by Jonathan Karp and Adam Sutcliffe, 149–69. Cambridge: Cambridge University Press, 2012.

Valman, Nadia. *The Jewess in Nineteenth-Century British Literary Culture*. Cambridge: Cambridge University Press, 2007.

Vickers, Emma. *Queen and Country: Same-Sex Desire in the British Armed Forces, 1939–45*. Manchester: Manchester University Press, 2013.

Walkowitz, Judith R. *Nights Out: Life in Cosmopolitan London*. London: Yale University Press, 2012.

Webster, Wendy. *Imagining Home: Gender, 'Race', and National Identity, 1945-64*. London: UCL Press, 1998.

Wolkowitz, Carol. *Bodies at Work*. London: Sage Publishing, 2006.

Zweiniger-Bargielowska, Ina. 'The Making of a Modern Female Body: Beauty, Health and Fitness in Interwar Britain'. *Women's History Review* 20, no. 2 (2011): 299–317. https://doi.org/10.1080/09612025.2011.556324.

3

Shop assistants, 'living-in' and emotional health, 1880s–1930s

Alison Moulds[1]

[B]eing always beside your work and associated with your work, has a very depressing effect upon you.

In 1908, Miss Pettigrew – who ran the boot department at Moore, Taggart & Co., manufacturers and wholesale warehousemen in Glasgow – reflected on the pressures of the 'living-in' system for retail workers. In her view, living and working in one space negatively impacted one's emotional health. She argued that it was better for shop girls to have 'outside interests' (beyond their work), and that she would be 'very unhappy' sharing accommodation.[2]

Miss Pettigrew was giving evidence to the Departmental Committee on the Truck Acts (1906–8). Appointed by the Home Secretary, the Committee was tasked with investigating the operation of the Truck Acts, which sought to curtail employers paying their workers in goods ('truck') rather than wages. As part of this, the Committee considered the living-in system, a practice whereby shop assistants received board and lodging – on the shop premises or in nearby accommodation – instead of part of their salary. Over two and a half years, the Committee heard evidence from employers and shop workers, including Miss Pettigrew. She conceded that she had 'not experienced' living-in herself (the system was not used by her employers) but that her arguments were based on what she had 'heard'.[3] The fact she had no direct experience did not discredit her claims, for she deployed common tropes about living-in. These spread not only by word of mouth but also permeated popular culture and public discourse.

At the *fin de siècle*, retail work was sometimes seen as genteel and even glamorous, offering the prospect of upward social mobility for men and women from working-class and lower-middle-class backgrounds. Yet it was also represented as injurious to shop assistants' physical, mental and moral health. There was growing concern about the long hours worked, the lack of seating available and the unsanitary and unseemly nature of shops and their accommodation. Campaign groups such as the Early Closing Association, the Shop Hours Labour League, and the National Union of Shop Assistants (hereafter 'the Union') initially directed their attention to working hours.[4] They gradually secured reforms – the 1886 Shop Hours Act limited the number of working hours to seventy-four for under-eighteens, with further legislation passed in the 1890s. When it came to the question of living-in, however, campaigners were less united.

In retail, as in many occupations, living-in was rooted in the apprenticeship system.[5] While learning their trade from an established shopkeeper, adolescent and teenage boys had traditionally lived with their master's family. By the close of the nineteenth century, apprenticeships were declining in retail, but the practice of living-in continued, particularly in the drapery and grocery trades. With the expansion of consumer culture, stores grew in size, becoming mass employers of both men and women. In these shops, employers usually no longer lived on the premises. Instead, a larger-scale (sometimes compulsory) living-in system developed, with 'an institutional form of life'.[6] There were marked regional differences, however; living-in was widespread in London and Wales but uncommon in Liverpool and practically 'unknown' in Scotland, as the Truck Committee heard.[7]

Abolishing living-in became one of the Union's main objectives in the 1890s,[8] but the Early Closing Association – which was dominated by philanthropists and larger employers and lacked representation from retail workers[9] – insisted that some assistants preferred the system.[10] The fact that resistance lay with the unionists arguably curtailed political intervention. The Truck Committee's final report concluded that living-in had advantages as well as disadvantages and called for improved regulation and inspection, rather than abolition. Unimpressed, the Union redoubled its conviction that 'the whole system of living-in must go'.[11] Critics associated living-in with overcrowded, poorly ventilated accommodation and low-quality food. Some claimed it aggravated the problem of unpaid overtime and that employers used it to suppress salaries. Politically, it disenfranchised shop workers, since they could not take advantage of the lodger franchise. Further, if live-in employees were dismissed, they could be left homeless. Within this constellation of issues, workers' 'emotional health' (as it would now be termed) emerged as a significant part of the discourse.

Scholarship on Victorian and Edwardian retail work has typically concentrated on philanthropic campaigns, trade unionism and legislative change. Socio-economic historians have considered some of the privations of living-in. Wilfred B. Whitaker presents it as part of a broader culture of overwork, describing how – in the eyes of employers – '[b]eyond a place to sleep and eat, little was needed' for live-in workers.[12] More recently, scholars have considered living-in through the lens of gender and sexual politics. Christopher Hosgood argues that it was an infantilizing experience, which compromised workers' masculinity or femininity, keeping them in a state of 'suspended adolescence',[13] while Lise Shapiro Sanders and Katherine Mullin show how the system stimulated anxieties about the shop girl's perceived sexual improprieties.[14]

This chapter reorients attention to how the affective side of living-in was represented. Drawing on a range of literary, medical, campaigning and parliamentary sources, I focus on cultural constructions of shop life between the 1880s and 1930s, asking to what extent debates about retail workers' welfare explored and prioritized their feelings of happiness and contentment, or their anxieties and frustrations. Living-in was of course not unique to shop assistants – in this period, many occupations (from domestic service to teaching) involved living on-site, in employer-provided accommodation. Experiences of living-in were bound up with specific working conditions and occupational identities, though common themes emerged across professional groups. Agnes Arnold-Forster's chapter on hospital residences for doctors and nurses illustrates the enduring nature of many of the tropes surrounding living where you work.

Representations of retail workers living-in were not purely negative and the Truck Committee heard arguments both for and against the system. While I examine how living-in might be seen as depressing and stultifying, and as producing stress, anxiety or even fear, I also consider more affirmative responses to the practice, which was sometimes seen as offering a support system for shop workers. Living in proximity to one's colleagues might engender feelings of loneliness and isolation or – conversely – friendship and camaraderie. More broadly, this chapter considers how debates about the emotional rewards and challenges of living-in were inflected with assumptions about class and gender and how they were bound up with ideas about the rights, duties and sensibilities of employers and employees.

Living spaces

In 1892, the medical journal the *Lancet* published the findings of its 'Sanitation in the Shop' inquiry. Across two leading articles, it lambasted the retail industry as a public health crisis, one which caused physical and mental degeneration among shop workers. Turning its attention to the living-in system, the inquiry complained that assistants 'have no residence, no home, but merely a room at the top of the house – sometimes a mere attic'. Meanwhile, others 'have no bedrooms at all, but are expected to sleep in the shop under the counter'.[15] The privations of inadequate accommodation and lack of dedicated sleeping space were seen as robbing shop workers of their dignity and right to a home life.

Contemporary literature featured similarly forlorn images of shop assistants' living spaces. In Émile Zola's novel *Au Bonheur des Dames* (1883) – which was immediately translated into English – the heroine Denise Baudu lives in the attic above a grand department store.[16] Her room is portrayed as 'a narrow cell' leading off a 'convent-like corridor'.[17] Tropes of live-in accommodation as ascetic single-sex environments remained pervasive; Zola's description prefigures images of the twentieth-century hospital residence as a 'monastic cell', as explored by Arnold-Forster. Unlike most shop girls (who shared bedrooms), Zola's heroine has her own space, which – though meagre – provides a 'refuge' where she can 'give way to tears' after a demanding day on the shop floor, in which she has to 'smile' despite her 'continual fear of being brutally dismissed'.[18] William Reddy argues that, within an emotional regime, 'emotional refuge[s]' offer a 'safe release from prevailing emotional norms' and a 'relaxation of emotional effort'.[19] For many commentators, however, living-in extended (rather than relaxed) the shop's emotional regime.

This is thrown into sharp relief in Cicely Hamilton's play *Diana of Dobson's*, first performed in 1908. It opens in a shop assistants' dormitory in a fictional suburban establishment, Dobson's Drapery Emporium. The stage directions describe the set as a 'bare room', with '[v]ery little furniture' and 'everything plain and comfortless'.[20] The titular heroine rails against the setup of a 'stuffy dormitory' with 'mean little rules to obey' and against the '[g]rind and squalor and tyranny and overwork' of shop life (40, 38). The dormitory emblematizes her feelings of constraint but is also a space in which she can air her protests. The play follows Diana as she comes into an unexpected inheritance and triumphantly departs the business, a familiar arc in literature about retail work. Her renunciation of the shop's stultifying regime is liberating – the next scene shows her exulting in a trip to the Swiss Mountains, their sublimity a radical departure from her claustrophobic experience of living-in.

The way in which shop assistants interacted with their living spaces was unpacked by trade union activist Margaret Bondfield in an 1899 article for *The Economic Journal*. Bondfield derived authority from her past experience as a shop worker,[21] and the article combined general observations with several anonymous case studies of live-in accommodation. The piece began by sharing a 'typical' set of House Rules for live-in employees. In addition to an 11.00 pm curfew and a prescribed bedtime, these strictures mandated that no pictures or photos were 'allowed to disfigure the walls' and no flowers could be displayed.[22] By preventing workers from adorning or personalizing their living space, employers deprived assistants of self-expression and stimulation. The case studies offered a more complex portrait of shop life, however. A 'high-class drapery and outfitting business' in south-west London, for instance, featured bedrooms which were 'made pretty and homelike by the assistants who occupy them' (presumably they were permitted some form of decoration) but others which were 'dingy and overcrowded'.[23] In a 'middle-class drapery and outfitting business', one bedroom had a 'dirty, dilapidated appearance' but another was 'pleasant' and 'well-furnished', and the assistants had use of 'a delightfully pleasant sitting-room'.[24] The interrelationship between the sensory and affective aspects of live-in accommodation is a theme I explore elsewhere.[25] As Bondfield's article suggests, living conditions varied considerably across and even within establishments.

When it came to what standard of living space shop assistants required or deserved, opinions varied. As part of its inquiry, the Truck Committee visited staff accommodation. The final report conceded that some 'certainly lacked brightness and cheerfulness' and were even 'shabby', but it suggested that the rooms were of a similar quality to that which workers might find if they were living outside the shop, in lodgings. Further, the report contended that 'assistants are drawn from different grades' and 'the difference between, say, a West End establishment and an East End establishment corresponds to differences in the homes from which the assistants come'.[26] The report suggested that variations in living standards replicated what assistants had experienced before or would encounter elsewhere, ignoring the fact that – for many shop assistants – retail work was aspirational, offering the prospect of social mobility. In the same year the Committee presented its report, the Union magazine, *The Shop Assistant*, published a Christmas cartoon special on living-in. According to an advert previewing the issue, the aim was 'to deepen the indignation by showing the supremely ridiculous restrictions and impositions of the system'.[27] The magazine capitalized on familiar tropes – such as poor-quality food and being locked out after curfew – to incite its readers, hoping that 'indignation' would turn to protest. While the Truck Committee constructed a hierarchy of retail workers, with different needs and expectations, *The Shop Assistant* sought to unite its readers and inspire collective action.

Family support or moral surveillance?

Like the apprenticeship system, living-in was rooted in notions of paternalism, with masters expected to act in loco parentis for their young recruits. Giving evidence to the Truck Committee, Henry Robson – a member of the Federation of Grocers' Associations and the proprietor of a grocer's and provisions dealer in Bournemouth – crafted an image of living-in which suggested it was a replication or extension of family life. Robson had experience of accommodating between four and six boys in his home; in many cases, he claimed, they were 'friends of the family'. He endorsed the Committee's suggestion that arrangements in his business were 'really those of a rather large family'.[28] While it is unsurprising that Robson represented himself as a benevolent employer, this was an image of living-in with which the Committee readily presented him.

Abuses of the system were increasingly reported, however, with some suggesting that living-in did not facilitate, but rather undermined, the tenets of family life. The *Lancet's* 1892 inquiry, for example, reported that one assistant complained that his employer would not grant him even a 'few hours' leave of absence' when his mother was dying.[29] For the author H. G. Wells, being apprenticed to a draper at age thirteen meant the end of childhood and leaving the family home, as he reflected in his 1934 autobiography. The news of his second posting produced an 'unhappiness and dismay' so visceral he could apparently still 'feel' it fifty years later.[30]

Some commentators implied that modern business practices were altering the emotional regime of shop life. There were fears that an oversupply of shop assistants and the system of commissions were creating a competitive atmosphere. The emotional labour of retail – vividly illustrated by Grace Whorrall-Campbell in Chapter 2 – was both celebrated and critiqued. In *A Young Draper's Guide to Success* (1901), W. M. Naismith counselled readers that 'a cheerful temper' should be accompanied by 'obedience' towards their employer and customers.[31] This demand to be 'polite and obliging' exerted considerable pressure, however, as detailed in a pamphlet entitled *Behind the Counter: Sketches by a Shop Assistant* (1888). The anonymous author described how assistants were expected to 'preserve a cool temper' when faced with difficult customers and had to remain 'all smiles and sunshine' even when verbally abused or fined by their employer. This emotional regime was unsustainable, the author claimed: '[u]nless assistants are well cared for, they cannot possibly be expected to retain that happy disposition which is so necessary to success.'[32]

For live-in assistants, this disciplinary control apparently extended to non-working hours. *Behind the Counter* described how

> These poor mortals are always within the glance of their master's eye [. . .]. He does not forget or scruple to question his assistants as to their mode of life, and severely criticises any act which is not in touch with his narrow ideas of human existence.

Further, even 'a claim to the rights and privileges of manhood' did not prevent an assistant having 'the manner in which he spends his leisure hours' dictated by his employer. The author implied that such experiences of surveillance could be infantilizing, as Hosgood has argued, and claimed that it 'restrain[ed] the natural hilarity of young manhood'.[33] By presenting domestic rule as an emotionally impoverished regime, antithetical to 'natural' pleasures, the pamphlet countered suspicions that unsupervised youths might engage in more immoral past-times.

Other commentators insisted that living-in provided a support system, particularly for young people who moved from the countryside to the metropolis, who did not have ready access to accommodation with family or friends. An article in the *Cambria Daily Leader* in 1913 acknowledged that 'public opinion' had turned against the system as being 'a restriction of personal liberty'. However, it suggested that there was 'something to be said for it in the case of juniors, under a management which takes a real concern in the well-being of the youths who come to the shops from country homes'.[34] The reference to 'well-being' (rather than physical health or moral welfare) implied that the employer's responsibility extended beyond providing meals and accommodation and regulating workers' conduct.

Gender differences were also evoked, with some commentators arguing that living-in protected women's moral welfare. Giving evidence to the Truck Committee, Margarita Oliver – who worked in a silk department – spoke favourably of the system. She described how it 'would be bad morally and physically' for girls to live out but exempted 'young men' who, she claimed, were 'different and look at things in a different light'. Deploying common tropes, Oliver argued that employers would struggle to attract respectable female workers without offering some supervision. She insisted that, if living-in was abolished, then the 'parents of the better class girls would not allow their daughters to come up and take lodgings in London'. Further, she claimed that older shop women had a steadying influence, providing a 'moral check' upon the younger girls.[35]

Critics debunked this idea that the system safeguarded workers' morality and welfare. In George Gissing's novel *The Odd Women* (1893), shop life entails a climate of permissiveness and promiscuity. At the start of the narrative, Monica Madden works for a drapery establishment in Walworth Road, London. Gissing satirizes the laxity of her employers, describing how these 'large-minded men' were 'so generous' that they granted each young person a latchkey and allowed them to go out in the evenings.[36] This lack of supervision enables men like Bullivant and Widdowson to pursue Monica. Further, her sense of lassitude – cultivated by shop life – means that she tolerates Widdowson's courtship, despite her absence of '[e]motional interest in him' (46). Due to the public nature of the shop, he can loiter outside her accommodation uninvited, an act which produces a 'fit of trembling' in her (73), and he becomes the subject of gossip among her colleagues, which leaves Monica lying awake with 'tear-stained eyes' (58). In these passages, Gissing emphasizes the pressures of shop life, its threat to respectable female conduct and emotional welfare. He also refutes the idea that older female workers might provide a moralizing influence over shop girls.

For many commentators, living-in did not protect, but rather jeopardized, shop assistants' moral welfare. While Bondfield's article recorded some positive aspects of living-in, it refuted the idea that the system 'provides both home and guardians' for young people, noting that – in most cases – 'this impression is entirely erroneous'. Rather, she claimed, workers' 'moral calibre [was] weakened by the absence of proper social or home life'.[37] Critics suggested that employers used 'moral care' as a smokescreen to justify an exploitative system, an argument crystallized in Thomas Spencer Jones's campaign pamphlet *The Moral Side of Living-In* (1907). Spencer Jones (editor of *The Shop Assistant* magazine) castigated the fact that 'morality is regarded as a matter of restraint', a blunt instrument of control emblematized by 'locked doors'. Painting an emotionally deleterious image of shop life, he complained that '[t]he atmosphere is demoralizing. The surroundings are miserable.'[38] Further, the system was seen to drive shopworkers to pursue more clandestine amorous encounters and to hamper them from saving money to start their own families and building the skills required for domestic life.[39]

Despite these challenges, living-in was often represented as a transitional stage, in which the young assistant would save money and develop the expertise needed to establish his or her own shop. Independent shopkeeping was aspirational because it promised greater autonomy and self-sufficiency. This fantasy was enacted in popular fiction, such as Wells's novel *Kipps* (1905). At the start of the narrative, the eponymous hero is apprenticed to Shalford, a draper in Folkestone. Drawing on his own experiences, Wells describes how the teenaged Kipps finds shop life tedious and dispiriting, feeling a 'vague self-disgust that shaped itself as an intense hate of Shalford and all his fellow-creatures'.[40]

Dismissed after a night of drunkenness with an eccentric acquaintance, Kipps is saved from poverty after inheriting a fortune. Yet he remains mired in shame at his inability to attain gentility. After losing his wealth, the story ends with Kipps setting up a bookshop, where he lives with his family. 'He wonders how it was he ever came to fancy a shop a disagreeable place', though he reasons that 'being on your own' is 'different' (410). Whereas Kipps flounders as a man of leisure, he finds mental and emotional well-being in the rhythms of shop life. His motto – '[k]eep a shop and the shop'll keep you' – shows how he derives satisfaction from work and self-sufficiency (423). The book closes with an idyllic scene in which the protagonist and his wife are rowing on the Hythe canal, '[o]ne early-closing evening in July' (424). With Kipps able to control his working hours, he can manage his leisure time and prioritize his family over business.

Wells presents a much less sentimental vision of shopkeeping in *The History of Mr Polly* (1910). In this novel, the titular protagonist feels so restricted by shop life that he decides to burn down his business (also his home) and desert his wife. The narrative opens by explaining how Polly 'hated his shop and his wife and his neighbours' and how he resents his own 'stagnation'.[41] This dual rejection of his place of work and his domestic space shows how deeply his personal and professional lives intersect. Despite his relative autonomy, Polly experiences similar feelings of constraint to live-in assistants. In response to emotional and financial pressures, he fakes his own death and becomes a nomad, finding work as a handyman at a rural inn. While Kipps merges family life and retail business, Polly rejects both to find independence and self-fulfilment.

Work and leisure time

Historians such as Hosgood have suggested that living-in 'broke down the barriers' separating work, sleep and leisure, with all three conducted in the same place.[42] In this period, however, many workers – ranging from domestic servants to agricultural labourers – would not have experienced a clear demarcation between these activities. Yet commentators increasingly argued that living and working in one space was injurious to emotional health and that boundaries between work and leisure time were central to feelings of well-being – ideas which prefigure modern-day conceptions of 'work–life balance'. Within the context of debates about living-in, anxieties were shaped by perceptions that retail exerted a contaminating influence. This is implicit in Bondfield's critique that living-in meant '[t]he atmosphere of "shop" is always with [the workers]'.[43]

Critics emphasized that long working hours and curfews left little time for recreation. The *Lancet* inquiry complained that '[t]here is no time for reading or self-culture; it means practically life from bed to the counter and from the counter back to bed'.[44] By presenting the counter and bed as almost contiguous, the author highlighted the lack of leisure time available to shop assistants and the monotony of their existence. These images recall those found in *Death and Disease behind the Counter* (1884), a sensationalist exposé of the dangers of retail written by Thomas Sutherst, a barrister and President of the Shop Hours Labour League. Characterizing shop life as being 'simply from bed to work and work to bed the year round', Sutherst's book bemoaned that there was little opportunity for self-improvement, since '[t]hrough sheer physical exhaustion and want of time the mental powers are utterly paralyzed'.[45]

Campaigners calling for reduced working hours highlighted the importance of assistants using their leisure time responsibly and respectably, through visiting libraries and lectures, rather than public houses or music halls.[46] Sutherst presented myriad case studies of assistants who claimed that if they had more free time they would use it for self-improvement. Meanwhile, writers who did discuss shop workers' dissipation implied that it was the drudgery of shop life that drove emotionally and mentally starved workers to indulge in vulgar pleasures. In *The Counter Exposed* (1896), Will Anderson recalls his time as a live-in shop assistant at a grocer's in Kent. He describes returning home one day to find that the teenage apprentice had 'fallen down in a drunken fit, and vomited'. For Anderson, it was not a lack of supervision but rather the 'grinding monotony' and 'cheerless work' that invited such debauchery.[47]

The *Lancet* equivocated on the subject of retail workers' right to unfettered leisure time. Its 'Sanitation in the Shop' articles concluded by enthusiastically asserting that assistants

> demand to be free when their work is done, and they urge that hours of work should not be so long and the pay so slight as to debar them from the possibility of living healthy, useful, enjoyable lives.[48]

This recalls the rhetoric of commentators such as Sutherst, who merged ideas of physical health and self-improvement with happiness. However, a later piece in the *Lancet* suggested that the Union's resolution to abolish living-in went too far. This article, printed in 1907, instead called for the system to be regulated, to curtail its 'sanitary defects' and to bring about 'reasonable liberty' for those presently 'deprived' of it. The writer suggested that employers should 'find no sympathy' if they 'curtail' workers' 'liberty to such an extent as to injure their health, or even to deprive them of reasonable enjoyment'. Yet the repetition of the caveat 'reasonable' indicates anxiety that greater freedom would lead to licentiousness. Moreover, the article endorsed the idea that employers should be able to extend their 'supervision and control [. . .] beyond the duration of the working day', implying it was they who were best placed to determine what pleasures workers might 'reasonably' undertake.[49] The previous endorsement for assistants to lead 'enjoyable lives' has been restrained. The *Lancet*'s shift could be explained by the use of a different author (both pieces appeared anonymously), though the journal remained under the same editor (Thomas Wakley junior). Of course, by framing living-in primarily as a sanitary issue – an idea which informs both articles – the *Lancet* brought it within the remit of medical authority and expertise.

Critics challenged this idea that employers were well-suited to regulate workers' leisure time, however. *Behind the Counter* suggested that puritanical employers averse to the theatre or reading would expect their employees to shun such entertainments, and that this left assistants with few alternatives except to 'wander about [the streets] in a shiftless and purposeless manner' or 'be kept at the grindstone until it is time for bed'.[50] Meanwhile, radical campaigners such as Clementina Black lambasted the notion that 'an employer has some quasi-royal or quasi-paternal right to guide and regulate the lives of employees out of working hours' as one which 'ought, at this time of day, to be strenuously resisted'.[51] She presented this as anathema to modern sensibilities.

Leisure time was being conceptualized as a fundamental right. Sutherst's moralizing undertone can be detected in his preoccupation with self-improvement, but he also argued that nature demanded time for exercise, relaxation, nourishment and mental culture. He offered a pitiable portrait of shop life, describing how the youth who entered retail 'bids adieu to exercise, fresh air, friends, books, and all that makes life worth having'.[52] Similar images are found in Wells's autobiography, when he narrates his transition from childhood to apprenticeship, freedom to labour:

> Now it was my turn to put the [. . .] books away, give up drawing and painting and every sort of free delight, stop writing stories and imitations of *Punch*, give up all vain hopes and dreams, and serve an employer.[53]

He suggests that an apprenticeship thrust him into a world of business which denied him simple pleasures.

Popular literature forged a link between leisure and emotional health by showing how shop assistants greeted even short-lived respite with pleasure. In *The Odd Women*, Gissing describes how when Monica leaves 'the big ugly "establishment" [of the shop], her heart beat cheerfully, and a smile fluttered about her lips' (32). Though her pleasures are few, the shift from her space of work to the outside world is gratifying, linked to feelings of freedom and (relative) independence. In Dorothy Whipple's novel *High Wages* (1930), the shop assistant Jane Carter is 'beside herself with joy' while on holiday, relishing '[e]ach golden minute'. In a moment of free indirect discourse, the narrator notes, 'when you only have a holiday once in a while, what a happiness it is!'[54] This fantasy of escapism is enacted on a grander scale in *Diana of Dobson's*. Even after the heroine has frittered away her windfall and is living on the streets, she insists that she does not 'regret' her 'one glorious month' of travel, adventure and independence (74).

Wells's social comedies about shop work depict men who experience the drudgery and shame of retail and indulge in fantasies of escapism and romance. *The Wheels of Chance* (1896) follows a draper's assistant on his eagerly awaited cycling holiday. The narrator reflects,

> Only those who toil six long days out of the seven, and all the year round, save for one brief glorious fortnight or ten days in the summer time, know the exquisite sensations of the First Holiday Morning.[55]

Mr Hoopdriver regards his vacation as a brief interlude of freedom, for shop life is presented as a degradation which constrains his independence and undermines his masculinity. While engaging with the privations of retail work, the novel's comedic plot centres on Hoopdriver's holiday adventures which – it is implied – will sustain him when he returns to the world of the shop. As Richard Higgins identifies, Wells is 'never quite sure if he wants recklessness or only the idea of recklessness'.[56] While Hoopdriver (re)submits to the privations of shop life, Kipps remodels his role within the retail industry, and Polly absconds for a radically new life. Like his protagonists, Wells found dreaming to be a form of rebellion and escapism. His autobiography recalls how, during his apprenticeship, his 'disposition to reverie increased'. These daydreams were linked to feelings of loneliness; finding that his colleagues are now 'blank nameless figures', Wells concludes that he 'made no friends'.[57]

Companionship and solitude

The impression that shop life was lonely and without enjoyment has been reinforced and challenged by historians. Hosgood contends that shop assistants led an 'isolated existence', separated from their local communities, and describes them as 'the most pitiable of the lower middle class'.[58] By contrast, while Sanders reflects on shop girls' struggles, she tempers this by exploring their leisure pursuits, from their consumption of popular periodicals to music-hall entertainment. While living-in was associated with emotional hardships, many commentators (both past and present) suggested that shop life offered opportunities for recreation and camaraderie.

Shop assistants were often represented as finding fulfilment in sociability. Giving evidence to the Truck Committee, Arthur Unwin Cole – the director of Cole Brothers in Sheffield – expressed his support for the living-in system, particularly for 'young assistants'. He claimed that '[t]he social element in the living-in system is a very powerful element and means a very great deal to these people'.[59] His argument drew on assumptions that working-class men and women (which he disassociated from himself and the Committee with the phrase 'these people') would find pleasure in socializing. Through his focus on companionship, he constructed shop assistants as an 'emotional community' – to draw on Barbara Rosenwein's concept – which derived value and meaning from interpersonal interactions.[60]

Another witness – Mr Cormack, partner of Jenners department store in Edinburgh – also supported living-in, though he felt the system should be optional. He contended that their workers had 'more home comforts' living-in than in lodgings. When asked about his assistants' well-being, he replied, 'I think they are very happy. They have cricket clubs and football clubs, as well as concerts and theatricals [. . .]; we give them every facility for recreation.' The Committee's question and Cormack's response show that there was a concern not simply with the standard of accommodation provided but workers' emotional well-being and access to recreational activities. It was in Cormack's interests to present himself as a humane employer and to suggest that his workers were content. However, his claims that he had lived-in for thirteen years suggest he may have had intimate knowledge of the conditions needed to support workers' well-being. He endorsed the popular view that living-in was 'even more favourable' among women and that, without it, a company would struggle to attract the 'same class' of workers.[61]

Those who defended the system suggested that it offered particular advantages to young workers and a mobile workforce, not simply because it provided a form of supervision but because it offered a social network. If Wells's autobiography recalls his apprenticeships as a largely friendless and lonely time, his fiction presents more romanticized and nostalgic images of the camaraderie of shop life. Mr Polly looks back fondly on his time as an apprentice at the Port Burdock Drapery Bazaar, remembering 'there were girls! And friendship! In the retrospect Port Burdock sparkled with the facets of quite a cluster of remembered jolly times'. Although the sleeping accommodation is a 'bleak' place, the shop is where he 'first tasted the joys of social intercourse' (20). Polly's memories are coloured by his later despondency, however. He concedes that, after one friend departed, and another became a more 'tiresome companion', the shop became 'a dreariness full of faded memories' (46).

Protest writing emphasizing the frustrations of retail work similarly acknowledged some of the more affirmative aspects of shop life, which largely related to social intercourse. The author of *Behind the Counter* reflected that '[t]here are a few situations in which you can enjoy yourself very well indeed', namely where the employer lived off-site and the assistants lived-in 'under the management of a sympathetic housekeeper'. The pamphlet described some of the personalities encountered in shop life, including the 'stage-struck' assistant who loves the theatre and who 'thinks it is his imperative duty to be happy under all circumstances'. This 'jolly associate' 'transforms his bedroom into a miniature theatre' and '[w]ith the assistance of a few bedfellows, an impromptu drama is produced every night'. Another character sketch represented 'the practical joker of the establishment' who 'is always in trouble, yet [. . .] is a very happy individual', and who stays in his employer's good graces by being a talented salesman.[62] While some writers romanticized a paternalistic style of living-in, this author celebrated one where colleagues lived more freely, as equals. He showed how, under the right circumstances, shop life could become emotionally satisfying or even rewarding. For this writer, the ideal situation was not necessarily one where living-in was abolished but where it was practised with more freedoms.

Many commentators warned that social mixing could be dangerous, however, since undesirable colleagues could jeopardize the moral character of more genteel employees. In fiction, shop-assistant protagonists are often represented as intellectually, socially or emotionally superior to their colleagues. In *The Odd Women*, Monica is contrasted with the 'showily dressed' and 'coarse-featured' Miss Eade, who later moves into prostitution (55). Giving evidence to the Truck Committee, Margarita Oliver accepted that there were circumstances where roommates may not get on, in which 'different temperaments are thrown together where they are not comfortable'. However, she suggested that, in such cases, it was possible to change rooms – a claim that other witnesses denied.[63] By contrast, Bondfield recalled her experience of being 'put into a room with a woman of mature age who led a life of a most undesirable kind' and with a girl suffering from consumption.[64] The dual image of exposure to moral and physical corruption was stark enough to be cited in the Committee's final report, which reiterated the idea that 'evil moral effects of a serious nature may result from undesirable companionship'.[65] Such portraits emphasized that living in close proximity to one's colleagues did not always mitigate, but could even enhance, feelings of isolation and vulnerability. The sexualization of service workers and the elision between retail and sex work, intimated here, are discussed in greater depth by Whorrall-Campbell in Chapter 2.

Commentators also debated whether solitude (rather than sociability) might be positive for mental well-being. Questioning William Alexander Sergeant, the manager of Peter Robinson's in Oxford Street, the Truck Committee asked whether live-in workers might 'lose the advantages of seclusion', since 'they have no time to think'. Sergeant responded dismissively, suggesting that assistants did 'not want much time to think when they have been in business all day', though he conceded they sometimes sought 'fresh air'. The Committee persisted, asking whether employees should have 'a life with a greater freedom [. . .] accompanied by seclusion'. Sergeant replied that

> [i]t seems to me to be rather a new idea that seclusion would be a good thing for one. It may be in some cases; there may be a few men who are fond of study and they may not have the opportunities, but as a rule they are not that sort of men at all in our trade.[66]

The Committee constructed solitude as a right, but Sergeant resisted this as a peculiarly 'modern' notion and implied that shopworkers were 'not [the] sort' who appreciated opportunities for contemplation and introspection. The fact he associated seclusion with study indicates a narrow view of the benefits of solitude, for the Committee evoked images of a richer and more rewarding personal life that went beyond the rhetoric of self-improvement. Just as the *Lancet* suggested that employers had the right to determine what enjoyments were 'reasonable', Sergeant implied that he understood what level of solitude his workers needed.

Other commentators supported the idea of a link between solitude and well-being. In her evidence to the Truck Committee, Miss Pettigrew critiqued the fact that living-in required always being in the company of one's colleagues. She reflected it would make her 'very unhappy' to share a room with 'strange girls' and to have 'no place of [her] own'. She also noted that it would involve 'a certain amount of restriction': 'If you are fond of reading or anything like that it might be a nuisance to somebody else.'[67] Living-out had apparently given Miss Pettigrew greater freedoms for managing her space and leisure time and she struggled with the idea of these simple pleasures being curtailed. Similar ideas appeared in fiction. In Somerset Maugham's novel *Of Human Bondage* (1915) – set at the *fin de siècle* – Philip Carey forsakes his medical studies for retail work after becoming destitute. He struggles with living-in after his experiences of lodging, finding that '[t]he sensation of other people sleeping in the room was inexpressibly irksome' for he 'had been used to solitude'. Thus 'to be with others always, never to be by himself for an instant' was 'horrible to him'.[68] Meanwhile, in *High Wages*, Jane finds her transition from living-in to owning her own shop emotionally rewarding. Talking to herself, she reflects that the highlight is 'being *alone*. *That's* why I'm so happy' (193), and the narrator describes how she sleeps above her shop in 'precious solitude' (245). In these novels, having one's own domestic space marks both social status and emotional health. In public discourse and popular culture then, solitude was increasingly represented as an aspiration or even entitlement.

Conclusion

Living-in declined in the opening decades of the twentieth century. Neither Harrods (founded 1849) nor Selfridges (established 1909) – major London department stores – used the system, and this shifted the expectations of employers and employees. Meanwhile, store owners who moved away from living-in reported favourably on the results. At Debenham's, the practice was largely ended by 1905. When the Truck Committee asked Ernest Debenham, the owner, if the assistants were 'brighter' and had 'more energy' as a result, he agreed, and he endorsed the suggestion that living-out allowed for a 'freer' and 'more human' lifestyle.[69] While the Committee's report fell short of recommending the abolition of living-in, it repeated Debenham's statements, supporting a vision of health which fused physical and emotional well-being.[70] Living-in came under increasing criticism after a series of fires exposed the risk to life[71] and was ended by more shops during the First World War, since rising food prices meant it was difficult to sustain financially.

By the mid-twentieth century, living-in was recalled both contemptuously and nostalgically by former shopworkers. In *They Also Serve: The Story of the Shop Worker* (1949), P. C. Hoffman railed against the system, comparing its successful overthrow by the unionists to the storming of the Bastille.[72] His emotionally charged account shows how abolishing living-in was central to the self-respect of many unionized workers. In 1973, Miss Harnaman recalled her experiences of living-in at David Morgan's between 1914 and 1935. She described how the 'discipline and control was very severe' but she fondly recalled 'many good times when someone would play [the piano] and sing' in the sitting room. Weighing up the disadvantages and advantages, she concluded, 'I personally liked living-in.'[73] Her nostalgia recalls that of the former Nippy Josephine Heslit, cited by Whorrall-Campbell in Chapter 2. Harnaman's letter was reproduced in a history of David Morgan's (prepared by the store owner's descendants), used to endorse a rose-tinted (though not uncritical) view of living-in, where any privations were tempered by good humour and camaraderie.

Competing representations of living-in are unsurprising; conditions varied between different stores, and workers responded according to their own temperaments and prior experiences of domestic life. Some commentators insisted that the pains and indignities of living-in were felt acutely, while others suggested that there was solace or pleasure in the social side of the arrangement. Many shifted between these views, exploring both the struggles and rewards of living-in. While questions of physical, mental, moral and emotional health were often interwoven in debates, certain categories of well-being were sometimes prioritized over others. Representations of living-in were underpinned by age, class and gender prejudices; some suggested that young apprentices, the working classes and women did not have the same expectations, aspirations or sensibilities as older middle-class men – the presumed interlocutors and audiences for many of these debates.

Despite the persistence of such prejudices, commentators carved out a place for emotional health within broader conceptions of welfare. While its importance was contested by some, it emerged as a category of health to be recognized and valued. Different interpretations and understandings of emotional health took shape – opinions varied on whether sociability or solitude was crucial to feelings of fulfilment. Within these discussions of living-in, new ideas about work–life balance were being constructed. Time and space away from one's work and colleagues were increasingly fashioned as rights and even as preconditions to emotional health. These living standards were seen as modern, progressive and aspirational for an upwardly mobile workforce.

Notes

1 This research is a product of a large European Research Council project, 'Diseases of Modern Life: Nineteenth-Century Perspectives', led by Professor Sally

Shuttleworth and funded from the European Research Council (ERC) under the European Union's Seventh Framework Programme ERC Grant Agreement number 340121.
2. Departmental Committee, *Minutes of Evidence*, III, 340–1.
3. Departmental Committee, III, 341.
4. Since it underwent several name changes in quick succession, I refer to it here simply as 'the Union'.
5. Departmental Committee, *Report of the Truck Committee*, I, 68.
6. Whitaker, *Victorian and Edwardian Shopworkers*, 8.
7. Departmental Committee, I, 68.
8. See, for example, 'National Union of Shop Assistants', 3.
9. Whitaker, *Victorian and Edwardian Shopworkers*, 52.
10. Stacey, 'The Government Shop Hours Bill', 9.
11. 'Shop Assistants and the Living-In System', 8.
12. Whitaker, *Victorian and Edwardian Shopworkers*, 9.
13. Hosgood, 'Mercantile Monasteries', 336.
14. Sanders, *Consuming Fantasies*. Mullin, *Working Girls*, 97–163.
15. 'Report of the Lancet' (27 February 1892), 491.
16. Mullin, *Working Girls*, 130.
17. Zola, *Ladies' Paradise*, 88.
18. Zola, *Ladies' Paradise*, 123.
19. Reddy, *The Navigation of Feeling*, 129.
20. Hamilton, *Diana of Dobson's*, 35. All subsequent references to this edition are noted parenthetically in the text.
21. Bondfield continued her campaigns in Parliament and later became the first woman cabinet minister.
22. Bondfield, 'Conditions', 278–9.
23. Bondfield, 'Conditions', 279.
24. Bondfield, 'Conditions', 282.
25. Moulds, 'Behind the Scenes'.
26. Departmental Committee, I, 75.
27. 'Next Week', 448. The British Library's bound volume for the year does not feature the cartoon special, but some of the images appeared in previous (extant) issues.
28. Departmental Committee, III, 184, 186.
29. 'Report of the Lancet' (27 February 1892), 491.
30. Wells, *Experiment in Autobiography*, 114.
31. Naismith, *A Young Draper's Guide*, 34.
32. *Behind the Counter*, 2–3, 5.
33. *Behind the Counter*, 4, 8.
34. 'Living-In', 4.

35 Departmental Committee, III, 315.
36 Gissing, *The Odd Women*, 31. All subsequent references to this edition are noted parenthetically in the text.
37 Bondfield, 'Conditions', 277.
38 Spencer Jones, *Moral Side*, 9, 13.
39 Hosgood, 'Mercantile Monasteries', 331.
40 Wells, *Kipps*, 46. All subsequent references to this edition are noted parenthetically in the text.
41 Wells, *The History of Mr Polly*, 9, 175. All subsequent references to this edition are noted parenthetically in the text.
42 Hosgood, 'Mercantile Monasteries', 331.
43 Bondfield, 'Conditions', 277.
44 'Report of the Lancet' (27 February 1892), 491.
45 Sutherst, *Death and Disease*, 10, 9.
46 Whitaker, *Victorian and Edwardian Shopworkers*, 41.
47 Anderson, *The Counter Exposed*, 37, 39.
48 'Report of the Lancet' (12 March 1892), 602.
49 'Shop Assistants and Living In', 1310.
50 *Behind the Counter*, 4.
51 Black, 'Report of the Departmental Committee', 315.
52 Sutherst, *Death and Disease*, 17.
53 Wells, *Experiment in Autobiography*, 88.
54 Whipple, *High Wages*, 173.
55 Wells, *The Wheels of Chance*, 17.
56 Higgins, 'Feeling Like a Clerk', 472.
57 Wells, *Experiment in Autobiography*, 89, 94.
58 Hosgood, 'Mercantile Monasteries', 335, 323.
59 Departmental Committee, III, 308, 311.
60 Rosenwein, *Emotional Communities* and 'Worrying about Emotions'.
61 Departmental Committee, III, 323.
62 *Behind the Counter*, 8.
63 Departmental Committee, III, 316.
64 Departmental Committee, III, 119.
65 Departmental Committee, I, 71.
66 Departmental Committee, III, 199.
67 Departmental Committee, III, 341.
68 Maugham, *Of Human Bondage*, 517.
69 Departmental Committee, III, 192–4.
70 Departmental Committee, I, 73.
71 Horn, *Behind the Counter*, 108.

72 Hoffman, *They Also Serve*, 47.
73 Quoted in: Morgan, *David Morgan*, 175–6.

Bibliography

Anderson, Will. *The Counter Exposed: An Appeal to Shop Assistants, Clerks, Warehousemen and All Others*. London: Klene & Co, 1896.

Behind the Counter: Sketches by a Shop Assistant. Aberdare: George Jones, 1888.

Black, Clementina. 'Report of the Departmental Committee on the Truck Acts'. *The Economic Journal* 19 (June 1909): 315–19.

Bondfield, Margaret. 'Conditions Under Which Shop Assistants Work'. *The Economic Journal* 9 (June 1899): 277–86.

Departmental Committee on the Truck Acts. *Report of the Truck Committee*. Vol. 1. London: HM Stationery Office, 1908.

Departmental Committee on the Truck Acts. *Minutes of Evidence Taken Before the Truck Committee*. Vol. 3. London: HM Stationery Office, 1908.

Gissing, George. *The Odd Women*, edited by Patricia Ingham. Oxford: Oxford University Press, 2008.

Hamilton, Cicely. 'Diana of Dobson's'. In *New Woman Plays*, edited by Linda Fitzsimmons and Viv Gardner, 27–77. London: Methuen, 1991.

Higgins, Richard. 'Feeling Like a Clerk in H.G. Wells'. *Victorian Studies* 50 (Spring 2008): 457–75.

Hoffman, P.C. *They Also Serve: The Story of the Shop Worker*. London: Porcupine Press, 1949.

Horn, Pamela. *Behind the Counter: Shop Lives from Market Stall to Supermarket*. Stroud: Sutton, 2006.

Hosgood, Christopher P. '"Mercantile Monasteries": Shops, Shop Assistants, and Shop Life in Late-Victorian and Edwardian Britain'. *Journal of British Studies* 38 (July 1999): 322–52.

'Living-In'. *Cambria Daily Leader* (24 November 1913): 4.

Maugham, W. Somerset. *Of Human Bondage*. New York: Modern Library, 1999.

Morgan, Aubrey Niel. *David Morgan, 1833–1919: The Life and Times of a Master Draper in South Wales*. Risca: Starling Press, 1977.

Moulds, Alison. '"Behind the Scenes of a Retail Shop": Sensory Experiences of Living-In, c.1880s-1920s'. In *Shopping and the Senses: A Sensory History of Retailing and Consumption*, edited by Serena Dyer. London: Palgrave, 2022.

Mullin, Katherine. *Working Girls: Fiction, Sexuality, and Modernity*. Oxford: Oxford University Press, 2016.

Naismith, W.M. *A Young Draper's Guide to Success*. Paisley: Alexander Gardner, 1901.

'National Union of Shop Assistants: Swansea Branch'. *South Wales Daily Post* (18 July 1894): 3.

'Next Week and the Week After'. *The Shop Assistant* 20 (19 December 1908): 448.
Reddy, William. *The Navigation of Feeling: A Framework for the History of Emotions*. Cambridge: Cambridge University Press, 2001.
'Report of the Lancet Sanitary Commission on Sanitation in the Shop'. *Lancet* (27 February 1892): 490–2.
'Report of the Lancet Sanitary Commission on Sanitation in the Shop'. *Lancet* (12 March 1892): 600–02.
Rosenwein, Barbara. *Emotional Communities in the Early Middle Ages*. Ithaca: Cornell University Press, 2006.
Rosenwein, Barbara. 'Worrying About Emotions in History'. *American Historical Review* 107 (June 2002): 821–45.
Sanders, Lise Shapiro. *Consuming Fantasies: Labor, Leisure, and the London Shop Girl, 1880–1920*. Columbus: Ohio State University Press, 2006.
'Shop Assistants and Living In'. *Lancet* (11 May 1907): 1310.
'Shop Assistants and the Living-In System'. *The Times* (12 April 1909): 8.
Spencer Jones, T. *The Moral Side of Living-In*. London: Shop Assistant Publishing, 1907.
Stacey, J.A. 'The Government Shop Hours Bill and "Living In"'. *The Times* (7 January 1910): 9.
Sutherst, Thomas. *Death and Disease behind the Counter*. London: Kegan Paul, Trench, 1884.
Wells, H.G. *Experiment in Autobiography. Discoveries and Conclusions of a Very Ordinary Brain (Since 1866)*. Philadelphia: J. B. Lippincott, 1967.
Wells, H.G. *The History of Mr Polly*. London: W. Collins, 1920.
Wells, H.G. *Kipps: The Story of a Simple Soul*. London: Macmillan, 1905.
Wells, H.G. *The Wheels of Chance: A Bicycling Idyll*. New York: Macmillan, 1913.
Whipple, Dorothy. *High Wages*. London: Persephone Books, 2016.
Whitaker, Wilfred B. *Victorian and Edwardian Shopworkers: The Struggle to Obtain Better Conditions and a Half-Holiday*. Newton Abbot: David & Charles, 1973.
Zola, Émile. *The Ladies' Paradise*, translated by Brian Nelson. Oxford: Oxford University Press, 2008.

4

The emotional landscape of the hospital residence in post-war Britain

Agnes Arnold-Forster[1]

In the 1950s and 1960s, British hospitals were places to live as well as sites of work, care and recovery. Both doctors and nurses would live in hospital-supplied housing, and it was thought to be 'in the interests of hospitals and their patients that doctors [were] made resident'.[2] Pay was minimal beyond room, board and laundry services, and it was assumed that most young healthcare practitioners had few other obligations outside of medical or nursing training at that stage of their careers. Trainee doctors and nurses also worked very long hours. In 1963, Ronald Macbeth described hospital clinical work as 'quite literally full-time'.[3] Writers to the *British Medical Journal's* (*BMJ*) letters page alerted readers to the 'somewhat unique condition which doctors have accepted without demur'.[4] This excessive temporal commitment and the dual nature of the hospital blurred boundaries between professional and domestic space, undermining distinctions between home and work.

Histories of hospitals, their buildings and inhabitants have tended to focus on architectural design, patient experience or medical advances. In contrast, the impact of changes to hospital infrastructure on healthcare professionals' experiences of work has been of less concern. To expand on existing literature by scholars such as Annmarie Adams, this chapter will explore the emotional landscape of the hospital residence in mid- to late-twentieth-century Britain.[5] Drawing on emotions history, I argue that this little-studied story can tell us much about the quotidian or 'ordinary' working and living experiences of hospital staff and allow us to interrogate the affective dimensions of labour and examine the emotional communities developed in certain environments.[6] Using accounts of doctors' and nurses' experiences of hospital residences published in medical journals and oral history interviews, I will interrogate the meanings, representations and emotions of living on hospital sites, thereby continuing Alison Moulds's discussion of 'living-in' and 'work–life balance'.

Beginning in the 1970s, British hospital residences began to be sold off or repurposed. Their closure prompted fierce debate in the pages of the medical press. Advocates commented on the protective sense of belonging fostered by employees living and working together, and detractors deplored their capacity to erode inhabitants' personal lives and free time, and decried their exclusionary nature (residences were difficult or impossible to occupy if you were married or had children). Today, the notion of 'work–life balance' is ubiquitous in discussions of labour, gender and professional identity, and anxieties about work-related stress pervade contemporary society. Some of the sources of these anxieties – smartphones and Covid-19 – are peculiar to the twenty-first century and some of the precise language – 'work–life balance' and 'burnout' – post-date the period discussed here. However, the equilibrium between home life and work life was attracting increased attention in the decades following the Second World War. In the 1950s, 1960s and 1970s, employers, feminists and psychologists were investigating the importance of effective spatial and temporal boundaries in maintaining workers' emotional health.[7]

In addition, while the emerging specialty of occupational health was primarily preoccupied with the dangers and risks of manual labour and factory settings, with the transformation of the UK labour market and the demise of the industrial sector, there was a corresponding decline in physical illnesses and disabilities linked to work. Instead, there was a surge in diagnosed or observed mental health issues associated with the rise of the service sector and changing workplace cultures, such as longer working hours, zero-hour contracts and a blurring of boundaries between home and work.[8] This chapter explores these trajectories, using the hospital as a case study. It argues that healthcare professionals – and particularly doctors – used debates over living on-site to delineate concerns about working conditions and well-being. In addition, they used those same debates to articulate and reinforce ideas and ideals about clinical labour and identities. These debates faded from view as hospital residences were closed and repurposed in the 1970s and 1980s. However, recent consternation about doctors' rest and social spaces – emerging in the twenty-first century – demonstrates that working conditions, well-being and clinical identities remain live topics and that many of the issues posed by those debating the pros and cons of hospital residences are still unresolved.[9] While both doctors and nurses lived on-site, this chapter focuses on doctors' experiences for the sake of space.

Hospital residences

Doctors, nurses and other healthcare professionals have been living on hospital sites for centuries. Traditionally, and since well before the foundation of the NHS, board and lodging were given free to make allowances for trainees' enforced residence in hospitals.[10] In the eighteenth century, general hospital nurses rested in small rooms adjacent to the wards and in the early nineteenth century, hospitals began to build extensions to house larger bedrooms, kitchens, washing rooms and bathrooms for their resident staff. Nurses' accommodation was styled with obvious nods towards domestic aesthetics. Operating as residences for single women, they were accompanied by flower beds and traditional domestic architecture, often situated on the outskirts of the hospital site.

By the 1860s, new trends in nursing education and professionalization meant that the provision of sleeping quarters was considered essential to the preservation of discipline and respectability among the young, predominantly working-class, women who worked in the hospital. For instance, the absence of dormitories was thought to 'lower the standard of the women who can be obtained for night duty' and diminish their clinical efficiency.[11] Despite these concerns, nurses were accustomed to 'boxing and coxing' or occupying beds at different hours between shifts. In the second half of the nineteenth century, purpose-built residential homes for nursing staff, containing dormitories, dining rooms and dedicated quarters for the matron, began to be built on British hospital sites. The combined priorities of health, respectability and discipline among the nursing staff provided the main impetus to build residences on adjoining hospital grounds and shaped their configuration.[12]

At the London Hospital in Mile End, bedrooms allocated to senior nurses were interspersed between nurses' dormitories to secure a degree of surveillance. Despite these authoritative measures, the nurses also gained several amenities for their enjoyment and relaxation. Their homes contained a range of leisure spaces, including dining halls, sitting rooms and libraries. A public garden in Stepney Way was also provided and in 1936, an indoor swimming bath was added.[13] By the early twentieth century, the quality and variation of nurses' accommodation was frequently deployed as part of advertising campaigns designed to attract nursing students to different institutions for their training. One prospectus directed at St George's nursing students depicted the nurses' residence at Atkinson Morley's Hospital. Similarly, a photo story published in *Nursing Times* in 1951 printed images of 'one of the nurse's cheery bedrooms', 'a corner of the nurses' dining room', 'the fine new Nurses' Home, opened by

Princess Mary in 1938' and 'Nurses off duty in the spacious sitting room of the Nurses' Home'.[14]

Doctors also lived on hospital sites, particularly when they were at the beginning of their careers. The terminology we still colloquially use to describe different junior doctor positions – house officer, senior house officer, resident – is an inheritance of an earlier period when young clinicians were expected or required to live in hospital accommodation so that they could be contacted at all hours and monitor patients overnight. As indicated in the introduction, accommodation, along with food and laundry services, was frequently offered for free – perks designed to compensate doctors for the excessive temporal commitment living on-site demanded. In an oral history interview I conducted with a plastic surgeon who moved from Egypt to England in 1961, he described his experiences of living on the hospital site: 'We were paid £30 a month but we had board, we had accommodation, food, laundry, everything.'[15] From the 1950s onwards, however, the Ministry of Health began to mandate that charges be deducted from junior doctors' salaries to pay for their food and lodgings.[16]

In response, the British Medical Association (BMA) began to defend the interests of their junior members and demanded that to ensure the residence of doctors, hospitals must maintain adequate accommodation. The BMA's responses to the Ministry's mandate revealed the less than salubrious living conditions of mid-century resident doctors. In 1963, R. M. Forrester – a doctor from Wigan – heralded a new dawn in hospital residency: 'The time has come when hospitals must make their jobs, and their accommodation, attractive. The grubby monastic cell, with its worn lino, cracked lampshade, and iron bedstead, is slowly on the way out.'[17] Rooms must not just be adequately furnished; they should also be big enough to live in comfortably. The BMA called on the Ministry of Health to specify a minimum size for a room and at one meeting the Chairman invited the submission of 'horror pictures', which showed 'accommodation which fell short of the standard'.[18] In 1964, the BMA's Hospital Junior Staffs Group Council passed a resolution, 'affirming that where standards of hospital residential accommodation fell short of Ministry memorandum HM (58) 68 a reduction of charges should be made'.[19] At that meeting, one member said that he had had 'a room which contained all the things the Ministry said it should contain, only it was so small that he could hardly get in'.[20] One *BMJ* article described nurses' homes as simply 'abysmal'.[21]

Quality of accommodation was not, however, the only issue affecting healthcare professionals' living conditions. As intimated, British hospital residences began to be sold off or repurposed in the 1970s. The plans for the new

Royal London Hospital, for example, precipitated the large-scale demolition of the nurses' homes built between 1884 and 1918. Other residential blocks were converted into administrative offices and the population of hospital employees who lived on-site declined after most of the buildings dedicated to staff accommodation were sold to a private developer. For nurses, the changes to their hours of work and annual leave entitlements that took place in the 1970s – combined with broader social and cultural transformations in the British workforce – meant that fewer lived on-site than ever before. The introduction of eight-hour shifts after the first major reorganization of the NHS in 1974 reflected the needs of married and non-resident nurses, tipping the balance away from those who lived in hospital nurses' homes and towards the men and women who lived in private accommodation.[22] The debates around these trends – about charges in the 1950s and 1960s, and then about the potential closure of hospitals residences in the 1970s – tell us much about how members of hospital staff felt about their environments and working cultures.

Advocates for resident life commented on the protective sense of belonging fostered by employees living and working together. In contrast, critics argued that they were not suitable for junior doctors with husbands, wives or children. They all, however, demonstrated the immersive experience of hospital life and attested to the importance of intangible, ephemeral interaction – social or professional – in the construction of identity and workplace cultures. In his speculative account of clinical life, hospital chaplain George Day described the strategies he would use to gain a full understanding of an institution and its employees:

> I would make a point of lunching and dining quite frequently in the resident house doctors' mess, and keeping my ears open. I would even drop in for a late-night beer or coffee – or even lose half a crown to them at their poker school. In this way, I would come to learn more about the hospital than the matron, the medical superintendent, and the hospital secretary all rolled into one: more about the things that matter – that is, the personalities, the clash of personalities, and the fluctuating morale. For these young chaps are in the front line of the battle, holding the fort during the hours of darkness and at week-ends, when their chiefs are away.[23]

In this description, he alluded to the emotional value of the clinical community. This is a portrait not just of working life but also of friendship. He identified these informal interactions, the intangible exchanges, and the subtle texture of social life as 'the things that matter'.

Support for the importance of these informal interactions was clamorous in the debates over hospital quarters for married junior doctors that emerged in the 1960s. Earlier in the twentieth century, doctors tended to marry late – after they had finished their itinerant training and once they had settled on a long-term post. By the 1960s, however, more and more doctors were marrying young, some even before they had finished medical school. D. W. Dingwall conducted a survey for the *BMJ* about the provision of married quarters for house officers in 1963. He found that 'To-day many doctors are married at the very beginning of their graduate career and . . . a considerable number of final-year medical students throughout the country are already married'.[24] This proved problematic for the 'life of collegiate monasticism' that had been traditionally expected of trainees.[25] References to religious orders in correspondence about hospital residences were rife and pregnant with meaning. Not only did they imply a kind of religious devotion to the job on behalf of the trainee surgeons and physicians, but they made assumptions about the gender and sexuality of these doctors. In all the letters sent to the editor of the *BMJ* and other healthcare journals, the trainee doctor was assumed to be male and married to a woman who waited at home.

For doctors, hospitals cultivated the kind of single-sex, masculine culture and community more usually seen in monasteries or even boys' public schools. As one correspondent put it in 1963, 'The outlook of many hospital management committees that it is immoral for any houseman to have sexual relations in the hospital, be he married or no, persists.'[26] Once students had graduated, they then embarked on a programme of training that required them to live on the hospital site, attend to patients overnight and move from institution to institution every six months or so. Few, if any, hospitals provided residential quarters for married couples and local, short-term rental accommodation was hard to find.[27] Junior doctors must either live apart from their spouse for several months at a time or live together outside the hospital walls.

Neither of these solutions was popular. As early as 1954, a doctor from Hillingdon in Middlesex, W. Arklay Steel, complained about the financial consequences of married couples living apart: 'Many young married doctors have to contribute to the upkeep of two establishments when they become resident, and the financial hardship and privations they must experience to make ends meet can be imagined.'[28] Nine years later, the problem remained unresolved and doctor Michael Heston deplored the 'considerable hardship during the pre-registration year' suffered by married junior doctors 'due to the paucity of married quarters'. This hardship was both financial and a product of the 'imposition of relative chastity'. He wrote, '[the junior doctor] is unlikely in London to be paying less than £250 per annum for his flat where his wife waits patiently for the precious half-day and the two week-ends in five which should bring her husband home.'[29] Advocates for married quarters argued that trainees should be able to combine married life with hospital life:

> A married man wishing to continue in the hospital service cannot apply for more than 25% of the junior hospital posts advertised if he wishes to remain living with his wife. Why should a man have to choose between leaving his wife or pursuing his profession?[30]

These arguments for married quarters circulated around two key points. First, that regardless of whether a doctor and their spouse lived apart (with the doctor staying on hospital property and the spouse living elsewhere) or if they both lived off-site, both options meant that families would see little of the working parent: 'It is indefensible to expect children to understand why they should have to answer the question, "When did you last see your father?"'[31] Second, both meant that junior doctors were not fully embedded within the hospital culture, a distance that might prove pedagogically problematic and curtail future career development. In 1967, 'A General Practitioner's Wife' wrote to the *BMJ* lamenting the living arrangements her and her husband had been forced to adopt while he completed his training, 'I speak with authority – and bitterness – as we were pushed out of hospital work altogether in order to keep our family together and properly fed and clothed – redeployed into general practice and suburbia after a keen and ambitious start in surgery; frustrated for life, for our temerity in marrying and begetting children.'[32] Instead, she argued for dedicated junior doctor residences, with space for spouse and child:

> If junior doctors had their own flats, and in between dealing with patients 100 hours a week could sit down with their own kids, have coffee made by their own wives, the long hours would irk so much less that they would almost cease to be a problem.[33]

In similar terms, Clarice A. Baker – a female non-resident registrar at the Mile End Hospital – thought that the 'hospital as a whole would benefit greatly' if 'a modest type of married quarters were provided on hospital territory'. She suggested that this would have positive results:

> the young houseman's energies could be concentrated on treating his patients, without the need to worry about a pregnant wife or sick baby in a distant flat. The communal property would be better cared for, and . . . the doctor would not

feel obliged to rush off the minute he was officially 'off duty' if home were near by.[34]

This anxiety about junior doctors rushing off as soon as the working day was officially over was shared both by those advocating *for* married quarters and those advocating *against*. Doctor John Shepherd wrote to the *BMJ* in 1967,

> Already there is a tendency for a '9 to 5' attitude to prevail, and I believe this is quite contrary to all that is best in surgical or medical practice. To maintain a high standard of work in hospitals it is imperative that junior staff are trained and encouraged in the idea of continuity of care.[35]

He viewed 'with much disquiet' the trend, as he saw it, 'by which registrars in the major specialties are discouraged from living in hospital except on their emergency nights'.[36] Addressing similar issues, Dr Ronald Macbeth also wrote to the *BMJ* to caution against the introduction of married quarters to hospitals. Like Shepherd he was concerned about the recent tendency of trainee doctors to live in private accommodation, but he was also concerned that the introduction of double beds to hospital residencies might have pernicious consequences: 'There are two aspects of this matter – duty to one's patients and education of oneself.'[37] He insisted that duty to one's patient turned 'upon the concept that as a resident one is available to them at all times at a minute's notice'.[38] Commitment to the hospital and its inhabitants must be total and the line between personal life and professional engagement should be fine and easy to blur:

> It may be argued that this can be achieved if one lives in suitably placed married quarters in hospital. I doubt, however, if engrossment with purely domestic personal matters can always be laid aside as briskly as when one lives bachelor-style in the mess.[39]

The second 'aspect of this matter' – 'the education of oneself' – was more important to Macbeth than the first, however. And it was here that he emphasized the importance of 'the firm' and demonstrated the value that many mid-century practitioners ascribed to the participation in this social organization and to an adherence to a certain culture and community. 'The firm' was (and in some places still is) the key mechanism and organizational unit for the type of apprenticeship-style learning common in modern British hospitals. Broadly speaking, the firm refers to a unit of doctors working together. It is usually made up of a single profession and has one or occasionally two permanent members – a consultant – after whom it is named. It also includes other grades of doctors who join temporarily and for varying lengths of time. There is a clear hierarchy and distribution of roles and for many it connotes a military-style structure.

Macbeth described the 'educational value' of 'living with the job, even when not actively seeing one's own patients', and insisted on the value of 'being around in the mess for the casual discussion of cases and for consultation at resident level – where, for example, a colleague is uncertain what he should do with a patient sent up to the casualty department'. Macbeth argued that these experiences were 'the stuff whereof the training of a good doctor is made' and that 'one cannot receive this sort of education if one is in the married quarters feeding the baby or washing the nappies'.[40] He was concerned that these distractions were harming the development of doctors' professionalism: 'It seems to one such that medicine is coming to be regarded more and more as "a job like any other", and less and less as a vocation.'[41] He cautioned young doctors against marriage before they were fully trained, as it might prove distracting. He said that there was no reason for junior doctors to 'prematurely [assume] marital responsibilities' as they must be 'shared with a job which is quite literally full-time'.[42] He concluded his letter with the insistence that 'If people wish to marry young they should not aim to be doctors; they will neglect one or other assignment'.[43]

Social spaces

The 'literally full-time' nature of clinical training was made even more explicit by the debates about hospital cafeterias. In 1960, the BMA's Hospital Junior Staffs Group Council received complaints from medical officers at the Dorset County Hospital, 'where a cafeteria-style communal dining-room had recently been established'.[44] This marked a change from tradition. For much of the twentieth century, junior doctors ate, relaxed and socialized in dedicated spaces on the hospital site – spaces closed off to patients and visitors. The Hospital Junior Staffs Group Council was concerned that a cafeteria, open to both doctors and patients, was a 'retrograde step'.[45] The doctors at Dorset County Hospital had not been consulted beforehand and they thought that the cafeteria system was 'undesirable' because there were 'often matters doctors wanted to discuss among themselves'. Various Group members thought that residents should retain a dining room of their own and many believed that the opportunities for knowledge exchange that these spaces afforded were 'vital for the success of the hospital'.[46] In dedicated dining rooms, doctors could 'discuss their problems' and solicit advice from one another about tricky cases or recalcitrant patients.[47] These spaces also had an educative function. Various interested parties advocated for the traditional practice of trainee doctors living and socializing on the hospital site by insisting on the professional and pedagogical value of the opportunities for informal exchange that being a hospital *resident* produced. Ronald Macbeth particularly emphasized the value of eating together. He wrote to the *BMJ* in 1963, 'Being around in the mess for the casual discussion of cases and for consultation at resident level ... these are the stuff whereof the training of a good doctor is made'.[48]

Similar concerns were expressed by A. M. Cantor in his 1978 essay on a new hospital. He was troubled by the fact that meals were provided in a 'common dining room for non-medical as well as medical personnel' and that there was 'no dining area allocated specifically to medical staff'. He lamented,

> The usual opportunities for discussion, interchange of ideas and experience, and mutual help, which are such a valuable feature of the doctors' mess, are sacrificed in the interests of doctors for their patients, and it will be regrettable if this is to be the pattern for hospitals in the future.[49]

Critics of the new and redesigned hospitals that failed to accommodate dining, rest and relaxation facilities for trainee doctors sometimes (and increasingly) framed their complaints in terms of worsening working conditions. In response to A. M. Cantor's lamentation, junior doctors who had, until its recent closure, worked at the Royal Portsmouth Hospital levied similar critiques at the new Queen Alexandra Hospital in Cosham, into which they were due to move.[50] This new hospital had a mess room, but it was only 14 feet by 24 feet and supposed to house over sixty junior doctors. Even worse, it was located opposite the patients' library, presumably problematic because patients might overhear the staff's discussions of their sensitive cases.[51] The new hospital had 'totally inadequate telephone facilities' in the resident doctors' accommodation, 'no separate dining-room facilities of medical staff' and doctors shared residential blocks with nursing and other staff.[52] The junior doctors concluded their letter with: 'we have resolved not to accept the continued decline of our working conditions in this way'.[53]

However, this was not just a problem of adequate working conditions and there was more to the doctors' mess and dining room than just education and the sharing of patient information. They were also places where friendships were made, where professional communities were built and where the culture of the institution was shaped. One now-retired surgeon I interviewed reflected on his experience of training in the 1960s: 'First of all we had the social life in the hospital and so even though we worked, there was a community, there was a community in the hospital. We had a party every Saturday.'[54] This could only happen in places dedicated to doctors – clinical 'club houses' within hospital walls. The Chairman of the Hospital Junior Staffs Group Council believed that it was 'important that a resident should have a mess life'. A 'mess life' implied all those things – friendship, community and culture, not just work. The Chairman also believed that this 'life' had been under threat since 1948 – 'the National Health Service had partly destroyed it' – and the redesign of hospitals was delivering 'the final death blow'.[55]

Crucially, hospitals that provided no dedicated space for doctors to eat also denigrated their professional exceptionalism, upsetting the conventional hierarchies. The 'final death blow' was to 'treat resident doctors in the same way as resident typists and resident nurses' (who, presumably, had less of a right to a communal, collegiate professional life than their medical counterparts).[56] A hospital without a mess was just like any other place of ordinary work. In fact, two members of the Hospital Junior Staffs Group Council thought that doctors who were compulsorily resident should not have to pay board and lodging charges at all; instead, they 'should have been thrown in when the NHS came into being, "as in the Army"'.[57]

As before, these references to 'mess life', monasticism and the army were not coincidental. They underscored the intentional similarities between the post-war British hospital and other places where affluent white men socialized. In cultivating and defending rest, residential and social spaces for doctors, hospitals and their inhabitants were also cultivating and defending a workplace culture – one that inculcated trainee clinicians into a pattern of behaviours and attitudes that served to strengthen connections within the profession and demarcate its boundaries. Medical and surgical cultures were created inside the hospital – and maintained as much by the physical buildings as they were by the people who inhabited them.

Indeed, much of the critique of the redesigned hospitals in the 1970s circulated the damaging effects the loss of dedicated space for rest and relaxation would have on the workplace culture and on the feelings of belonging, commitment and collegiality experienced by trainees.[58] As A. M. Cantor lamented, 'The most serious fault is in the arrangements for junior medical staff.' There was no provision for a doctors' mess in the original plans and 'the accommodation for junior medical staff [was] haphazardly dispersed in residential blocks which are also used by nursing and other staff'.[59] The residential quarters had 'no doctors' common room' and they were located far from the main hospital building.[60]

He noted that 'the effect will be unfortunate because junior staff will be isolated from each other during leisure hours, and they will lose many of the traditional and more pleasant aspects of hospital life'.[61] This sense that ill-conceived hospital architecture could foster isolation and despair was widespread in the letters pages of medical journals and attests to the value doctors ascribed to spending social time together. As Cantor insisted, 'The dining arrangements also militate against the growth of normal working and social relationships among junior (and senior) medical staff'.[62]

Rest and social spaces in the twenty-first century

Scant and often poor-quality hospital accommodation is still provided for resident junior doctors. However, the campaigns to retain rest and social spaces for all hospital staff in the 1960s, 1970s and 1980s were largely unsuccessful. Accommodation for nurses was sold off or repurposed, residences for junior doctors reduced and places dedicated to the rest and relaxation of staff were phased out. Recently, however, the issues have re-emerged. In early 2019, the *BMJ* launched a campaign calling for doctors to be able to take the breaks that they required for their 'well-being and patient safety'.[63] Later that year, a report by Health Education England said that all staff should have access to 'good occupational health, psychological support, and rest facilities'.[64] The NHS Staff and Learners' Mental Wellbeing Commission set out a range of recommendations to improve the mental health of healthcare workers, including that they all have 'suitable, accessible, psychologically safe, and confidential spaces in which to socialise, share and discuss experiences, and to rest'.[65] These recommendations echoed the spirit of the debate that raged in the 1960s and 1970s over charging for, and then the closure of, hospital residences and cafeterias but reframed it using twenty-first-century terminology. Issues shared by doctors in the 1970s and in the 2010s include the importance of rest to the emotional health of NHS workers; the value of private, confidential spaces separate from those dedicated to patients; and the usefulness of places where doctors and nurses can discuss clinical experiences.

The *BMJ*'s campaign and the Health Education England report did not, of course, come from nowhere. Throughout the early twenty-first century, the medical press regularly published experiences of healthcare professional fatigue and calls for the reinstatement of on-call rooms and the doctors' mess. In 2005, a trainee physician published a short piece entitled, 'Junior doctors' shifts and sleep deprivation: Please make on-call rooms available to doctors at night'. He described how he had recently worked nights as a medical registrar at a university hospital and was 'shocked to see the notice on the door to the on-call rooms, saying that on-call rooms are not provided any more'. He framed this as a safety and well-being issue and pitted the ordinary junior doctor against 'NHS policy makers', who might be 'persuaded to give doctors a room for half an hour to help us to freshen up?' He also observed that the lack of rest spaces was a problem for recruitment to his specialty: 'How can I convincingly persuade my juniors to take up general medicine as a career full of variety and challenges? No wonder general medicine has slipped down the priority list in favour of specialist interests, despite remaining in the front line.'[66]

In 2012, junior doctors demanded that hospitals reinstate free on-call rooms so that trainees could rest during or after night shifts. Doctors regularly try to get some sleep before driving home at the end of their working day to reduce their risk of car accidents. Susannah Patey, a foundation year two doctor in Birmingham, told the BMA's junior doctors conference that she had to pay £37 a time for a room with a reclining chair if she wanted to sleep after a night shift: 'I think people who are trying to sleep before driving are not being allowed to by hospital trusts.... I don't think that's reasonable, and I don't think that's fair.' Unlike debates in the middle of the twentieth century, these campaigns focus on healthcare professionals' need for sleep and spend less time attending to the spatial dynamics of doctors' and nurses' social and professional needs.

In contrast, debates about the doctors' mess feature many of the same lines of argument as offered by proponents of dedicated social spaces for hospital staff in the 1960s and 1970s. In an article published in 2003, the author describes the negative connotations of the doctors' mess:

> The doctors' mess has always been associated with junior doctors hiding from work or eating their lunches. It is often a drab room, with the same facilities – usually a pool table, a drinks machine, and sometimes nowadays a computer, sofas (falling to pieces), and a satellite television (if you are lucky).[67]

And yet, 'there is, however, one other thing in every mess: doctors'. Reflecting on the importance of intangible, ephemeral interaction in hospital life, the author reflected, 'The mess has always been a major point of social interaction for doctors. They come to talk about other staff they like or dislike, football, going out at the weekend, and, sometimes, politics.'[68] For this junior doctor, the mess played a crucial role in his social life, medical education and career progression.

The recent medical press is full of articles describing the resurrection of the doctors' mess. In 2019, the *BMJ* argued that while junior doctors' hours are now restricted, and socializing and networking have largely moved online, 'a private space for doctors to rest is still a vital resource for both the doctors, and their patients'.[69] Two trainees at one hospital in Bristol had used one of their study days to work on the mess. It had not been updated for a decade and was looking 'slightly worse for wear'. It took them fifteen hours to clean, with more work the following morning to complete the renovation. They were both former mess presidents, responsible for the space and related social activities for junior doctors. They were, therefore, clear about its value:

> The reason we worked on making the space nice was because if a space is cluttered you don't want to rest in it, you don't want to be in it, and it doesn't clear your mind . . . we wanted a space where people could breathe and then restart. Decision making is paramount to what we do. If you can't make a decision about whether you want a cup of tea or what you want to eat then how are you going to make clear clinical decisions?[70]

Much like material from the mid-twentieth century, this quotation attests to the perceived importance of space dedicated to rest and relaxation for the clinical competence and emotional well-being of doctors.

Conclusion

In spring 2020, the Policy Exchange – a UK-based, centre-right think tank – launched a call for evidence to 'inform a major piece of research into how we should build the next generation of hospitals'. The proposed lines of inquiry drew on the experiences of the NHS in responding to Covid-19, and the think tank promised it would 'explore whether the Government's new building programme could potentially mark the most comprehensive reform of hospital building in England since the 1960s'.[71] One of the key questions the Policy Exchange set out to investigate was, 'what provision should new hospitals make for key worker / affordable housing?' This is a very good question. However, any consideration of this proposal should include an assessment of the history of hospital accommodation. If it did, then planners and policymakers might reflect on the impact of residencies on the culture and community of hospital work; the potentially damaging effect they have on people with caring responsibilities (and that those effects are, unfortunately, profoundly gendered); and the influence they exert on temporal commitment, 'work–life balance' and workplace well-being.

In this chapter I have shown how the dual nature of the hospital – a place to both live and work – blurred boundaries between professional and domestic space and undermined distinctions between home and work. Published in 2019, the NHS Long Term Plan prioritized worker well-being, made repeated recourse to the idea of a 'modern' employment culture and proposed to tackle problems it saw as peculiar to the twenty-first century. However, the issues it identified were not new. Instead, the rhetoric of the Plan is the apotheosis of a long process by which healthcare institutions have not only become increasingly managed workplaces but have also attempted to manage the feelings of their employees. Contrary to the pervasive insistence on the novelty of recent interventions – and contrary to the nostalgia that permeates professional recollections of late-twentieth-century healthcare working conditions – for the duration of the NHS's history, there have been complaints about the welfare of hospital workers, anxiety about declining morale and repeated suggestions for reforms to ameliorate staff well-being. And, since the service's inception, hospitals have operated as incubators for new ideas about organizations' roles and responsibilities towards the well-being or morale of their staff. Hospital rest and social spaces are just one example of issues that prompted fervent debate about the meanings and emotions of healthcare labour, well before explicit notions of staff 'well-being' entered the public and professional lexicon.

Notes

1 This research was funded by the Wellcome Trust Investigator Award, Surgery & Emotion (108667/Z/15/Z).
2 Whiteley et al., 'Correspondence', 129.
3 Macbeth, 'Married Quarters in Hospital', 1674.
4 Whiteley et al., 'Correspondence', 129.
5 Adams, 'Rooms of Their Own'.
6 Hamlett, 'Space and Emotional Experience', 119–38.
7 Cooper, 'Medical Feminism', 1–11; Jackson and Moore, *Balancing the Self*.
8 Long and Brown, 'Conceptualizing Work-Related Mental Distress', 2.
9 Rimmer, 'Provide Doctors with Rest Spaces', 354.
10 Whiteley et al., 'Correspondence', 129.
11 'The Royal London Hospital'.
12 Chaney, 'Before Compassion'.

13 Survey of London, 'The Royal London Hospital'.
14 'St Luke's – The First Municipal General Hospital', 140.
15 Oral history interview conducted by Agnes Arnold-Forster.
16 Whiteley et al., 'Correspondence', 129.
17 Forrester, 'Married Quarters in Hospital', 51.
18 'Hospital Junior Staffs Group Council', 231.
19 'Hospital Junior Staffs Group Council', 231.
20 'Hospital Junior Staffs Group Council', 231.
21 Arnold, 'Where have all the Nurses gone?', 200.
22 Rivett, '1978–1987: Clinical Advance and Financial Crisis'.
23 Day, 'Personal View', 182.
24 Dingwall, 'Special Article', 1664.
25 Heston, 'Married Quarters in Hospital', 1475.
26 Heston, 'Married Quarters in Hospital', 1475.
27 Dingwall, 'Special Article', 1664.
28 Arklay Steel, 'Correspondence', 129.
29 Heston, 'Married Quarters in Hospital', 1475.
30 Johnson, 'Married Quarters', 507.
31 Cromwell, 'Married Quarters in Hospital', 52.
32 A General Practitioner's Wife, 'Married Quarters', 507.
33 A General Practitioner's Wife, 'Married Quarters', 507.
34 Baker, 'Married Quarters in Hospital', 51.
35 Shepherd, 'Married Quarters', 507.
36 Shepherd, 'Married Quarters', 507.
37 Macbeth, 'Married Quarters in Hospital', 1674.
38 Macbeth, 'Married Quarters in Hospital', 1674.
39 Macbeth, 'Married Quarters in Hospital', 1674.
40 Macbeth, 'Married Quarters in Hospital', 1674.
41 Macbeth, 'Married Quarters in Hospital', 1674.
42 Macbeth, 'Married Quarters in Hospital', 1674.
43 Macbeth, 'Married Quarters in Hospital', 1674.
44 Macbeth, 'Married Quarters in Hospital', 1674.
45 Macbeth, 'Married Quarters in Hospital', 1674.
46 'Annual Representative Meeting, Swansea 1965', 270.
47 'Annual Representative Meeting, Swansea 1965', 270.
48 Macbeth, 'Married Quarters in Hospital', 1674.
49 Cantor, 'Personal View', 1224.
50 Tweedie et al., 'Facilities for Junior Doctors', 1503.
51 Tweedie et al., 'Facilities for Junior Doctors', 1503.
52 Tweedie et al., 'Facilities for Junior Doctors', 1503.
53 Tweedie et al., 'Facilities for Junior Doctors', 1503.

54 Oral history interview conducted by Agnes Arnold-Forster.
55 'Hospital Junior Staffs Group Council', 231.
56 'Hospital Junior Staffs Group Council', 270.
57 'Hospital Junior Staffs', 260.
58 Arnold-Forster, 'A Small Cemetery', 284.
59 Cantor, 'Personal View', 1224.
60 Cantor, 'Personal View', 1224.
61 Cantor, 'Personal View', 1224.
62 Cantor, 'Personal View', 1224.
63 Rimmer, 'Provide Doctors with Rest Spaces', 354.
64 Rimmer, 'Provide Doctors with Rest Spaces', 354.
65 Health Education England, 'NHS Staff and Learners' Mental Wellbeing Commission', 11.
66 Varughese, 'Junior Doctors' Shifts', 515.
67 Raw, 'The Doctors' Mess', 689.
68 Raw, 'The Doctors' Mess', 689.
69 Rimmer, 'The Future of Doctors' Messes', 364.
70 Rimmer, 'The Future of Doctors' Messes', 364.
71 Policy Exchange, 'Call for Evidence'.

Bibliography

A General Practitioner's Wife. 'Married Quarters'. *British Medical Journal* 1 (1967): 507.
Adams, Annmarie. 'Rooms of Their Own: The Nurses' Residences at Montreal's Royal Victoria Hospital'. *Material History Review* 40 (1994): 29–41.
'Annual Representative Meeting, Swansea 1965'. *British Medical Journal* 2 (1965): 29–68.
Arklay Steel, W. 'Correspondence'. *British Medical Journal* 2 (1954): 128–9.
Arnold, Nancy. 'Where have all the Nurses gone?' *British Medical Journal* 280 (1980): 199–201.
Arnold-Forster, Agnes. 'A Small Cemetery: Death and Dying in the Contemporary British Operating Theatre'. *Medical Humanities* 46 (2020): 278–87.
Baker, Clarice A. 'Married Quarters in Hospital'. *British Medical Journal* 2 (1963): 51–2.
Cantor, A. M. 'Personal View'. *British Medical Journal* 2 (1978): 1224.
Chaney, Sarah. 'Before Compassion: Sympathy, Tact and the History of the Ideal Nurse'. *Medical Humanities*. Online First (2020): 1–10.
Cooper, Frederick. 'Medical Feminism, Working Mothers, and the Limits of Home'. *Palgrave Communications* 2 (2016): 1–11.
Cromwell. 'Married Quarters in Hospital'. *British Medical Journal* 2 (1963): 51–2.
Day, George. 'Personal View'. *British Medical Journal* 3 (1968): 182.

Dingwall, D. W. 'Special Article: Provision of Married-Quarters for House Officers'. *British Medical Journal* 1 (1963): 1664–5.

Forrester, R. M. 'Married Quarters in Hospital'. *British Medical Journal* 2 (1963): 51–2.

Hamlett, Jane. 'Space and Emotional Experience in Victorian and Edwardian English Public School Dormitories'. In *Childhood, Youth and Emotions in Modern History: National, Colonial and Global Perspectives*, edited by Stephanie Olsen, 119–38. London: Palgrave, 2015.

Health Education England. 'NHS Staff and Learners' Mental Wellbeing Commission' (2019).

Heston, Michael. 'Married Quarters in Hospital'. *British Medical Journal* 1 (1963): 1475.

'Hospital Junior Staffs'. *British Medical Journal* 1 (1963): 260–61.

'Hospital Junior Staffs Group Council'. *British Medical Journal* 2 (1960): 269–71.

'Hospital Junior Staffs Group Council'. *British Medical Journal* 2 (1964): 229–31.

Jackson, Mark, and Martin D. Moore. *Balancing the Self: Medicine, Politics and the Regulation of Health in the Twentieth Century*. Manchester: Manchester University Press, 2020.

Johnson, P. A. 'Married Quarters'. *British Medical Journal* 1 (1967): 507.

Long, Vicky, and Victoria Brown. 'Conceptualizing Work-Related Mental Distress in the British Coalfields (c.1900-1950)'. *Palgrave Communications* 4 (2018): 1–10.

Macbeth, Ronald. 'Married Quarters in Hospital'. *British Medical Journal* 1 (1963): 1673–74.

Oral history interview conducted by Agnes Arnold-Forster. (2021).

Policy Exchange. 'Call for Evidence: Building Hospitals in the Post-Covid Era' (2020).

Raw, Jason. 'The Doctors' Mess: The Unsung Resource'. *British Medical Journal* 327 (2003): 689.

Richardson, Harriet, ed. *English Hospitals, 1660–1948: A Survey of their Architecture and Design*. Swindon: Royal Commission on the Historical Monuments of England, 1998.

Rimmer, Abi. 'The Future of Doctors' Messes'. *British Medical Journal* (2019): 364.

Rimmer, Abi. 'Provide Doctors with Rest Spaces and On-call Rooms, Says Mental Health Review'. *British Medical Journal* (2019): 354.

Rivett, Geoffrey. '1978–1987: Clinical Advance and Financial Crisis'. The Nuffield Trust. https://www.nuffieldtrust.org.uk/chapter/1978-1987-clinical-advance-and-financial-crisis (accessed 28 April 2021).

Shepherd, John. 'Married Quarters'. *British Medical Journal* 1 (1967): 507.

'St Luke's – The First Municipal General Hospital'. *Nursing Times* (10 February 1951): 140.

Survey of London. 'The Royal London Hospital'. https://surveyoflondon.org/map/feature/1230/detail/#fn:105 (accessed 24 March 2021).

Tweedie, J. H., A. Milosevic, and D. Shuttleworth. 'Facilities for Junior Doctors in New Hospitals'. *British Medical Journal* 2 (1978): 1503.

Varughese, George. 'Junior Doctors' Shifts and Sleep Deprivation: Please Make On-Call Rooms Available to Doctors at Night'. *British Medical Journal* 331(2005): 515.

Whiteley, J. Stuart, et al. 'Correspondence'. *British Medical Journal* 2 (1954): 128–9.

5

Negotiating deindustrialization
Emotions and Ahmedabad's textile workers
Rukmini Barua

On 27 March 1983, nearly 150 workers marched towards the Kankaria Lake in the western Indian city of Ahmedabad for an act of mass suicide in protest against the closures of two textile mills, Monogram and Marsden. The two mills had been shut down a few months earlier, leaving nearly 7,000 workers unemployed.[1] This protest was led by a newly formed trade union, the Bharatiya Kamdar Parishad of the then relatively nascent Bharatiya Janata Party (BJP). In anticipation of this heavily publicized event, the police cordoned off the lake. The workers never reached the water and were arrested.[2]

This incident, dismissed as a mere theatrical protest at the time, foregrounds two significant historical processes that frame this chapter. The early 1980s marked the beginnings of a debilitating process of industrial restructuring that transformed working lives in Ahmedabad. This was part of a broader movement of deindustrialization that unfolded across India, culminating in the liberalization policies of the early 1990s. Large-scale job losses, informalization and casualization followed, accompanied by widespread despair, anger and frustration. Simultaneously, the protest signalled the arrival of a new political player in Ahmedabad. The industrial belt of the city had long been the stronghold of the Gandhian labour union, the Textile Labour Association (TLA), and its political ally, the Indian National Congress. This protest – led by a rival trade union – thus foreshadowed the rapid ascent of the Hindu nationalist BJP in the textile mill neighbourhoods and ultimately in state- and national-level politics.

Deindustrialization in twentieth-century India followed a somewhat divergent pattern from similar phenomena globally. Instead of marking a transition to a 'post-industrial' society, deindustrialization in India precipitated the displacement of workers from large (often formal sector) factories to informal, poorly paid and precarious work arrangements. This did not so much mean capital flight to other locations with cheaper reserves of labour but rather implied a dislocation of the sites of industrial production and a restructuring of employment regimes.

Recent scholarship on deindustrialization has shifted from a focus on its political and economic causes and impact to a consideration of its cultural meanings.[3] Within this framework, deindustrialization is viewed as a dynamic emotional and affective process that shapes memory and animates notions of class and community.[4] This chapter builds on this existing body of work by placing emotions centre stage in its examination of the history of Ahmedabad's 'deindustrialization'. Such an approach allows us to trace the heterogeneous experiences of workers facing industrial restructuring and casualization and complicates the often uniform narrative of loss that dominates accounts of deindustrialization. In doing so, this chapter considers the history of deindustrialization as an ongoing process (or to use Alice Mah's term, industrial ruination) rather than a discrete event,[5] outlining the variegated spectrum of feelings that are tied to the changing dynamics of work. Finally, by teasing out the interaction between structural transformations and individual subjectivities, the social, political and spatial underpinnings of feelings and emotional styles are addressed.

This chapter will proceed in three interconnected steps. First, I consider the ways in which emotions were framed around work relations and workers' politics in the textile industry of Ahmedabad. Second, I trace the graded structures of anxiety and precarity that emerge at the moment of the factory closures. And third, I examine ways of remembering and forms of nostalgia (focusing particularly on the notion of harmony) that shape contemporary emotional landscapes of labour in the city. I draw on published interviews of former mill workers and oral historical and ethnographic research conducted in Ahmedabad between 2011 and 2013 to explore how emotions were mobilized, experienced and articulated in the making and remaking of working lives.

From 1861 onwards, when the first textile mill was established in Ahmedabad, the city acquired a reputation as the Manchester of the East. Mill chimneys and workers' neighbourhoods bloomed in a crescent along the eastern banks of the river Sabarmati. At its peak, there were sixty-three composite textile mills operating, employing roughly 155,000 workers daily.[6] Ahmedabad's mill workers, though living and labouring under distinctly trying conditions, were among India's best-paid industrial workers.[7] The 1980s, however, marked a period of social and economic upheaval in Ahmedabad; along with large-scale mill closures resulting in over 100,000 job cuts, the city witnessed long periods of caste and religious violence. The responses to deindustrialization in Ahmedabad appeared to be dramatically different from those in Bombay, which was also undergoing an acute industrial crisis. Textile mill workers in Bombay banded together for an eighteen-month-long strike against factory closures, even in opposition to the stand taken by their representative trade union.[8] In contrast to this militant collective action, contemporary observers saw Ahmedabad's workers as 'docile'.[9]

In order to understand this representation of Ahmedabad's workers (and its connected emotional registers), we must begin by examining the dominant (if not hegemonic) conceptualization of working-class politics in the city. The story of Ahmedabad's mills and those who worked in them was inextricably tied to the story of the city's main trade union, the Textile Labour Association (henceforth TLA). And to grasp the emotional dynamics of deindustrialization, it is to the TLA that we must first turn.

The TLA and its emotional style

Born of Gandhi's first political fast in 1918, the TLA established itself by the early 1920s at the forefront of the labour struggle – a move that Breman points out was actively encouraged by the industrialists.[10] The union established a model of arbitration and negotiation between labour and capital that has partly contributed to the image of Ahmedabad's working classes as peaceful or even 'passive'.[11] This model of arbitration had an impact far beyond that of the city's textile industry, forming the basis of the national-level Industrial Relations Act, shepherded into existence in 1947 by Gulzarilal Nanda, the labour minister for the Bombay province and TLA general secretary.

The militancy that engendered the formation of the TLA was gradually replaced by an unwavering commitment to arbitration[12] that did not sway even during the crisis of the textile industry. The union cast the mill workers as members of a *parivar* or family, encompassing the owners, managers and workers, and sought to instil obedience and docility in them by emphasizing their duties towards their employers and a reciprocal responsibility of the management towards the workers. The language of kinship thus worked to imbricate the control of workers' lives and spaces with a sort of filial duty. Emotions were clearly implicit in the union's view of industrial relations, which were geared towards harmony between labour and capital and encouraged a collaborative, peaceful and righteous approach to industrial disputes. Strikes were only to be used as the last resort, when all peaceful and constitutional methods of negotiations had been exhausted. Even on strike (which was exceedingly rare under the aegis of the TLA), workers were enjoined to be peaceful and non-violent and to 'bear no ill-will towards their employer or their officials'.[13] The union was convinced that a harmonious atmosphere in the mills would not only encourage higher productivity and enable the workers to 'render valuable service to the industry' but also make the experience of working itself 'lighter and more pleasant'. The intertwined logics of emotionality and productive efficiency in this case produced specific forms of workers' subjectivities that would support the needs of capital.[14]

As part of its 'righteous struggle', much of the union's efforts were directed towards the material, moral and social upliftment of textile workers. This was aided in no small measure by the TLA's prodigious political presence. From 1924, the union began participating in electoral politics, contributing large numbers of representatives to the municipal bodies, up until the late 1960s. With connections in politics and civic administration and armed with a well-oiled network of neighbourhood-level union representatives, the TLA embarked on its goal of 'all around progress'.[15] The TLA negotiated for the provision of civic amenities, mediated quotidian conflicts, appealed for better housing, and ran libraries, dispensaries and gymnasiums. In short, the union operated a sort of 'parallel government' in the mill districts.[16] Through such a presence in working-class neighbourhoods and its role as the sole representative union (and therefore the only union authorized to negotiate with mill owners), the union retained a tenacious hold over the textile workers, despite several challenges to its authority. As part of its efforts towards the material improvement of workers' lives, the union carried out its social reformist agenda of remaking Ahmedabad's workers into responsible and respectable citizens.[17] Central to this civilizing mission was a focus on developing a specific emotional repertoire for the working classes that spanned spaces of work and home. It emphasized non-violence, restraint, moral virtue, temperance, prudence and civility, with an aim towards building workers' self-respect and dignity.[18]

Work in the textile mills

While the TLA's own reportage and occasionally nostalgic accounts of the past tend to render textile workers as a unified body, divisions did exist and were reinforced by the TLA's very mode of functioning. I take a brief detour here to outline the composition of the workforce to better contextualize the discussions that follow. Work in the textile mills was historically segregated by caste and religion, with each department drawing labour from particular groups.[19] For instance, Dalit[20] subcastes were employed primarily in the spinning departments, Vaghris in the frame departments and upper castes such as Brahmins and Vanias in bundling and reeling. The weaving sheds were staffed mainly by Muslim workers, with a gradual increase of middle-caste Patels and Patidars. Among others, Bavchas, Marathas and Kolis (a numerically dominant but lower-caste group) also formed a fair proportion of the workforce. While there were changes in the caste-based occupational groupings of textile mills, much of the earlier segmentation persisted and was, in fact, strengthened by the TLA's structure as a federation of various departmental unions and by its mode of organizing.[21] The bulk of the union's membership was composed of Dalit workers, while the often better-paid Muslim weavers remained somewhat distant from the TLA.[22] This constellation of caste, community and regional ties resulted in somewhat heterogeneous workers' settlements. Workers lived in poorly serviced *chawls*[23] and for the better part of the twentieth century Dalits and Muslims – the two groups that dominated millwork in Ahmedabad – lived in close proximity.

Women workers, who had formed a considerable proportion of the workforce in the early decades of the twentieth century, had been whittled down to 3 per cent by the early 1980s.[24] The TLA actively encouraged women to withdraw from waged labour and supported the rationalization of female workers by promoting an ideology of feminine domesticity that called for women to emotionally sustain the home.[25] Many of the women workers retrenched in the rationalization drives of the 1930s and the 1960s returned to the mills as contract or *badli* (substitute) workers. Thus, at no point was the workforce an entirely secure, 'formal' one. Nearly half of the mill workers by the late 1970s were non-permanent workers, who laboured with meagre protection.[26] Nevertheless, there was an overarching security offered by textile mills that distinguished mill work from forms of casual labour – the fact that it 'effectively guaranteed work every day'.[27]

The 'shock' of the closures

When the mill closures happened, it came as a 'shock', even though the textile industry had been sputtering for several years. Indications of impending closures were signalled when the third shift in the mills was discontinued, vacancies no longer filled and entire departments shut down. Between the early 1980s and mid-1990s, the composite textile mill industry was dismantled almost entirely. However, as the closures unfolded, anxieties and uncertainties were more finely graded – with the possibility of certain mills reopening, certain segments of the workforce were more secure, certain skills more valued. Political connections, for instance, influenced which textile mills managed to evade regulations governing closures and also, perhaps, their selection for reopening.[28]

Another layer of tension was introduced by the staggered layoffs during this period. *Badli* (substitute) and contract workers, for instance, were often the first to be dismissed.[29] In Abhay Mills, first *badli* work was stopped, then the third shift, followed by large-scale retrenchment and finally, a complete shut down in early 1984.[30] With the very survival of the composite mill in doubt, additional pressures were placed upon the work process and the production units. *India Today* reported that while the spinning departments remained reasonably profitable, the costs incurred by the weaving units were partly responsible for the textile crisis. Some mill owners had indicated that the mills could be reopened if the weaving units were scrapped.[31] For instance, Ashok Mills retained only the spinning department, liquidating its weaving, processing and dyeing units.[32] Differential anxieties and apprehensions were thus generated by one's place in the hierarchy of work, often articulated in the idiom of caste and religion. These anxieties were reflected, for instance, in Valirambhai's account of his work life in Ahmedabad:

> I worked at the Silver Mills for one and a half years. After the closure of the third shift, I worked in a factory for one month or so. For Muslims, it is very difficult to get work in some mills. Everywhere, one will find nepotism, casteism, communalism. In mills, there will be back-door recruitment.[33]

The Muslim workforce in the textile mills had been gradually shrinking, and the weaving departments were increasingly being staffed by middle-caste workers (in particular, Patidars).[34]

Similarly, Dalit workers recognized stigmatization, discrimination and increasing vulnerability as stemming from their caste position. Despite the TLA's public posturing of inter-caste unity, forms of untouchability persisted in the establishment of separate drinking water facilities and rest spaces, among others.[35] As Danabhai of Marsden Mills reflected,

> In the textile industry, we Dalits are the worst hit sufferers during the last 20 years. The reason is the most of the Dalits are in spinning-throstle department only. In this departments, single row of machines was doubled . . . doubled was made

four-fold ... six-fold ... and eight-fold ... obviously an axe of retrenchment will fall on the Dalits only. Is it not so?[36]

The tensions over industrial restructuring and shrinking mill employment, expressed in terms of community, thus indicated deepening schisms between various groups of mill workers. Such concerns tied together questions of work segmentation in textile mills, experiences of systemic prejudice and the sense of discrimination that marked working lives.

Simultaneously, a pervasive sense of anger and betrayal surfaced against the TLA. The union had retreated from taking any kind of militant stand and concerned itself with appealing to the principles of trusteeship. Social activist Manishi Jani's fact-finding report on retrenchment (which included a series of interviews conducted with former mill workers) commented on the union's attitude during the most intense period of unemployment:

> they believe the textile industry is one big family and the mill owner is the head of the family, while the worker is the younger brother. That is why the worker must request the family head with folded hands. And if he is not satisfied, he should seek help from the Sarkar mabaap.[37]

Referencing the union's well-established emotional repertoire of harmony, such commentaries foreground the practices of supplication and paternalism that marked the TLA's relationship with the state and capital.[38]

The union, at this point, was 'deaf and dumb' and busy trying to 'persuade the workers not to wash dirty linen in public by getting excited and angry'. The TLA's stand as perceived by retrenched workers was to 'remain peaceful and starve', reinforcing widely held assumptions that 'the workers of Gujarat are mild natured, peace loving and not struggle minded'.[39] For the workers, however, the TLA appeared as their 'weak point'. As Amrutbhai, a former worker at Tarun Mills mentioned, 'If I was a TLA president, all the mills of Ahmedabad would have gone on strike! The Government would get baffled!'

Emotions (or, more precisely, appropriate ways of feeling) in the face of extreme economic crisis emerged as the site on which workers and the union were pitted against each other. The disillusionment with the TLA's response was exacerbated by rumours circulating around the union's complicity in the closures. Workers reported that their concerns over imminent mill closures were deliberately dismissed by the TLA.[40] Contemporary reportage suggests that the TLA did not merely take a passive position in the face of mass retrenchment but was actively involved in the corruption that surrounded mill closures. Workers' feelings of discontent were not just directed towards the union but were also aimed at broader institutional structures that they had so far been part of. Social insurance schemes that they had contributed to failed to provide any support once the mills closed down. Similarly, acts of solidarity extended by workers during previous moments of crisis (such as donating a day's wages or working on holidays to raise funds for floods) were not reciprocated. As Mithabhai of Monogram Mills put it, 'Now when we are jobless, why is there no relief fund for us?'

It was under these circumstances that the workers' mass suicide attempt (with which I began the chapter) took place. It was an attempt to call attention to their suffering and hardship and articulate it in a visible, public form. It was also an occasion for the BJP to signal that they were listening. Ashok Bhatt of the BJP, who orchestrated this protest, responded to Congress Party leaders who dismissed the incident as a political stunt: 'It will sound like a joke to all insensitive people. But to those whose kitchen fires are dead, this may mean many things.'[41]

After the mills

The anger, resentment and sense of betrayal that former mill workers felt towards the TLA is perceptible in present-day conversations about the past. 'It was less of trade unionism and more of brokering deals', Jigneshbhai told me,

> But after the mills closed down, did the workers die? Or did they become completely destitute? No, this didn't happen. We all went into different lines of work – some got jobs in power looms and workshops, other started hawking or began petty trades, like running phone booths, or driving rickshaws.

This shift towards informal employment or the 'fall from paradise', as Breman put it, was accompanied by profound emotional upheavals. 'These neighbourhoods became "dull" once the mills closed', Amritbhai recalled, 'that kind of *mahaul* (atmosphere, ambience) was lost forever'. The *mahaul* that Amritbhai was referring to was one that is remembered as brimming with vitality, oriented by the rhythms of the mills and framed by bonds of sociality and conviviality between mill workers. The mill sirens, likened to a mother's call to come home, governed everyday life – structuring domestic chores and meal timings and directing the bustle of large groups of workers on foot or cycles from their *chawls* to the mills.[42] The loss of this *mahaul* was felt as a sensory one.

As contemporary reportage and oral narratives point out, the emotional implications of the mill closures were felt across generations. For older male workers, deindustrialization signalled an enduring trauma. It was articulated as an embodied loss: 'I did not know how to live, where to go and what to do. It was like losing my hands.'[43] They spoke of the closures in the language of bereavement, 'as if somebody had died in the family', in terms of 'a shock like a parent's sudden death' and as a form of intimate grief, 'of feel[ing] like becoming a widower'.[44]

Having to then find employment in unskilled or otherwise poorly paid jobs (sometimes doing the same work they did in the mills) was perceived as shameful.[45] Female work participation increased, and while women were considered to be more 'resilient' in weathering the crisis of deindustrialization, there was a shift towards work that had been previously considered humiliating or degrading.[46]

In other contexts, scholarship on deindustrialization has shown that unemployment produced a crisis of masculinity and a loss of male pride.[47] 'Now *every* member of the household has to work', Jigneshbhai told me, 'and even then, this household won't ever be able to afford jaggery or ghee or seasonal vegetables'. Jigneshbhai's conversation betrays a nostalgia towards the past that is fairly common among older residents of the mill neighbourhoods in particular. In such recollections of life during the peak of the textile industry, the trope of the male breadwinner that Jigneshbhai recalled was seen as a measure of a good life. Although women in the mill neighbourhoods had been involved in waged work throughout (often in home-based, casual or contract work), there was a transformation in the dynamics of work following the mill closures. The fiction of feminine domesticity and the sole male earner, thus punctured, unsettled notions of masculinity in this social milieu.

Deindustrialization not only transformed employment regimes but also unsettled a way of life. The network of institutions that was largely mediated by the TLA – access to credit, dispensaries, reading rooms – disintegrated. As workers turned to lower-paying, more precarious jobs, there was a collective drop in the standard of living, which had generational repercussions:

> Along with higher salaries in the textile mills, there used to be a lot of support – scholarships and so on. And mill workers' children benefitted from this. You see, earlier, with education you could see the birth of a new 'middle class'. Now, this [kind of upward mobility] has become very difficult for the working classes.[48]

The new middle class that Jigneshbhai referred to was an entire generation of Dalit workers who acquired economic prosperity through stable mill employment and government affirmative action, often physically relocating from the cramped quarters of the mill districts to the suburbs.[49] Even workers like Jigneshbhai, who were never made permanent in the mills, felt this loss of possibility and connected it to diminishing social respectability more broadly. Jigneshbhai's concerns are not so much a sentimentalized longing for the past but rather the 'occupation of past possibilities in the present moment'.[50] They lament the loss of possibilities, opportunities and a vision of the future that was conceivable in the past.[51]

The emotional attachment that (especially the older generation of) workers retained with the materiality of the mills was visible decades after the closures. Mill identity cards are safely stored away inside trunks and cupboards and brought out with some reverence to show researchers. As are curfew passes, which allowed mill workers some mobility during intermittent episodes of violence. The mill compounds – whether desolate and overgrown or 'rejuvenated' as shiny new commercial, industrial or residential complexes – remain part of the emotional geography of these neighbourhoods. Jeevanbhai, a former TLA representative and worker in Sarangpur Mill No. 2, would etch out the contours of his spinning department onto the flattened, empty landscape as he recalled his work life. Other workers would conjure their mill gates out of thin air, as they outlined their daily commute to the mills. This sense of place is one that is clearly grounded in their historical experiences of work and its everyday rhythms.[52]

Yet, there were other ways in which workers related to the spaces of the closed mills. The mill structures and boundary walls were gradually dismantled by the local residents.

> Everyday people . . . you know, poor people like me . . . would set out in the morning with their lunch boxes, combing through the mill buildings to forage bricks, iron scrap, anything that could be used or sold. There was no work at that time, and a kilo of scrap would fetch Rs. 12, 13. If one could find 5-6 kgs, they could take home Rs. 60.[53]

The material remnants of the mills thus found their way into workers' housing and formed a tenuous safety net during the harshest period of the crisis.

The process of compensation for retrenched workers was a fraught one – the textile mills had declared bankruptcy, the mill lands were caught between competing claims and the TLA was routinely accused of corruption. However, as compensation trickled in, one of the first investments was made in housing.

Against the backdrop of declining standards of living and the loss of social prestige that followed the mill closures, these new material practices can be read as carrying profound emotional significance. Workers could, for the first time, afford to renovate their *chawls*. On the foundations of the original low-roofed structures, two or sometimes three storeys were added. Walls were cemented, floors were tiled and, gradually, other markers of relative affluence were added – attached toilets and bathrooms, a television, a fridge. Workers had lost the social and institutional support afforded by employment in the mills, but as Jigneshbhai put it, 'they had something to show for it'. The process of deindustrialization and the emotions embedded in it were not necessarily consistent but rather gave rise to spatially and temporally contingent feelings of ambivalence.

Coeval to the collapse of the textile industry, there were tremendous changes unfolding in the political realm. The TLA's electoral presence had diminished considerably and its political ally, the Congress Party, was rapidly losing its grip on municipal politics. In the meantime, the nascent Hindu right-wing Bharatiya Janata Party (and its umbrella organization, the Sangh Parivar) stepped up efforts to broaden its initial upper-caste, middle-class constituency.[54] In the wake of its involvement in caste violence in the mid-1980s, the BJP embarked on a nationwide effort to embrace Dalits into the greater Hindu fold. BJP-affiliated trade unions proliferated across Gujarat as the party aimed to reach the urban poor.[55]

Once the BJP entered the Ahmedabad Municipal Corporation in 1987, party officials opened local offices in the mill neighbourhoods. In this way, the party penetrated existing arenas of urban sociality – the street life of the mill areas, the *addas* – historically forged and finessed by the TLA and its representatives. At these *addas*, sites of male sociality, large numbers of men would linger for hours, chatting, playing board games and discussing the state of the world. While the TLA was embedded in this form of public life through its vast network of worker representatives, the BJP's mode of functioning relied on an engagement of senior party members with local youth. A new channel of proximate intimacy was inaugurated, offering closeness to political leadership and the state.[56]

Beginning with widely established techniques of gaining neighbourhood support – organizing health camps and distributing school supplies and books to students – the party moved on to incorporating young Dalit men into the lower rungs of its leadership.[57] At a time when the first shock of mill closures had sent the industrial districts into a crisis – of livelihoods, social identity, reputation and social honour – this move can be seen as offering a space in which young working-class men could make an attempt to reclaim some degree of social respectability.

The BJP's presence and success in the mill neighbourhoods thus knitted together a range of (complementary and sometimes contradictory) sentiments. These included specifically local and classed feelings of isolation from networks of political power and visibility, resentment (as a form of perceived injustice) against the TLA and feeling 'useless'.[58] The Gujarati legacies of non-violence and connected practices of vegetarianism were paradoxically mobilized into a sacrificial imaginary by employing a rhetoric of disgust against Muslims (and their supposedly carnivorous appetites).[59] At the same time, it also drew on national-level emotive strategies of being and feeling part of a unified Hindu body.[60]

Harmony, nostalgia and memory

In post-independence India, Ahmedabad acquired the reputation of being one of the most 'riot-prone' cities in India – major episodes of religious and caste violence occurred in 1969, 1981, 1985–6, intermittently through the 1990s and reaching its horrific peak during the anti-Muslim pogrom of 2002. Much of the scholarship on Ahmedabad tends to view the collapse of the textile industry (and the TLA's decline) as a crucial factor in the communalization of the city's politics. Varshney, for instance, contends that organizations like the TLA constituted a 'bulwark of peace' and were instrumental in establishing 'civic contact between Hindus and Muslims';[61] hence, the disintegration of the city's formerly 'harmonious' social fabric can be dated to the collapse of the textile industry. Breman suggests that the TLA diffused communal tensions by appealing to 'working-class solidarity'. This form of social consciousness rested on 'communal harmony', which was replaced by an attachment to 'primordial loyalties' with the decline of the mills.[62] Spodek understands endemic urban violence, in part as a consequence of criminalization that surfaced once 'civic order' – fostered by institutions such as the TLA – eroded. Violence was an effect of the 'breakdown of institutional and moral cohesion'.[63] It is not my intention to suggest that deindustrialization did not precipitate profound transformations with far-reaching social, political and emotional consequences – much of this chapter has argued that new emotional registers emerged to articulate the changed relationship with work and trade unionism. Rather, it is to prise open the category of harmony, which seems to colour so much of how the past is seen. What does it mean to say that mill workers were a more harmonious lot in the past? Or that the TLA promoted social harmony?

At one level, the narrative of harmony appears not only in scholarly accounts but also in popular memory in the mill neighbourhoods of contemporary Ahmedabad. Jasani sees an 'almost tangible desperation' to believe in and represent a 'once peaceful past that has progressively decayed'.[64] I noticed a similar tendency during my own conversations with residents of the mill localities. In every conversation that I had with Imdadbhai, then Congress municipal councillor and the son of Muslim migrant mill workers, he would repeat, 'Have you written down that earlier there was a spirit of harmony? Make sure you write that down.' Another resident remarked, 'There was so much camaraderie amongst people then. We would celebrate festivals together and all three faiths [Hindus, Christians and Muslims] lived together.' The memory of the 'mixed neighbourhood' surfaced time and again, counterposed against the much more starkly segregated living arrangements of the present. This image of the past linked together work in the mills with feelings of neighbourliness, implying that a shared work culture translated into social warmth and cohesion outside the mills. These narratives of an idealized working-class community certainly elide both the social divisions that existed and the drudgery and hardship of work in the mills but nevertheless offer a counterpoint to talk about[65] or even critique sociopolitical dynamics of contemporary Ahmedabad.

Even in these nostalgic accounts of harmony we can find traces of other more ambivalent and contradictory feelings, however. One of the crucial ways in which harmony is conceptualized in Ahmedabad is related to intercommunity support and mutual protection (bolstered by the TLA) during episodes of violence.[66] This understanding of harmony implies that violence came from 'elsewhere' and its perpetrators were 'outsiders'. Jeevanbhai's recollections of the violence of 1969 complicate this. Jeevanbhai is a former TLA representative and a Congress municipal councillor who has built his political career on the plank of 'communal harmony'.[67] During the riots of 1969, when there were months of unrest and curfew, Jeevanbhai recalled that he would slip through the warren of streets behind his home at Kundawali chaali, making straight for Sarangpur No. 2 Mill. Workers of each shift would move together, 50–100 people at a time. 'The ones who would live amongst their own community managed to go to work.... Here, we [Dalits] were in the majority, so we would cut through the *gallis* and get to the mill.' Muslim workers from Bapunagar, for instance, could not come to work in Gomtipur mills, for they would have to cross three or four Hindu areas on their way. Neither could Hindu workers from Gomtipur go towards Ajit Mill in Rakhiyal, crossing the Muslim neighbourhood of Rajpur on the way. But there was no violence within the mills.[68] Jivan Thakore makes a similar observation:

> Hindu and Muslim friends met and discussed what was happening in their respective localities . . . [workers] refrained themselves and saw to it that their family members did not participate in the violence . . . The supervisors and jamadars feared that the outrage outside might creep into the mill and its premises. But we had communal harmony inside the [mill] compound.[69]

However, while Thakore relates peace within the mill to 'feelings of brotherhood', Jeevanbhai sees it as a function of distance: 'their departments and our departments were separate.' He presents an entirely different profile of the perpetrators – local strongmen who were his friends and fellow TLA representatives who 'cleared out' neighbourhoods of Muslim mill workers:

> For 2-3 months afterwards, Hindu and Muslim workers would not talk to each other while at work. After that the sense of brotherhood was repaired a bit . . . you know, Hindus are very forgiving. Muslims never forget or forgive . . . say their wife or child has died [killed], they hold on to that anger, to that enmity and always nursing vengeful feelings.

To my mind, there is often a slippage in the ways in which the operations of the TLA are understood, in the accounts that posit the union as the keeper of social cohesion and harmony. Or in other words, accounts that suggest that the TLA's emotional repertoire that emphasized non-violence and harmony was not contested. Elsewhere, I have argued that the TLA's extensive apparatus of grassroots control was often buttressed by precisely the kind of 'unruly' worker that it was publicly committed to sanitizing.[70] Thus, even as the union urged the (male) workforce to be non-violent and respectable, its actual operations on the ground depended on those who embodied fearlessness, aggression and the ability to inflict violence and inspire respect. The TLA was not, as other scholars have also suggested, an institution separate from the textures of everyday life in the workers' neighbourhoods.[71] But if this was so, then the argument that harmony was something that the union fostered and disharmony something external to it does not hold. Indeed, in Jeevanbhai's nostalgic recollections of the past, it is the feelings associated with virile, aggressive (and clearly bigoted) masculinity (and the social bonds that came with it) that he highlights.

This chapter offers a long history of working-class politics, trade unionism and its discontents by looking at the emotional dynamics of deindustrialization.

By focusing on the broad range of feelings that emerged following the closure of mills, I suggest that emotions of loss, betrayal and despair were framed by the communally segmented structures of the work process. These feelings had a spatial location and a sensory dimension. Life in the mill neighbourhoods following deindustrialization reconfigured workers' emotional practices, combining working-class anxieties with Hindu nationalist militancy. Deindustrialization did not just manifest in emotions of loss and resignation but also in complex and often troubling registers of feelings. Finally, this chapter has critically evaluated the nostalgic rendering of a harmonious past in light of recurrent sectarian conflict, suggesting that harmony and disharmony, unity and disunity were enmeshed even in the 'glory days' of mill work. As Ahmedabad remakes itself as India's first Heritage City, there have been renewed efforts to preserve its industrial past.[72] Memorializing and aesthetizing the city and its mills as sites of peaceful coexistence runs the risk of erasing the violence and dispossession that has marked the city's twentieth-century history.[73]

Notes

1 *India Today*, 31 January 1983.
2 *The Times of India*, 28 March 1983; *India Today*, 31 January 1983.
3 See for instance Mah, *Industrial Ruination*; High and Lewis, *Corporate Wasteland*.
4 High, 'The Wounds of Class'; Strangleman and Rhodes, 'The "New" Sociology'; Bonfiglioli, 'Post-Socialist Deindustrialisation'.
5 Mah, *Industrial Ruination*.
6 Spodek, *Ahmedabad*, 195.
7 Spodek, 'Manchesterisation'.
8 Representative trade unions in India are those that have been granted exclusive rights of collective bargaining.
9 *India Today*, 15 January 1985.
10 Breman, *The Making and Unmaking*, 46.
11 Patel, *Industrial Relations*.
12 Patel, 'Class Conflict'.
13 TLA, 'Six Decades of the TLA', 3–4.
14 TLA, 'Annual Report 1950–51', 12. See also Donauer, 'Emotions at Work'.
15 TLA, 'Six Decades of the TLA', 16.
16 Spodek, 'From Gandhi to Violence'.
17 TLA, 'Annual Report 1950', 2.
18 See select TLA Annual Reports 1924–81.

19 Lakha, 'Character of Wage Labour'.
20 Formerly untouchable caste groups, in this case mostly Hindu.
21 See Lakha, 'Character of Wage Labour'; Breman, *The Making and Unmaking*; Gillion, *Ahmedabad*. See also Royal Commission of Labour in India, Vol. 1, Part 1. 7 ff.
22 Breman, *The Making and Unmaking*.
23 One or two room dwellings, with shared facilities, common in industrial cities across India.
24 Jhabvala, *Closing Doors*.
25 Barua, 'Feminine Domesticity'.
26 Breman, *The Making and Unmaking*, 204.
27 Breman, *The Making and Unmaking*, 28.
28 *India Today*, 31 July 1984.
29 Breman, *The Making and Unmaking*.
30 Jani, *The Textile Workers*.
31 *India Today*, 29 February 1984.
32 Howell and Kambhampati, 'Liberalization and Labour'.
33 Jani, *Textile Workers*, 11.
34 Muslim workers nevertheless constituted nearly 7 per cent of the retrenched workforce in the mid-1980s, as opposed to 3 per cent in Bombay. See Patel, *Workers of Closed Textile Mills*; Mhaskar, 'Indian Muslims in a Global City', 17; Breman, *The Making and Unmaking*.
35 Breman, *The Making and Unmaking*, 57.
36 Jani, *Textile Workers*, 7–8.
37 Jani, *Textile Workers*, 3. 'Mabaap' lit. translates as 'mother-father'. This term suggests an engagement with the state in terms of goodwill or benevolence rather than through rights and entitlements.
38 *India Today*, 31 July 1984.
39 The interviews cited in this section have been drawn from Jani, *Textile Workers*.
40 Interviews Ahmedabad, 2011–12.
41 *India Today*, 30 April 1983. Ashok Bhatt went on to serve as a member of the Gujarat Legislative Assembly for nearly two decades. Formerly an employee of Arvind Mills, he is widely credited with building the BJP's support base in Ahmedabad. He was accused of inciting anti-Muslim violence in 1985 and 2002.
42 Breman and Shah, *Working in the Mill*.
43 Noronha, 'Duration of Unemployment'.
44 Noronha, 'Duration of Unemployment'.
45 Breman, *The Making and Unmaking*, 214.
46 Shah, *Ahmedabad*, 119; Jhabvala, *Closing Doors*.
47 Joshi, 'On "De-Industrialization"'.
48 Jigneshbhai, interview.

49 Banerjee and Mehta, 'Caste and Capital'.
50 Finkelstein, *The Archive of Loss*, 92.
51 See also Boym, *The Future of Nostalgia*.
52 Meier, 'Encounters'. A broader literature exists on the relationship between social space, emotions and affect. See for instance Khan, 'The Social Production'; Bondi, Davidson and Smith eds., *Emotional Geographies*; Thien, 'After or Beyond Feeling?'.
53 Jeevanbhai, interview.
54 Nandy, *Creating a Nationality*.
55 Shah, 'Tenth Lok Sabha Elections', 2924.
56 See also Berenschot, *Riot Politics*, 143.
57 In other contexts, organizations of the Hindu right have deployed similar techniques of mobilization. For instance, in Bombay, the Shiv Sena entered mill neighbourhoods through social and community work. See, for instance, Menon, *One Hundred Years One Hundred Voices*; and Hansen, *Wages of Violence*, 53–7.
58 For resentment as injury and injustice, see Fassin, et al., 'On Resentment and Ressentiment'. See also Jasani, 'Violence, Urban Anxieties and Masculinities' for an analysis of the aftermath of violence and feelings of 'being used'.
59 Ghassem-Fachandi, 'Ahimsa, Identification and Sacrifice'.
60 In particular, reclamation of Hindu masculinity against the Muslim 'other' is a common trope employed by Hindu fundamentalism. An extensive body of work exists on this subject, including Hansen, 'Recuperating Masculinity'; Sarkar, 'Semiotics of Terror'; Gupta, *Justice before Reconciliation*.
61 Varshney, *Civic Life and Ethnic Conflict*, 231.
62 Breman, 'Communal Upheaval as Resurgence', 1485–8.
63 Spodek, 'From Gandhi to Violence'.
64 Jasani, 'A Potted History of Neighbours', 160.
65 Jasani, 'A Potted History of Neighbours', 160.
66 Breman, 'Communal Upheaval as Resurgence'.
67 Jeevanbhai and Imdadbhai have contested municipal elections together for over a decade, neatly dividing the Dalit and Muslim constituencies in Gomtipur. Their commitment to communal harmony was mentioned in *The Indian Express*, which noted that their 'firm resolve to maintain peace meant that no untoward incident took place'. *The Indian Express*, 8 March 2002.
68 Jeevanbhai, interview.
69 Thakore, cited in Breman, *The Making and Unmaking*, 223.
70 Barua, 'The Textile Labour Association'.
71 See Breman, *The Making and Unmaking*; Spodek, *Ahmedabad*.
72 *The Times of India*, 27 April 2010; *The Hindu*, 9 July 2017.
73 For other discussions of Ahmedabad's remaking of heritage, see Da Costa, 'Sentimental Capitalism in Contemporary India'.

Bibliography

Banerjee, Dyotana, and Mona G. Mehta. 'Caste and Capital in the Remaking of Ahmedabad.' *Contemporary South Asia* 25, no. 2 (2017): 182–95.

Barua, Rukmini. 'Feminine Domesticity and Emotions of Gender: Women and Work in 20th and Early 21st Century India.' *L'Homme. Zeitschrift für feministische Geschictswissenschaft* 21, no. 2 (2021): 59–77.

Barua, Rukmini. 'The Textile Labour Association and Dadagiri: Power and Politics in the Working-Class Neighborhoods of Ahmedabad.' *International Labor and Working Class History* 87 (2015): 63–91.

Berenschot, Ward. *Riot Politics: Hindu–Muslim Violence and the Indian State*. Rupa Publications, 2013.

Bondi, Liz, Joyce Davidson, and Mick Smith, eds. *Emotional Geographies*. New York: Routledge, 2016.

Bonfiglioli, Chiara. 'Post-Socialist Deindustrialisation and its Gendered Structure of Feeling: The Devaluation of Women's Work in the Croatian Garment Industry'. *Labor History* 61, no. 1 (2020): 36–47.

Boym, Svetlana. *The Future of Nostalgia*. Basic Books, 2001.

Breman, Jan. 'Communal Upheaval as Resurgence of Social Darwinism'. *Economic and Political Weekly* 37, no. 16 (2002): 1485–8.

Breman, Jan. *The Making and Unmaking of an Industrial Working Class: Sliding Down the Labour Hierarchy in Ahmedabad, India*. Delhi: Oxford University Press, 2004.

Breman, Jan, and Parthiv Shah. *Working in the Mill No More*. Delhi: Oxford University Press, 2004.

Da Costa, Dia. 'Sentimental Capitalism in Contemporary India: Art, Heritage, and Development in Ahmedabad, Gujarat'. *Antipode* 47, no. 1 (2015): 74–97.

Donauer, Sabine. 'Emotions at Work-Working on Emotions: The Production of Economic Selves in 20th Century Germany'. PhD Dissertation, Freie University, 2015.

Fassin, Didier, Thomas Brudholm, Michael Lambek, Amelie Rorty, Bhrigupati Singh, and C. Jason Throop. 'On Resentment and Ressentiment: The Politics and Ethics of Moral Emotions'. *Current Anthropology* 54, no. 3 (2013): 249–67.

Finkelstein, Maura. *The Archive of Loss: Lively Ruination in Mill Land Mumbai*. Durham: Duke University Press, 2019.

Ghassem-Fachandi, Parvis. 'Ahimsa, Identification and Sacrifice in the Gujarat Pogrom'. *Social Anthropology* 18, no. 2 (2010): 155–75.

Gillion, Kenneth L. *Ahmedabad: A Study in Indian Urban History*. Berkeley: University of California Press, 1968.

Gupta, Dipankar. *Justice before Reconciliation: Negotiating a 'New Normal' in Post-Riot Mumbai and Ahmedabad*. London: Routledge, 2013.

Hansen, Thomas Blom. 'Recuperating Masculinity: Hindu Nationalism, Violence and the Exorcism of the Muslim "Other"'. *Critique of Anthropology* 16, no. 2 (1996): 137–72.

Hansen, Thomas Blom. *Wages of Violence: Naming and Identity in Postcolonial Bombay*. Princeton: Princeton University Press, 2001.

High, Steven C., and David W. Lewis. *Corporate Wasteland: The Landscape and Memory of Deindustrialization*. Ithaca, NY: Cornell University Press, 2007.

High, Steven. '"The Wounds of Class": A Historiographical Reflection on the Study of Deindustrialization, 1973–2013'. *History Compass* 11, no. 11 (2013): 994–1007.

Howell, Jude, and Uma Kambhampati. 'Liberalization and Labour: The Fate of Retrenched Workers in the Cotton Textile Industry in India'. *Oxford Development Studies* 27, no. 1 (1999): 109–27.

Jani, Manishi. *The Textile Workers: Jobless and Miserable*. Ahmedabad: SETU, 1984.

Jasani, Rubina. 'A Potted History of Neighbours and Neighbourliness in Ahmedabad'. In *The Idea of Gujarat: History, Ethnography and Text*, edited by Edward Simpson and Aparna Kapadia, 153–67. Orient Blackswan, 2010.

Jasani, Rubina. 'Violence, Urban Anxieties and Masculinities: The "Foot Soldiers" of 2002, Ahmedabad'. *South Asia: Journal of South Asian Studies* 43, no. 4 (2020): 675–90.

Jhabvala, Renana. *Closing Doors: A Study on the Decline of Women Workers in the Textile Mills of Ahmedabad*. Ahmedabad: SETU, 1985.

Joshi, Chitra. 'On "De-Industrialization" and the Crisis of Male Identities'. *International Review of Social History* 47 (2002): 159–75.

Khan, Razak. 'The Social Production of Space and Emotions in South Asia'. *Journal of the Economic and Social History of the Orient* 58, no. 5 (2015): 611–33.

Lakha, Salim. 'Character of Wage Labour in Early Industrial Ahmedabad'. *Journal of Contemporary Asia* 15, no. 4 (1985): 421–41.

Mah, Alice. *Industrial Ruination, Community, and Place: Landscapes and Legacies of Urban Decline*. Toronto: University of Toronto Press, 2012.

Meier, Lars. 'Encounters with Haunted Industrial Workplaces and Emotions of Loss: Class-Related Senses of Place Within the Memories of Metalworkers'. *Cultural Geographies* 20, no. 4 (2013): 467–83.

Menon, Meena. *One Hundred Years One Hundred Voices: The Millworkers of Girangaon: An Oral History*. Calcutta: Seagull Books, 2004.

Mhaskar, Sumeet. 'Indian Muslims in a Global City: Socio-Political Effects on Economic Preferences in Contemporary Mumbai'. MMG Working Paper 13-04, Max Planck Institute for the Study of Religious and Ethnic Diversity (2013).

Nandy, Ashis, et al. *Creating a Nationality: The Ramjanmabhumi Movement and Fear of the Self*. New Delhi: Oxford University Press, 1998.

Noronha, Ernesto. 'Duration Of Unemployment And Re-employment: Part–I'. *Management and Labour Studies* 24, no. 2 (1999): 96–112.

Patel, BB. *Workers of Closed Textile Mills*. New Delhi: Oxford/IBH Publishing, 1988.

Patel, Sujata. 'Class Conflict and Workers' Movement in Ahmedabad Textile Industry, 1918–23'. *Economic and Political Weekly* 19, no. 20–21 (1984): 853–64.

Patel, Sujata. *The Making of Industrial Relations: The Ahmedabad Textile Industry, 1918–1939*. Oxford: Oxford University Press, 1987.

Report of the Royal Commission on Labour, Vol. I (Bombay Presidency, including Sindh). London, 1931.
Sarkar, Tanika. 'Semiotics of Terror: Muslim Children and Women in Hindu Rashtra'. *Economic and Political Weekly* 37, no. 28 (2002): 2872–76.
Shah, Amrita. *Ahmedabad: A City in the World*. London: Bloomsbury, 2015.
Shah, Ghanshyam. 'Tenth Lok Sabha Elections: BJP's Victory in Gujarat'. *Economic and Political Weekly* 6, no. 21 (1991): 2924.
Spodek, Howard. *Ahmedabad: Shock City of Twentieth Century India*. Bloomington: Indiana University Press, 2011.
Spodek, Howard. 'From Gandhi to Violence: Ahmedabad's 1985 Riots in Historical Perspective'. *Modern Asian Studies* 23, no. 4 (1989): 765–95.
Spodek, Howard. 'The Manchesterisation of Ahmedabad'. *Economic and Political Weekly* 17, no. 13 (1965): 483–90.
Strangleman, Tim, and James Rhodes. 'The "New" Sociology of Deindustrialisation? Understanding Industrial Change'. *Sociology Compass* 8, no. 4 (2014): 411–21.
Textile Labour Association. 'Annual Reports 1924–1981.' Ahmedabad: TLA.
Textile Labour Association. *Six Decades of the Textile Labour Association (1917–1977)*. Ahmedabad: TLA, 1977. https://indianlabourarchives.org/handle/123456789/1794?mode=full (accessed 26 September 2021).
Thien, Deborah. 'After or Beyond Feeling? A Consideration of Affect and Emotion in Geography'. *Area* 37, no. 4 (2005): 450–4.
Varshney, Ashutosh. *Civic Life and Ethnic Conflict: Hindus and Muslims in India*. New Haven: Yale University Press, 2002.

Part II

Professional and personal identities

6

Education, work and self-worth in women's letters to Soviet authorities, 1924–32

Hannah Parker

Five days after *Pravda*'s publication of an article titled 'Cultural Poverty' on 10 April 1929 by Deputy Minister for Education Nadezhda Krupskaia – about the spread of literacy skills across the Union and political work in libraries – Elizaveta, a twenty-two-year-old library worker from Ulianovsk region, on the Volga River, wrote her a letter.[1] Elizaveta's letter expressed a litany of anxieties about her abilities and credentials as a librarian. Largely self-educated, required to work from a young age to support her family and now working as a librarian (*bibliotekar'*), Elizaveta's biography describes a path of proletarian self-improvement common to biographical statements written by citizens in the period.[2] Yet, she claimed, she was 'semiliterate' and did not deserve her post in the library, a thought which caused her great distress.

> The thing is that I had to study for three years only, because my father died (and in general in 1917-18 studies were bad) and then I had to go to work to support my family [. . .] now, now I'm already an employee and [so] the path to learning is closed to me. I'm self-educated [. . .] But now I'm faced with the fact that I do not deserve my post as a librarian, I'm poorly acquainted with literature, I know hardly any literature, I'm semiliterate, and I'm a librarian but I can't satisfy [the job's] demands, instruct their interests, and teach them systematically to read about reading [which] is what I need [to do] – it torments me terribly.[3]

The anxieties embedded in Elizaveta's statement are striking; her own perceptions of her limited knowledge or understanding of the key political literature of the period, she explained, meant that she was out of her depth and unable to fulfil the obligations such a job entailed. This was a failure, Elizaveta reasoned, which called into question her participation in Soviet education altogether.

Though popularly known as Lenin's widow, Krupskaia maintained an active lifelong commitment to the education of workers, taking a special interest in libraries as public institutions. Krupskaia's commitment to the personal development of workers has been considered a 'conservative' counterpart to the pure productionism of the 1920s and 1930s.[4] However, as Christopher Read has pointed out, her emphasis upon the significance of 'consciousness' and the creativity of communist – as opposed to bourgeois – labour in Marxism perhaps indicates a utopianism regarding the transformative power of education.[5] These ideas underpinned her article published almost one week prior, which lamented that the lack of funding for adult education had allowed the 'ice of illiteracy' to 'freeze to the shores of an impoverished life', and called for immediate attention to adult education in literacy, politics and technical skills through libraries and reading rooms.[6] Elizaveta, concerned about the consequences of her missed schooling and educational inadequacies for her participation in the education of the workers in her locale, asked for advice, framing her dilemma explicitly in terms of knowledge, utility and belonging.

> The further I read about library affairs, the more I see myself disappearing, it turns out I have no idea and do not understand many branches of library work, what do you advise to me? Would it not be more honest on my part to say that I am not fit for purpose and leave? Answer me please and advise me.[7]

Apparently overwhelmed by the expectation that she would be responsible for acquainting workers with important literature, and its relevance to their lives, Elizaveta expressed that her sense of belonging in her workplace was shaken by these feelings of technical inadequacy. Requesting reassurance from Krupskaia, she explained the discussions she had had at work in this vein.

> I've already talked about it for a long time with the head of the regional CPSU Ushakova, but she advises me to stay on and says that if I have the desire, a real librarian will emerge from me, especially in our workers' libraries where I feel that with my own weight with the workers I can give something. But in fact desire alone does very little.[8]

The emphasis placed by Ushakova upon Elizaveta's 'desire' to work as a librarian and the virtue of her proletarian background as mutually dependent attributes of her suitability to the role in the education of workers sheds light upon the significance of notions of emotional and biographical 'authenticity' that were crucial to the construction of knowledge in the Soviet Union.[9] While a citizen's class background might be key to civic belonging and professional authority, without an equivalent emotional investment in socialist construction, one's authenticity as an educator was not secure. This mutual dependence was not lost upon Elizaveta, who evidently felt insecure in the degree of political consciousness afforded her by her background.

Emotions were critical to the success of the Bolshevik project. In this chapter, I argue that the emotional engagements of citizens were critical to notions of socialist mobilization, and the productive labour required for socialist construction, and that their emotional experience was delineated sharply by binary notions of gender. Women were both beneficiaries of Soviet educational policies and, due to their association with nurture and mothering, expected to possess the innate qualities necessary to facilitate them, as mothers and educators, mobilizing the Soviet population behind the state's rapid industrialization programmes. Against the context of a complex and fluctuating system of rights, obligations and belonging, which were contingent upon productive labour, education became a cornerstone of women's feelings of self-worth. As this chapter will discuss, women, who had been liberated from the dual oppressions of capitalism and 'domestic slavery' by the Revolution, were a key target for adult education and the liquidation of illiteracy, which aimed to raise their 'low cultural level', engage them in productive labour and facilitate their social and emotional transformation into the New Soviet Woman.[10]

The October Revolution promised the pursuit of 'happiness', an ideal which necessarily combined collective and individual experiences, and required the reconstruction of public values, which were embodied by the New Soviet Person.[11] The role of the Bolshevik Party as benefactor to its citizens established expectations of gratitude, with the consequence that belonging and inclusion hinged upon the performance of certain emotions – among them joy, gratitude, righteous anger and collective spirit – in their public, private and professional conduct.[12] This mobilization of the population, and the generation of its emotional allegiance to the revolutionary state, required the monitoring of the 'public mood', to which end the inculcation of 'conscious and vigilant citizens', who could police the boundaries of the Soviet emotional community.[13] This priority was particularly important towards the end of the 1920s, as the decade's future-oriented utopianism was replaced with the assertion that socialist happiness was already present.[14] A key tenet of the Revolution in culture, education was critical to the political mobilization of the proletariat across the Soviet Union, which would deconstruct the pre-revolutionary attitudes of the population and reorient them towards the Soviet collective. Nadezhda Krupskaia suggested that a true 'collectivist' could only be mobilized through the 'education of a multi-faceted, internally disciplined person, capable of deep feeling, clear thought and organised action'.[15] Considered both facilitators and guardians of the October Revolution, librarians were crucial to this emotional process of mobilization.[16] Elizaveta's letter clearly manifests the complexities of the relationship between education, self-worth and productive labour as the latter solidified the boundaries of belonging in the decade following the Civil War, which culminated with the First Five Year Plan. Accordingly, perhaps most evident in Elizaveta's text is the tension between emotional engagement and the demands of Soviet productivism.[17]

Literacy also enabled the population of the Soviet Union to engage with political leaders as patrons, or what Alexey Tikhomirov has termed 'personified trust', which offered feelings of protection or security, softening the material and political insecurity amidst which they lived.[18] Letters were sent in the thousands, solicited from citizens as correspondents to the press and in consultations on policy, and volunteered for a variety of functions.[19] Often adopting and reproducing the ideological vernacular of the state, a process described by Stephen Kotkin as 'Speaking Bolshevik', letters have provided a rich, if controversial, source for the study of Soviet history.[20] Building upon a rich scholarship, I argue that through their errors, idiosyncrasies and priorities, letters indicate the author's sense of their own social identity, the boundaries of ideological acceptability and the emotional conventions of Soviet society.[21] Moreover, as objects, letters establish a tangible emotional connection between the citizen and state across the vast distances of the Soviet Union.[22] The process of writing invested letters both with social and emotional agency, manifesting one's membership of the Soviet emotional community.[23] Elizaveta's correspondence demonstrates the expectations that the state's liberation of women placed upon them and the emotional burden this could generate. While the biography she outlined followed the conventional trajectory of revolutionary emancipation, the emotional states Elizaveta described indicate the tension between the emancipation of Soviet women, their obligations to socialist construction through participation in the workforce and the struggle for belonging this tension generated, worked out on the page.

The New Soviet Woman: Emancipated and educated

Following the revolutions of 1917 and the years of Civil War that followed, women in the new Soviet state were 'emancipated' from the drudgery of domestic labour that had characterised their daily lives under tsarism and were drawn into the workplace, education and public life in unprecedented numbers. Though these measures were racked with assumptions about women's physiologies and capabilities, and underpinned by the demand for an expanded labour force, policymakers sought both to dismantle the obstacles to women's participation in the public workforce, legalizing divorce, and at least attempting to provide creches and cafeterias, and to protect this participation, legislating against pay inequality and against dismissal on the grounds of pregnancy or dependent children, and discussing menstrual leave throughout the 1920s and 1930s.[24] The Zhenotdel, or 'women's department', was established in 1919, focused on improving the lives of women through literacy and education, spreading awareness of the new emancipatory laws in place, activities described as 'work amongst women'.[25]

To facilitate the population's enthusiastic participation in the construction of socialism, literacy drives were undertaken on a remarkable scale across the Union, which sought to mobilize the population behind the Soviet state and reconstruct pre-Revolutionary attitudes. The *likbez* campaigns (an amalgam of *likvidatsiia bezgramotnosti*, or 'liquidation of illiteracy') formally commenced on 26 December 1919 with the Decree 'On the liquidation of illiteracy among the population of the RSFSR', which required all people between the ages of eight and fifty-nine to become literate in their native language.[26] Literacy drives prioritized the mobilization of allegedly 'backwards' elements of society such as women, of whom only 12.5 per cent were able to read in 1917.[27] Public education and literacy campaigns also instructed citizens' acquisition of 'political literacy', necessary to properly fulfil the obligations associated with full citizenship and inclusion in Soviet society.

Women's low educational status was frequently associated with anti-revolutionary potential, particularly in the form of religious belief, which was positioned as the antithesis of political literacy and scientific knowledge, and a scourge to which women were especially susceptible.[28] The 'task [of replacing] a religious explanation of the world with a scientific one' was a common theme in letters to *Krest'ianka* and to Nadezhda Krupskaia; one account titled 'Belief in religion and the break with it', sent to *Krest'ianka* in 1925 by '*krest'ianka* Panina' from Kanishevo, Ryazan, opened with an anecdote from childhood, whereby 'the priest said: thunder and lightning are from god, but the teacher said: it is an accumulation of gases'.[29] Education through the Zhenotdel and the expansion of the Soviet education system offered the solution to these opposing forces, framed in the language of nurture and development. The 'instructor of the Belgorod district Zhenotdel', one L. Chubareva, explained that when her village's 'backwater non-party peasant women begin to outgrow the intoxication of religious prejudices' they no longer 'envelop the new generation in papal magic'.[30] Once in possession of literacy, women acquired the responsibility to organize and advise those women in their villages and towns who were still learning or who remained 'illiterate'. A peasant delegate to the Zhenotdel in Maliushino, a village near Krasnopole in Belarus, Liza Trifanova, described the enthusiastic reception of the women's conferences (*babskie konferentsii*) that had recently been held in Krasnopole and requested support from the district Zhenotdel.[31] Recommending the expansion of work among women in the area throughout winter (when there was less agricultural work to be completed), Trifanova proposed the establishment of *babskie* committees composed of 'the more literate peasant women, who are able to give some kind of advice to the peasant women, and clarify the difficult questions, of which there are many'.[32] Present in these discussions of women's literacy and illiteracy are two implications: that, as Elizaveta's concerns about 'semi-literacy' convey, 'literacy' was measured by one's grasp of key political concepts and literature; and that education imbued women with the social role of educator.

With the structural causes of their oppression dismantled, the emotions associated with the rapid 'modernization' of women and their mobilization behind socialist construction were construed as pride, joy and, crucially, gratitude to the Party as benefactor, in what Jeffrey Brooks has termed a 'moral economy of the gift'.[33] Enthusiastic participation in socialist construction – through public labour and formal political participation – was critical to the enjoyment of full Soviet citizenship and the rights it entailed. The Soviet conception of rights was not static – especially during the years following the Revolution. In essence, although the potential for 'fundamental human uniformity' underpinned the Russian socialists' understanding of equality, citizenship operated within set boundaries and functioned on the principle of exclusion.[34] The substance of the Soviet constitutions in 1918 and 1936 applied a gradated exclusionary system of citizens' rights, according to which those deemed 'representatives of the exploiting classes' were subject to a reduction in economic, social and legal status and protection. In theory, this model of Soviet rights would by 1936 ensure that full citizens had the right to a job and quality-dependent pay – which, in practice, was a duty as well as a right. The fulfilment of this right established access to workers' clubs, sanatoriums, annual leave, medical care, limited social pensions and the rights to education in preparation for work, and to the vote; the humanity of the social 'alien' who failed or refused to fulfil these duties, however, was questionable. The rights won by Soviet liberation were construed both as an inalienable right and a generous gift bestowed by the party. As a result, Golfo Alexopoulos has argued that 'Soviet society consisted of citizens who experienced various and often paradoxical states of civic belonging'.[35] These rights were dependent upon the fulfilment of duty to actively participate in the construction of socialism through labour and political activism, a concept which (along with membership of the 'exploiting classes') was subject to political manipulation.[36]

A matter of life or death: Political consciousness, power and the negotiation of belonging

Having been 'liberated' from the domestic sphere and the obligation to motherhood by the October Revolution, the doors to the professions had been flung wide open. Although motherhood was not women's only role, mothering remained important, and women working as educators and librarians often stressed the skills and achievements associated with the 'social mothering' enacted in their professional lives, its contribution to the socialist development of children and citizens.[37] Education constituted a constant theme in women's letters: women wrote to request assistance in acquiring education, to plead for the reinstatement of their education following a reduction in civic status or to report on their progress; otherwise, they used their educational status as ideological leverage for material or legal interventions.

Letters from women in educational roles frequently also conveyed a thorough knowledge of their rights and self-worth – and a sense of their own importance as educators, responsible for the moral and political development of the population.[38] Both facets often manifested in their writing as righteous anger over working conditions, pay and the prioritization of children. A series of requests for advocacy sent to the trade journal *Red Librarian* (*Krasniy bibliotekar'*) in the wake of a series of decrees from the Commissariat for Education and Central Committee seeking to expand the library network and promote the importance of library work perhaps mostly clearly encapsulates the ways in which women working in public education could employ their social status to assert certain material rights to which they felt entitled, both on the basis of law and the political value of their profession.[39] Responding to a provocation from the journal for reports of all local violations of the government directive raising the status and rate of pay for librarians to that of teachers, P. Maksimtseva asked directly for help from the journal in chasing an overdue wage increase for her staff in 1930: 'I hereby request the editor of *Red Librarian* to assist me in obtaining a salary from the village Council at the rates established and published in the resolution of the Central Committee and Sovnarkom of the RSFSR [. . .] Ask the editors not to refuse my request.'[40] Another letter from the same collection, signed by the Head of the District Library and three other women, on the same matter reads:

> We ask that you immediately inform us whether this situation is a violation of TsIK and Sovnarkom [decree] from 10/08/1930, and if so, to take action to correct this violation, since here in Aleksin [a town in Tula, Russia], we were unable to do anything, despite the fact that we ourselves and our Groups sent information of a corresponding character to the City Soviet.[41]

The Head of the Inter-Library Union, Timofeeva, called for 'assistance in creating favourable conditions for political education workers' stating that without these conditions, few if any workers would be willing to do this work.[42] For librarians, the publication was evidently seen as able to advocate effectively for the members of its profession where their union – among which women were well represented and organized – could not.[43]

According to Natalie Delougaz's 1945 review of *Red Librarian*, its list of contributors included a considerable proportion of 'non-librarians', indicating a relatively broad readership to whom issues relating to libraries were pertinent and a broad perception that, though not factory or agricultural labour, education work was a field vital to the socialist future.[44] It was not insignificant that education librarianship was a profession in which women were well represented and able to reach positions of status. Accordingly, traces of scorn and indignation can be detected in the workers' commentaries on their employment. The regional librarian V. Feskova closed her letter with remarks about her current and prospective rates of pay: 'I am a regional librarian, I receive a salary of 43 rubles, with 66 rubles planned from January 1. Now tell me, does a regional librarian get to use an apartment? What kind of holiday do I get?'[45] Another letter from L. F. Trefilova, Head of the Nizhkraia Factory Library, reported that her library's factory committee refused to pay her and her assistants according to the new decree because 'they allegedly didn't have enough money to pay for our labour (*truda*) according to the estimate. Strange!' Trefilova requested that any reply be sent both to her and the factory itself.[46] By contrast, letters to industrial trade journals did not reflect the same sense of status and expertise, evoking instead a sense of revolutionary rhetoric. In a file of letters to the editor from the same year to a trade journal for sugar factory workers, 'Voice of the Sugar Worker' (*Golos sakharnika*), only one female-authored letter is held, and signed only anonymously by a 'girl from the factory', calling attention to her factory's abuse of the working conditions of a blind, elderly, male colleague. Rather than basing her allegations on the grounds of legal rights, the girl rooted her complaint in the revolutionary credentials of the man's background: a Civil War veteran, whose defence of the sugar factory from the Whites meant that he deserved comfort, rather than 'unnecessary suffering and torment' – negotiating his place in Soviet society based on his biographical credentials, not unlike Elizaveta's evocation of her family's hardship during the Revolution.[47]

Evidently, many women in educational professions appeared to find pride, purpose and entitlement in their roles, constructing a strong sense of self- and social worth in their letters. However, the emotional picture was rather more multifaceted. Though the reception of public education by women across the Soviet Union was by no means uniform, its value and uses among women who acquired it reflected an awareness that, as Sheila Fitzpatrick has demonstrated, in the new Soviet state, education – and the political criterion of 'consciousness' that it implied – was, along with one's basic occupation, key to social (and political) belonging.[48] Writing to *Krest'ianka* in 1924, Anastasia L. related this social mobility with eschatological tropes of darkness and light, remarking, 'you know, that literacy (*gramota*) is a ray, which illuminates the path of your life!'[49] Correspondingly, *downwards* social mobility, or one's exclusion from certain rights, could cause extreme emotional distress. Her education having been terminated due to her father's previous occupation as a priest, in 1934, Maria Gokhorova petitioned Krupskaia for the continuation of her studies, in the language of its emotional toll upon her: 'I don't work anywhere, I am burning with shame in front of my girlfriends, because they are continuing their education, while I am deprived of this.'[50] Maria's letter suggested the emotional internalization of her exclusion from Soviet society's primary means of accessing the full rights of a citizen and, accordingly, social belonging – productive work and socialist education.

As a consequence of the hierarchies of value and belonging institutionalized by the obligation to productive labour, and the state's arbitrary identification of enemies, symptoms of what China Mills has called elsewhere an 'affective economy of anxiety' are visible in the relationship between structural conditions and psychic well-being, fundamental to Marxism and Marxism Leninism, and their manifestation in Bolshevik ideology after 1917.[51] In this formulation, the relationship manifested in anxieties over the 'public mood': with capitalism, and therefore the structural causes of alienation and suffering, dismantled, unhappy feelings should have become obsolete, and so unhappiness under or with Soviet power could be perceived as dissent, or 'distrust', in turn generating by the constant proximity of many to what Tikhomirov has termed the 'boundaries of distrust'.[52] This phenomenon was related to the pathologization of symptoms of psychic distress, as attributable to the 'pathogen' of anti-Soviet sentiment. This was embodied most clearly by the taboo of suicide, which as Kenneth Pinnow has shown was considered to represent the individual 'opting out' of Soviet society.[53] The mental and physical exhaustion caused by the fear of being caught in the escalating search for internal enemies among 'those who belonged' is known to have caused the suicide deaths of waves of those disenfranchised, and their children.[54]

Though the act of suicide itself was considered 'evidence' of an individual's rejection of the collective, for which responsibility lay with the kin of the deceased, representatives of the state are known to have responded with sympathy to threats of suicide as negotiations for personal salvation.[55] Two-thirds of the way through her letter, Elizaveta recounted an incident in the workplace, whereby an auditing error had led to allegations of theft: 180 books worth 130 roubles had gone missing, for which the library board had suspended and threatened to sue her. The books had eventually been located at the library at the time of writing, and Elizaveta had been rehired (albeit at a lower salary), but the psychic effect of the case on Elizaveta was made clear, as she described in her own words:

> I was close to suicide [. . .] for me, to leave the organization was equal to death, I became nervous, and I was only 21 years old, and I used to be an utterly calm person.

Though not a 'threat' of suicide in the sense discussed earlier, Elizaveta's admission was a striking reflection of the importance of mobilization and productivity within the workforce to one's sense of civic belonging and social identity, and of Elizaveta's fear of the consequences of social and ideological ostracization, upon the boundary of which she saw herself as existing – equated in her letter with death. Elizaveta's letter was not intended for publication, which arguably explains the more emotional character of her missive: unlike those writing to *Red Librarian*'s editorial board, Elizaveta wrote directly to Krupskaia, prompted by the latter's article for *Pravda*. By the same token, unlike the other librarians, her letter doesn't contain a direct request, beyond an agreement or suggestion that training provisions for library workers be increased. Rather, it is otherwise an attempt to negotiate belonging, through a request for advice or reassurance from a head of state with direct ties to Lenin, the 'grandfather' of the Revolution. In comparison to the letters written to *Red Librarian*, the significance of the intended audience of the letters should not be underestimated. Indeed, Delougaz notes that the most frequently covered topic in *Red Librarian* was the general 'role' of the library in public life, with the majority of these articles – both by the publication's editorial team and its contributors – dealing with the importance of libraries in political education.[56] We might also submit, then, that the high worth afforded to political education led (at least among the readership of *Red Librarian*) to a sense of confidence in the claims made by library workers to certain rights. Yet, with reference to Elizaveta's 'semi-literacy', these claims were contingent upon a particular standard of professional competence dependent upon political knowledge, as evidenced by her pleas for assistance in raising herself to the standard of literacy and professional ability that she saw to be appropriate.[57]

* * *

Towards the end of her letter, Elizaveta asked if she could send Krupskaia 'as a tribute' some poems she had written about Lenin, with whom she shared a birthplace – the oblast' was named after him. She also explained the enjoyment she found in the activities associated with her work, in particular in anti-religious work and its literature, which she loved and undertook almost every day. Reading, writing and working at such a standard, Elizaveta obviously *wasn't* semi-literate. Although the emotional states described by letter writers such as Elizaveta, while vivid, are ambiguous, the emotional 'frames of reference' employed by the letter writers in this chapter indicate their collective knowledge of the contours of the Soviet emotional landscape, while also expressing a sense of place upon it. Based on her literary interests and abilities, it would not be unreasonable to entertain the thought that the self-deprecation expressed in Elizaveta's letter was instrumental and aimed at the restoration of her reputation following a scandal in the workplace. Yet, at the core of the anxieties articulated by Elizaveta is an awareness both of the importance of *political* literacy to the definition of one's education and to the 'cultured-ness' of Soviet citizens – as well as the necessity of education and 'cultured-ness' to one's social worth and belonging, a notion complicated by the gendered field of librarianship.

Krupskaia did respond to Elizaveta, imploring her to remain in her post, restating the productiveness of an emotional commitment to self-improvement and socialist construction.

> Dear comrade, I read your letter. In my opinion, you should not leave library work in any way. It is necessary now, that we deploy [library work] as widely as possible. It doesn't matter that you do not have enough knowledge, if you'd be

willing to learn – to learn from books and even more from life. The setting you have, [there and] with the party seems to be correct, you only need the skill, and the ability to listen to the feedback of the workers.[58]

Perhaps reflecting her own beliefs in the importance of the individual to the collective, Krupskaia acknowledged the biographical information Elizaveta provided, underlining the educational potential of a proletarian background. She did not respond to Elizaveta's disclosure of suicidal ideation, nor did she address the scandal which caused Elizaveta so much distress, omissions which might be read as a tacit absolution of the incident, or, as an effort to re-incorporate Elizaveta in the Soviet order, by extending the state's cultural monopoly over Elizaveta's skills and life experience.[59] Notwithstanding the ambiguity of Elizaveta's intention in extending her plea for Krupskaia's reassurance, the 'imposter syndrome' displayed in Elizaveta's writing sheds light upon the conflicting emotional implications of emancipatory rhetorics of productive participation in socialist construction, and work more broadly, bringing emotional histories of capitalist work and social class into fruitful conversation with non-capitalist contexts, by considering the boundaries of socialist belonging and the 'work' done by and for different feelings.[60] While many women found a sense of pride in their educational feats and new social identities as Soviet workers, for others the gendered contingency of their social and political belonging upon their abilities to nurture the political consciousness of their communities constituted a heavy psychological burden.

Notes

1 'Kul'turnaia nishcheta', *Pravda*, 10 April 1924, 6.
2 Soviet citizens were expected to provide autobiographies and autobiographical statements in relation to most institutional and organizational practices. For more on citizen autobiographies, see Fitzpatrick, *Tear off the Masks!*; Halfin, *Terror in My Soul*.
3 Gosudarstvenniy Arkhiv Rossiskoi Federatsii (GARF), fond. 7279, opis. 7, delo. 18, list. 56.
4 The relationship between 'productionism' and cultural revolution after the Bolshevik Revolution is covered in more detail in Read, 'Krupskaya, Protekul't, and the Origins of Soviet Cultural Policy', esp. 254.
5 Read, 'Krupskaya, Protekul't, and the Origins of Soviet Cultural Policy', 254.
6 Nadezhda Krupskaia, 'Kul'turnaia nishcheta', *Pravda*, 10 April 1924, 6.
7 GARF, f. 7279, op. 7, d. 18, l. 56.

8 GARF, f. 7279, op. 7, d. 18, l. 56.
9 The significance of 'desire' to the consolidation of one's proletarian background echoes findings elsewhere in this volume about the gendered experiences of performance anxiety and imposter syndrome to the social construction of scientific knowledge in post-war Britain. Merchant and Horrocks, 133–150.
10 For more on early Soviet gender ideology and the New Soviet Woman, see Goldman, *Women, the State and Revolution*; Parker, 'Voices of the New Soviet Woman'.
11 Balina and Dobrenko, 'Introduction'. The New Soviet Person was the embodiment of the proletariat after the October Revolution: A renewal of the social body according to progressive and collectivist ideals, and which practised an ideal proletarian culture, and new moral and emotional standards. For more on the evolution of the concept, see Soboleva, 'The Concept of the "New Soviet Man"'. On the emotional intensity of political mobilization in social movements and the context of the Revolutionary period, see: Balina and Dobrenko (eds), *Petrified Utopia*; Fitzpatrick, 'Happiness and Toska'; Jasper, 'The Emotions of Protest'; Stockdale, 'My Death for the Motherland is Happiness'; Vasilyev, 'Revolutionary Conscience, Remorse and Resentment'. On emotion, obligation and duty and the social cohesion of early Soviet society, see Tikhomirov, 'The Regime of Forced Trust'.
12 Brooks, *Thank You Comrade Stalin!*.
13 Rosenwein, 'Worrying About Emotions', 85.
14 Tikhomirov, 'The Regime of Forced Trust', 87; Balina and Dobrenko, 'Introduction', xviii.
15 Nadezhda Krupskaia, (1988), 180, cited in Read, 'Krupskaya, Protekul't, and the Origins of Soviet Cultural Policy', 253.
16 Richardson Jr., 'The Origin of Soviet Education for Librarianship'.
17 The First Five Year Plan was a state-centralized economic plan for the modernization of the Soviet economy through rapid industrialization and collectivization of agriculture, implemented from 1928 to 1932. For more on this, see chapter 1 of Kotkin, *Magnetic Mountain*.
18 Tikhomirov, 'The Regime of Forced Trust', 85.
19 Soviet publications were frequently overwhelmed by citizen requests to become correspondents. Dobrenko (trans. Savage) in *The Making of the State Writer*, 91.
20 For 'Speaking Bolshevik' as a means of appropriating the bases of social solidarity, see Kotkin, *Magnetic Mountain*; for discussion of letters to the press as an 'instrument of power', and their effect on propaganda production, see Lenoe, 'Letter-Writing and the State'.
21 Dobson, 'Letters'; Krylova, 'Identity, Agency, and the First Soviet Generation'; Fitzpatrick, 'Supplicants and Citizens', 78–105.
22 Tikhomirov, 'The Regime of Forced Trust', 83.

23 Rosenwein, 'Worrying About Emotions'. My treatment of letters as textual and material sources has been influenced by Wassell Smith, 'The fancy work what sailors make'. The letters informing this chapter were written to Nadezhda Krupskaia, and to the editorial boards of *Red Librarian* trade journal and *Krest'ianka*, the women's supplement of the peasant newspaper *Krest'ianksaia gazeta*, which are held in the State Archive of the Russian Federation, and the Russian State Archive of the Economy, respectively. The letters consulted for this article were written in Russian and were sent primarily from women based in Russia, Ukraine and Belarus. While nationality and language policies in the Soviet Union did protect national rights, across the Union Russian remained the dominant nationality and language, and the officials and organs of the central state possessed relatively little knowledge of eastern languages. For more on this see Brandist, *The Dimensions of Hegemony*, esp. chapter 6. The picture for non-Russian women was complicated by nominally anti-imperial, if still colonial or postcolonial, assumptions about oppression, backwardness and Otherness. For more on the Bolshevik emancipation of Muslim women in Central Asia and the Caucasus, see Gradskova, 'Opening the (Muslim) Women's Space'; Kamp, *The New Woman in Uzbekistan*.

24 Ilič, 'Equal Pay for Equal Work', 104, and 'Soviet Women Workers and Menstruation', 1409-15.

25 For more on the Zhenotdel and its activities, see Stites, 'Zhenotdel'.

26 'On the liquidation of illiteracy' (29 January 1919); for more on literacy, education, and 'the national question', see Brandist, *The Dimensions of Hegemony*, chapter 6.

27 Literacy among men is accepted to have been three times higher at 37.5 per cent, though this was unevenly distributed across social groups. Vincent, *The Rise of Mass Literacy*, 9–13.

28 See, for example, Central Committee RKP 'On Anti-religious propaganda among Women Workers and Peasants' (15 September 1921).

29 Rossiskiy Gosudarstvenniy Arkhov Ekonomiki (RGAE), fond. 392, opis. 2, delo. 31, list. 155.

30 RGAE, f. 396, op. 2, d. 31, l. 140.

31 Liza described the initiatives in her village with the adjective *babskie*. A generally derogatory expression in Russian, in which her letter was written, the use of this term is understood to reflect the common usage of Polish and Belarusian in the region. According to Dobrenko in *The Making of the State Writer*, 195, Maliushino was 40 miles from a city and 26 miles from the railroad.

32 RGAE, f. 396, op. 2, d. 21, l. 164.

33 Brooks, *Thank You Comrade Stalin!*, 83.

34 Alexopoulos, 'Soviet Citizenship, More or Less', 212; Zaharejivić, 'How to know a citizen when you see one?', 72.

35 Alexopoulos, 'Soviet Citizenship, More or Less'.

36 Smith, 'Social Rights in the Soviet Dictatorship', 387.

37 Rebecca Balmas Neary has developed the idea of 'social mothering' compellingly in relation to the wife-activists movement of the 1930s. In relation to the persistence of essentialist notions of gender and care, I argue that this concept can be traced back to the early years of Soviet power. Balmas Neary, 'Mothering Socialist Society'. For further discussion of the similarities drawn between mothering and educating, see Parker, 'My old eyes weep but I am proud of my children'.
38 Richardson Jr., 'The Origin of Soviet Education for Librarianship', 114.
39 In addition to those discussed here, the majority of letters from the file demanded advocacy on the same issue GARF, f. 5462, op. 12, d. 226, ll. 2-4, 13, 15, 22, 30, 31, 33, 35, 40, 47, 51, 52, 59, 60, 61, 64, 72, 73, 76, 77, 78, 85, 89, 103, 104, 105, 113a.
40 GARF, f. 5462, op. 12, d. 226, l. 35.
41 GARF, f. 5462, op. 12, d. 226, ll. 6-8.
42 GARF, f. 5462, op. 12, d. 226, l. 50.
43 A letter from one L. Lavrentieva proposed the need for a trade union encompassing all library workers, in order to be able to effectively protect the rights and material interests of library workers over the interests of the All-Union Central Council of Trade Unions, GARF, f. 5462, op. 12, d. 226, l. 29; another letter, from three female library workers in Nizhnii Novgorod, included several quotations from their local committee's refusal to pay at the new rate for publication, also requesting clarity over whether technical workers in libraries were also entitled to the same rate of pay, GARF, f. 5462, op. 12, d. 226, l. 45.
44 Delougaz, 'Some Problems of Soviet Librarianship', 214.
45 GARF, f. 5462, op. 12, d. 226, l. 89.
46 GARF, f. 5462, op. 12, d. 226, l. 10.
47 GARF, f. 5463, op. 7, d. 261, l. 59.
48 Fitzpatrick, *Education and Social Mobility in the Soviet Union*, 4.
49 RGAE, f. 396, op. 2, d. 29, l. 394.
50 Letter from M.S. Gorokhova petitioning Krupskaia to continue her studies, 13 November 1934, RGASPI, f. 78, op. 1, d. 524, ll. 99-99ob., in *Stalinism as a Way of Life*, 408.
51 Mills, 'Dead People Don't Claim', 307.
52 Tikhomirov, 'The Regime of Forced Trust', 112.
53 Pinnow, *Lost to the Collective*.
54 Tikhomirov, 'The Regime of Forced Trust', 113-14.
55 Pinnow, *Lost to the Collective*; Tikhomirov, 'The Regime of Forced Trust', 113-14.
56 Delougaz, 'Some Problems of Soviet Librarianship', 214.
57 GARF, f. 7279, op. 7, d. 18, l. 56.
58 GARF, f. 7279, op. 7, d. 18, l. 55.
59 Tikhomirov, 'The Regime of Forced Trust', 114.
60 See, for example, Langhamer and Barron, 'Children, Class, and the Search for Security', or Matt, *Keeping Up with the Joneses*.

Bibliography

Alexopoulos, Golfo. 'Soviet Citizenship, More or Less – Rights, Emotions, and States of Civic Belonging'. *Kritika* 7, no. 3 (2006): 487–528.

Balina, M. and E. Dobrenko. 'Introduction'. In *Petrified Utopia: Happiness, Soviet Style*, edited by M. Balina and E. Dobrenko, xv–xxvi. Ontario: Anthem Press, 2009.

Balmas Neary, Rebecca. 'Mothering Socialist Society: The Wife-Activists' Movement and the Soviet Culture of Daily Life, 1934–1941'. *The Russian Review* 58, no. 3 (1999): 396–412.

Brandist, Craig. *The Dimensions of Hegemony: Language, Culture and Policy in Revolutionary Russia*. Leiden: Brill, 2015.

Brooks, Jeffrey. 'Public and Private Values in the Soviet Press, 1921–1928'. *Slavic Review* 48, no. 1 (1989): 16–35.

Brooks, Jeffrey. *Thank You Comrade Stalin! Soviet Public Culture from Revolution to Civil War*. Princeton: Princeton University Press, 2001.

Delougaz, Natalie. 'Some Problems of Soviet Librarianship as Reflected in Russian Library Periodicals'. *The Library Quarterly: Information, Community, Policy* 15, no. 3 (1945): 213–23.

Dobson, Miriam. 'Letters'. In *Reading Primary Sources: The Interpretation of Texts from Nineteenth and Twentieth Century History*, edited by M. Dobson and B. Ziemann, 57–73. London: Routledge, 1998.

Fitzpatrick, Sheila. *Education and Social Mobility in the Soviet Union, 1921–1934*. Cambridge: Cambridge University Press, 2009.

Fitzpatrick, Sheila. 'Happiness and Toska: An Essay in the History of Emotions in Pre-War Soviet Russia'. *Australian Journal of Politics and History* 50, no. 3 (2004): 357–71.

Fitzpatrick, Sheila. 'Supplicants and Citizens: Public Letter-Writing in Soviet Russia in the 1930s'. *Slavic Review* 55, no. 1 (1996): 78–105.

Fitzpatrick, Sheila. *Tear Off the Masks!: Identity and Imposture in Twentieth-Century Russia*. Princeton: Princeton University Press, 2005.

Goldman, Wendy Z. *Women, the State and Revolution, 1917-1936*. Cambridge: Cambridge University Press, 1993.

Halfin, Igal. *Terror in My Soul: Communist Autobiographies on Trial*. Cambridge, MA: Harvard University Press, 2003.

Ilič, Melanie. '"Equal Pay for Equal Work": Women's Wages in Soviet Russia'. In *The Palgrave Handbook of Women and Gender in Twentieth-Century Russia and the Soviet Union*, edited by Melanie Ilič, 101–15. Basingstoke: Palgrave Macmillan, 2017.

Ilič, Melanie. 'Soviet Women Workers and Menstruation: a Research Note on Labour Protection in the 1920s and 1930s'. *Europe-Asia Studies* 46, no. 8 (1994): 1409–15.

Ingold, Tim. *Making: Anthropology, Archaeology, Art and Architecture*. London: Routledge, 2013.

Jasper, James M. 'The Emotions of Protest: Affective and Reactive Emotions in and Around Social Movements'. *Sociological Forum* 13, no. 3 (1998): 397–434.

Kamp, Marianne. *The New Woman in Uzbekistan: Islam, Modernity and Unveiling under Communism.* Seattle: University of Washington Press, 2006.

Kotkin, Stephen. *Magnetic Mountain: Stalinism as a Civilisation.* Oakland: University of California Press, 1997.

Krylova, Anna. 'Identity, Agency, and the First Soviet Generation'. In *Generations in Twentieth Century Europe*, edited by Stephen Lovell, 101–21. Basingstoke: Palgrave Macmillan, 2007.

Langhamer, Claire and Hester Barron. 'Children, Class and the Search for Security: Writing the Future in 1930s Britain'. *Twentieth Century British History* 28, no. 3 (2017): 367–89.

Lenoe, Matthew. 'Letter-Writing and the State: Reader Correspondence with Newspapers as a Source for Early Soviet History'. *Cahiers Du Monde Russe* 40, no. 1 (1999): 139–69.

Matt, Susan. *Keeping Up With the Joneses: Envy in American Consumer Society, 1890–1930.* Philadelphia: University of Pennsylvania Press, 2003.

Mills, China. '"Dead People Don't Claim": A Psychopolitical Autopsy of UK Austerity Suicides'. *Critical Social Policy* 38, no. 2 (2017): 302–22.

Parker, Hannah. '"My old eyes weep but I am proud of my children": Grief and Revolutionary Motherhood in the Soviet 1920s'. In *Gender, Emotion and Power*, edited by Hannah Parker and Josh Doble (forthcoming).

Parker, Hannah. 'Voices of the New Soviet Woman: Gender, Emancipation and Agency in Letters to the Soviet State, 1924–1941', unpublished PhD thesis, University of Sheffield (2018).

Pinnow, Kenneth. *Lost to the Collective: Suicide and the Promise of Soviet Socialism.* Ithaca: Cornell University Press, 2010.

Read, Christopher. 'Krupskaya, Protekul't, and the Origins of Soviet Cultural Policy'. *International Journal of Cultural Policy* 12, no. 3 (2006): 245–55.

Richardson Jr., John V. 'The Origin of Soviet Education for Librarianship: The Role of Nadezhda Konstantinovna Krupskaya, Lyuobov' Borisovna Khavkina-Hamburger, and Genrietta K. Abele-Derman'. *Journal of Education for Library and Information Science* 41, no. 2 (2000): 106–28.

Rosenwein, Barbara H. 'Worrying About Emotions in History'. *The American Historical Review* 107, no. 3 (2002): 821–45.

Rowley, Alison. 'Spreading the Bolshevik Message? Soviet Regional Periodicals for Women, 1917–1941'. *Canadian Slavonic Papers* 47, no. 1/2 (2005): 111–26.

Smith, Mark. 'Social Rights in the Soviet Dictatorship: the Constitutional Right to Welfare from Stalin to Brezhnev'. *Humanity: An International Journal of Human Rights, Humanitarianism and Development* 3, no. 3 (2012): 385–406.

Soboleva, Maja. 'The Concept of the "New Soviet Man" and Its Short History'. *Canadian-American Slavic Studies* 51 (2017): 64–85.

Stites, Richard. 'Zhenotdel: Bolshevism and Russian Women'. *Russian History* 3, no. 2 (1976): 174–93.
Vincent, David. *The Rise of Mass Literacy: Reading and Writing in Modern Europe.* Cambridge: Cambridge University Press, 2000.
Wassell Smith, Maya. '"The Fancy Work what Sailors Make": Material and Emotional Creative Practice in Masculine Seafaring Communities'. *Nineteenth-Century Gender Studies Special Issue: Making Masculinity: Craft, Gender and Material Production in the Long Nineteenth Century* 14, no. 2 (2018), http://ncgsjournal.com/issue142/PDF/smith.pdf (accessed 6 October 2020).

7

Money, emotions and domestic service in Buenos Aires, 1950–70

Inés Pérez[1]

Francisca was born in 1939 on the outskirts of Castelli, a small town 170 kilometres south of the City of Buenos Aires. When her parents separated, her mother sent her to live with María and Antonio Fernández, a couple from Dolores, the largest town in the area. Francisca was somewhere between the ages of six and nine, according to the different versions of her story.[2] At the Fernández house, Francisca had no specific tasks assigned to her but instead helped with whatever was needed, especially housework. From that point on, according to everyone who was asked, she became part of the Fernández family. As one of María's granddaughters recalls, 'Francisca arrived and [. . .] quickly earned herself a place in all of our hearts.'[3] Francisca spent her entire life with María and Antonio's family: she lived with the couple until their deaths; then with Chela, one of their daughters; and then with Chela's daughter María Isabel, whom she also took care of until she died. Francisca, who never married or had children of her own, died in 2015.

In Argentina, domestic service underwent a process of commercialization in the early decades of the twentieth century, which some historians have described as the modernization of domestic service.[4] Some 400,000 people were estimated to have been employed in domestic service in 1947, 91 per cent of whom were women. By 1970, there were 610,000 employees in the sector, 93.7 per cent of whom were women. Between these two dates, live-in employment went from representing 62 per cent of all jobs to 29.3 per cent. Towards the end of the 1930s, employment by the hour began to become more commonplace, and this trend increased over the following decades.[5] The passing of Decree-Law 326 in 1956 was a major milestone in this process because although it only acknowledged limited rights for household workers, it enabled them to defend these rights before the Domestic Labor Tribunal (DLT), which was also created that year.[6] However, domestic work was performed within a variety of relationships that were hard to define using the terms set out in the law, as was the case with Francisca and the Fernández family. What role did money and emotions occupy in these relationships, and how did it affect the ways the different parties conceptualized them and what they could expect from them?

When I conducted the interviews, which were used in an earlier research project, one of the questions that interested me was whether or not Francisca received a salary, given that she did not work outside the Fernández house until the 1970s. Francisca completed her high school diploma as an adult, and then trained as a teacher, although she never worked as one. She was employed at various municipal offices, at a children's home and ran two libraries after training as a librarian. But all of this happened after she turned thirty, and it was not clear how she had supported herself up to this point. According to Sergio, María Isabel's son and María and Antonio's great-grandson, 'she never lacked for anything' and she likely received money of some sort to cover her personal expenses, but as a kind of allowance rather than as a salary. Francisca may have received money from the Fernándezes, but to maintain her role as 'part of the family' it was essential that this not be viewed as a salary:

> she was never thought of as an employee. She was always my aunt, my mother's sister. In fact, you often had to explain to people outside the family that she was my aunt but an aunt of the heart. She wasn't actually a blood relation, because her last name was Bravo, her father was of Portuguese descent, and my mother's surname was Aguilar. I mean, they weren't actually related.... My grandmother was a Fernández and she came from the Franco family, so there was no shared surname, but their relationship was a family one. She was always my great-grandmother's little girl, or my grandmother's daughter, and my mother's sister. [...] there was never any talk of it being a form of employment, it was always a question of family.[7]

Indeed, the economic exchanges between Francisca and the Fernández family did not stop at the money she received from them. When Chela's husband died, Francisca was given a car. This inheritance is described in interviews as proof of the family ties that connected them and how fond they were of her. However, although Sergio claims that Francisca was like a sister to his mother, the car was not comparable to the inheritance that María Isabel received (which included property and other assets). Nor were the conditions of the inheritance the same: regardless of the family's will, María Isabel would receive that which was her legal right; Francisca, on the other hand, would only receive anything if the deceased and the rest of the family so wished. Her status was inferior and conditional: her role as a daughter, sister or aunt included the clarification 'of the heart'.

The distinction between an employment relationship and family ties generally rests on the separation of love and money. However, as Viviana Zelizer has shown, not only are modern family relationships based on exchanges of money and goods, often the legitimacy of these exchanges derives from the people involved viewing themselves as part of the family, and the exchange of goods and money can even be used as a language of affection.[8] The car that Francisca received and the money that María and Antonio gave her to cover her needs when she was young are presented as signs of affection and proof of a family bond. All the same, this affection did not water down the asymmetries in the relationship nor did it simply serve to justify them. Instead, it was an intrinsic part of how the different parties constructed and negotiated the social distances that mediated between them.

Anthropological, sociological and historical studies have noted the significance of emotions in domestic service.[9] Relationships in which domestic work and care are exchanged tend to be characterized by marked physical and emotional proximity between the parties. In the case of domestic service, the intense asymmetries that define the positions of employers and workers imply a complex bond that is conceptualized as emotional 'ambiguity' or 'ambivalence'.[10] Within domestic service, money can have different meanings that transcend its exchange value and convey a variety of emotions, such as affection and gratitude, but also indignation and resentment. These meanings and the ways in which money circulates between employers and workers can define the types of relationship they have.

In this chapter, I will explore the emotions that both workers and employers assigned to money within domestic service relationships in order to reflect on the place that emotions and money occupied in the construction of social hierarchies in the City of Buenos Aires between the mid-1950s and the 1970s, in other words, a time and place in which salaried employment was the norm in this sector. By analysing cases that were filed before the DLT, I will focus my analysis on the emotional meanings assigned to lack of payment and the expectations of remuneration for work that had been performed. I will begin by addressing the voices of the workers, before moving on to those of the employers.

Indignation

In 1966, Amalia Tiscornia filed a lawsuit against her former employers, claiming 200,000 pesos in wages for the time she had spent at Pablo and Esther Varela's home, where her father had left her 'to perform all manner of work' before returning to Paraguay for good in 1955, when Amalia was ten years old.[11] Between then and September 1965, she had cleaned a seven-storey building that belonged to the Varelas while also working as a domestic worker at the apartment where the family lived. In the suit, she stated that they had 'never paid her a penny for the work she had done' and that, instead, knowing that she was about to get married, they 'had promised her an apartment on the eighth floor in return for services rendered' but then failed to keep this promise.

Amalia was going to get married but was unable to because she did not have her paperwork in order and was struggling to obtain this from Formosa, the province she was from, and it is not clear whether she ultimately managed to get married or not. When she filed the suit, on 16 September 1966, her son was just seventeen days old. She justified her actions before the DLT by saying that she was 'forced by the circumstances of having to support her child'.[12] Although the suit was based on the lack of payment for legally established items pertaining to an employment relationship (wages, bonuses, vacation pay) and the conflict ultimately revolved around a specific sum of money, the promise of an apartment suggests a relationship that transcends a mere employment contract. Just as the car that Francisca received was presented as an 'inheritance', the promise of the apartment conjures up the idea of a dowry or asset through which the family supports the creation of a new home, both in terms of the timing (around Amalia's marriage) and its significance in material and symbolic terms. Even though the money for unpaid wages that she was claiming through the lawsuit could be thought of as equivalent to the value of the apartment in question, the promise that Amalia invoked transformed this asset into a home such that attaining it would make her not just an owner but also a housewife. In Amalia's terms, the money was not only a way of looking out for her son financially, it was also a ticket to respectability, which gender and class played a central role in defining.[13]

The prolonged lack of payment over the course of these years carries a distinct emotional burden. The legal case files are made up of polyphonic texts in which the voices of the different stakeholders can be traced. In the foreground are the robust, eloquent turns of phrase of lawyers and other professionals who were well versed in the law and legal language, but these are intertwined with more unusual expressions, detailed descriptions of specific situations and personal narratives that contain the voices of both plaintiffs and defendants that, while not using the legal register, are nonetheless framed by this. In Amalia's suit, she argues that she had not been 'paid a single penny' for all her years of work. The expression is a colloquial one. It is generally used to indicate the low value of something ('that's not worth a penny') or someone's greed ('he didn't give me a penny'). The emphasis expresses indignation: the lack of payment was a form of humiliation; the lawsuit a demand for compensation for that moral damage.

The relationship between Amalia and the Varelas had begun as one of guardianship: her father had left her with them in exchange for education, shelter and food, not a salary. Although arrangements of this sort had declined since the early decades of the twentieth century, they were still common in both the City of Buenos Aires and Buenos Aires Province.[14] The placement of minors in such positions continued to produce meaning around domestic service, although these were not always accepted by the workers in question.

In 1966, for instance, Miriam appeared before the DLT to claim wages for the three years and five months she had worked for Azucena Boca. According to the lawsuit, Azucena had not paid her wages but instead promised she would deposit them in a bank account to help Miriam save and to prevent 'some *chinito* [boy from the sticks] from getting her to fall in love with him and then taking her money'. She did not let Miriam out on her day off nor did she give her vacations to avoid her being taken for a ride, given that she was '*una provinciana de tierra adentro* [a country bumpkin]'. Although Miriam was between twenty-one and twenty-two when she started working for Azucena, according to her reports she was treated as though she was a minor, incapable of handling money, and whose sexual honour had to be protected via extreme measures such as not being allowed out.

Miriam was placed in an inferior position that brought together class, gender and migratory origin. As recent studies on the middle class have shown, the racialization of social distance was key to the configuration of class and political identities in contemporary Argentina. In contrast to the image of the melting pot and the notion of a 'white' Argentina built through the great waves of migration from Europe to the country between the final decades of the nineteenth century and the middle of the twentieth, these studies have highlighted how the racialized contrast between the areas around Buenos Aires and the centre-east of the country (ambitious, developed, democratic) and the rest of the country (poor, backward) took on a key role in how these identities were defined following the increase in internal migration to Buenos Aires that began in the 1930s. The middle class perceived itself as 'white' and of European descent, in contrast to the *'cabecitas negras* [little black heads, a pejorative expression in Spanish]' from the provinces.[15] The indignation that appears in some of Miriam's remarks is a response to treatment that racialized and infantilized her, the most extreme manifestations of which were the reluctance to pay her and let her out of the house, which was justified through judgements on her sexual honour.[16]

As in Amalia's case, the lawsuit can be interpreted as a quest for reparation for moral damages. Was it resentment that prompted Miriam's actions? This emotion is not referred to explicitly in her claim or in the position papers submitted by her lawyer, but as Elisa Deamineur has pointed out, 'resentment was almost always represented as an intimate sentiment or feeling, one that was only shared through actions, gestures, and expressions that could take different shapes and significations'.[17] It was reprehensible and thus hard to express in the context of the trial, when it was essential for plaintiffs to adapt to the emotional expectations of judges and other legal professionals. Resentment was only explicitly referred to by employers and was used to delegitimize workers' demands.

Resentment and compassion

In 1975, Augusto Saranda ascribed the lawsuit that Esther Colombo had brought against him at the DLT to the resentment that she harboured. According to Augusto, Esther had lived in his father's house until he died and had then moved to his, where he took her in 'out of a voluntary sense of humanity', given that Esther was a single mother. He had intended to hire her as a domestic worker but Esther, who had migrated from Paraguay, did not have her papers in order and so he did not do so, which 'angered the plaintiff and revealed how resentful she was'.[18] In his response, Augusto claimed:

> Merely coming to live in my home does not justify her believing herself to be my domestic servant. I let her live in my house out of a voluntary sense of humanity because she was a single mother, without a home or any way to support her child. I never used her domestic services. [. . .] This claim owes exclusively to a social grudge borne by a mind sullied by the life she has lived, which finds joy in biting the hand that feeds her because it could not or cannot bite the hand that caused the harm she has suffered or believes she has suffered.[19]

The idea of the 'social grudge' emerges here as an illegitimate reason for bringing a lawsuit against Augusto but not as an illegitimate feeling. What is at issue is the fact that the grudge is directed against the defendant rather than against 'the hand that caused the harm she has suffered or believes she has suffered'. Although it is not clear who this statement refers to, it may be the father of Esther's child, and the 'sullied life' he speaks of may refer to the fact that she was a single mother. Once again, the worker's sexual honour becomes significant in the negotiation of the asymmetries that lay between the workers and their (alleged) employers. Grudges and resentment are presented as misplaced emotions, as female feelings typical of women like Esther whose lives (and honour) had been sullied and whose experiences sparked compassion in those who were now forced to defend themselves against false accusations.

This reference to a social grudge was made at a time in which social hierarchies in Argentina were still undergoing enormous transformations as a result of the policies implemented during Juan Domingo Perón's first two administrations. Starting in the early 1940s, during his time as Labour Secretary and then Labour Minister, Perón promoted several bills that incorporated a variety of labour rights to the Argentinean legal system and built a social movement supported by workers' organizations and unions. Peronism generated a deep resistance in the middle class, which was focused on totalitarian features of his government but which also reflected the anxieties generated by the possibility of the eventual 'revenge of the proletariat'.[20] According to Omar Acha, class resentment was at the core of the configuration of relationships between employers and domestic workers during the Peronist administrations, examples of which can be found both in crimes carried out by workers (robberies and, in more serious cases, murders) and in discourses written by or for employers (literary or psychological texts, journalism, cartoons and comic strips, etc.). However, the word 'resentment' was rarely used by workers themselves; it was rather used by middle- or upper-class agents who talked about domestic workers, sometimes in sympathetic terms. In the cases presented before the DLT, resentment was only referred to by employers. Although in recent years numerous studies have pointed to the significance of emotions in legal proceedings and in the configuration of the law itself, and although, as in this case, the defendants themselves evoked emotions such as compassion in their defence, the mention of resentment sought to present the workers' claims as illegitimate, unfounded and false.[21]

What did employers mean when they spoke of resentment? As Javier Moscoso has pointed out, resentment is 'a highly intellectual passion linked to the denial of fortune as a form of retribution [and] to the promise of an egalitarian and meritocratic society' which 'called into question the merits of those who enjoyed a privileged position'.[22] In this sense, resentment, defined as a form of hatred mixed with fear and indignation directed at the oppressor, has been identified as a key emotion in various revolutionary processes and the formation of a range of social and political movements demanding more egalitarian societies.[23] In Friedrich Nietzsche's exploration of resentment, which was later taken up by Max Scheler, resentment (*ressentiment*) is defined with different overtones, as a 'very strong feeling of inferiority and source of mystification' and as a leaning towards frustration and bitterness.[24] It is the latter sense that emerges most clearly in these employers' discourses. In the workers' suits, in contrast, we can infer indignation and the quest for reparation as a way of calling inequality into question, starting from the moment when a public authority established that workers are deserving of respect (i.e. when the DLT was created).

Resentment is not the only emotion discussed by employers and associated with money – or more specifically, the non-payment of this. In the fragment cited above, Augusto is described as someone who helped Esther by letting her live in his home 'out of a voluntary sense of humanity' even though she did not work for him. The expression itself is suggestive. The voluntary aspect seems to refer to the decision to let Esther live in his house and thus to the lack of a subsequent sense of obligation to deliver what she claimed he owed her. The 'humanity', in contrast, conjures up a sense of compassion that also emerges in other employers' discourses. This combination, however, seems to suggest that the gesture he made and the emotions that prompted it were at the same time voluntary and an inevitable part of the human condition.

Based on an analysis of lawsuits filed before the DLT in the first decade of the twenty-first century, Santiago Canevaro has shown that employers continue to build a position of moral superiority in their responses to employee demands, invoking feelings such as indignation and presenting themselves as being the 'saviours' of their workers and as helping them out of compassion.[25] Augusto's 'voluntary sense of humanity' can be read in this key, in which the emotions that are attributed to the defendants place them in different, distant social positions using terms that articulate class, gender and migratory origin. The fact that the plaintiff was a foreigner, a single mother and poor made her someone worthy of compassion, but a 'mind sullied by the life she had lived' transformed her into a 'poisonous snake' who 'deserved her suffering'.[26]

What is interesting is that the compassion evoked by the employers in their statements is what justifies the absence of payment, because it allows them to frame the relationship between them and their employees as not being a working one. Augusto explained that Ramona lived in his home because of his 'humanity', not because there was an employment contract between them. The same argument emerges in other cases, such as the one cited below, in which María Vintana explains that Elena Navarra lived in her house because she had decided to let her stay in one of her bedrooms out of the compassion she felt for Elena's financial circumstances, without expecting anything from her in return, and not because there was a domestic work arrangement between them, as Elena herself argued:

> The truth of the matter is that the plaintiff and her family lived in the defendant's house for a few months in 1971 [. . .]. This room was provided to her free of charge by the undersigned, who was sympathetic ('compadecida') to the economic hardship the plaintiff's family was experiencing, without anything being provided in exchange for this. She particularly emphasizes that neither the plaintiff nor any of her family members ever performed any work for either the undersigned or her family.[27]

Money borrowed, money advanced, money paid to support workers' children and money not paid are all cited in the proceedings not only as signs of trust and affection but also as part of narratives that place employers in positions of moral and social superiority. Lack of payment is proof of compassion in the eyes of one party and a reason for indignation – or resentment, in the employers' terms – in the other's view. However, these emotions are not reflected in similar terms in these trials. Compassion could be expressed because it was presented as a moral virtue, but resentment was only evoked explicitly to delegitimize the demands of the workers on whom the feeling was projected.

Was what the employers expressed really compassion? According to Martha Nussbaum, compassion is 'a painful emotion directed at another person's undeserved misfortune or suffering',[28] which rests on three cognitive elements:

> *the judgement of size* (a serious bad event has befallen someone), *the judgement of nondesert* (this person did not bring the suffering on him or herself), and *the eudaimonistic judgement* (this person, or creature, is a significant person in my scheme of goals and projects, an end whose good is to be promoted).

Nussbaum argues that class difference impedes compassion because it implies a distance from the sufferer that prevents them from being perceived as someone whose well-being is to be promoted. In the discourse of those involved in legal proceedings at the DLT, compassion is the term that appears most frequently. However, what is meant by this term can be more accurately described as pity, which is a similar emotion but has, since the Victorian era, acquired overtones of condescension and superiority, or even of charity or mercy. Nussbaum notes the kinship between these terms and the complexities around translating them, given that their meanings overlap significantly.

In this case, 'compassion' can be also translated as sympathy. In her study of British nurses in the interwar period, Sarah Chaney has distinguished sympathy from compassion, showing that sympathy was part of middle-class ideals of femininity.[29] While using words such as 'compasión' or 'compasivo', plaintiffs were also positioning themselves as part of the middle class and stating their distance from those who had driven them into court. As Margrit Pernau has pointed out, compassion is more than simply a benign emotion: just as it upholds moral communities, it also allows the exclusion of those whose pain becomes invisible, while reinforcing the hierarchies within the community.[30] Significantly, in the employers' discourse, the workers' demands were described as harmful, as damaging to their honour, making them unworthy of compassion while also demonstrating that they themselves had caused the suffering they were experiencing, casting them out of the moral and emotional community that the employers and judges were part of.

Final remarks

The labour trials analysed in this chapter reveal the different emotional meanings that are assigned to money and, more specifically, to the absence of a remuneration that the plaintiffs had expected and were demanding, which was delegitimized and resisted by the defendants. It is possible to trace emotions in the voices of both workers and employers, although the specific emotions evoked by each party were different and were not presented in the same way. Lack of payment could be grounds for indignation on the part of workers, because it expressed a form of treatment that called their respectability into question and subordinated them through a logic that articulated gender, class and migratory origin and positioned them as minors that needed to be protected. What is interesting is that this happened in a time and place in which salaried relationships were the norm within domestic service (and within the broader world of work). These were times when labour rights, albeit limited ones, had been officially recognized for the sector – and in which an institution like the DLT had been created to resolve conflicts arising from labour relations.

From the employers' point of view, lack of payment was explained by reframing their relationship with the plaintiffs: the latter's presence in their homes was not due to an employment contract between them but rather because they had decided to offer them shelter, moved by the compassion they felt for the difficulty of their circumstances. In these terms, the lawsuit against them was illegitimate, the fruit of resentment that made the plaintiff unworthy of the compassion the defendants had once felt for them. Indignation, resentment and compassion are moral emotions that imply a negotiation of social asymmetries. However, if indignation and resentment called the privileged position of one party into question, compassion helped to sustain these hierarchies and redraw the boundaries of emotional-moral communities by excluding those who sought to dispute them.

It is interesting that when negotiating these asymmetries, both parties referred not only to these emotions but also to sexual honour. This is particularly significant given that this notion is evoked in discourse intended to be heard by a legal authority that had been created as part of a movement to bring domestic service on to equal terms with other labour relationships that took place within the labour market. This movement was limited – the supposed uniqueness of domestic service was used to justify the fact that only limited rights were recognized for domestic workers and that a specific authority was created to resolve conflicts around this work, one that lay outside of the labour courts and even the judiciary itself.[31] Despite these limitations, the DLT was established after the first comprehensive legal regime for the sector was passed, which acknowledged labour rights such as limitations on working hours, paid vacation and sick leave, thus framing the relationship between workers and their employers as a contractual, commercial one. However, the respectability that was disputed at the DLT depended on positions within the family, relationships that were hierarchical and revolved around status.[32] In this sense, it may be useful to follow Simona Cerruti's line of thought on how appeals to positive law and natural law are articulated in lawsuits and demands for justice 'from below'.[33]

What does this tell us about the broader historical narrative? The social construction of work as a field that is free of emotions rests on a narrative that presents the increasing predominance of wage work as the outcome of dependent relationships with significant personal and emotional content being displaced by impersonal, commercial ones. By examining the role of emotions in the world of work, we can call this narrative into question by pointing out the overlap between personal and labour relations, probing the emotional burdens of different kinds of work, raising the visibility of emotional labour and analysing the role of emotions in the construction of asymmetries in this sphere.³⁴ The commercial nature of an exchange depends less on the presence or absence of money than on other factors such as the value of the goods or services being defined independently of the relationship between those who participate in the exchange and the transaction exhausting the meaning of the relationship between them. However, as Florence Weber notes, to understand some exchanges we need to move beyond the opposition between commercial and personal meanings to attempt to identify the moments in which one of these imposes itself on the other and in both meanings need to be included to 'shed light on the different facets of an event'.³⁵ In this sense, analysing emotions in the world of work can help us explore how personal and commercial logics are articulated within labour relations and the implications of these for how parties understand and negotiate their relationship and the inequalities that these gave rise to.

Notes

1. I am very grateful to María Bjerg, Débora Garazi and Valeria Pita for their careful reading and suggestions. I also want to thank Victoria Patience for her translation of the chapter.
2. I first heard Francisca's story after her death. I was able to interview one of her closest friends, one of her nieces and the granddaughter and great-grandson of her erstwhile guardians. I examined this case in greater detail in Pérez, 'Fronteras'.
3. Interview with María Angélica, Dolores, 2 December 2017.
4. Remedi, 'Las trabajadoras'; Zurita, *Trabajo*.
5. Acha, *Crónica*.
6. Decree-Law 326 included rights such as paid vacations and sick leave, implemented severance pay and prior notice, restricted the working day to eight hours for live-out staff and established a minimum of twelve continuous hours of time off per day for live-in staff, among other things. These rights were limited in comparison to those that were enshrined for other types of workers at the time. The DLT (which was initially known as the Domestic Labor Council) was created through Decree 7979 of 1956 by the Ministry of Labor and Social Security, which depended on the Office of the President. Pérez, Cutuli and Garazi, *Senderos*.
7. Interview with Sergio, Dolores, 17 December 2016.
8. Zelizer, *La negociación*; Zelizer, *El significado*.
9. Steedman, *Labours*; Todd, 'Domestic Service'; Hochschild, *The Managed Heart*; Canevaro, 'Afectividad'.
10. Goldstein, *Laughter*.

11 Acta 332/1966, TTD, AGN.
12 Acta 332/1966, TTD, AGN.
13 This case was explored in greater depth in Pérez, '¿Criadas o trabajadoras?'.
14 Cases of girls being placed in domestic service appear up until the late 1960s in the files of minors in juvenile institutions and files from juvenile courts in Buenos Aires Province. Agostina Gentili has come across similar set-ups for the same period in Córdoba Province. Gentili, 'Veladuras'.
15 Adamovsky, *Historia*; Visacovsky and Garguin, *Moralidades*.
16 This case was explored in Pérez and Canevaro, 'Languages'.
17 Deamineur, 'Mechanisms', 115.
18 Acta 3/1975. TTD, AGN.
19 Acta 3/1975. TTD, AGN.
20 Acha, *Crónica*, 117. Juan Domingo Perón reached the presidency on three occasions: 1946, 1952 and 1973. His second administration was ended by a military coup in 1955.
21 There is a broad body of literature that addresses the role that emotions play in legal proceedings. See, for example, Bandes, *The Passions*; Muravyeva, 'Emotional'; Vidor, 'The Press'; Barclay, 'Performing'; Bjerg, *Lazos*.
22 Moscoso, 'The Shadows', 20.
23 Fantini, Moruno and Moscoso, *On Resentment*.
24 Oudai Celso, 'Nietzsche', 38.
25 Canevaro, 'Juicios'.
26 Acta 3/1975. TTD, AGN. Quote from the defendant's response to the claim initiated against him.
27 Acta 48/1972, TTD, AGN.
28 Nussbaum, *Upheavals*, 315.
29 Chaney, 'Before'.
30 Pernau, 'Love'.
31 As was mentioned above, the DLT depended on Argentina's Ministry of Labor and Social Security, rather than on the judiciary. Labour courts were created in 1944 in the City of Buenos Aires and in 1948 in Buenos Aires Province, both of which were part of the judiciary. Stagnaro, *Y nació*.
32 In her analysis of the defilement cases filed in Rio de Janeiro in the early decades of the twentieth century, Sueann Caulfield found similar tensions between efforts to modernize the defence of sexual honour through judicial institutions with public authority, which expressed growing respect for citizen equality, on the one hand, and the defence of women's honour based on corporate institutions such as the family and on racial and gender inequalities, on the other: 'the notion of honour often obscured the contradictions between the official principles of universal citizenship, equal rights, and democracy with the realities of discrimination based on gender, race, and class relations.' Caulfield, *Em defensa*, 34.

33 Cerruti, 'Who is below?'.
34 Langhamer, 'Feelings'.
35 Weber, 'Transacciones', 68.

Bibliography

Acha, Omar. *Crónica sentimental de la Argentina peronista. Sexo inconsciente e ideología, 1945–1955*. Buenos Aires: Prometeo, 2014.

Adamovsky, Ezequiel. *Historia de la clase media argentina. Apogeo y decadencia de una ilusión, 1919–2003*. Buenos Aires: Planeta, 2009.

Bandes, Susan. *The Passions of Law*. New York and London: New York University Press, 1999.

Barclay, Katie. 'Performing Emotion and Reading the Male Body in the Irish Court, c. 1800–1845'. *Journal of Social History* 51, Issue 2 (2017): 1–20.

Bjerg, María. *Lazos rotos. La inmigración, el matrimonio y las emociones en la Argentina entre los siglos*. Buenos Aires: Universidad Nacional de Quilmes Editorial, 2019.

Canevaro, Santiago. 'Afectividad, ambivalencias y desigualdades. Apuntes para pensar los afectos en las relaciones sociales en el servicio doméstico de Buenos Aires'. In *Emociones, afectos y sociología. Diálogos desde la investigación social y la interdisciplina*, edited by Marina Ariza (coord.), 241–78. México: Universidad Autónoma de México, 2016.

Canevaro, Santiago. 'Juicios, acusaciones y traiciones. Moralidades en disputa en el servicio doméstico en Buenos Aires'. *Revista Século XXI. Revista de Ciencias Sociais* 5, no. 1 (2015): 26–52.

Caulfield, Sueann. *Em defensa da honra. Moralidade, e nação no Rio de Janeiro (1918–1940)*. Río de Janeiro: Universidade Estadual de Campinas, 2000.

Celso, Yamina Oudai. 'Nietzsche: The "First Psychologist" and Genealogist of Ressentiment'. In *On Resentment: Past and Present*, edited by Bernardino Fantini, Dolores Martín Moruno, and Javier Moscoso, 37–54. Newcastle: Cambridge Scholars, 2013.

Cerruti, Simona. 'Who is below? E. P. Thompson, historiador de las sociedades modernas: una relectura'. In *Historia pragmática. Una perspectiva sobre la acción, el contexto y las fuentes*, edited by Mariana Garzón Rogé, 79–104. Buenos Aires: Prometeo, 2018.

Chaney, Sarah. 'Before Compassion: Sympathy, Tact and the History of the Ideal Nurse'. *Med Humanities* (2020): 1–10 (Published Online First: 30 July 2020. doi: 10.1136/medhum-2019-011842).

Deamineur, Elise. 'Mechanisms of Collective Resentment: Gender Wars and the Alteration of Patriarchy in Eighteenth-Century Rural France'. In *On Resentment:*

Past and Present, edited by Bernardino Fantini, Dolores Martín Moruno, and Javier Moscoso, 113–34. Newcastle: Cambridge Scholars, 2013.

Fantini, Bernardo, Dolores Martín Moruno, and Javier Moscoso. *On Resentment: Past and Present*. Newcastle: Cambridge Scholars, 2013.

Gentili, Agostina. 'Veladuras. El servicio doméstico de niñas y jóvenes en la narrativa judicial de los años sesenta en Córdoba, Argentina'. *Secuencia. Revista de Historia y Ciencias Sociales*, edición especial (2018): 85–118.

Goldstein, Donna. *Laughter Out of Place: Race, Class, Violence, and Sexuality in a Rio Shantytown*. Berkeley: University of California Press, 2003.

Hochschild, Arlie. *La mercantilización de la vida íntima. Apuntes de la casa y el trabajo*. Buenos Aires: Katz, 2008.

Langhamer, Claire. 'Feelings and Work in the Long 1950s'. *Women's History Review* 26, Issue 1 (2017): 1–17.

Moscoso, Javier. 'The Shadows of Ourselves: Resentment, Monomania and Modernity'. In *On Resentment: Past and Present*, edited by Bernardino Fantini, Dolores Martín Moruno, and Javier Moscoso, 19–36. Newcastle: Cambridge Scholars, 2013.

Muravyeva, Marianna. 'Emotional Environments and Legal Spaces in Early Modern Russia'. *Journal of Social History* 51, Issue 2 (2017): 1–17.

Nussbaum, Martha. *Upheavals of Thought. The Intelligence of Emotions*. Cambridge: Cambridge University Press, 2001.

Pérez, Inés. '¿Criadas o trabajadoras? Lenguajes, representaciones y estrategias frente a la justicia laboral (Buenos Aires, 1956–1970)'. *Revista de Historia y Justicia* 11 (2018): 101–24.

Pérez, Inés. 'Fronteras y jerarquías familiares en casos de colocaciones domésticas en la ciudad y la provincia de Buenos Aires, 1940–1960'. *Secuencia. Revista de Historia y Ciencias Sociales*, no. 106 (2020): 1–29.

Pérez, Inés and Santiago Canevaro. 'Languages of affection and rationality: household workers' strategies before the Tribunal of Domestic Work (Buenos Aires, 1956–2013)'. *International Labor and Working Class History* 88 (2015): 130–49.

Pérez, Inés, Romina Cutuli, and Débora Garazi. *Senderos que se bifurcan. Servicio doméstico y derechos laborales en la Argentina del siglo XX*. Mar del Plata: Eudem, 2019.

Pernau, Margrit. 'Love and Compassion for the Community: Emotions and Practices among North Indian Muslims, ca. 1870–1930'. *The Indian Economic and Social History Review* 54, no. 1 (2017): 21–42.

Remedi, Fernando. 'Las trabajadoras del servicio doméstico: entre la subordinación y la negociación en una modernización periférica. Córdoba (Argentina), 1910–1930'. *Historia Regional y de las Fronteras*, no. 19 (2014): 423–50.

Stagnaro, Andrés. *Y nació un derecho. Los tribunales del trabajo en la provincia de Buenos Aires*. Buenos Aires: Biblos, 2018.

Steedman, Carolyn. *Labours Lost. Domestic Service and the Making of Modern England*. Cambridge: Cambridge University Press, 2009.

Todd, Selina. 'Domestic Service and Class Relations in Britain 1900–1950'. *Past and Present* 203 (2009): 181–204.

Vidor, Gian Marco. 'The Press, the Audience, and Emotions in Italian Courtrooms (1860–1910)'. *Journal of Social History* 51, Issue 2 (2017): 1–24.

Visacovsky, Sergio, and Enrique Garguin. *Moralidades, economías e identidades de clase media. Estudios históricos y etnográficos*. Buenos Aires: Antropofagia, 2009.

Weber, Florence. 'Transacciones económicas y relaciones personales. Una etnografía económica después de la gran división'. *Revista Crítica en Desarrollo*, no. 2 (2008): 63–91.

Zelizer, Viviana. *La negociación de la intimidad*. Buenos Aires: Fondo de Cultura Económica, 2009.

Zelizer, Viviana. *El significado social del dinero*. Buenos Aires: Fondo de Cultura Económica, 2011.

Zurita, Carlos. *Trabajo, servidumbre y situaciones de género. Algunas acotaciones sobre el servicio doméstico en Santiago del Estero, Argentina*. Santiago del Estero: Universidad Nacional de Santiago del Estero, 1997.

8

Managing feeling in the academic workplace

Gender, emotion and knowledge production in a Cambridge science department, 1950–80

Sally Horrocks and Paul Merchant

A wealth of research in the social sciences and humanities has shown that scientific work has significant affective and subjective dimensions, frequently concealed to bolster the public authority of science and scientists.[1] However, there have been no sustained examinations of the management of feeling and emotion by those working in scientific workplaces and ways in which such emotion work formed part of the everyday working world of science.[2] Detailed historical and anthropological studies of particular laboratories and field sites have not focused on the management of feeling of the scientists present.[3] Meanwhile, sociological and biographical studies of scientists include attention to matters of pleasure and satisfaction but without locating these feelings in the experience of particular workplaces.[4] Studies of other workplaces in the period include analyses of the management of feeling that can be usefully applied to academic and scientific workplaces, in particular Arlie Hochschild's concept of 'emotional labour' and Michael Roper's development of this concept in relation to forms of male insecurity among senior managers.[5] But recent sociological studies of academic work that deal with emotions, particularly those of Charlotte Bloch, suggest that academic workplaces may involve specific forms of emotion work, connected to the production of knowledge, communicated in named publications.[6] Bloch's work draws attention to the ways in which management of feeling shapes academic careers but locates this in the contemporary neoliberal university.[7] This chapter instead focuses on an academic workplace of the recent past and considers ways in which the management of feeling was closely tied to the production of particular kinds of scientific knowledge.

The Department of Geodesy and Geophysics

We focus on the University of Cambridge's Department of Geodesy and Geophysics during a period in which its members contributed to radical new interpretations of the earth's geology. From 1955, the Department was based in a large Victorian house in the west of Cambridge, called Madingley Rise.[8] The rooms of the house formed offices, a library, a map room, a room filled with calculating machines and a coffee room. In our period, it was occupied by a small number of permanent scientific staff (all male), a few technicians and assistants, a secretary and a small population of research students. Sir Edward ('Teddy') Bullard was Head of the Department for a large part of our period (1960–73). Much of the work of the Department was concerned with the analysis of geophysical data collected by research ships describing the earth's crust under the Atlantic and Indian Oceans. In the 1960s this work brought the Department considerable scientific fame as Fred Vine and Drummond (Drum) Matthews reported their theory of 'sea-floor spreading', and then Dan McKenzie and Robert (Bob) Parker published the first paper describing 'plate tectonics'. The chapter draws on extended life story interviews with several members of the Department: David Davies (1961–70), Anthony Laughton (1951–4), Dan McKenzie (1963–2007), Fred Vine (1962–5), Sue Vine (1963–5) and Carol Williams (1965–73 and 1978–90s).

Using these interviews, we explore ways in which the management of feeling was integral to the Department's success in producing new knowledge in the earth sciences.[9] It is clear that the Department can be thought of as a particular 'emotional community' where certain 'norms' (or 'standards' or 'rules') operated, as in other workplaces.[10] But rather than attempting to describe these norms, our attention remains with the individual scientists who worked in the Department but whose emotional lives also took place elsewhere, and at other times, before and after their employment. In particular, we are interested in the way in which feelings such as insecurity, as a feature of all human experience *and* as a product of particular biographies, were activated in this specific workplace.[11]

The interviews were not recorded in order to explore the emotions of scientists, and so their use here may be considered a form of reuse.[12] Our analysis does not depend on the coding for particular emotion words or 'statements about emotions';[13] we listen to the full interviews to identify – from a range of clues – the experience of emotion in the past (when employed in the Department, but also since) and in the act of the interview itself. This means that though we of course pay attention to moments in the interviews when scientists tell us that they 'felt' X or Y, we are also alert to all the audible signs of 'composure' and 'discomposure' in interview,[14] to the more directly psychoanalytical signals of past 'emotional investments' stressed by Michael Roper that may not ever have been 'consciously articulated by the actors *as* emotion' and which involves 'imaginative connection with the subjectivities of the people in the past'[15] and to indications of past expressions of emotions in practice and 'demeanour'.[16]

First, we examine the emotion work required by female scientists working for the Department in order to 'fit into' a predominantly male environment in which women, including wives, were often understood to be in supportive roles. Secondly, we consider efforts of male scientists to manage their fear of failure and the pressure to live up to high expectations of family and peers. In the conclusion, we consider the different ways in which men and women managed feelings in this Department. We then consider questions of time and timing in the experience and memory of emotions at work that are revealed by life story interviews.

Women scientists in the Department

The Department was primarily a masculine, homosocial environment. There were no female permanent members of academic staff. Women whose presence was noted in the interviews were PhD students, scientific assistants, secretaries, tea ladies and family members of male scientists, especially wives and daughters. In this environment, managing feeling was highly gendered and reflected the status differences between men and women. It is clear from the way in which male scientists talk about their wives – for example, 'she kept me sane' – that women were valued for their nurturing roles outside the workplace.[17] This contributed to the tendency *in* the workplace for women scientists to take on responsibility for tasks that supported the psychological needs of others, placing these needs above their own. At the same time their own feelings remained unnoticed because they lacked what Hochschild termed a 'status shield' which both increased their exposure to poorer treatment and reduced the extent to which their own feelings were considered important or even considered at all.[18]

These themes will be explored through the interviews with Sue Vine and Carol Williams. Sue Vine studied geology at the University of Cambridge and on graduating got a job working with Drum Matthews processing data from research ships and using it to build models. She was also the girlfriend, later wife, of Fred Vine, one of the PhD students. Carol Williams took over from Sue Vine as Matthews's assistant in 1965, having recently completed a degree in geology at the University of Leicester. In 1966 she was the first female geophysicist allowed to join a research cruise on the Royal Research Ship Discovery. Later she completed a PhD in the Department and spent five years working in the United States before returning as a research assistant in 1978, a role that lasted until the mid-1990s.

Both interviews provide evidence of how these women scientists were under constant pressure to manage their feelings in order to find a place for themselves in this environment, even women such as Sue Vine, whose educational background was similar to that of many of the men. Reflecting on her two years in the Department, Sue recalled that she did not at the time feel she was on the same level as the men around her:

> The place was full of bright – bright young research students and I think I thought I wasn't quite up to that grade but I don't think that was to do with being a woman, I think it was just that I wasn't quite on that level intellectually, you know, I was sort of at a more mediocre sort of level.[19]

Asked to reflect on why she saw herself in this way, she suggested that in retrospect it was not so much that these men were necessarily cleverer than her, it was that at the time they 'seemed more able' because of their greater self-confidence, 'because they were more sort of full of it'.[20] These reflections hint at the work she had to do to manage her feelings in this situation, which she had at the time resolved by accepting her own mediocrity, something she now doubted was actually the case. By interpreting her own situation at the time as being one of not being 'bright' enough, she was able to avoid confronting highly gendered schemes of value and forms of social display.

Like Sue Vine, Carol Williams constantly had to manage her feelings of insecurity about her academic ability, something that was not helped by having arrived at university via a secretarial course and A-levels at night school. She felt particularly acutely that her mathematics was not as strong as that of the men around her, commenting, 'I probably thought I was the thickest person in the room and I definitely felt a lack of mathematics.'[21] This led her to take additional A-levels in mathematics and physics to add to her existing qualifications. Throughout her time in the Department she continued to feel that 'my lack of mathematics was a big liability' and that 'this made me feel inferior to many of the others who were good at maths'.[22] She also attributes her lack of confidence to her family background, suggesting that 'my parents hadn't given me a lot of confidence'.[23]

The self-confidence of women scientists and PhD students was not helped by instances where it was made clear by the actions of senior men that women's academic ability was less valued than their physical attractiveness or their role as potential partners for male scientists. Two examples relating to the recruitment of PhD students stand out. The first was the story, regularly repeated as a humorous anecdote, of a Brazilian female PhD student who reputedly had been recruited on the basis of a photograph sent with her application rather than a rigorous appraisal of her academic ability. The second was the presence of Monica Dirac, daughter of Nobel Prize-winning Cambridge physicist Paul Dirac. Despite her relatively poor academic record, a fourth from Oxford according to Bullard, her parents seem to have encouraged her studies as a means of securing a husband sufficiently clever to be relied upon to make intelligent conversation with her father.[24] In this she was successful, marrying Bob Parker.

When Sue and Carol were first recruited to work for the Department it was to process data collected by male scientists aboard research ships that spent extended periods of time at sea. In 1966 Carol became the first woman to join one of these research cruises. This provoked implied hostility from some of the crew: 'being a girl on board I was told that I was bringing the ship bad luck.'[25] In response, Carol describes herself keeping a 'low profile' which she explains here involved avoiding the unnecessary attention that might have resulted from missing a shift in the on-ship laboratory or from entering spaces in which she felt she might not be welcome:

> I think initially I kept a low profile and I watched my Ps and Qs and I wasn't outspoken, and I just conformed to as much of what I thought was the plan as I could.... I suppose I was also feeling a bit seasick... but I've never, ever missed a watch. I'm very proud of this, never missed a watch on a scientific ship.... I've sort of staggered on. So I guess I didn't go into the bar for the first two or three days before because I was feeling a bit queasy and then I guess I sort of played it gently as to wondering how welcome I would be in there.[26]

Carol's account of her experiences points to the pressure she felt to fit in and the hard work she put in to do so. As we go on to show, fitting-in on ships and in the Department didn't just involve not standing out. It involved taking on certain kinds of emotion work.

Being nice

Although Carol Williams was employed for her scientific skills, her interview is replete with examples of the many ways in which she took on tasks in the workplace that involved looking after the well-being of others that called for skills in personal relations. The ways in which these activities became intertwined was revealed clearly when she said,

> I just got back into assisting with the cruises and helping a field course. I was a co-examiner for the field course projects. I was supervising students, occasional external examiner. I used to organise the colloquia and then there was my archiving of marine data as always, and my own bits and pieces of research. And I used to recycle the paper and organise the parties.[27]

Many of these tasks, not least the parties, were concerned with the intellectual and emotional well-being of others, with 'bits and pieces' of her own scientific work, as well as her own feelings, seemingly secondary.

This sense of Carol as someone who put the needs of others above her own is echoed in her memories of using her typing skills to relieve male colleagues of what to them was unwelcome labour:

> And I remember that Drum had just written a paper which he wanted me to type quickly and put in the post. So I sat down in my cabin and typed Drum's paper, and then I went and popped out into Plymouth and posted it and – *Why didn't Drum type it?*
> Drum – Drum was a one finger typist and my dreaded secretarial course that my parents had pushed me into actually came in a little useful. I could use all my fingers, so I probably volunteered to type it knowing it would save Drum a lot of time.[28]

Such work clearly contributed to the status of others and took her away from other activities that were more prestigious in this environment, such as original research and named publication. At sea, Carol also saw it as part of her role to make life easier for others by taking responsibility for maintaining a notice board to share information between those on board doing research and those crewing the ship: 'I was happy to do things like this, and if there were maps or illustrations required I was very happy to draw pictures and something I liked doing, so I probably volunteered to do that.'[29] When she says that this notice board work was 'a welcome distraction', it is others, rather than herself, that she has in mind:

> We had a competition, we put up a diagram of the internal structure of the airgun and asked for suggestions of how people thought it operated. And we had a surprising number of comments and suggestions and – which showed that people took an interest and read the bulletins and, you know, this – you need some little distractions on days at sea and so this was a – seemed to be a welcome distraction.[30]

The overwhelming impression is of Carol taking on extra emotion work to support others, without this being in any way reciprocated. She was noting the feelings of others, while making her own as unlikely to be noted as possible.

Not having a 'status shield'

In her analysis of the gender dimensions inherent in the management of feeling, Hochschild argued that women regularly had to manage the additional burdens that arose from their lack of a 'status shield'. This, she suggested, meant that their own feelings were rarely acknowledged or respected while 'high status people tend to enjoy the privilege of having their feelings noticed and considered important'.[31] In the academic workplace this could lead not just to women moderating their behaviour to accommodate what they saw as the expectations of others but also to their inability to claim full credit for themselves and ultimately to gain respect for their expertise and job security. Carol Williams's interview is replete with examples of moments when her feelings remained unnoticed or where she modified her actions to avoid confrontation with more powerful colleagues. A striking example comes from the period during which she completed a PhD. She was an expert rower and her status as a student meant that she was eligible to compete for the university in the prestigious women's boat race, for which she was selected in 1972. Throughout the period of intensive training leading up to the event she concealed her involvement from Drum Matthews because she felt he would have disapproved of the amount of time it was taking away from her academic work. To do this she would leave the Department 'looking hopefully as if I was going to the library or something' and change en route. When asked why she felt the need to do this she responded:

> Well, I don't know, I can't – I can't imagine Drum actually sort of coming – you know, thumping on my office door and stamping up and down saying, 'I hear you've gone rowing after all'. I suppose I just didn't want to displease him and if he didn't know about it, well, so much the better.[32]

Despite these difficulties, Carol's crew went on to win the race by three lengths.[33] Instead of making her own desires and aspirations known, and inviting colleagues to share in her achievements, Carol opted to prioritize avoiding confrontation and accommodating their feelings. Perhaps she judged that less emotion work was required to avoid conflict with a senior colleague than would be required to navigate conflict successfully.

This power imbalance was evident a decade later when Carol was one of a team of four, alongside Sir Peter Kent, Martin Bott and Dan McKenzie, who organized an important meeting at the Royal Society on sedimentary basins. Afterwards it was decided to produce a book of papers from the meeting, but as Carol recalls:

> The Royal Society were going to produce a book of this meeting and I was asked to edit it, but I was left to edit it. This is another of my really naïve moments. And so I received all these papers and I was working really, really hard and we were meant to be going away on holiday, and I just couldn't do it and I put the holiday off for three or four days just to get all this editing finished and sent it all in. And, you know, and the way it was typed, it was 'edited by Kent, Bott, McKenzie and Williams'. I didn't dream of putting 'meeting organised by, edited by Carol Williams', I just didn't dream of doing it; I was so stupid. So anyway, that's how it went in, and in due course a nice book was produced.[34]

Here, those who were already considered important gained further credit and prestige without sharing in the editing work, while Carol had to manage her time and her feelings unnoticed.[35] Reflecting on these events, she clearly felt a keen sense of injustice but acknowledged that at the time a different course of action had been unthinkable. Her description of herself as 'stupid' for not challenging this seems to reflect not only her repeated ascription of blame to herself for opting not to take on the emotional burdens that such challenges would have entailed but also her knowledge of the long-term negative consequences of not receiving the level of credit her actual contributions warranted.

A lack of public credit and acknowledgement of her expertise in the form of promotion was another feature of Carol's career. After she was awarded her PhD she considered applying for promotion – from research assistant to associate – but did not do so because she was waiting for encouragement, even though she was aware that others with fewer qualifications were employed at a higher grade. When asked why this was she reflected, 'I kind of thought if other people considered me worth it they'd offer it, which is a very old fashioned way of looking at things.'[36] She also commented that she was not sure if there were sufficient funds in the grant to increase her salary and described herself at the time as 'naïve' and 'very unpushy'.[37] Later on, when Drum Matthews was about to retire she contemplated applying for the post, despite being aware that a male member of staff was already under consideration but seen as rather young. At the time she saw a possible solution: to apply but offer to stand down later:

saying, well, after three or five years I would stand down and if they wanted to apply Bob White in it – but somehow I didn't apply. I think I had the naïve notion that if the Department thought me good enough they would invite me to apply, and of course they didn't invite me to apply, so I remained a research assistant.[38]

Perhaps the most challenging moments for Carol came when it became apparent to her that the continuation of her post was in doubt. The first hint of this, in 1982, caused Carol some anxiety ('that worried me a bit') but she was able to continue. Her post was then moved to a part-time one, something she presents as having been, to some extent at least, imposed on her rather than actively sought: 'I'd foolishly talked about taking up art part time and doing much more oil painting. And he said, "Oh, well, you want to go part time. I'm going to cut you down now to part time."'[39] Later it was decided to eliminate her post entirely, something she described as 'absolutely shattering'.[40] This feeling of rejection and hurt was compounded by the discovery that the university did not hold any formal paperwork relating to her employment, so she just had the word of her boss that she had to leave and 'I didn't even get my P45', the tax form usually given to employees when their employment is terminated in the UK. Her boss suggested a leaving party to mark her long service to the Department, but Carol was reluctant, arguing, 'I can't accept a party. I feel so ashamed to be leaving.'[41] Eventually she relented and 'they did have a little mini, mini presentation after a few weeks and I went back and I said thank you and went home [laughs]. So I was – I was very shattered at all this.'[42] These reflections suggest the extent to which Carol continued to manage her own feelings in order to accommodate those of others, even at the point of leaving the Department.

For Carol, working for the Department was a constant balancing act, a process of carefully meeting the expectations of the others, being helpful and supportive without appearing to have too many expectations of her own. Her recollections of her period in the Department indicate that at the time she chose not to acknowledge the difficulties she faced or the work that went into managing her feelings. In hindsight, however, she chastised herself for being 'naïve' and even 'stupid' by accepting the gendered expectations ascribed to her. It also seems likely that this stance arose from an implicit recognition that managing her feelings in this way was what enabled her to participate in scientific work that she enjoyed and valued. This analysis is supported by her comments on what life outside science might have entailed for a woman from her background, saying,

'I have a fear of, you know, sitting next to someone and having to talk about washing powder or something.'[43]

Male roles and anxieties

There is strong evidence in the interviews that male scientists in the Department worried about their intellectual performance in relation to others and that they acted in a variety of ways to manage feelings of inferiority or insecurity. Carol Williams remembers that Drum Matthews, head of the Department's 'marine group' from 1966 to 1982, introduced her to his group by saying, 'we don't really do anything very clever here'[44] and that in general:

> Drum was a very modest person. He was always describing himself as 'a bear of little brain', after Pooh Bear, and scratching his head and saying, 'Oh, I don't know what to think of that'. He was determined that science should be fun and he'd invent sort of jollies to go alongside the work. . . . He didn't have a lot of confidence, I don't think, in himself because he had struggled a bit with his thesis.[45]

Dan McKenzie also uses the word 'modest' to describe Drum but suggests that this was not a modesty expressed in any tendency to give way to colleagues on questions of science. He says that he was 'very, modest, quite quiet, absolutely un-shiftable in his opinions on everything' including approaches to interpreting geophysical data.[46] In the light of this, we might interpret self-deprecating comments about not 'very clever' work and identification with Pooh Bear – reinforced by books taken on every cruise and a toy left out at a dinner party for senior colleagues – as strategies for managing feelings of intellectual insecurity without losing any actual scientific and social capital in the Department:

> There were six chairs and Pooh Bear was sitting on one . . . and none of these quite important people dared to take Pooh Bear off the chair and so we could all sit down. . . . . So we had to wait until Drum came back with the drinks and said, 'Oh, I'll move Pooh Bear' [laughs].[47]

Another scientist, David Davies, decided to take on what he saw as an important but secondary care-taking role in the Department because he regarded himself as less 'brilliant' than Teddy Bullard and a new research student, Dan McKenzie:

> I think my job at the Department was – I sort of knew I wasn't going to be a brilliant scientist. 'I sort of knew'! I knew I wasn't! And I knew that there were

good, really good, people coming through all the time, like Dan for instance, who – but all departments in every scientific discipline . . . need somebody in the department who will make things happen, you know, who will organise the symposia, who will meet the visitors, who will organise the expeditions, this, that and the other. . . . . And I suppose I slipped into that role 'cause nobody else did it, but – you know, inviting speakers to colloquia and driving people from the station [laughs], all that kind of stuff. So – and departments do need that as well as brilliant minds, they do need people who will do the donkey work.[48]

Davies left the Department in 1970 and by 1980 was no longer working in science. Doing departmental 'donkey work' and leaving the Department are understood by Davies as logical responses to what he took to be 'clear' differences between himself and others:

Well, at Madingley Rise it was clear Teddy was brilliant and that Dan McKenzie was brilliant. . . . . . I mean, I've thought quite a bit about this, about what sort of career I would have been heading for if I'd stayed at Madingley Rise, and I am convinced I might have ended up as, you know, Head of Department, but it would have been Head of Department making sure that the Department ran properly, not Head of Department doing brilliant things. [49]

His statement that he has 'thought quite a bit about this' points to – we suggest – the extent to which this decision as a young scientist to give way to others happened as part of a process of managing feelings of self-doubt that has continued in moments of reflection and reassessment since.

Being regarded by others as brilliant was no defence against worrying feelings. Dan McKenzie himself operated with feelings of anxiety – even, as he puts it, 'dread' – concerning his work. In a digression from a discussion of the mix of applied and theoretical work in the Department, he says:

I like to be involved in the observations, I like to do field work. I like to do the theory, I don't mind if I get things wrong provided I'm not stupid, right, that's what I dread, right.
What is it you dread?
Being stupid. Don't mind being wrong. . . . What you hope is that you don't make any simple errors in coding and mathematics, and that you hadn't done something which is just plain stupid.[50]

This admission of dreading being stupid echoes earlier sections of the life story interview in which he recalls his memories of finding school work difficult: 'up until, really I was thirteen or fourteen, I didn't do well at school.

I was, was frightened and nervous, and couldn't understand a lot of what was going on.'[51] This period of his life is captured in his mother's book *Children in the House* (1954) of which he says 'parts of it show me absolutely as I remember myself at that stage, of, of being uncertain about, you know, my human relations with other people, and not knowing when I was going to get laughed at'.[52]

Discussion of his plate tectonics paper of 1967 reveals other worries. Though Davies had regarded him as an exceptional PhD student, he himself had doubts about his future employment in science that were only eased by this high-profile publication:

> What it did do was to convince me that I didn't really have to worry very much about whether I was going to get a job doing scientific research, and that certainly had been a concern of mine when I was a graduate student.[53]

And even after it was published and it 'made the splash it did', there was another reason to worry. Plate tectonics, once discovered, seemed so straightforward that it was quickly taught to school children:

> when it first happened [being taught in schools] I was extremely alarmed because, I thought, you know, how in the world am I going to earn a living, you know, [laughs] if this just becomes, you know, if all that I know is, is obvious to people who are taught at school.[54]

In 1966 – with Dan recently awarded his PhD and still a year off his submission to *Nature* on plate tectonics, Drum Matthews continuing to lead the collection of data at sea with Pooh Bear books on board and David Davies a year into his self-appointed role as departmental organizer – a senior scientist in the Department and Fellow of the Royal Society (FRS), Maurice Hill, died by suicide, aged forty-seven. Carol Williams remembers, 'I walked into a full but very silent coffee room one morning and I in a whispered voice asked what the problem was, and I was told.'[55] Interviews in the collection contain a range of explanations for this suicide but a strong thread is the view that Maurice perceived his work in science as falling short of expectations set by those around him. In the Department, he had Teddy Bullard to compare himself to, as David Davies explains: 'Maurice knew that Teddy was a mega brain compared with – Maurice was not intellectually incredibly high powered but he was very good at making things happen and making people feel they wanted to do things for him.'[56] And others point out that he was working under the wider shadow cast by his father:

He of course had a very distinguished father, AV Hill, who was president of the Royal Society and a Nobel Prize winner. And Maurice always, I think, felt that it was difficult to live up to his father's reputation and this partly I think was why his life ended tragically. . . . We went to sea together . . . and you get to know people very well at sea socially as well as through the work, and he talked about his father and I very much sensed that he was somewhat living in his father's shadow. . . . One might have thought, well, becoming an FRS would have been a great achievement but then he had another achievement way above him.[57]

Teddy Bullard's Royal Society biographical memoir for Maurice Hill hints at some kind of cognitive deterioration, stressing that he 'was driven, entirely by things within himself' to end his life.[58] In this way, Bullard's memoir conveys no sense that Hill's overwork and self-doubt might have been connected to the Department as a place of work where performance anxiety would seem to have been widespread and in which the experience of loss of intellectual function must have been especially difficult to live with.

Conclusion

Our discussion of women scientists', especially Carol Williams's, experience of the Department sheds new light on women's scientific careers, drawing attention to the ways in which knowledge production depended on their emotion work and management of their own feelings. The interviews with male scientists reveal that they too were constantly engaged in the management of feeling, especially feelings of performance anxiety, and could take on forms of emotion work as part of their jobs. Management of one's own and others' feelings was a substantial factor in the production of new knowledge about the earth, suggesting that emotion should more often be explored as an aspect of the social construction of scientific knowledge.

Male and female scientists seem to have managed feeling in the Department in different ways. With some simplification, we might suggest that Sue Vine and Carol Williams experienced a form of 'imposter syndrome', a feeling that they did not deserve a position – certainly not a permanent position – in the Department. Male scientists, on the other hand, would seem to have been satisfied that they deserved to hold permanent positions but worried about their 'position' in another sense: their placing on an imagined hierarchy of intellectual brilliance in the Department and to some extent beyond it. Like Michael Roper's managers, they experienced 'anxiety . . . about whether or not they measured up'.[59]

Interviews reveal a *continuous* process of management of feeling over time. The experience of exclusion is remembered vividly; feelings of insecurity and difficulty seem to have had a lasting effect or are at least memorable. There is evidence that interviewees have thought about their emotional lives in the Department over the years since, in moments of reflection, with David Davies's remark 'I've thought quite a bit about this' being perhaps the clearest indication. Interviewees seem occasionally uncomfortable with the version of the self that is revealed in the interview, especially a tension between their willingness to behave in a particular way in the past and a new understanding of those actions that has developed over time, and perhaps during the interview conversation itself. Doing departmental 'donkey work', feeling not 'bright' or volunteering for emotion work are parts of a past self which do not fit easily with current understandings of themselves. Finally, it is clear that the experience of emotion at work cannot be easily separated from life outside work, including life *before* paid work. Feelings of anxiety have roots in family, for example, in Carol Williams's comments on self-confidence and the perception of others that Maurice Hill compared himself not just to other scientists in the Department but also to his father. With all of this temporal complexity, it is clear that studies of emotion and work need to do more than consider 'lapses of time' between 'the experience of an emotion and the memory of an emotion'.[60]

Notes

1. For example Jones, *Femininity, Mathematics and Science*; Daston, 'The Moral Economy of Science'; Keller, *A Feeling for the Organism*.
2. We follow Langhamer in using emotion and feeling synonymously in part because no distinction is made between emotions and feelings by interviewees themselves: Langhamer, 'Feelings, Women and Work', 90. Delap suggests too that affect and emotion cannot be clearly distinguished: Delap, 'Feminism, Masculinities and Emotional Politics', 574.
3. Gould, 'Women and the Culture of University Physics', 127–49; Traweek, *Beamtimes and Lifetimes*; Latour, *Pandora's Hope*, 24–79.
4. For example Hermanowicz, 'Scientists and Satisfaction', 45–73; Söderqvist, *Existential Projects,* 45–84; Turkle, *Falling for Science*, 3–38.
5. Clance and Ament, 'The Imposter Phenomenon'; McDowell, *Capital Culture*; Morris and Feldman, 'Managing Emotions in the Workplace'; Hochschild, *The Managed Heart*; Roper, *Masculinity and the British Organization Man*, especially 2, 10, 128, 163–4.

6 Bloch, *Passion and Paranoia* and Bloch, 'Managing the Emotions'. See also Ehn and Löfgren, *Emotions in Academia*.
7 And Karlsohn's historical contribution takes us back to the mid-1700s: Karlsohn, 'The Academic Seminar'.
8 In this chapter we refer to the Department of Geodesy and Geophysics as 'the Department'. Interviewees sometimes refer to it as 'Madingley Rise'. For a detailed history of the Department, see Williams, *Madingley Rise and Early Geophysics at Cambridge*. Following Linda McDowell's arguments about the effect of space on the performance of gender, it seems possible that the domestic setting of the Department may have contributed to management of feeling by men and women, but this is not easily judged from our sources. McDowell, *Capital Culture*, 166–7.
9 The interviews, all but one of which is over ten hours long, were each recorded between 2010 and 2012 by *National Life Stories* at the British Library for the project An Oral History of British Science and are available online at https://sounds.bl.uk/.
10 These terms in the field of the history of emotions are discussed by Plamper, *The History of Emotions*, especially 56–9, 67–74 and 251–90.
11 As Roper puts it, 'what emerges from this kind of approach is a sense of subjectivity ... as a matter of personality formed through lived experience and the emotional responses to those experiences ... a means of apprehending the significance of earlier life experiences, whose conscious and unconscious effects are always working away within the mind.' Roper, 'Slipping Out of View', 65–6.
12 Bornat, 'Remembering and Reworking', 43–52.
13 Plamper, *The History of Emotions*, 252.
14 Dawson, *Soldier Heroes*; Summerfield, *Reconstructing Women's Wartime Lives*; Summerfield, 'Culture and Composure', 65–93; Roper, 'Slipping Out of View', 57–72; Roper, 'Re-remembering', 181–204; Abrams, *Oral History Theory*, 48–9, 57–8, 87–8, 100.
15 Roper, 'The Unconscious Work of History', 174.
16 Delap, 'Feminism, Masculinities', 574.
17 Interview with Dan McKenzie by Paul Merchant, 2010, reference C1979/24, Track 11, British Library Sound Archive.
18 Hochschild, *The Managed Heart*, 174–5.
19 Interview with Sue Vine by Paul Merchant, 2011, reference C1979/39, Track 1, British Library Sound Archive.
20 C1979/39, Track 1.
21 Interview with Carol Williams by Paul Merchant, 2012, reference C1979/67, Track 4, British Library Sound Archive.
22 Interview with Carol Williams by Paul Merchant, 2012, reference C1979/67, Track 9, British Library Sound Archive.
23 C1979/67, Track 9.
24 C1979/67, Track 4.

25 C1979/67, Track 4.
26 C1979/67, Track 4.
27 C1979/67, Track 5.
28 C1979/67, Track 6.
29 C1979/67, Track 8.
30 C1979/67, Track 8.
31 Hochschild, *The Managed Heart*, 174–81.
32 C1979/67, Track 5.
33 'Cambridge University Women's Boat Club 1941–2014', http://cuwbchistory.org/crew-lists/crew-lists-1970s#BB1971 (accessed 16 November 2020).
34 C1979/67, Track 5.
35 This phenomena in the history of science was labelled as the 'Matilda effect' by Margaret Rossiter: Rossiter, 'The Matthew Matilda Effect'.
36 C1979/67, Track 5.
37 C1979/67, Track 5.
38 C1979/67, Track 9.
39 C1979/67, Track 9.
40 C1979/67, Track 5.
41 C1979/67, Track 5.
42 C1979/67, Track 5.
43 C1979/67, Track 9.
44 C1979/67, Track 3.
45 C1979/67, Track 4.
46 C1979/24, Track 11.
47 C1979/67, Track 4.
48 Interview with David Davies by Paul Merchant, 2011–12, reference C1979/50, Track 4, British Library Sound Archive.
49 Interview with David Davies by Paul Merchant, 2011–12, reference C1979/50, Track 5, British Library Sound Archive.
50 C1979/24, Track 7.
51 C1979/24, Track 1.
52 C1979/24, Track 5.
53 C1979/24, Track 8.
54 C1979/24, Track 7.
55 C1979/67, Track 4.
56 C1979/50, Track 3.
57 Interview with Anthony Laughton by Paul Merchant, 2010–11, reference C1979/29, Track 3, British Library Sound Archive.
58 Bullard, 'Maurice Neville Hill', 192–203.
59 Roper, *Masculinity and the British Organization Man*, 128.
60 Plamper, *The History of Emotions*, 290.

Bibliography

Abrams, Lynn. *Oral History Theory*. London: Routledge, 2010.

Bloch, Charlotte. 'Managing the Emotions of Competition and Recognition in Academia'. In *Emotions and Sociology*, edited by Jack Barbalet, 113–31. Oxford: Blackwell, 2002.

Bloch, Charlotte. *Passion and Paranoia: Emotions and the Culture of Emotion in Academia*. Farnham: Ashgate, 2012.

Bornat, Joanna. 'Remembering and Reworking Emotions: The Reanalysis of Emotion in an Interview'. *Oral History* 38, no. 2 (2010): 43–52.

Bullard, Edward C. 'Maurice Neville Hill, 1919–1966'. *Biographical Memoirs of Fellows of the Royal Society* 13 (1967): 192–203.

Clance, Pauline Rose, and Suzanne Ament Imes. 'The Imposter Phenomenon in High Achieving Women: Dynamics and Therapeutic Intervention'. *Psychotherapy: Theory, Research and Practice* 15, no. 3 (1978): 241–47.

Daston, Lorraine. 'The Moral Economy of Science.' *Osiris* 10 (1995): 2–24.

Dawson, Graham. *Solider Heroes: British Adventure, Empire and the Imagining of Masculinities*. Abingdon: Routledge, 1994.

Delap, Lucy. 'Feminism, Masculinities and Emotional Politics in Late Twentieth Century Britain'. *Cultural and Social History* 15, no. 4 (2018): 571–93.

Ehn, Billy, and Orvar Löfgren. 'Emotions in Academia'. In *The Emotions: A Cultural Reader*, edited by Helena Wulff, 101–18. Oxford: Berg, 2007.

Fox Keller, Evelyn. *A Feeling for the Organism: the Life and Work of Barbara McClintock*. New York: WH Freeman, 1983.

Fraser, Erica L. 'Masculinity in the Personal Narratives of Soviet Nuclear Physicists'. *Aspasia* 8 (2014): 45–63.

Gould, Paula. 'Women and the Culture of University Physics in Late Nineteenth-Century Cambridge'. *The British Journal for the History of Science* 30, no. 2 (1997): 127–49.

Hermanowicz, Joseph C. 'Scientists and Satisfaction'. *Social Studies of Science* 33, no. 1 (2003): 45–73.

Hochschild, Arlie Russell. *The Managed Heart: Commercialization of Human Feeling*. California: University of California Press, 2003 [1983].

Jones, Claire. *Femininity, Mathematics and Science, 1880–1914*. Basingstoke: Palgrave Macmillan, 2009.

Karlsohn, Thomas. 'The Academic Seminar as Emotional Community'. *Nordic Journal of Studies in Educational Policy* (2016): 2–3. https://www.tandfonline.com/action/showCitFormats?doi=10.3402%2Fnstep.v2.33724.

Langhamer, Claire. 'Feelings, Women and Work in the Long 1950s'. *Women's History Review* 26, no. 1 (2017): 77–92.

Latour, Bruno. *Pandora's Hope: Essays on the Reality of Science Studies*. London: Harvard University Press, 1999.

McDowell, Linda. *Capital Culture: Gender at Work in the City*. Oxford: Blackwells, 1997.
Morris, J. Andrew, and Daniel C. Feldman. 'Managing Emotions in the Workplace'. *Journal of Managerial Issues* 9, no. 3 (1997): 257–74.
Plamper, Jan. *The History of Emotions: An Introduction*. Oxford: Oxford University Press, 2015.
Roper, Michael. *Masculinity and the British Organization Man since 1945*. Oxford: Oxford University Press, 1994.
Roper, Michael. 'Re-remembering the Soldier Hero: the Psychic and Social Construction of Memory in Personal Narratives of the Great War'. *History Workshop Journal* 50, no. 1 (2000): 181–204.
Roper, Michael. 'Slipping Out of View: Subjectivity and Emotion in Gender History'. *History Workshop Journal* 59 (2005): 57–72.
Roper, Michael. 'The Unconscious Work of History'. *Cultural and Social History* 11, no. 2 (2014): 169–93.
Rossiter, Margaret W. 'The Matthew Matilda Effect in Science'. *Social Studies of Science* 23 (1993): 325–41.
Söderqvist, Thomas. 'Existential Projects and Existential Choice in Science: Science Biography as an Edifying Genre'. In *Telling Lives in Science*, edited by Michael Shortland and Richard Yeo, 45–84. Cambridge: Cambridge University Press, 1996.
Summerfield, Penny. 'Culture and Composure: Creating Narratives of the Gendered Self in Oral History Interviews'. *Cultural and Social History* 1 (2004): 65–93.
Summerfield, Penny. *Reconstructing Women's Wartime Lives: Discourse and Subjectivity in Oral Histories of the Second World War*. Manchester: Manchester University Press, 1998.
Traweek, Sharon. *Beamtimes and Lifetimes: The World of High Energy Physicists*. London: Harvard University Press, 1988.
Turkle, Sherry. *Falling for Science: Objects in Mind*. London: The MIT Press, 2011.
Williams, Carol. *Madingley Rise and Early Geophysics at Cambridge*. London: Third Millennium Publishing, 2009.

9

Control your feelings and be a leader

Representations of women, emotions and career in Brazilian media

Tatiane Leal

An image illustrates a 2010 cover of *Veja*, Brazil's leading weekly magazine: female legs crossed, wearing black shoes with very high heels, occupying the entire cover space, next to the headline 'The Heiresses of a Revolution'.[1] A similar allegory appears on the cover of another weekly magazine, *Época*, in 2012. This time, the giant female shoe steps on the tie of a prostrated man, who venerates her with his eyes, accompanied by the title 'The women won the war of the sexes'.[2]

It is not a coincidence that these covers resemble each other. The imaginary universe of majestic high heels marked the early 2010s in Brazilian media. Music, soap operas, commercials, self-help books and reports announced a new female identity: *the powerful woman*. Icon of a post-feminist sensibility, the new millennium's Brazilian woman would achieve a balance between traditional femininity and contemporary empowerment, reconciling desires (or demands) that society traditionally attributes to women, such as marriage, family and beauty, with success and power at work.[3] This powerful woman would reap the fruits of the liberation brought by the feminist movement, echoing McRobbie's thesis of a 'mediatic post-feminism' that celebrates feminism from the assertion that it is not necessary anymore.[4] The 'heirs of a revolution' did not achieve equality but something better: they overcame men, combining power and femininity.

These new women were different from previous generations because they occupied higher positions in the job market, justified by an alleged contemporary predilection for female leaders by Brazilian companies. It is no coincidence that the man's formal shirt and tie trodden on by the elegant black shoe on the cover of *Época* made direct reference to the corporate world. In the same period, covers such as 'The lessons of the women big bosses'[5] (*Veja*, 2012) and 'The secret of women who got there'[6] (*Época*, 2014) used testimonies from women who rose to prominent positions in the corporate world. They work both as evidence for the thesis defended by the magazines and as pedagogical models to follow. The magazines attribute the recent success of women leaders to a growing recognition by companies of an essential female competitive advantage: their emotions. More sensitive than men, they would be more attentive leaders to their employees and run more empathic companies. The magazine articles follow a model that Freire Filho calls self-help journalism and attempt to teach the 'correct' handling of emotions.[7]

This chapter investigates how Brazilian media represented the relationship between gender, emotions and work in the early 2010s. The aim is to understand how these journalistic discourses engender contemporary female subjectivities and negotiate socio-historical visions about emotions and gender identities. Brazil is a country marked by social inequality and a series of barriers faced by women, such as the persistence of domestic and sexual violence, sexism in institutions and cultural discourses, the low political representation of women, the precariousness of reproductive rights and the wage discrepancy between men and women[8] – a set of factors that is intensified for Black women.[9] Therefore, it is essential to uncover how Brazilian media discourse understands the idea of female power and negotiates traditional and contemporary aspects in (re) producing values about women, work and emotions, and to investigate how these discourses address (or do not address) the persistence of these inequalities in Brazilian reality.

Women, emotions and media

Western culture has historically defined women as emotional beings. In both 'common sense' and 'scientific thinking', both emotions and women are considered natural entities, therefore chaotic, irrational and potentially dangerous. They must be managed and instrumentalized, subordinated to reason's design. Medical and psychological discourses established distinctions between ideal femininity, with characteristics such as sensitivity, meekness and passivity, and pathological femininity, related to madness and hysteria.[10]

This conception is also present in Brazilian culture but with specificities. The supposed 'emotional Brazilian' historically represents the cultural identity in this country. This stereotype, present in the Portuguese colonizers' speeches and, later, explored by Brazilian social scientists, also appears positively in 'common sense': a self-image of an affectionate, sociable and cheerful people, in contrast to the alleged coldness of Europeans and Americans.[11] However, if Brazilian men can be associated with emotions, it happens only according to explicit cultural rules. While emotionality is considered a positive sign of masculinity in specific contexts such as among passionate football fans, Brazilian culture still perpetuates hegemonic masculinities that associate sensitivity with male homosexuality or women.[12] In turn, Brazilian women are traditionally associated with sensible subjectivities, appropriated to caring for others and domesticity, reinforcing the gender division between public and private.[13]

The association between women, the body and a lack of emotional control is also historically situated in Brazil. Vieira's analysis of the theses defended by gynaecology students at Brazilian universities in the nineteenth century reveals how this imagery appears in scientific discourse.[14] The female body, it was held, would make women more susceptible to pathological states, like 'menstrual madness'. The result is the recommendation that they remain in the private sphere: 'Given the psychic status of women in these conditions, Icard, Berthier and Lawson Tait even say that women should stay away from public affairs.'[15]

In this context of moral condemnation of women's work and the appreciation of motherhood as their natural objective, the female labour force was gradually expelled from Brazilian factories. In 1872 they constituted 76 per cent of the factories' workforce, but by 1950 they represented only 23 per cent. Occupation outside the home was classified as a threat to honour and family.[16] Medical and popular discourses converged on the universalization of emotions as phenomena of the body and women as subjects whose social role should be defined by this corporeality.

Studies within history, social sciences and feminist theory refute the idea that emotions are essential and universal phenomena, pointing out how emotionality is historically and socially constructed and how emotion expression protocols are learnt inside a culture, even when perceptions about feelings are internalized as 'natural'.[17] The micropolitical dimension of sentimental discourse is essential to understand how power relations permeate the production of emotions relating to gender identities.[18] From men, society expects courage, rationality and disciplined aggressiveness. On the other hand, women need to demonstrate kindness, compassion and optimism. It is from the reproduction of this emotional culture that these distinctions are built and maintained. Historically, Western society considers rationality more reliable and professional than sensibility, reserved for the domain of the home.[19]

In this perspective, discourses produce not only the emotions they talk about but also the subjects themselves. For Ahmed, emotions act discursively and politically, shaping male and female bodies from the constant repetition of performative acts.[20] This process's cultural construction becomes erased, and this emotional culture 'sticks' to these bodies, being understood as natural expressions, which contributes to the maintenance of the power structures.[21]

The construction of female subjectivity involves a rhetoric of controlling emotions.[22] Freire Filho points out the media's centrality in the discursive production of emotions, gender and sociability.[23] The proliferation of magazines and television programmes aimed at women is part of this pedagogy of behaviours. From an early age, the girl is surrounded by media that promise to teach her how to act and behave to adapt to the social parameters that will make her feel included and desired.[24] In this way, we can understand media as a teaching device, whose discourses contribute to classifying emotional experiences and behaviours as desirable or dangerous, healthy or pathological, productive or unproductive.[25]

In a cultural context in which neoliberalism becomes more than an economic system, constituting a dominant *ethos*, each subject is called to reach success individually by finding the emotional and subjective instruments for this achievement within oneself.[26] This imperative calls on women to engage with post-feminist discourses that reinforce that barriers to gender equity must be overcome based on individual empowerment, an ethos that also influences contemporary Brazilian culture.[27] Thus, media narratives dedicated to advising women on their work relationships offer an opportunity to glimpse contemporary discourses on gender and emotions. How are women, traditionally seen as emotional beings and, therefore, locked up in the private space, called upon to manage their affective lives in order to become business leaders?

Methodology and notes on the Brazilian context

This chapter analyses representations of gender, emotions and work in reports published between 2010 and 2014 in the Brazilian magazines *Veja* (Look) and *Época* (Epoch). These media outlets were chosen because they are, respectively, the leader and vice leader among the country's most widely circulated weekly magazines.[28] The oldest is *Veja*, from *Editora Abril* (Abril Publishers), launched in 1968, inspired by the American magazine *Time*. Although much more recent, *Época*, launched in 1998 by *Editora Globo* (Globo Publishers), reached prominence by becoming the main competitor of *Veja* in the Brazilian market. They position themselves as opinion makers and key media outlets to understand and discuss society.[29]

Their target audience includes men (*Veja*: 51 per cent; *Época*: 50 per cent) and women (49 per cent; 50 per cent), reaching mainly adults, from thirty to more than fifty years old (*Veja*: 69.3 per cent; *Época*: 72 per cent). However, the magazines also reach young people up to thirty years old, teenagers and even children, groups that share the remaining percentages (*Veja*: 30.7 per cent; *Época*: 27 per cent). Upper- and upper-middle-class readers are the majority (55 per cent; 67 per cent), followed by the lower-middle class (36.6 per cent; 29 per cent). The poorest represent only 8.4 per cent of readers of *Veja* and 4 per cent for *Época*.[30] The magazines address various themes such as politics, economics, science, culture and society.

For this chapter, I have selected five cover stories about women in the labour market for qualitative analysis: 'Screams that made history' (*Veja*, 2010);[31] 'The lessons of the presidents' (*Veja*, 2012);[32] 'Is the war of the sexes over?' (*Época*, 2012);[33] 'How to make a truce for the sexes' (*Época*, 2013);[34] and 'They want the top' (*Época*, 2014).[35] The cover stories stand out in these magazines, with higher visibility and bigger size than the others. These five articles vary between four and ten pages.

I selected the period 2010–14 because it was just before the outbreak of the so-called Feminist Spring in Brazil, a series of demonstrations that proliferated in 2015, and which included street protests and online campaigns around feminist issues.[36] Therefore, among other discourses that highlight the enduring nature of gender inequalities in Brazil, it is important to understand the magazines' discourses about the supposed overcoming of the 'war of the sexes'.

I analyse these articles from a Foucauldian perspective, understanding that discourse is a practice that builds this reality while naming it.[37] To study media representations based on Foucault is to investigate how the media works by constructing the world that it says it objectively portrays.[38] Thus, analysing the conceptions of women, work and emotions that magazines produce means to investigate, qualitatively, how these discourses promote certain concepts of feminine subjectivity as ideal, normal or desirable, based on continuities and discontinuities between them and with other statements that historically circulated in a culture.

Periodical studies also provide a theoretical-methodological basis for this investigation. They understand magazines as *cultural objects* that can be privileged materials to investigate modern and contemporary cultures since they articulate political, social, economic, scientific and cultural discourses that circulate at a place and a time.[39] From this perspective, I consider a set of visual and textual aspects within the chosen articles and their placement in the magazines: the article's structure; chosen words, arguments and images; interviewed specialists; readers' letters; and advertisements, since all these elements produce meanings in dialogue. The discussion goes on two sides: female emotions as powerful and risky in the workplace.

Carved to lead: Female emotions as powerful

'Big bosses', 'powerful', 'winners'. These are some of the adjectives used by the texts analysed to describe the new generation of women leaders. In 'They want the top' (*Época*, 2014), an engineer, a military woman, a legal director and a businesswoman illustrate the secrets to women achieving success: *gender cannot be an impediment*; *do not give up in fear of what will go wrong*; *believe in your ability*; and *it takes dedication and persistence*. Época celebrates a scenario of possibilities open to women, who may have depended on changes in society in the past but now would need only themselves to 'get there':

> Never have women gone so far: to the Republic's Presidency or Petrobras, the country's largest company. Achievements, as always, give rise to new and even more ambitious aspirations. Women want to stay in the lead and advance in many other areas. They conquered male-dominated territory. They counted on society changes (which allowed women aviator officers) and a high dose of personal determination. Their stories contain lessons for other pathfinders – and men as well.[40]

Published two years earlier, 'The lessons of the presidents' (*Veja*, 2012) was structured around the description of the individual trajectories of eight women 'big bosses' (managers and presidents of Brazilian companies). The article includes fifteen secrets to achieve success, such as: *use female characteristics in a balanced way to lead your team*; *use femininity to your advantage – invest in looking good*; *do not play the victim – sexism is not always the source of your failure*; and *accept criticism – your boss is not your husband*. Veja's article states that the big bosses' trajectories reflect a reality widely spread among Brazilian women:

> The era when women sought to match men at work is over. In a short time, this idea will only exist in the minds of old-fashioned feminists and some men. Armed

with intrinsically feminine skills – such as the ability to build relationships, work in groups, and communicate – they shattered the invisible barrier that separated them from the best and best-paid positions. In Brazil, women are the majority in universities and the workforce. They have spread across all departments, from sales to the most technical areas, such as engineering. Little by little, they move towards top organizations.[41]

The news story alternates individual trajectories with the voices of experts and figures from scientific studies, such as one that states that out of sixteen key competencies to exercise a commanding role, women would be better than men in twelve, they would tie in three and lose in only one ('to develop strategic perspective'). These results would mean, in the words of the magazine, that women were *naturally* leader material.

The articles are based on what Freire Filho calls 'self-help journalism', a type of journalism that offers quick guides to solving problems and conquering psychic and emotional goals. This type of reporting emulates techniques and aesthetics of self-help literature, reinforcing a conception of the self as an easily accessible and manageable repository. Often, the text presents some steps to be followed by the reader to achieve, for example, happiness, self-esteem and success. Specialists (usually from psychology or psychiatry) support the journalistic argumentation with the authorized voice of science. Furthermore, stories of ordinary individuals overcoming struggles exemplify and legitimate the advice presented.[42]

The notion of overcoming past difficulties does not appear only in the interviewees' trajectories. The article 'Screams that made history' (*Veja*, 2010) compares women's situation today with their social place in the middle of the twentieth century. The text begins by describing the hardships of a not-too-distant past in which 'the house was the rule'. This past scenario contrasts with the present when 'all that was left behind'. The entry of women into the labour market has transformed this context. The story evokes both feminism and the post-industrial economy to explain its causes. According to the magazine, 'if there is still sexism, at least on this scale, society has antibodies to fight it.'[43]

This transformation of the economy is presented as flattering for women. If they were confined for centuries to the private space due to their inherent sensitivity, that same nature has now become the justification for this meteoric rise to power: they are 'armed with intrinsically female skills'.[44] *Época* also presents this alleged innate aptitude of women for contemporary corporate style to justify why 'The woman won the war of the sexes' (*Época*, 2012): 'companies have been eagerly looking for characteristics considered, wrongly or not, more feminine than masculine – versatility, empathy with different groups, ability to perceive and reconcile different interests.'[45]

This appreciation of traditional female subjectivity at the workplace can be attributed to the development of affective capitalism throughout the twentieth century. For Illouz, the articulation between the affective life and the ethos of capitalism enabled the understanding of emotions based on the language of investment and profit. Individuals are called to manifest emotions in the right ways in order to establish better interpersonal relationships. Consequently, well-managed emotions can generate symbolic and financial gains, producing happy and successful individuals. At the workplace, leaders and employees should be empathetic, control anger and demonstrate sensitivity. Attributes previously considered feminine and reserved for the domestic space are now valued as assets in the corporate world.[46] This discourse continues to influence contemporary subjectivities, including in Brazil, where emotions management has won a prominent space in self-help literature and media, with discourses specifically addressed to women.[47]

However, it is crucial to analyse how these magazine articles redefine public and private boundaries. Professional success is just one of the pillars that keeps powerful presidents at the top. Returning to 'The lessons of the presidents', *Veja*'s concern was not only to obtain valuable lessons for the management of companies or to structure a good relationship with employees but also to show that these women are *more than executives*: they have families, hobbies, relationships. Furthermore, it is precisely from this private universe that they extract the feminine characteristics that would make them such good leaders, like the ability to care for others. This association is evident in the images that make up the story: they do not portray the 'big bosses' in their work environments but in moments of distraction in their private lives: cooking, doing Pilates, posing with ballet slippers, performing gardening activities, walking the dogs.

> Comfortable in her position, the woman who commands millionaire budgets is no different from the one who takes care of the garden, the one who walks dogs in the park, or the one who likes to cook for friends – as the eight women in charge of large corporations prove, in the pages that follow, they reveal their secrets to reaching the top of their career.[48]

Work is treated here as an extension of the private world. Inextricably linked to women, the private is where they can truly express their natural characteristics. There is a reinforcement of the idea of feminine essence. The magazines constantly affirm the power of 'female characteristics' without raising questions about how society produced these conceptions and without considering that women can be different from each other. To exalt positive skills among stereotypes established in a patriarchal society does not fail to reinforce them, as both emotions and women are reinforced, in this discourse, as natural and essential entities.[49]

These tensions also appear in other elements of the magazines. Advertising also celebrates powerful women: 'Whenever they look in the mirror, women find themselves more and more independent and successful', says an ad for a clothing store.[50] However, other ads reinforce traditional demands of femininity, especially beauty care. A shampoo ad equalizes beauty and success in importance ('Your hair must shine as much as your achievements').[51] A tampon ad redirects empowerment to romantic relationships: an image of a man observing a woman appears beside the text 'Confidence makes you more beautiful day and night'.[52]

A skinny model in a supplement advert illustrates the imperative: 'Eliminate the extra pounds from your body and your conscience.'[53] This calling also appears in other magazines, as shown by *Época*'s announcement of women's magazine *Marie Claire*. A Brazilian celebrity with a sexy dress illustrates the slogan: 'With everything on! In October, a special issue on the body for you to take care of yours'.[54] Therefore, along with the imperatives of success in the cover stories, there are demands of attaining the perfect body and the desired man, demonstrating that new aspirations of femininity coexist with traditional models.

Working women also appear in advertising, but before discussing these images, it is important to return to the news stories to highlight the race and class intersections in their gender representations. Concerning the production of a reality in which female career success is ubiquitous, it is essential to emphasize that the magazines' portraits of leaders represent a particular feature: all the characters mentioned are white upper-class women. Maids and nannies do not appear as subjects in labour but as instruments for powerful leaders' success. As *Veja* says, 'One in four Brazilian mothers who work full time has the support of nannies or maids, which allows them to take on greater professional challenges [. . .] These domestic services are still cheap in Brazil, especially compared to Europe.'[55] In Brazil, 92 per cent of domestic workers are women and 63.4 per cent are Black women. The role is precarious: 71.6 per cent of domestic workers do not have a formal contract and labour rights.[56] The celebration of 'cheap services' demonstrates that the promotion of women's victories at work universalizes white upper-class women's experience compared to the complex Brazilian reality, erasing inequalities.

These images are in contradiction with some present in the advertisements of these editions. Eight photographs of different women – Black, white, indigenous, women with disabilities, mothers, scientists and professionals – illustrate an advertisement by the federal government: 'In today's Brazil, women conquer their space and participate in building a stronger Brazil.'[57] Here, propaganda exalts Brazilian women's diversity, with strength being the common element. In another advertisement, by a Brazilian private entity that supports small businesses, the image of a smiling Black woman is accompanied by the text 'I believe in myself, in my business, that I will sell everything, that I will kill a lion a day, that tomorrow everything starts again'.[58] A Black woman represents the entrepreneurial woman capable of conducting her own business successfully. Although cover stories portray subjects in privileged positions, advertising presents empowerment as achievable for all women.

Readers' letters about 'The lessons of the presidents' (*Veja*), published in the next edition of the magazine, reinforce this perception: of the nine letters, only one presents an opposing view, reinforcing that the perfect balance between personal life and leadership proposed by the magazine is unattainable and subjects women to a double or triple workday. The eight others celebrate a new world where conquests are open to all women who work hard and trust in their own capacities. One of the readers shares her own story of conquering a large company's management, and two male readers extol the effort of these women, one stating that they 'proved that they do not need quotas to reach the top'.[59]

Therefore, the arguments of the magazines follow a contradictory path. The mention of gender, when associated with structural difficulties, is quickly dismissed. Supported by individual success stories, the articles respond to the neoliberal ethos by calling on individual women to take responsibility for pursuing their success, reinforcing the post-feminist rhetoric that collective mobilizations for structural transformations would no longer be necessary.[60]

On the other hand, this individual success is credited to gender itself, reinforcing the conception of a feminine nature. The apparent contradiction produces a discourse that maintains power structures. The relationship between female subjectivity, a more prominent emotionality and the natural relationship with the private world is maintained, updating itself only to meet neoliberal capitalism's demands. Emotionality shapes the female bodies in this discourse.[61] Women have always been like that, but only now do companies recognize these natural advantages. Each woman would be responsible for turning their emotions into productive assets; otherwise, they turn into a risk.

The rhetoric of control and the risks of femininity

The stories treat female emotions as a competitive differential in building a successful life. However, women need to manage these emotions to correspond to an adequate pattern of behaviour. When out of control, femininity can pose a potential danger. There is a frequent warning that women must not get carried away by emotions and must use them in a balanced way. There is a pedagogy that teaches women to express their emotions correctly.[62]

In 2013, *Época* published 'Men & women: the war of the sexes at work'.[63] If the magazine presented the war as won in the previous year, this new report analyses the 'blind spots' that would hinder the professional relationship between men and women, in another example of 'self-help journalism'. If women's presence at the workplace is now a reality, they are still considered the *second sex* in these spaces – they got there later and brought difficulties for themselves and men. Explanatory boxes detail the main reasons for disagreements between men and women at work: 'women talk too much'; 'men do not listen to women'; 'women want to change men'; 'men are afraid to speak to them'; 'women feel excluded'; 'men do not value women'; 'women are too emotional'; 'men are insensitive'. The key to overcoming these obstacles, according to *Época*, is to know these *natural* differences and manage them to increase productivity at work.

The rhetoric of control aimed at women involves the idea of an out-of-control counterpoint, something wild that can be a threat to order, which is evident in this news story.[64] Although the advice also addresses men, their job is mostly understanding the needs of (often excessive) female emotional expression. Women would always be at risk of emotionality outside the tone of the corporate environment. Their uncontrollable streams could quickly turn into hysterical aggression or fragility that could burst into tears. As the problem 'they are afraid to talk to them' shows, 'men need to overcome this fear', and 'women must try to contain their emotions and separate the personal from the professional'. Here, the private and the public again appear inseparable from the female, but this time, negatively.[65]

One of the problems is, precisely, 'they are too emotional'. Therefore, women must be aware of how they express emotions in the workplace. An exaggerated sensitivity ('they feel excluded') or an excessive display of dissatisfaction ('they talk too much') could generate unproductive and stressful work environments. The news story exemplifies these concerns with a problematic coexistence between two executives of a company, a man and a woman. The image accompanying the narrative shows a woman laughing wildly with her mouth open and her eyes closed – a graphic sign typical of comics to emphasize the feeling of noise – wearing a misaligned outfit, touching a man's arm who cringes, scared, bringing his hands to his face to protect himself. He has his eyes closed and an expression of suffering.[66] These discourses reinforce the idea that work is a space of rationality – therefore, a masculine place par excellence. They maintain traditional hierarchies between reason/emotion and male/female. If emotions can be potent for women, this is possible only after emotional work that transforms them into capital.

The other extreme of hysterical aggressiveness would be the risk of excessive sensitivity. The story calls men to 'police themselves so as not to leave them [*women*] unattended'.[67] This feminine fragility would lead to problems since men fear that women are offended by receiving negative feedback, so 'they [*men*] are afraid to talk to them [*women*]'.[68] Men also 'do not value women enough' since their emotionality demands constant demonstrations and women need praise and recognition at each step of the job.[69]

In 'The lessons of the presidents', *Veja* also identifies a series of deviations in female subjectivity. Women would always be on the threshold between the positive expression of emotions and the lack of control that generates weakness, distrust and risk. *Veja* teaches, for example, the importance of holding back tears in the workplace, a problem presented as susceptible to happen at any time with women ('crying is allowed but at the right time'):

> Some professional moments can be exciting, such as when a boss receives a tribute from his team or when colleagues congratulate an executive who is going to retire. In these moments, expressing sensitivity by shedding tears is opportune and even beneficial for the career. Showing emotion in the workplace generates empathy, one of the great skills for any leader. As they are more sensitive than men, women should take advantage of this. However, it is worth remembering that the right cry is that of emotion, not weakness, and it needs to be in proportion. 'It is not good crying at all in times of high pressure, or when faced with a new goal or challenge', says Sérgio Averbach from São Paulo, from the consultancy Kom / Ferry, specialized in training leaders.[70]

Thus, the uncontrollable character of the passions would make the emotional person (woman) at the same time more vulnerable and more dangerous than the rational individual (man).[71] Despite all the celebratory discourses about female leadership, the stereotype of hysteria would haunt these leaders, who should follow the magazines' advice and 'mix female and male characteristics' to avoid an overly emotional reaction, leading to tears and aggressive reactions. To *Veja*, this risk is evident, and the big bosses' secrets tell women what not to do:

> If someone interrupts or steals your idea, you must repeat your opinion and make it clear that the proposal in question is yours, in a polite way and *without becoming hysterical* (my emphasis).[72]
>
> Even though *women are more depressed* and feel emotions at twice the intensity of men, criticism can help them grow and improve a blind spot in their career (my emphasis).[73]

The choice of the words *hysterical* and *depressive* demonstrates the construction of a female subjectivity in which the emotional lack of control could assume pathological contours. This uncontrolled woman echoes the stereotype present in nineteenth-century sentimental literature: women who let themselves be 'out of control', 'sad' and 'temperamental' lived in disarray and were responsible for the unhappiness of their husbands and children.[74] At the same time that they announce an era in which women have overcome gender inequalities and conquered the highest positions in the corporate world, these magazines reverberate traditional discourses that reinforce female subjectivity as potentially inadequate. If the risks were applied to the domestic space before, they now extend to the work universe.

Therefore, the barrier to female success would not be in structural inequalities but in the incorrect handling of emotions that would make it impossible for women to overcome the risks inherent in their own nature. The discourse valorizing female aptitudes has clear limits. Only individual emotional work could overcome the potential risk, transforming this dangerous essence into affective capital. Therefore, this discourse maintains the hierarchies of power between men and women at work and transfers to the individual the responsibility for her own success or failure.

Final considerations

The powerful women can do everything and still be in high heels. The image of these shoes, so often used in Brazilian media in the early 2010s, represents the maintenance of femininity in women's rise in the workplace. The *Veja* and *Época* stories reinforce a traditional view of female subjectivity in which both femininity and emotions are natural and universal entities. The novelty of magazines' discourse is that female emotion becomes powerful when managed, constituting an affective capital. However, if they do not respond to strict control practices, emotions (and women) can become dangerous and inappropriate. Thus, always working from dichotomies, magazines continue to oppose rational men – therefore, constant and reliable – to emotional, potentially hysterical, tearful and weak women, that is, unpredictable.

These stories, imbued with the aura of journalistic objectivity, act discursively as instruments of neoliberal rationality, helping to inscribe in the individual the imperative of self-government to capitalize emotions, producing a female subjectivity conformed to the demands of performance at work, without changing the traditional gender hierarchy. Thus, at least in these magazines, the beginning of the 2010s was represented as the advent of a new era in which oppressions were behind, and each woman would have powerful leaders as inspirational role models to follow her own path. Other prominent inequalities in Brazil, such as race and class, were not addressed by these articles.

Shortly after, the same country saw an explosion of feminist discourses in which one of the main tenets is the right to be in the public space.[75] The coexistence of celebratory speeches about women who dominated the workplace and claims denouncing that women can be the target of violence for their simple presence on the streets seems contradictory. However, these contradictions point to a discursive battlefield in which different forms of being a woman in society are in dispute. Recognizing the complexity of these flows of power provides tools to question ideals of female success and freedom present in the media, especially in discourses that do not alter traditional representations about women and their emotions.

Notes

1   *Veja*, 'As herdeiras de uma revolução', 1.
2   *Época*, 'A mulher venceu a guerra dos sexos', 1.
3   Gill, *Gender and the Media*, 249.
4   McRobbie, 'Post-feminism and Popular Culture', 255–6.
5   *Veja*, 'As lições das chefonas', 1.
6   *Época*, 'O segredo das mulheres que chegaram lá', 1.
7   Freire Filho, 'The Power Itself', 720.
8   Miguel and Biroli, *Feminismo e Política*, 9–16.
9   Ribeiro, *O que é lugar de fala?*, 40–2.
10 Freire Filho, 'Chains of Happiness', 65–71; Lutz, 'Engendered Emotion', 70–3.
11 Rezende, 'O brasileiro emotivo', 94–5.

12 Rios and Coelho, 'Emotion and Masculinity', 31–2; Bento, *Homem Não Tece a Dor*, 95.
13 Freire Filho, 'Chains of Happiness', 78.
14 Vieira, *A medicalização do corpo feminino*, 27–46.
15 Silva, 'Da menstruação', 83. Quoted in Vieira, *A medicalização do corpo feminino*, 43.
16 Rago, 'Trabalho feminino e sexualidade', 582.
17 Frevert, *Emotions in History*, 3–18; Illouz, *O Amor nos Tempos do Capitalismo*, 7–13; Rezende and Coelho, *Antropologia das emoções*, 9–17.
18 Rezende and Coelho, *Antropologia das emoções*, 75–8.
19 Illouz, *O Amor nos Tempos do Capitalismo*, 7–59.
20 Ahmed, *The Cultural Politics of Emotions*, 13; Butler, *Problemas de Gênero*, 240.
21 Ahmed, *The Cultural Politics of Emotions*, 8.
22 Lutz, 'Engendered Emotion', 71–3.
23 Freire Filho, 'Chains of Happiness', 68–70.
24 Fischer, *Trabalhar com Foucault*, 113–32.
25 Freire Filho, 'Chains of Happiness', 68.
26 Ehrenberg, *O Culto da Performance*, 9–14.
27 McRobbie, 'Post-feminism and Popular Culture'; Castellano, 'Be a Winner Woman', 1.
28 Nascimento, 'Brazilian Press and Denunciation', 68.
29 Benetti and Hagen, 'Journalism and the Itself Image', 129–33.
30 *Veja*, 'Mídia kit Veja'; *Época*, 'Mídia kit Época'.
31 Góes, 'Gritos que fizeram história', 18–22.
32 Gianini, 'As lições das presidentes', 82–91.
33 Coronato, Lins and Yuri, 'A guerra dos sexos acabou?', 68–74.
34 Oliveira, 'Como fazer a trégua dos sexos', 84–91.
35 Buscato, 'Elas querem o topo', 60–5.
36 Bogado, 'Rua', 23–42.
37 Foucault, *Arqueologia do Saber*, 60; Foucault, *História da Sexualidade I*, 111–13.
38 Fischer, *Trabalhar com Foucault*, 133–4.
39 Latham and Scholes, 'The Rise of Periodical Studies', 517–31; Hammill, Hjartarson, and McGregor, 'Introduction', iii–xiii.
40 Buscato, 'Elas querem o topo', 61–2.
41 Gianini, 'As lições das presidentes', 82.
42 Freire Filho, 'The Power Itself', 717–45.
43 Góes, 'Gritos que fizeram história', 22.
44 Gianini, 'As lições das presidentes', 83.
45 Coronato, Lins and Yuri, 'A guerra dos sexos acabou?', 71.
46 Illouz, *O Amor nos Tempos do Capitalismo*, 7–59.
47 Castellano, 'Be a Winner Woman', 1.

48 Gianini, 'As lições das presidentes', 83.
49 Wittig, 'One is not Born a Woman', 103–9.
50 *Veja*, Renner Advertisement, 1 March 2010, 21.
51 *Veja*, Seda Advertisement, 1 March 2010, 9.
52 *Veja*, Intimus Advertisement, 1 March 2010, 88.
53 *Veja*, Nutrilipo Advertisement, 2 May 2012, 99.
54 *Época*, Marie Claire Advertisement, 8 October 2012, 110.
55 Gianini, 'As lições das presidentes', 83.
56 Brasil, *Relatório anual socioeconômico da mulher*, 17–19.
57 *Época*, Brazilian Federal Government Advertisement, 10 March 2014, 38–9.
58 *Época*, Sebrae Advertisement, 8 October 2012, 102–3.
59 Renato M P (Águas Claras), Rosana C (Goiânia), Vitória D (Curitiba), Gênys A (São Paulo), Melissa D (Curitiba), Jacqueline C (by email), Rafael A P (São Paulo), Vítor Hugo S A (Divinópolis), *Veja*, 9 May 2012, 42–4, comments on *Veja*, 'As lições das presidentes'.
60 McRobbie, 'Post-feminism and Popular Culture', 259.
61 Ahmed, *The Cultural Politics of Emotions*, 4.
62 Freire Filho, 'Chains of Happiness', 70–1.
63 *Época*, 'Homens & mulheres', 1.
64 Lutz, 'Engendered Emotion', 71–3.
65 Oliveira, 'Como fazer a trégua dos sexos', 84–91.
66 Oliveira, 'Como fazer a trégua dos sexos', 84–5.
67 Oliveira, 'Como fazer a trégua dos sexos', 87.
68 Oliveira, 'Como fazer a trégua dos sexos', 89.
69 Oliveira, 'Como fazer a trégua dos sexos', 90–1.
70 Gianini, 'As lições das presidentes', 84.
71 Rezende and Coelho, *Antropologia das emoções*, 25.
72 Gianini, 'As lições das presidentes', 88.
73 Gianini, 'As lições das presidentes', 88.
74 Schnog, 'Changing Emotions', 84–109.
75 Bogado, 'Rua', 33–4.

Bibliography

Ahmed, Sara. *The Cultural Politics of Emotions*. Edinburgh: Edinburgh University Press, 2014.

Benetti, Marcia, and Sean Hagen. 'Journalism and the itself Image: The Institutional Discourse of the Weekly Magazines'. *Estudos em Jornalismo e Mídia* 7, no. 1 (January/July 2010): 123–35. https://doi.org/10.5007/1984-6924.2010v7n1p123.

Bento, Berenice. *Homem Não Tece a Dor: Queixas e Perplexidades Masculinas*. Natal: EDUFRN, 2015.

Bogado, Maria. 'Rua'. In *Explosão Feminista: Arte, Cultura, Política e Universidade*, edited by Heloisa Buarque de Hollanda, 23–42. São Paulo: Companhia das Letras, 2019.

Brasil. Presidência da República. Secretaria de Políticas para as Mulheres. *Relatório Anual Socioeconômico da Mulher*. Brasília: Secretaria de Políticas para Mulheres, 2015.

Buscato, Marcela. 'Elas querem o topo'. *Época*, 10 March 2014.

Butler, Judith. *Problemas de Gênero: Feminismo e Subversão da Identidade*. Translated by Renato Aguiar. Rio de Janeiro: Civilização Brasileira, 2016.

Castellano, Mayka. '"Be a Winner Woman!": Gender Peculiarities and Success Definitions on Self-Help Literature'. *E-Compós* 18, no. 2 (May/August 2015): 1–16. https://doi.org/10.30962/ec.1131.

Coronato, Marcos, Marina Navarro Lins, and Flávia Yuri. 'A guerra dos sexos acabou?' *Época*, 8 October 2012.

Ehrenberg, Alain. *O Culto da Performance: da Aventura Empreendedora à Depressão Nervosa*. Translated by Pedro F. Bendassolli. Aparecida: Ideias e Letras, 2010.

Época. 'A mulher venceu a guerra dos sexos'. 8 October 2012.

Época. 'Homens & mulheres: A guerra dos sexos no trabalho'. 2 December 2013.

Época. 'Mídia kit Época'. https://irp-cdn.multiscreensite.com/43f3dabf/files/uplo aded/midia%20kit%20%C3%A9poca%202020-atualizado_14.07.pdf (accessed 16 December 2020).

Época. 'O segredo das mulheres que chegaram lá'. 10 March 2014.

Fischer, Rosa Maria Bueno. *Trabalhar com Foucault: Arqueologia de uma Paixão*. Belo Horizonte: Autêntica, 2012.

Foucault, Michel. *A Arqueologia do Saber*. Translated by Luiz Felipe Baeta Neves. Rio de Janeiro: Forense Universitária, 2016.

Foucault, Michel. *História da Sexualidade I: A Vontade de Saber*. Translated by Maria Thereza da Costa Albuquerque and J. A. Guilhon Albuquerque. São Paulo: Graal, 2011.

Freire Filho, João. 'Chains of Happiness: Emotions, Gender, and Power'. *Matrizes* 11, no. 1 (January/April 2017): 61–81. http://dx.doi.org/10.11606/issn.1982-8160.v11i1p61 -81.

Freire Filho, João. 'The Power Itself: Journalism Self-help and Building Self-Esteem'. *Famecos* 18, no. 3 (2011): 717–45. https://doi.org/10.15448/1980-3729.2011.3.103 79.

Frevert, Ute. *Emotions in History: Lost and Found*. Budapest: Central European University Press, 2011.

Gianini, Tatiana. 'As lições das presidentes'. *Veja*, 2 May 2012.

Gill, Rosalind. *Gender and the Media*. New Hampshire: Polity, 2007.

Góes, Marta. 'Gritos que fizeram história'. *Veja*, 1 March 2010.

Hammill, Faye, Paul Hjartarson, and Hannah McGregor. 'Introduction–Magazines and/as Media: Periodical Studies and the Question of Disciplinarity'. *The Journal of Modern Periodical Studies* 6, no. 2 (2015): iii–xiii. https://doi.org/10.5325/jmodeperistud.6.2.iii.

Illouz, Eva. *O Amor nos Tempos do Capitalismo*. Translated by Vera Ribeiro. Rio de Janeiro: Zahar, 2011.

Latham, Sean, and Robert Scholes. 'The Rise of Periodical Studies'. *PMLA* 121, no. 2 (March 2006): 517–31. https://www.jstor.org/stable/25486329.

Lutz, Catherine. 'Engendered Emotion: Gender, Power and the Rhetoric of Emotional Control in American Discourse'. In *Language and the Politics of Emotion*, edited by Catherine A. Lutz and Lila Abu-Lughod, 69–91. New York: Cambridge University Press, 1990.

McRobbie, Angela. 'Post-feminism and Popular Culture'. *Feminist Media Studies* 4, no. 3 (2004): 255–64. https://doi.org/10.1080/1468077042000309937.

Miguel, Luis Felipe, and Flávia Biroli. *Feminismo e Política*. São Paulo: Boitempo, 2014.

Nascimento, Solano. 'Brazilian Press and Denunciation: an Analysis of Two Decades in the Predilection for Showing Problems'. *Verso e Reverso* XXVII, no. 65 (2013): 68–76. https://doi.org/10.4013/ver.2013.27.65.01.

Oliveira, Graziele. 'Como fazer a trégua dos sexos'. *Época*, 2 December 2013.

Rago, Margareth. 'Trabalho Feminino e Sexualidade'. In *História das Mulheres no Brasil*, edited by Mary del Priore, 578–606. São Paulo: Contexto, 2012.

Rezende, Claudia Barcellos, and Maria Claudia Coelho. *Antropologia das emoções*. Rio de Janeiro: FGV, 2010.

Rezende, Claudia Barcellos. 'O brasileiro emotivo: Reflexões sobre a construção de uma identidade brasileira'. *Revista Brasileira de Sociologia da Emoção* 2, no. 4 (April 2003): 93–112.

Ribeiro, Djamila. *O que é Lugar de Fala?* Belo Horizonte: Letramento, 2017.

Rios, Fábio Daniel da Silva, and Maria Claudia Pereira Coelho. 'Emotion and Masculinity in Brazilian Soccer World'. *Pagu*, no. 58 (August 2020): 1–35. https://doi.org/10.1590/18094449202000580007.

Schnog, Nancy. 'Changing Emotions: Moods and the Nineteenth-Century American Woman Writer'. In *Inventing the Psychological: Toward a Cultural History of Emotional Life in America*, edited by John Pfister and Nancy Schnog, 84–109. New Haven: Yale University Press, 1997.

Silva, Henrique Wenceslau. 'Da menstruação'. Faculdade de Medicina do Rio de Janeiro, 1891: 83. Quoted in Elisabeth Meloni Vieira, *A Medicalização do Corpo Feminino*. Rio de Janeiro: Fiocruz, 2015.

Vieira, Elisabeth Meloni. *A Medicalização do Corpo Feminino*. Rio de Janeiro: Fiocruz, 2015.

Veja. 'As herdeiras de uma revolução'. 1 March 2010.

Veja. 'As lições das chefonas'. 2 May 2012.

Veja. 'Mídia kit Veja'. http://publiabril.abril.com.br/marcas/veja/plataformas/revista-im
 pressa (accessed 16 December 2020).
Wittig, Monique. 'One is not Born a Woman'. In *The Lesbian and Gay Studies Reader*,
 edited by Henry Abelove, Michele Aina Barale, and David M. Halperin, 103–09.
 New York: Routledge, 1993.

Part III

Emotions, politics and power

10

'Violent emotions'

Canine suffering, emotional communities and the emotionally charged work of (anti) vivisection in London, New York and Paris

Chris Pearson

Anti-vivisectionists located their movement within the new humanitarian age in which the 'sentiment of mercy', in feminist and novelist Mona Caird's words, had replaced older morality codes. For Caird and others, scientific experimentation on live animals challenged the whole idea of civilization. How could civilized men and women, who possessed emotional sensitivity, support the cruel pain inflicted on dogs and other animals during vivisection? According to Caird, vivisection undermined white racial superiority as it put Europeans on the same emotional and moral level as 'ferocious savages'. For Caird, civilized behaviour meant sympathizing with those beyond your kinship group. Vivisectionists and 'savages' were unable to do this due to their underdeveloped emotions. 'Savages' satisfied their 'appetites on roast relative or boiled stranger', and vivisectionists were unable to feel sympathy for the animals they experimented on.[1] As this racialized understanding of sympathy suggested, the scientific work of vivisection raised interlocking and emotionally charged questions about civilization, pain, medicine, progress and human–animal relations. For opponents of vivisection, it caused 'the most atrocious suffering known to-day' and they felt passionately its impact on themselves, modern society and animals.[2] The very existence of vivisection was experienced as personal emotional anguish. It entered the dreams of anti-vivisectionist doctor Anna Kingsford, who was moved to declare that she would rather offer her own body for experimentation than see animals writhing in pain on the vivisectionist's table. As Carol Lansbury observes, 'her anguish became a passionate hatred for the men she termed devils', and Kingsford believed that her occult powers had led to the deaths of French vivisectionists Paul Bert and Claude Bernard.[3]

The scientific practice of working on live animals provoked 'violent emotions' (in the words of noted Harvard physiologist Walter B. Cannon), which so marked the vivisection debates in late-nineteenth- and early-twentieth-century London, New York and Paris.[4] Vivisection and the campaigns against it constituted profoundly emotional work. Transnational 'emotional communities' developed across London, New York and Paris that laboured to defend and attack vivisection. Historian of emotions Barbara Rosenwein describes an emotional community as comprising individuals 'tied together by fundamental assumptions, values, goals, feeling rules, and accepted modes of expression' who are members of a social group in which they have a common stake and interests.[5] According to Rosenwein, such groups change over time, define what is emotionally acceptable and promote emotional norms. During the late nineteenth century, emotional communities coalesced and clashed around laboratory dogs and their real and perceived suffering, and the fraught issue of whether or not experimenting on them was emotionally acceptable work.[6] Anti-vivisectionists and vivisectionists formed two overarching and transnational emotional communities. But within each were overlapping and sometimes competing emotional communities delineated along the lines of nation, aims, tactics and approaches to animal pain and suffering.

All these emotional communities worked hard to promote or challenge vivisection. The work of the scientists was most often salaried, conducted in research laboratories and informed by scientific theories and practices. Their work was conducted on real animals and as such had a 'more-than-human' dimension. The work of the anti-vivisectionists was often voluntary and entailed writing and publishing articles, attending demonstrations and conferences and lobbying legislators. It was conducted with animals held close in hearts and minds and so too contained 'more-than-human' elements.

This chapter focuses on the 'violent emotions' sparked by experiments conducted on dogs. Of all the animals in research laboratories, experiments on dogs were the most emotionally charged. Dog owners, veterinarians, animal protectionists and dog breed specialists intensified long-standing narratives that dogs were emotionally sensitive animals who loved and felt loyalty towards humans.[7] For its opponents, vivisection severed the bonds between dogs and humans. For its supporters, vivisection offered dogs the opportunity to display their devotion to humankind.

As Rob Boddice has demonstrated, vivisectionists argued that vivisection was emotionally uplifting work that benefitted individuals and society, and they defended animal experimentation through transnational networks.[8] Members of these communities claimed that their work was informed by compassion and love for humans and animals. They dismissed their anti-vivisectionist critics as emotionally deviant and deficient, in often gendered ways.[9] At times they diverged along national lines and attitudes towards animal suffering. The emotional communities of anti-vivisectionists accused vivisectionists of inflicting unbearable pain and suffering on dogs through their experimental work. They argued that this work corrupted the emotions and characters of its practitioners. The anti-vivisectionists also asserted that their often unpaid labour was emotionally exhausting but necessary to secure personal and collective emotional well-being. They formed varied and sometimes overlapping emotional communities, divided according to nationality and aims (especially between those who wanted to regulate vivisection and those who wanted to abolish it). Anti-vivisectionists were often members of other emotional communities rooted in feminism, humanitarianism and animal protection. Linked to, but often more radical than, the mainstream animal protection societies, anti-vivisectionists believed that they laboured to save humanity itself.[10]

In tracking the 'violent emotions' of the vivisection debates, this chapter seeks to add to studies that stress the transnational dimensions of the history of emotions and those that bring together scholarship on the history of animals and the history of emotions. National divergences are apparent but so too are emotional narratives and practices that stretched across the Atlantic and the Channel.[11] With a particular focus on dogs, this chapter shows how emotional communities converged and clashed in relationship to real and imagined animals and how emotional labour was conducted through encounters with, and understandings of, animal emotional suffering. Animals informed and motivated emotional work.

Promoting vivisection

Both sets of emotional communities identified two French scientists as the fathers of modern vivisection. François Magendie promoted experimental physiology as a way of understanding the workings of organisms, such as the nervous system. Vivisection, alongside chemistry, physics and anatomy, lay at the heart of his scientific method in which repeated experimentation on living creatures was deemed essential. On Magendie's death in 1855 the vivisection baton passed to his protégé Claude Bernard (1813–78), as did his chair at the prestigious Collège de France in Paris. Bernard continued in Magendie's footsteps but placed greater emphasis in his work on applying the knowledge gleaned from animal experimentation to humans and medical applications. For Bernard, it was morally justifiable to experiment on an animal 'even though painful and dangerous to him' as long as it was 'useful to man' [sic]. It would be more immoral for a doctor to try a treatment on a human that had not already been tested on a dog or other animal. He saw no need to justify his methods in response to the 'sensitive cries of people of fashion' who could not understand his methodology. The vivisector's pursuit of scientific knowledge overrode any emotional or sensory disturbance in the laboratory: 'he no longer hears the cry of animals, he no longer sees the blood that flows, he sees only his idea and perceives only organisms concealing problems which he intends to solve.' Guided by this principle, Bernard outlined his experiments on dogs, including poisoning them with carbon monoxide and 'injecting ether into the intestinal canal of a dog kept without food' before dissection.[12]

Bernard's work heavily influenced experimental physiology in Britain. An 1860 *Lancet* editorial may have lamented how teaching demonstrations on live animals at Alfort veterinary school 'silence[d] feeling',[13] but vivisection soon gained a foothold across the Channel, with its practitioners asserting that they would adapt it to British conditions. Assumptions about national character came into play. Expressing a belief in British emotional superiority and exceptionalism that would later be shared by anti-vivisectionists, British vivisectionists believed that their refined sensibilities would act as a natural brake to the cruelties committed by vivisectionists working in continental Europe. Their scientific work would, they believed, fit with the emotional norms of Victorian Britain, in stark contrast to the emotionally cold community of French vivisectionists. Dr John Anthony claimed that he and other British students had felt 'a degree of indignation' on witnessing the experiments on live animals conducted in France. British vivisectionists were less cruel than their French counterparts, he argued, while making greater scientific discoveries.[14] Professor of Practical Physiology and Histology at University College London, John Burdon-Sanderson, similarly pointed to the 'sentimentality' of his own and his colleagues' character, which was 'quite different' to those in Germany. This was not a showy emotional style marked by tears but one characterized by sensitivity and calmness.[15]

From 1870, Burdon-Sanderson and other experimental physiologists, many of whom had trained in France and Germany, strengthened their position in British universities. Unlike in France, British regulations took into account the suffering of animals, calling for such measures as the use of anaesthesia and skilled practitioners to carry out the research in controlled laboratory conditions. But like Bernard, British vivisectionists outlined in stark detail the various experimental techniques that could be conducted on dogs (and other animals). Burdon-Sanderson's *The Handbook for the Physiological Laboratory* was published in the United States, where it influenced the small but growing circle of experimental physiologists in New York, such as Dr John C. Dalton and Dr Austin Flint whose *Physiology of Man* (1873) was replete with details of experiments on dogs. Vivisection became a common teaching practice in New York's medical schools, and it received further institutional support with the foundation of permanent premises for the Rockefeller Institute for Medical Research in 1906. This organization became a particular bugbear for anti-vivisectionists. Although celebrated as a leading centre for American medical research, it had close links to France: Alexis Carrel, one of its leading research stars, was born in Lyon; it compared its laboratories with those of the Pasteur Institutes in Lille and Paris, and journalists drew links between John D. Rockefeller and Pasteur as comparable players in the struggle against dangerous diseases.[16] Experimental physiologists paid close attention to developments and opportunities in other countries, with some leaving Britain to work in France after the introduction of the Cruelty to Animals Act of 1876 that regulated vivisection.[17] They also defended vivisection at international congresses, such as the one held in London in 1913 where a resolution was passed declaring that animal experimentation was crucial to the medical advances.[18]

Vivisection was a thoroughly transnational endeavour, and its practitioners forged emotional communities across these countries, presenting themselves as sympathetic scientists. Drawing on Charles Darwin's claim that sympathy was instinctive in humans and, when combined with reason, it represented the height of humanity (as embodied in Victorian culture), physiologists saw themselves as 'men of feeling'. As Boddice has argued, they treated vivisection as a scientific practice rooted in sympathy because it would lead to medical treatments that would alleviate the suffering of countless humans and animals. It was morally better, according to their view, to sacrifice animals for the greater social good: self-styled gentleman scientist George Romanes gave over his dog Major to a vivisectionist in what he considered to be a moral and useful act. Vivisectionists would draw on their reserves of calmness and self-control, qualities fostered in their clean and rational scientific laboratories, to restrain their emotions as they performed vivisection. They trod a fine line between displaying emotional restraint and expressing their refined emotional concern for society.[19] In this vein, John Anthony defended his former teacher Sir Charles Bell as a man who was 'most kind and most feeling', while Cambridge physiologist Michael Foster claimed that their dedicated and careful pursuit of scientific knowledge made vivisectionists more 'gentle'.[20] Such statements sit within a broader narrative of surgeons' self-fashioning as men 'of feeling who could not simply amputate a limb in under a minute, but who, in the most profound sense, [were] capable of sympathising with [their] patients and who sought at all times to minimise their pain and suffering', according to Michael Brown.[21] Similarly, Agnes Arnold-Forster has shown how surgeons displayed plural masculine identities in combining 'medical and scientific skill and interest with compassion and care'.[22] Their supporters claimed that vivisectionists shared with doctors and surgeons a mission to alleviating suffering, and their work likewise fostered the emotional qualities of 'sympathy' and 'tenderness' that sat alongside an ability to still strong emotions in the pursuit of science. They were people who had families and pets and who certainly did not enjoy inflicting pain on animals.[23] Vivisection became 'fundamentally humanitarian' work.[24] The vivisectionist emotional communities stressed the emotional healthiness of vivisectionists and their methods and integrated them into the prevailing culture of sympathy. Opponents of vivisection did not buy into this narrative. They saw the vivisectionists' labour as corrupting individuals and society as a whole.

Working to oppose vivisection

The work of opposing vivisection often began with trying to expose the cruel work of vivisectionists. The Société Protectrice des Animaux (SPA) (Animal Protection Society), the main French animal protection society, became concerned about vivisection and launched an investigation into the practice in 1860. It found that the work of vivisection was useful but that cruelty should be minimized as far as possible. Many of its members were far more perturbed, exposing the divisions within emotional communities. Doctor Roche argued that it was unacceptable 'to attach an animal to an operating table, to plunge a lancet into its palpitating flesh, to dissect it alive, to make its blood pour out, to elicit its cries or howls of pain, of rage or of fright, to incite its anger or stupefy it with terror'.[25] The French state launched an investigation that ultimately concluded that vivisection did not require regulation.[26] But this did not convince those who viewed vivisection as physical and emotional torture, especially for emotionally sensitive dogs, and representative of the harshness and moral decline of modern urban life. Its opponents saw vivisection as undermining the special bond between humans and dogs and an attack on creatures who were capable of experiencing a range of emotions. Dogs, according to their human aficionados, were capable of feeling subtle and deep emotions and, as pets, became ever more drawn into homes as members of the family deserving of care and compassion.[27]

Female members of the SPA, such as the comtesse de Noailles, became leading critics of vivisection in the 1870s. They were joined in their labours by more radical activists, such as Maria Deraismes, who often merged anti-vivisection with feminism, motivated by the sense that male-dominated science brutalized women and animals.[28] In the 1880s the Société française contre la vivisection (French Society against Vivisection) led the struggle.

Transnational anti-vivisection emotional communities emerged. Their members declared disgust at vivisection and compassion for animals. Women spearheaded its work in Britain. Feminist Frances Power Cobbe was at the fore. With the RSPCA mired in disagreements over vivisection, Cobbe founded the Victoria Street Society for the Protection of Animals from Vivisection. As in France, anti-vivisection campaigns allowed British and American women to enter public life more fully. Elizabeth Blackwell and Anna Kingsford were troubled by male doctors' treatment and attitudes towards female bodies and drew a link between experimentation on poor people and animals. Both had witnessed what they considered to be cruel experiments on animals in Paris. Blackwell was the first woman to gain a medical degree in the United States, and on moving back to Britain in 1869 she continued to oppose the use of vivisection in American medical schools.[29]

Cobbe was particularly active in promoting anti-vivisection across borders. She gave advice and encouragement to Philadelphian animal protectionist Caroline Earl White who established the American Anti-Vivisection Society in 1883. The New York Anti-Vivisection Society, led by Diana Belais, was established in 1908. Cobbe also published an exposé of vivisection in America, which highlighted particularly cruel experiments, such as those of a Jersey City doctor B. A. Watson who dropped an etherized dog from the ceiling onto iron bars to research concussion of the spine. Cobbe pleaded with Americans to rise against the 'new vice of scientific cruelty' taking root in their country.[30] Whether or not they directly heeded Cobbe's call, American female anti-vivisectionists joined their French and British colleagues in seeing themselves as working to save humanity. But they tended to situate themselves within Christian and social reform movements rather than feminism.[31]

Anti-vivisectionists in London, New York and Paris paid close attention to one another's labours. The Victoria Street Society's publication *The Zoophilist* carried detailed 'intelligence' on anti-vivisection activity throughout Europe and North America (Henry Bergh of the American Society for the Prevention of Cruelty to Animals was the corresponding member for New York) and carried advertisements for *Le Zoophile*, the French anti-vivisection magazine.[32] Anti-vivisectionists also forged connections through visits, talks and information gathering. British ones made the most overseas trips. British-based Swedish anti-vivisectionist Lizzy Lind af Hageby had initially been troubled and horrified after witnessing vivisection at the Pasteur Institute in Paris. She was then instrumental in erecting the anti-vivisectionist statue and drinking fountain dedicated to the 'Brown Terrier Dog Done to Death in the Laboratories of University College', the scene of a riot in 1907 between medical students and working-class Battersea residents. Lind af Hageby went on to give lectures in the United States.[33] The New York Anti-Vivisection Society also invited British barrister and leader of the National Anti-Vivisection Society Stephen Coleridge to speak at one of their meetings in February 1910 when its members grilled him on the situation in Britain, and the American Humane Society, founded in 1877 to protect children and animals, sought the views of British doctors, journalists and thinkers, as well as American doctors.[34] International anti-vivisectionist congresses forged and strengthened such connections, with the abolitionist and restrictionist wings of the movement holding separate international events.[35] Anti-vivisectionists thus forged transnational, if sometimes divided, emotional communities, often inspired by British expertise, enthusiasm and effort.

Emotional mud-slinging

The anti-vivisectionists challenged the claims that vivisectionists were sympathetic and humanitarian scientists. Deraismes denounced their callous disregard for animal suffering that 'anesthesized their hearts for ever'.[36] In an echo of French anti-vivisection rhetoric, *Women and Work* worried that vivisectors' emotional hardening would mean they would lose 'their sensitiveness with regard to suffering humanity that is indispensable to a medical practitioner'.[37] Some experimenters reportedly even took a 'light-hearted' delight in vivisection and felt no sense of shame. In making these claims, anti-vivisectionists placed vivisectionists within the narrative of surgeons and scientists as emotionally detached and unfeeling men.[38] Doctors and scientists who opposed vivisection worried too about the practice's impact on vivisectionists. Archibald T. Banning, a doctor from Mt. Vernon (an area north east of the Bronx), recalled with 'horror' the vivisections he had witnessed as a medical student and noted that such scenes had led to 'morbid psychopathic' symptoms in some fellow doctors. Anti-vivisectionists seized on such accounts as credible condemnations of vivisection. They endlessly quoted Harvard University professor Henry J. Bigelow's statement that 'vivisection deadens the humanity of students'. Their attacks on the vivisectionists' emotional community became gendered. A doctor from Massachusetts labelled vivisection an 'unmanly crime'.[39] So too did Coleridge who stated that 'physiology is not a very manly pursuit': How could vivisectors be brave when they inflicted so much pain on weak animals? Manliness instead meant protecting defenceless animals.[40] The modern vivisector had become emasculated and emotionally cold, driven by a perverted belief in science and by base emotions. They had become corrupted by their vivisectionist labours.

Such gendered attacks challenged the vivisectionists' sense of themselves as manly defenders of humanity whose scientific work was emotionally and morally beneficial. Other lines of attack chipped away at their scientific credentials, and anti-vivisectionists turned modern evolutionary ideas against them. Inspired by 'Oriental' and evolutionary theories, Caird argued that the cruelty of vivisection was such that it would spill out from the laboratories and infect human hearts and 'nerves'. In a kind of evolutionary karma, this leaking out of misery, cruelty and savagery would lead inexorably to moral and physical degeneration. Vivisection threatened progress, and there 'must be gathering an unspeakably awful inheritance of suffering for the race that is guilty of these deeds of selfishness and violence'.[41] Vivisectionists were out of step with evolutionary progress in the age of humanitarianism.

The vivisectionists also launched gendered attacks on the emotional communities of anti-vivisectionists. Dr Simon Flexner, director of the Rockefeller Institute and a leading meningitis researcher, claimed that 'most of the outcry against animal experimentation . . . is raised by women. They are sincere, but lack facts. They point to the suffering [of animals]. Almost without exception the operations are painless'.[42] Flexner was not alone in portraying himself as a rational male defender of medical progress battling against the opinions, feelings and labours of overly sentimental and misinformed women. A 'lady . . . eminent in philanthropy' was not qualified to pass judgement on modern scientific methods, according to renowned British surgeon Jonathan Hutchinson. Their concerns were 'sentimentalism run mad'.[43] Psychiatric theories and language lent weight to such attacks. New York researchers asked for precautions to be taken against 'hysterical and snooping or other sentimental investigators' from entering their laboratories.[44] Montana State College professor E. V. Wilcox went further in pathologizing them, suggesting that their stories offered 'abundant evidence of mental pathology, interesting material for the specialist in nerve-diseases'.[45] Another tactic was to turn the humanitarian narrative against anti-vivisectionists. William W. Keen accused his mainly female critics of displaying 'the most violent and vindictive passions' when they wrote him threatening letters. They put a love of animals above humans, laying bare their cruelty towards humanity. It was the work of anti-vivisection, rather than that of the vivisectionists, that was emotionally troubling.[46]

New York surgeon James Warbasse charged the anti-vivisectionists with placing their 'undisciplined emotions' above medical progress. He supported neurologist Charles Loomis Dana's identification of the 'zoöphilic psychosis, in which there is an inordinate and exaggerated sympathy for the lower animals'. Inspired by French psychologists and psychiatrists (one of whom had located anti-vivisectionist women's love for animals as a form of hereditary madness), Dana's invention of this condition, which was allegedly most common in women and sprung from female biological weaknesses and excessive sentimentality, lent intellectual weight to claims that anti-vivisectionists were hysterical. Dana asserted that this was a modern disease: the pressures of urban life had overwhelmed the susceptible minds of 'weak' and 'selfish' women, whose minds had perverted the noble cause of animal welfare to become fixated on animals. This reheated eighteenth-century attacks on supposedly soppy female dog owners who paid too much attention to their pet at the expense of finding a husband and repeated British vivisectionists' claims that female anti-vivisectionists were emotionally (and sexually) deficient women who had failed to find husbands, so turned their focus to animals and the exhausting and harmful work of anti-vivisection.

Warbasse gleefully deployed Dana's diagnosis against the anti-vivisectionists. Women felt too much sympathy for animals that they caressed and fawned over, placing the needs of pet dogs over human suffering and the misery of animals in the livestock industry. The absurdity and tragedy of this condition was shown in the way that female New Yorkers spent money on pointless luxury products for their pet dogs rather than care for the thousands of destitute orphans who lived in the city. Invoking madness and cruelty served to paint opponents of experimental physiology as irrational and deluded. Warbasse based his argument on an article in *Pearson's Magazine* that contrasted the miseries of New York's orphans with the luxurious lives enjoyed by the dogs of rich women. In ignoring the orphans' plight, these apparently dog-obsessed women displayed their selfishness and turned their back on their natural maternal instinct. By implication, Warbasse positioned the anti-vivisectionists' campaigns and work as selfish, inhumane and pathological.[47] Cannon was more even-handed. The anti-vivisectionists had a 'kindly motive' which was 'no doubt humane', but they were 'ignorant' and misguided in their views, which posed a threat to humanity itself.[48] Pro-vivisectionists saw the work of anti-vivisectionists as part of a wider battle between 'blind sentiment' and 'clear reason', with the former gaining ascendency in modern countries, which contained the potential for disaster.[49]

Anti-vivisectionists, in turn, sought to turn their emotional communities and labours into rational responses to the cruelty of vivisection. They claimed to be 'actuated by sentiment'. Feeling prevented humans from carrying out everyday social transgressions – from punching each other to smoking cigars in church – and was at the root of anti-vivisection: 'it is the sole safeguard that the individual possesses against the crude and ferocious instincts of the human animal.'[50] Sentiment was the necessary obstacle to suffering and acted as the glue that bound civilized people together and ensured the smooth running of modern societies. As the emotional communities laboured and clashed, canine suffering came under scrutiny.

Debating dogs in the laboratory

Dogs were central to the work of vivisection. They were pliable in the laboratory, and their physiology was sufficiently similar to humans for comparisons to be made (although anti-vivisectionists challenged this claim).[51] Anti-vivisectionists tapped into the long-standing narrative that dogs were creatures capable of feeling varied and refined emotions. They presented dogs as the animals most tortured by vivisection (alongside monkeys) and argued that their suffering symbolized all that was wrong with vivisection: what kind of society allowed the callous experimentation on and death of emotionally sensitive animals, particularly those, such as dogs, who belonged at humans' side as pets? For Caird, animals, like humans, had a right to be spared suffering, not for their 'intellectual or moral faculties' but because they possessed 'a sentient nervous system'. It was sinful to inflict almost unspeakable horrors on animals, such as dogs, who were 'capable of affection, of fear, of gratitude, of devotion, in short of suffering'.[52] One of the members of the 1876 Royal Commission on Vivisection, anti-vivisectionist and editor of the *Spectator* Richard Holt Hutton, called on dogs (and cats) to be excluded from vivisection because of their high emotional sensitivity and 'special ties' to humans.[53]

Anti-vivisectionists most commonly advanced the belief – bolstered by Darwinism and popular dog-loving narratives – that dogs and humans shared similar emotions. For Cobbe, two of these shared emotions – faith and affection – were manipulated and exploited on the vivisection table. The vivisector betrayed canine faith and love for humans. Depicting a distressing scene, she noted that dogs would lick the vivisectors' hands just before the moment of painful death.[54]

Stressing the dog's close bonds with humans added to the sense that vivisection was a betrayal of innocent and affectionate animals and a subversion of the natural order. A New York Anti-Vivisection Society publication contrasted two images to show two different 'silent appeals'. One showed a vivisectionist ignoring a dog's appeal for mercy, while the other depicted a dog jumping into a river to rescue a drowning person, desperately waving for help. The dog is shown to be emotionally superior to the vivisector, as they understand the true meaning of sympathy.[55] The severing of human–canine bonds became a common trope: experimental work on live dogs represented the ultimate betrayal of the human–dog relationship. Amadée Latour, editor of the *Union médicale*, stated that 'it is abominable that an animal so loyal and so loving is subjected to the knife and tongs'.[56] Here was human hypocrisy laid bare, lamented Cobbe. It was impossible for humans to love dogs if they allowed the 'heart of a dog' to be dissected 'even while yet it beats with affection'.[57]

As dogs held such emotional resonance, anti-vivisectionists frequently deployed detailed descriptions of experiments on dogs to persuade the public of the evils of vivisection. These included former Rockefeller Institute employee Mary Kennedy's account of Alexis Carrel's leg-grafting experiments on dogs. One dog was reportedly left in a neck strap for three weeks: 'it was such a human-like little dog – just like a baby in its sufferings. It would look up at you so pitifully.' As Kennedy's observations suggest, the apparent similarity between the defencelessness of dogs and children underscored much humanitarian work.[58] In line with the broader humanitarian movement, the anti-vivisectionist emotional communities worried about the potentially troubling affective and moral impact of reproducing graphic descriptions of suffering animals. But they still aimed to shock their readers through their humanitarian work and create a visceral emotional reaction that would spur humanitarian action. The factual accounts would make readers 'sick with horror'. Some descriptions were dubbed 'spectacles full of horror and dread', including those of French researcher Paul Loye's experiments that entailed the decapitation of dogs, that would lead to the sense that something must be done.[59] By implication, those readers who failed to feel revulsion were abnormal or morally suspect.

To counter the claims and campaigning work of the anti-vivisectionist emotional communities, defenders of vivisection attacked their opponents' sensationalist style that sprung, in the words of Wilcox, from a 'morbid imagination'. Anti-vivisectionists were nothing more than 'sensation-hunters' who published 'brainsickly accounts' that corrupted their readers.[60] The work of anti-vivisectionists was emotionally suspect, not that of vivisectionists. Pro-vivisectionists also portrayed experimentation as strengthening the bonds between dogs and humans. American vivisectionists acknowledged the special status of the dog and noted how many Americans' 'well-founded love' of dogs raised worries.[61] But they stressed the importance of dogs as experimental creatures and argued that physical and emotional commonalities between humans and dogs enabled the latter to make a major contribution to physiological knowledge and medical advances. The dog's purported affection for and devotion to humanity was thus repurposed as a defence of vivisection. In the words of Cannon, 'the loyalty, devotion and self-sacrifice of the dog have often been emphasized; these noble qualities have their loftiest and most perfect expression when life itself is surrendered for the sake of the object worshipped'.[62] Vivisectionists also sought to position themselves as the true friends of dogs as they worked to combat canine diseases. Victor Horsley used Pasteur's rabies vaccine as evidence that animal experimentation benefitted the 'lower animals'. It had saved the dog, the most 'useful' and 'faithful' of animals, from a terrible disease.[63]

Other pro-vivisectionists took a different tack over the question of animal pain. They downplayed the pain that dogs experienced to assuage concerns about the emotional distress caused by vivisection. One strategy reheated Cartesian ideas to deny that dogs could really feel pain. One pro-vivisection British text, that was republished in New York, challenged anti-vivisectionists' portrayal of dogs as deeply sensitive creatures. It asserted that like other animals they lacked the consciousness and intellect needed to feel pain to the same extent that humans could. Renowned St Bartholomew's surgeon James Paget tapped into one racialized evolutionary assumption that pain was linked to heightened intellects. He claimed that 'savages' experienced less pain than the 'higher races' who through generations of 'mental cultivation' had developed heightened sensory awareness and intelligence. Animals too were less able to feel pain than humans. This was also the view of Warbasse, who stated that 'pain is a psychic phenomenon, and lower men and animals have but little appreciation of it'. It was an anatomical accident that dogs' eyes resembled those of humans in pain, and claims that dogs felt pain were mistaken anthropomorphism.[64] In contrast, some vivisectionists admitted that animals could experience emotional and physical pain, which they could dull through the use of the anaesthetics that had transformed human medicine.[65]

Conclusion

The emotionally charged debates on vivisection put canine suffering under the microscope. For the anti-vivisectionist emotional communities, the work of vivisection represented the ultimate betrayal of human–canine bonds, and university and hospital laboratories became sites of torture that challenged London, New York and Paris' status as beacons of civilized urban modernity. For the vivisectionist emotional communities, the laboratories were humane centres of progress, refined feelings and modern science. These transnational emotional communities came together and clashed with canine suffering in mind. Real and imaginary encounters with laboratory dogs gave an emotional charge to the labours of these activists and intensified the 'violent emotions' of the vivisection debates. This chapter has articulated the emotion work of experimentation on animals and of animal rights activism and revealed how dogs inspired new ways of thinking about and practising these labours. This indicates the benefit of paying more attention to the place of animals in the changing and contested relationship between emotions and work.

Notes

1 Caird, *Sentimental View*, 6, 13–14.
2 Goodridge, *What is Vivisection?*, 4. See Meyer, 'Expression', 399; Hausmann, 'We Must Perform Experiments', 264–83.
3 Lansbury, *Old Brown Dog*, 92–3. On the emotional and psychological toil of political disagreements, see Harris, *Man on Devil's Island*.
4 Cannon, *Opposition to Medical*, 1.
5 Rosenwein, *Emotional Communities*, 24–5.
6 On pain and animals, see Gray, 'Body, Mind and Madness', 148–63; Meyer, 'Expression'; Ramsden and Wilson, 'Suicidal', 205–17; White, 'Experimental Animal', 60–81.

7 For this history in France, see Kete, *Beast in the Boudoir*.
8 Boddice, *Science of Sympathy*; Boddice, *Humane Professions*.
9 On the gendered dimensions of emotional labour, see the chapters by Grace Whorrall-Campbell, Claire English, Sally Horrocks and Paul Merchant and Hannah Parker in this volume.
10 Bourke, *Story of Pain*; Halttunen, 'Humanitarianism', 303–34; Donald, *Women against Cruelty*. On the emotional labour of protest and activism, see the chapters by James Brown, Claire English and Hannah Parker in this volume.
11 Haggis and Allen, 'Imperial Emotions', 691–716; Papadogiannis, '(Trans) National Emotional Community', 589–614; Gaynor, Broomhall and Flack, 'Frogs and Feeling Communities'; Jørgensen, *Recovering Lost Species*; Pearson, 'Four-legged *poilus*', 731–60; Saha, 'Among the Beasts of Burma', 910–32; Webb, Pearson, Summerfield and Riley, 'More-Than-Human Emotional Communities', 245–62.
12 Bernard, *Introduction to the Study of Experimental Medicine*, 102–3, 179. See also Guerrini, *Experimenting with Humans and Animals*; Kete, *Beast in the Boudoir*, 13–18.
13 'Ethics of Vivisection', 144.
14 *Royal Commission on the Practice of Subjecting Live Animals*, 130.
15 Quoted in Boddice, *Science of Sympathy*, 74. On different national emotional styles, see Dixon, *Weeping Britannia*, 195.
16 French, *Antivivisection and Medical*, 19, 38–48; Turner, *Reckoning with the Beast*, 92; Beers, *For the Prevention of Cruelty*, 123; Flint, *Physiology of Man*; Sanderson, *Handbook for the Physiological Laboratory*, 95, 331, 405, 476–7. This is the US edition: the British edition was published in 1873. On the Rockefeller's French links, see RAC, RURSEAAVA, FA142, box 19, Palmer, 'All the Health in the World'.
17 Wilks, 'Vivisection', 941; Hausmann, 'We Must Perform Experiments', 270.
18 Keen, *Animal Experimentation*, xvi.
19 Boddice, *Science of Sympathy*, 2, 11, 28–30, 49, 86–7; Boddice, 'Vivisecting Major', 237; Meyer, 'Expression', 408–11; Dixon, *Weeping Britannia*, 190–1; Humphry, *Vivisection*, 8; Cleland, *Experiment on Brute Animals*, 5; Warbasse, *Conquest of Disease*, 8.
20 *Royal Commission on the Practice of Subjecting Live Animals*, 130; Foster, 'Vivisection', 376.
21 Brown, 'Surgery and Emotion', 333.
22 Arnold-Forster, 'Gender and Pain', 14.
23 Philanthropos, *Physiological Cruelty*, 48.
24 Borel, *Sur le vif*, 8.
25 Quoted in Kete, *Beast in the Boudoir*, 10.
26 Baldin, *Histoire des animaux domestiques*, 166.

27 Grier, *Pets in America*; Howell, *Home and Astray*; Kete, *Beast in the Boudoir*; Quick, 'Puppy Love', 289–314.
28 Kete, *Beast in the Boudoir*, 16–18.
29 Guerrini, *Experimenting*, 89–92; Lansbury, *Old Brown Dog*, 85, 90; Bittel, 'Science, Suffrage, and Experimentation', 684; Kean, 'Smooth Cool Men of Science', 16–38.
30 Cobbe and Bryan, *Vivisection in America*, 23, 31–2.
31 Beers, *Prevention of Cruelty*, 123; Bittel, 'Science', 682; Buettinger, 'Women and Antivivisection', 863.
32 *The Zoophilist*, 1 January 1884; 'List of Honorary'.
33 Cronin, *Art for Animals*, 149–53, 162. On the brown dog statue, see Lansbury, *Old Brown Dog*.
34 *Abstract of the Report on Vivisection*; RAC, RURSEAAVA, FA142, box 2, 'Report of the Proceedings'. Coleridge had renamed the Victoria Street Society the National Anti-Vivisection Society in 1898 and took it in a restrictionist direction. Infuriated by this change, Cobbe founded the abolitionist British Union for the Abolition of Vivisection. French, *Antivivisection*, 163.
35 Beers, *Prevention of Cruelty*, 123; Cronin, *Art for Animals*, 162.
36 Deraismes, *Discours contre*, 14.
37 *Women and Work*, 35, 30 January 1875. See also Metzger, *Vivisection*, 99.
38 Caird, *Sentimental View*, 21. One American Anti-Vivisection Society publication asked its readers to 'note the cool, precise, heartless language' adopted by scientists when describing their experiments. RAC, RURSEAAVA, FA142, box 2, 'Shall Science to Murder?'. See also Arnold-Forster, 'Gender and Pain'; Brown, 'Surgery and Emotion'.
39 *Abstract of the Report on Vivisection Adopted by the American Humane Association*, 5–6, 12.
40 Quoted in Anti-vivisection Society of Maryland, *Dawn*, 1. See also Bittel, 'Science', 681.
41 Caird, *Sentimental View*, 17, 23, 25.
42 Quoted in Heinl, 'What Vivisection'.
43 Hutchinson, 'On Cruelty to Animals', 308–9. See also Buettinger, 'Women and Antivivisection', 867.
44 RAC, RURSEAAVA, FA142, box 2, Frederick Tilney to Simon Flexner.
45 Wilcox, 'Anti-Vivisection Agitation', 788.
46 Keen, *Animal Experimentation*, 234, 251.
47 Warbasse, *Conquest of Disease*, 159–61; 'Dogs and Rabies', 736; Buettinger, 'Antivivisection and the Charge of Zoophil-Psychosis', 277–88; 'Passion for Animals'; White, 'Sympathy under the Knife', 115; Traïni, 'Opposing Scientific Cruelty', 534.
48 Cannon, *Opposition to Medical Research*, 15.
49 Keith, 'Some Aspects', 4.

50 Caird, *Sentimental View*, 19-20.
51 Kingsford, 'Uselessness of Vivisection', 176-7.
52 Caird, *Sentimental View*, 9, 14.
53 *Royal Commission on the Practice of Subjecting Live Animals*, xxiii.
54 Cobbe, 'Consciousness of Dogs', 1872, 429; Meyer, 'Expression', 400-1.
55 RAC, RURSEAAVA, FA142, box 3, New York Anti-Vivisection Society, *Affidavits*.
56 Quoted in Kete, *Beast in the Boudoir*, 13.
57 Cobbe, 'Zoophily', 287.
58 RAC, RURSEAAVA, FA142, box 2, White, 'Is Vivisection Morally Justifiable?'; RAC, RURSEAAVA, FA142, box 3, *Endowment of Torture*; Pearson, *Rights of the Defenseless*.
59 *Women and Work*, 86, 22 January 1876; Metzger, *Vivisection*, 92-3, 98; Loye, *Mort par la Décapitation*; Halttunen, 'Humanitarianism', 330; Hamilton, 'Reading and the Popular Critique', 72, 77-8; Meyer, 'Expression', 414.
60 Wilcox, 'Anti-Vivisection Agitation', 787.
61 RAC, RURSEAAVA, FA142, box 3, *Second Statement*.
62 RAC, RURSEAAVA, FA142, box 11, Cannon, *Dog's Gift*.
63 Horsley, 'Morality of Vivisection', 804-5.
64 Paget, 'Vivisection', 922; Warbasse, *Conquest of Disease*, 16-20, 23. On racialized understandings of pain, see Bourke, *Story of Pain*, 192-9.
65 'Vivisection and Anaesthetics', 749. See also Borel, *Sur le vif*, 8; Philanthropos, *Physiological Cruelty*, 19; Gray, 'Body, Mind and Madness', 149; Snow, 'Surgery and Anaesthesia', 195-214.

Bibliography

Abstract of the Report on Vivisection Adopted by the American Humane Association, September 26, 1895. Chicago: American Humane Association, 1895.
Anti-vivisection Society of Maryland. *Dawn: Denouncing the Pollution, and Advocating the Total Suppression of Vivisection* 1, no. 1 (January 1901).
Arnold-Forster, Agnes. 'Gender and Pain in Nineteenth-Century Cancer Care'. *Gender and History* 32, no. 1 (2020): 13-29.
Baldin, Damien. *Histoire des animaux domestiques, XIXe-XXe siècle*. Paris: Seuil, 2014.
Beers, Diane L. *For the Prevention of Cruelty: The History and Legacy of Animal Rights Activism in the United States*. Athens: Swallow Press/ Ohio University Press, 2006.
Bernard, Claude. *An Introduction to the Study of Experimental Medicine*. Translated by Henry Copley Greene. New York: Henry Schuman, 1949 [1865].
Bittel, Carla. 'Science, Suffrage, and Experimentation: Mary Putman Jacobi and the Controversy over Vivisection in Late Nineteenth-Century America'. *Bulletin of the History of Medicine* 79, no. 4 (2005): 664-94.

Boddice, Rob. *Humane Professions: The Defence of Experimental Medicine, 1876-1914*. Cambridge: Cambridge University Press, 2021.

Boddice, Rob. *The Science of Sympathy: Morality, Evolution and Victorian Civilization*. Urbana: University of Illinois Press, 2016.

Boddice, Rob. 'Vivisecting Major: A Victorian Gentlemen Scientist Defends Animal Experimentation, 1876–1885'. *Isis* 102, no. 2 (2011): 215–37.

Borel, Frédéric. *Sur le vif: considerations sur la vivisection*. Paris: Sandoz et Thuillier, 1883.

Bourke, Joanna. *The Story of Pain: From Prayer to Painkillers*. Oxford: Oxford University Press, 2014.

Brown, Michael. 'Surgery and Emotion: The Era Before Anaesthesia'. In *The Palgrave Handbook of the History of Surgery*, edited by Thomas Schlich, 327–48. London: Palgrave Macmillan, 2018.

Buettinger, Craig. 'Antivivisection and the Charge of Zoophil-Psychosis in the Early Twentieth Century'. *The Historian* 55, no. 2 (1993): 277–88.

Buettinger, Craig. 'Women and Antivivisection in Late Nineteenth-Century America'. *Journal of Social History* 30, no. 4 (1997): 857–72.

Burdon-Sanderson, J., ed. *Handbook for the Physiological Laboratory containing an Exposition of the Fundamental Facts of the Science, with Explicit Directions for their Demonstration*. Philadelphia: P. Blakiston, Son & Co, 1884.

Caird, Mona. *A Sentimental View of Vivisection*, Bijou Library No.3. London: William Reeves, 1883.

Cannon, Walter B. *The Opposition to Medical Research*. Chicago: American Medical Association, 1908.

Cleland, John. *Experiment on Brute Animals*. London: J.W. Kolckmann/ Association for the Advancement of Medicine by Research, 1883.

Cobbe, Frances Power. 'The Consciousness of Dogs'. *Quarterly Review* 133, 1872.

Cobbe, Frances Power, and Benjamin Bryan. *Vivisection in America*. London: Swan Sonnenschein/Victoria Street Society, 1889.

Cronin, J. Keri. *Art for Animals: Visual Culture and Animal Advocacy 1870–1914*. University Park: Pennsylvania State University Press, 2018.

Deraismes, Maria. *Discours contre la vivisection*. Paris: Auguste Ghio/ Ligue populaire contre l'abus de la vivisection, 1884.

Dixon, Thomas. *Weeping Britannia: Portrait of a Nation in Tears*. Oxford: Oxford University Press, 2015.

'Dogs and Rabies'. *Pearson's Magazine*, December 1909.

Donald, Diana. *Women Against Cruelty: Protection of Animals in Nineteenth-Century Britain*. Manchester: Manchester University Press, 2020.

'The Ethics of Vivisection'. *The Lancet*, 11 August 1860.

Flint, Austin. *The Physiology of Man*. New York: D. Appleton, 1873.

Foster, Michael. 'Vivisection'. *Macmillan's Magazine* 29, 1874.

French, Richard D. *Antivivisection and Medical Science in Victorian Society*. Princeton: Princeton University Press, 1975.

Gaynor, Andrea, Susan Broomhall, and Andrew Flack. 'Frogs and Feeling Communities: A Study in History of Emotions and Environmental History'. *Environment and History* (2020), https://doi.org/10.3197/096734019X15740974883861.

Goodridge, A. R. *What is Vivisection?* New York: J. J. Little, 1907.

Gray, Liz. 'Body, Mind and Madness: Pain in Animals in Nineteenth-Century Comparative Psychology'. In *Pain and Emotion in Modern History*, edited by Rob Boddice, 148–63. Basingstoke: Palgrave, 2014.

Grier, Katherine C. *Pets in America: A History*. Chapel Hill: University of North Carolina Press, 2006.

Guerrini, Anita. *Experimenting With Humans and Animals: From Galen to Animal Rights*. Baltimore: Johns Hopkins University Press, 2003.

Haggis, Jane, and Margaret Allen. 'Imperial Emotions: Affective Communities of Mission in British Protestant Women's Missionary Publications, c.1880-1920'. *Journal of Social History* 41, no. 3 (2008): 691–716.

Halttunen, Karen. 'Humanitarianism, and the Pornography of Pain in Anglo-American Culture'. *American Historical Review* 100, no. 2 (1995): 303–34.

Hamilton, Susan. 'Reading and the Popular Critique of Science in the Victorian Press: Frances Power Cobbe's Writing for the Victoria Street Society'. *Victorian Review* 36, no. 2 (2010): 66–79.

Harris, Ruth. *The Man on Devil's Island: Alfred Dreyfus and the Affair that Divided France*. London: Allen Lane, 2010.

Hausmann, Stephen R. '"We Must Perform Experiments on Some Living Body": Antivivisection and American Medicine, 1850-1915'. *The Journal of the Gilded Age and Progressive Era* 16, no. 3 (2017): 264–83.

Heinl, Robert D. 'What Vivisection Is Doing for Humanity'. *Frank Leslie's Weekly*, 31 March 1910.

Horsley, Victor. 'The Morality of Vivisection'. *The Nineteenth Century* 32 (1892): 804–5.

Howell, Philip. *At Home and Astray: The Domestic Dog in Victorian Britain*. Charlottesville: University of Virginia Press, 2015.

Humphry, G. M. *Vivisection: What Good Has it Done?* London: J. W. Kolckmann/Association for the Advancement of Medicine by Research, 1882.

Hutchinson, Jonathan. 'On Cruelty to Animals'. *Fortnightly Review* 26 (1876).

Jørgensen, Dolly. *Recovering Lost Species in the Modern Age: Histories of Longing and Belonging*. Cambridge, MA: MIT Press, 2019.

Kean, Hilda. 'The "Smooth Cool Men of Science": The Feminist and Socialist Response to Vivisection'. *History Workshop Journal* 40, no. 1 (1995): 16–38.

Keen, William W. *Animal Experimentation and Medical Progress*. Boston and New York: Houghton Mifflin Company, 1914.

Keith, Arthur. 'Some Aspects of the Modern Conflict Between Sentiment and Reason'. *The Fight Against Disease: The Quarterly Journal of the Research Defence Society* (Summer 1932): 4.

Kete, Kathleen. *Beast in the Boudoir: Petkeeping in Nineteenth-Century Paris*. Berkeley: University of California Press, 1994.

Kingsford, Anna. 'The Uselessness of Vivisection'. *The Nineteenth Century* 11 (1882).

Lansbury, Carol. *The Old Brown Dog: Women, Workers and Vivisection in Edwardian England*. Madison: University of Wisconsin Press, 1985.

'List of Honorary Corresponding Members'. *The Zoophilist*, 1 October 1888.

Loye, Paul. *La Mort par la Décapitation*. Paris: Progrès medical, 1888.

Meyer, Jed. 'The Expression of the Emotions in Man and Laboratory Animals'. *Victorian Studies* 50, no. 3 (2008): 399–417.

Paget, James. 'Vivisection: Its Pains and its Uses I'. *The Nineteenth Century*, December 1881.

Papadogiannis, Nikolaos. 'A (Trans)National Emotional Community? Greek Political Songs and the Politicisation of Greek Migrants in West Germany in the 1960s and early 1970s'. *Contemporary European History* 23, no. 4 (2014): 589–614.

'Passion for Animals'. *New York Times*, 8 March 1909.

Pearson, Chris. '"Four-legged *poilus*": French Army Dogs, Emotional Practices and the Creation of Militarized Human-Dog Bonds, 1871–1918'. *Journal of Social History* 52, no. 3 (2019): 731–60.

Pearson, Susan J. *The Rights of the Defenseless: Protecting Animals and Children in Gilded Age America*. Chicago: University of Chicago Press, 2011.

Philanthropos, [Francis Heatherly?]. *Physiological Cruelty, Or Fact vs. Fancy: An Inquiry into the Vivisection Question*. New York: John Wiley and Sons, 1883.

Quick, Tom. 'Puppy Love: Domestic Science, "Women's Work", and Canine Care'. *Journal of British Studies* 58, no. 2 (2019): 289–314.

RAC, RURSEAAVA, FA142, box 19, Frederick Palmer, 'All the Health in the World'. *Collier's*, 28 October 1922.

RAC, RURSEAAVA, FA142, box 2, Frederick Tilney to Simon Flexner, 18 February 1932.

RAC, RURSEAAVA, FA142, box 2, Caroline Earle White, 'Is Vivisection Morally Justifiable?' [n.d.].

RAC, RURSEAAVA, FA142, box 3, *The Endowment of Torture: Revelations from the Rockefeller Hall, New York, 1909*. London: British Union for the Abolition of Vivisection/The British Anti-Vivisection Society, [n.d.].

RAC, RURSEAAVA, FA142, box 3, *Second Statement of the Committee for the Protection of Animal Experimentation*, January 1922.

RAC, RURSEAAVA, FA142, box 3, New York Anti-Vivisection Society. *Affidavits: Concerning the Atrocities and Abuses of Vivisection Laboratories* [n.d.].

RAC, RURSEAAVA, FA142, box 11, Walter B. Cannon. *The Dog's Gift to the Relief of Human Suffering*. New York: American Association for Medical Progress, 1926.

Ramsden, Edmund, and Duncan Wilson. 'The Suicidal Animal: Science and the Nature of Self-Destruction'. *Past and Present* 224 (2014): 205–17.
Report of the Royal Commission on the Practice of Subjecting Live Animals to Experiments for Scientific Purposes, with Minutes of Evidence and Appendix. London: HMSO, 1876.
Rockefeller Archive Centre (hereafter, RAC), Rockefeller University Records, Special Events and Activities, Anti-Vivisection Activities (hereafter RURSEAAVA), FA142, box 2, 'A Report of the Proceedings at a Mass Meeting Held by the New York Anti-Vivisection Society at the Berkeley Lyceum, New York City, 25 February 1910'.
Rosenwein, Barbara H. *Emotional Communities in the Early Middle Ages.* Ithaca: Cornell University Press, 2006.
Saha, Jonathan. 'Among the Beasts of Burma: Animals and the Politics of Colonial Sensibilities, c. 1840–1940'. *Journal of Social History* 48, no. 4 (2015): 910–32.
Snow, Stephanie J. 'Surgery and Anaesthesia: Revolutions in Practice'. In *The Palgrave Handbook of the History of Surgery*, edited by Thomas Schlich, 195–214. London: Palgrave Macmillan, 2018.
Traïni, Christophe. 'Opposing Scientific Cruelty: The Emotions and Sensitivities of Protesters against Experiments on Animals'. *Contemporary European History* 23, no. 4 (2014): 523–43.
Turner, James. *Reckoning with the Beast: Animals, Pain and Humanity in the Victorian Mind.* Baltimore: Johns Hopkins University Press, 1980.
'Vivisection and Anaesthetics'. *British Medical Journal*, 5 June 1875.
Warbasse, James. *The Conquest of Disease through Animal Experimentation.* New York: Appleton, 1910.
Webb, Tom, Chris Pearson, Penny Summerfield, and Mark Riley. 'More-Than-Human Emotional Communities: British soldiers and mules in Second World War Burma'. *Cultural and Social History* 17, no. 2 (2020): 245–62.
White, Paul S. 'The Experimental Animal in Victorian Britain'. In *Thinking with Animals: New Perspectives on Anthropomorphism*, edited by Lorraine Daston and Gregg Mitman, 60–81. New York: Columbia University Press, 2005.
White, Paul S. 'Sympathy Under the Knife: Experimentation and Emotion in Late Victorian Medicine'. In *Medicine, Emotion and Disease, 1700–1950*, edited by Fay Bound Alberti, 100–24. Basingstoke: Palgrave Macmillan, 2006.
Wilcox, E.V. 'The Anti-Vivisection Agitation'. *The Journal of Comparative Medicine and Veterinary Archives* 19, no. 12 (December 1898).
Wilks, Samuel. 'Vivisection: Its Pains and its Uses III'. *The Nineteenth Century*, December 1881.
Women and Work 35, 30 January 1875.
Women and Work 86, 22 January 1876.
The Zoophilist, 1 January 1884.

11

Whistleblowing, guilt and liberal democracy

James Brown

Whistleblowing in the UK's National Health Service (NHS) is not new. As Chris Hart has argued, on occasion, even before the advent of the NHS in 1948, nurses would seek to raise concerns in spite of their managers.[1] Instances of whistleblowing in the NHS in forms that exhibit worrying similarities with recent whistleblowing can be traced back at least to the 1960s, especially to attempts, such as Barbara Robb's, to expose abuses in under-resourced long-stay psychiatric care.[2] However, a series of reforms in the 1980s and 1990s intended to create an internal market in health care and to prioritize patient choice arguably exacerbated some of the tensions inherent in the NHS and resulted in situations in which senior managers could become somewhat remote from hands-on care, while being preoccupied with certain performance indicators (e.g. those to do with waiting lists) at the expense of others. Whistleblowing, while not a new phenomenon in the health service, assumed a new salience in these circumstances, especially in relation to a series of scandals, and various attempts have been made, such as that of Sir Robert Francis in *Freedom to Speak Up* (2015), to make institutional provision for speaking out within the NHS. Nevertheless, instances where whistleblowers are first ignored, then vilified, victimized and hounded out of the NHS continue to accumulate.

The first part of this chapter explores the emotional drama of whistleblowing in the NHS, dwelling on the case of the surgeon Peter Duffy, who in 2019 published an account of his experiences, on which the following essay draws heavily. The available accounts of incidents of whistleblowing have a tendency to be asymmetrical. This is partly because the whistleblower's opponents typically deny that anything untoward has taken place and therefore deny that the whistleblower really *is* a whistleblower. Where a whistleblower *does* then publish an account of their experiences this commonly indicates that they have gone through the legally prescribed procedures for having their concerns addressed, and those concerns have been repudiated, possibly not in open debate but by the exercise of managerial and legal power, which, as will appear, often seeks to push the whistleblower into a kind of exile and into silence. Where whistleblowers nevertheless speak out, often they are either seeking to speak over the heads of their immediate opponents to the public at large and thus open an alternative forum for the judgement of their claims, or seeking to make subjective sense of experiences that have disturbed their previous understanding of themselves and their world, and sometimes, as in Duffy's case, to do both these things. The second part of this chapter advances a hypothesis about guilt and the back-to-front world in which a whistleblower who suffers retaliation is liable to find themselves. That hypothesis especially concerns the emotions that might motivate that retaliation. The third part explores the underlying structures and predicaments of modern whistleblowing by reference to the emergence of bureaucracy and liberal democracy in order to grasp part of the reason why regulatory intervention often has difficulty working, leaving the way clear for essentially similar dramas of failure, avoidable suffering and retaliation to be repeated.

Case history: The emotional drama of whistleblowing

Happily, Peter Duffy is still a consultant surgeon. For many years he worked in the NHS, spending much of his career in the University Hospitals Morecambe Bay Trust (UHMBT). He now works for the health service of the Isle of Man. For several years at Morecambe Bay he was among those raising concerns about risky practice and clinical incidents in the urology department, as he was legally and professionally obliged to do.

In 2010 Duffy's concerns intensified. They related to staffing and workload and to the clinical competence of a small number of colleagues. On the day before Christmas Eve, his father died. Not feeling festive, Duffy worked on Christmas Day and Boxing Day. After Christmas he sought and was initially denied half a day's leave to attend his father's funeral. In January 2011, a story about Duffy that had run in the local papers in the spring of 2010 appeared in the national press. It concerned a teenager, one of whose testicles Duffy had removed because of a high risk that it was cancerous. Duffy had advised the patient that there was a chance that the lump would prove benign, but that it would be safest to operate. Nevertheless, the story ran in some national newspapers in January 2011, and it was implied that Duffy had been incompetent.[3] A couple of weeks later the General Medical Council (GMC) launched an inquiry, which could have caused Duffy to be struck off. He later recalled that his shock on opening the letter from the GMC announcing the inquiry 'had [him] instantly leaning over the kitchen sink, retching'.[4] At some point, those whose clinical competence he had challenged circulated accusations that Duffy was racist within the Trust – accusations that went unchallenged because, as Duffy reports, for a long time he was not confronted with them.[5] In 2012, after the GMC had exonerated him and after some of the tabloids had apologized for their reports of January 2011, his heart began to suffer episodes of irregular beating, after which it would stop and restart.[6] For the remainder of Duffy's time at Morecambe Bay, fear loomed large. He was troubled by the avoidable death in January 2015 of a man known as Patient 'A'. The case had come before the Coroner, and Duffy feared details of it were being covered up:

> I myself was simply too intimidated and frightened by the potential for more hostility and retaliation to put in a formal report regarding what was clearly an avoidable death and major incident following on from years of risk taking. To my intense shame, I allowed the incident to go past without formally alerting management, the GMC or the CQC about it.[7]

Later in 2015, he reports being 'so frightened of retaliation that I'd even taken the precaution of fitting extra fire alarms alongside our front and back doors, so fearful was I of some middle-of-the-night act of revenge'.[8] The early summer of 2016 was marked 'by a dread and constant sense of incipient disaster'.[9] At a meeting with the Medical Director in which he rehearsed his concerns about patient safety and the death of Patient 'A', he explained that he had at one point felt so crushed that he had planned suicide.[10]

Duffy took his concerns outside the Trust. From 2015 onwards, feeling he needed either to speak out about Patient 'A' or become complicit in a cover-up, he was in touch with the Care Quality Commission (CQC), whose timeline of events describes Duffy 'as being *terrified* that [his frankness] might end [his] career in the NHS'.[11] In July 2015 he called the GMC's helpline to voice concerns regarding Patient 'A', only to withdraw them the following day because, as he put it in an email to the GMC, 'the personal cost to myself of reporting these individuals is likely to be too high'.[12]

While he remained employed by UHMBT Duffy did not take his concerns directly to the media. Though he went outside the Trust, he did not go outside the healthcare system as a whole. However, as C. Fred Alford has argued, keeping one's concerns within the organization makes retaliation no less likely.[13]

It possibly makes more difference to the whistleblower, who in the UK, under the 1998 Public Interest Disclosure Act (PIDA), is expected first to raise their concerns internally or to a 'prescribed person', and to make them public only as a last resort.[14] Where retaliation ensues, this can mean that the whistleblower is isolated within their organization, with few allies outside it or even none. A report on whistleblowing in the NHS commissioned by Sir Robert Francis as part of his inquiry speaks of this as 'a particularly risky moment' for whistleblowers.[15] What Agnes Arnold-Forster describes (elsewhere in this volume) as 'the immersive experience of hospital life', at a period in the mid-twentieth century when junior doctors were normally resident in hospitals, is in some ways still a feature of modern hospitals because of the long hours, the need to display not just professional expertise but conformity to local culture and because of the peculiar and absorbing intensity of medical work.[16] When this immersive experience works well it can give rise to a 'protective sense of belonging'.[17] But it can go wrong, and protection and belonging can give way to victimization. Some little time after approaching the CQC, Duffy's overtime ceased to be paid, though he continued to work the extra hours. An accusation that he was making fraudulent claims was 'covertly circulated' in the Trust, though he learned of it only at his Employment Tribunal in 2018, when the Trust threatened to sue him for £100,000.[18] Having been thus isolated within the Trust, Duffy felt he had no option but to resign, which he did on 6 July 2016. In March 2016 he had been voted by his colleagues 'Doctor of the Year'.[19]

Everything alleged above – rounding on the messenger, the attempt to isolate, vilify and discredit them, keeping them within the organization for a period so as to find grounds for sacking or forcing them out not related to their whistleblowing, and then, finally, disposing of them in such a way as to deprive them of their career – often happens where whistleblowers suffer retaliation. These things are so common that the All Party Parliamentary Group on Whistleblowing has dubbed them the 'cycle of abuse'.[20] Some are illegal; others are manifestly unjust; but this narrative is, worryingly, *normal*.[21]

Duffy has ended up in a kind of exile that keeps him away from his family for much of the time. However, by comparison with what whistleblowers sometimes suffer, his case is, if anything, unusual in how comparatively well things have worked out. On leaving UHMBT, Duffy's attempts to get work elsewhere in the NHS came to nothing, but he has been able to continue to practise in the independent health service of the Isle of Man. In 2018 Duffy took UHMBT to an Employment Tribunal and won on several substantive issues. Because of that victory, one can speak with confidence of UHMBT unjustly withholding pay and constructively dismissing Duffy.[22] The Trust's counter-allegations against Duffy came to nothing. However, Duffy's claim to have suffered detriment as a whistleblower was not upheld, partly for want of evidence (no witness from UHMBT was willing to come forward, though several had indicated to Duffy an intention to do so),[23] partly because Duffy cut elements relating to this claim from his case to reduce his financial risk when UHMBT threatened to demand its costs from him, and partly because, while the judgement of the Tribunal was meticulous in citing legal precedent, it can sometimes seem curiously unaware of the way contested whistleblowing tends to work out. Perhaps the form of the legal reasoning of such a judgement precludes the use of such knowledge.

The fact that Duffy's claim to have suffered detriment as a whistleblower was not upheld in respect of the parts of that claim that he *did* pursue at the Tribunal does not mean that the Tribunal ruled that he had not made any protected disclosures or suffered detriment for them. In the Costs Judgment Employment Judge Franey, responding to the Trust's claim that Duffy should bear the costs it incurred in preparing to answer claims about detriment that were withdrawn just before the Tribunal sat, indicated,

> No determination as to the merits of the withdrawn complaints was made, and despite the analysis contained within the costs warning letter [sent by UHMBT's lawyers] the Tribunal has not been persuaded by the respondent that they must have had no reasonable prospect of success.

Though the Tribunal was cautious in expressing views about claims on which it had not adjudicated, and did not imply that they would necessarily have succeeded, it considered Duffy 'to be a genuine and credible witness'.[24] The Tribunal's judgement, therefore, arguably leaves the question of whether Duffy suffered detriment as a whistleblower in the sense recognized by PIDA unresolved. The GMC has yet to rule in several cases related to Duffy's allegations and to allegations against him.

However, in securing victory on other counts and an award of just over £100,000, Duffy did well, though not well enough to stop the Trust in the immediate aftermath of the Tribunal from taking public comfort in the fact that, in its view, the majority of Duffy's claims had not been upheld. Only recently, and then because of something else, has there been any indication that the Trust's position *might* change. I'll come back to that.

One of Duffy's advantages as a whistleblower may have been that he seems seldom to have been under any misapprehensions about how badly whistleblowing would be likely to work out for him. Perhaps he was thus inoculated against the kind of disillusionment that has pushed other whistleblowers not merely through an emotional cycle of fear, outrage and dismay but also into a kind of existential crisis in which the whistleblower finds 'that nothing he or she believed [about the world] was true'.[25] Reality for Duffy seems always to have been more to do with clinical facts and his obligations to patients. That part of his world remains intact. Even so, his story exhibits one of the hallmarks of whistleblowers' tales: a sense of living in two parallel, yet morally opposite, universes at once. In one universe he had been voted Doctor of the Year by his colleagues. In the upside-down version, he is vilified as a fraudster, defrauded, defamed, isolated and disposed of.

This sense of living in morally opposite universes is replicated in other whistleblowers' tales. For example, Julie Bailey, who played a crucial role in bringing failings in the Mid-Staffordshire NHS Trust to light, found herself simultaneously honoured for her campaign (created a CBE in 2014 and named by *The Independent* and by BBC *Woman's Hour* the second most powerful woman in Britain) and vilified, driven out of her home town, with her businesses having failed and her life savings lost. Even now, after several reports have upheld the substance of her claims, some still deny her credibility and insist that she was either lying or delusional. It is one thing to be a controversial figure, and to excite strong opinions for and against oneself, but it is stranger and less explicable to be simultaneously in some sense so powerful while being in another so obviously power*less*.

Guilt and moral inversion

Duffy's account points to several features of the emotional plight of the whistleblower. One is that taking on one's organization is so much a test of endurance as virtually to be trial by ordeal, and a good deal of suffering can be experienced as punitive without its being formally acknowledged as punishment. Such unacknowledged punishment contributes to a sense of the world bifurcating into an official world and a nastier but, at times, more real world in which public right is routinely bested. That nastier, other world often feels as if it has something archaic about it. Hence Alford's description of modern management as feudal.[26] In this inverted world, the rights that should protect us mean little and are apt to be replaced by guilt, while due process morphs into a Kafkaesque nightmare, in which the attempt to bring the truth to light gets smothered by proceduralism.

There have been some valuable attempts to explore the subjective and affective experience of whistleblowers, both in scholarship[27] and in several films.[28] It is harder to get at the experience of the people who close ranks to retaliate *against* whistleblowers. Some reluctantly go along with retaliation because they have been intimidated, which is what may have happened to several of the witnesses Peter Duffy intended to call at his Employment Tribunal.[29] The way bureaucracy and hierarchy numb moral intuitions has been invoked to explain why many turn from or even against whistleblowers.[30] But, while this might explain the willingness not just of senior managers, who might be threatened by the whistleblower's revelations, but also of other people within the organization to contribute to the victimization of the whistleblower, it doesn't explain the strange way in which management, supposedly committed to the organization's professed values, can support someone who may be guilty of betraying those values, while joining with them in seeking to destroy the professional life of the whistleblower who is seeking to uphold them. This is what allegedly happened in Peter Duffy's case. Similarly, Eileen Chubb, as a care worker in BUPA's Isard House, found herself under the supervision of a manager who, Chubb contends, 'needed to feel the power that came from inflicting pain and fear', and enjoyed making the residents suffer, yet the management closed ranks in support of that manager and against those who warned them about her.[31]

Another possibility, especially in relation to Duffy's acknowledgement of a sense of shame regarding his failure formally to register his concerns over the death of Patient 'A', is that feelings associated with wrongdoing do not necessarily correlate to an objective state of being guilty. So far from existing in a world in which everyone is innocent until proven guilty, it's possible for organizations to lapse into a condition in which feelings of being compromised, complicit and vulnerable can ensnare almost anyone. At the outset of his career at Morecambe, a colleague at Duffy's leaving party at his previous hospital warned him that in dealing with certain allegations (such as a hypothetical, retaliatory accusation of racism) 'the NHS's knee-jerk response . . . tends to be *guilty until proven guilty*'.[32] Conversely, others can do reprehensible things while appearing curiously untouchable. The most notorious instance of this phenomenon is the self-image Himmler offered to the SS in the Posen speeches in October 1943, regarding the 'final solution' whereby they were invited to think of themselves as maintaining their essential decency and humanity while standing beside 100, 500, 1,000 corpses, whose murder constituted (in Himmler's view) a painful duty and an act of extraordinary self-sacrifice on the part of the SS. This repulsive phrase-making may also have marked an attempt on Himmler's part to bind the

Nazi elite in complicity in this most hideous of crimes, and, if so, the speech's disavowal of guilt betrays precisely the opposite. Guilts of various kinds can have powerful and perverse effects in the ways in which they help to constitute groups, by binding some people together, while excluding and sacrificing others.

This phenomenon of guilt being disavowed and yet embraced by a group, perhaps even inflicted on them by each other, is perverse by the standards of the 'official' world of law, morality and the presumption of innocence. In ways that rational policymaking over whistleblowing has difficulty dealing with, this phenomenon arguably contributes to the problems whistleblowers encounter. Even though by its nature it is usually hidden, there are several well-attested instances of it, though the ones that come to public attention are often in extreme situations, such as during war. There is some evidence, for example, that atrocities such as those committed by American forces at My Lai in Vietnam were more common than has been generally acknowledged and involved some recruits being inducted into combat units precisely by being *required* to commit murder and rape.[33]

The idea that everyone is in some sense guilty can exercise extraordinary power, sometimes for good and often for ill. Some whistleblowers profess to have been motivated by guilt. Julie Bailey, who campaigned to expose failings in the Mid-Staffs NHS Trust after the death of her mother in Stafford Hospital, admits that at times 'Guilt consumed me . . . for allowing Mom to die' in ghastly circumstances, and it could be debilitating, and yet, though she still struggles with that guilt, it has also spurred her on.[34] However, if everyone feels or fears themselves to be guilty of something, it might make dealing with *specific* and actual wrongdoing almost impossible: the sinner can hide in a forest of supposed sins and take refuge in the fatalistic notion that, since everyone errs, they individually are not particularly to blame.

One might interpret the retaliation that Duffy experienced from 2011 onwards as a trial of strength, whose purpose was to remind him that he was a vassal at the mercy of the powerful. The assertion of personal domination can sometimes manifest itself in supposedly impersonal hierarchies (in sexual harassment, for example). But a scenario in which ethical concerns are simply silenced by the abuse of power risks being too crudely wrong to be psychologically plausible. However, what if one posits a cadre of managers and staff who in some sense *already* feel ensnared in generalized complicity? When inspectors or regulators arrive it is easy for an understandable impulse to put on a good show to go a fateful step further and to become an exercise in which the inspected betray a resentful sense of their own vulnerability and a determination not to be found out. In other words, they start acting fearfully and guiltily, and at that point one's world splits into a real but concealed world of suspected culpability and failure and an official world in which all is well, provided one gets the now psychologically needed clean bill of health from the inspectors. Tracy Coates, speaking of her experience as a regulator visiting NHS hospitals, remarks that in toxic workplaces one can feel the fear among the staff almost immediately, and I'd add that behind that fear there may loom the spectre of generalized guilt.[35] Duffy recalls having been in a meeting in his last fortnight at Morecambe Bay with CQC inspectors where the collective fear was palpable and made him feel so ill he had to leave the room.[36]

What happens if one posits that the whistleblower is trying to raise concerns in an organization that already feels such generalized guilt? First, an allegation of *any* shortcoming becomes anathema. Among the few things that might alleviate this nagging sense of complicity are external recognition and reward, and the whistleblower threatens those things. By comparison, someone with real and specific failings is probably safe: they need managerial cover, and (in this scenario) the management identifies with them in their shared vulnerability. Their alleged wrongdoing is easily discounted, because everyone is assumed already to be guilty of *something*, and so the obvious response to an accusation from a whistleblower is to set about revealing *their* guilt and to show them what it means to suffer the consequences of it without managerial protection. That protection, available only to the 'good team-player', is on this hypothesis the only salve for one's failings, even as the organization as a whole needs approval from above (coincidentally, UHMBT was applying for Foundation Trust status when Duffy raised his concerns, and this would give it the prestige of official approval and a degree of financial autonomy within the NHS). The hypocrisy of the common retaliatory move whereby the staff evaluation of the whistleblower goes abruptly from being excellent to being so bad as to justify disciplinary action and dismissal would be hard for those guilty of it to swallow without some such psychological excuse.

What this speculation points to is an inversion of the professional and ethical world as we normally think of it, and one which, for the retaliators, has a compelling logic, obscuring some guilts and conjuring up others. If retaliation is conceived *merely* as nefarious self-interest on the part of managers, the conviction with which it is pursued becomes implausible. But conceived in the terms outlined here, self-interest becomes wrapped around with a perversely soteriological disguise and a spirit of solidarity. If one believes that only thus can we all live with ourselves and receive such absolution as the rites of modern managerialism afford, the whistleblower is a heretic. Hence, perhaps, the way Duffy was exposed to trial by public opinion for his operation to remove a possibly cancerous testicle from a teenager in 2010. Public opinion, in the shape of the press, duly condemned him in January 2011, and, as noted above, the GMC set about investigating. It is possible, in effect, that the first act of *public* whistleblowing in the drama Duffy was part of at Morecambe Bay (i.e. whistleblowing that ignores the law's schedule of 'prescribed persons' to whom disclosure should first be made and instead appeals directly to the public at large) was undertaken by someone else *against* him. If so, the symmetry of allegation being met by allegation points to this odd sense of the world having doubled so as to have acquired a grotesque mirror image of itself.[37]

Whistleblowing and liberal democracy

The idea of a group or organization being defined by complicity or shared guilt inverts one of the founding myths of liberal democracy. Contractarian political theory tells stories of the origin of political authority in which we enjoy certain rights *prior* to its constitution, which have to be respected *after* it. This is a key move in generating limited government and some sense of everyone within a state enjoying formal equality with each other. At the heart of contractarian theory, therefore, is the idea of universal, individual and innate rights.

One way of negating contractarianism's myth of political origin is to posit that, instead of enjoying inherent rights, we are instead burdened with original guilt and moral indebtedness. In lieu of rights that power must uphold and respect, one posits instead a condition that calls for punishment and makes us vulnerable to the worst that power can do.

A world of universal guilt is, historically, precisely what underlies contractarianism's founding assumption of universal rights: the pre-Enlightenment Europe of religious strife and terror of damnation. The role that Christian belief in humanity's inherent sinfulness played in giving rise to forms of modern life that proceed on a completely different assumption has been much debated. Max Weber gave an account of the role of Protestantism in the emergence of capitalism, which he saw as having been assisted by a 'spirit' or attitude of mind that sought relief from anxiety about salvation in systematic, unremitting, ascetic, this-worldly economic endeavour. In this way, profits accumulated, Weber argues, and were ploughed back into businesses, because, though they were a sign that God *might* save you, self-indulgence was not. Weber doesn't see this intense spiritual drama with its almost incidental contribution to capitalism's birth as having to continue indefinitely. Once the superior business efficiency of rationalized, systematic endeavour has been established, and it has outcompeted less efficient forms of economic activity, what was once accomplished as a result of an inner and spiritual drama will be accomplished instead by merely external compulsion, and we will find ourselves in what he calls 'a steel-hard casing' in which rationalization presents itself as a merely external constraint. [38]

Weber's work shows a way of questioning the values and founding myths of liberal democracy by going back from the world of the Enlightenment, which did much to formulate those values and myths, to the bloodier world of Reformation Europe. I have raised the possibility in this chapter that there may be some sense in which anxiety about guilt and the possibility of a kind of redemption, so far from being confined (in their sociological effects) to the past may still – in a toxic workplace, for example – continue to make themselves felt, albeit disconnected from theology, in ways that impinge on whistleblowers. If so, then one of the reasons why policymaking has difficulty making adequate provision for whistleblowing is that the dramas of whistleblowing can unfold according to a logic of which liberal reason is ignorant, revealing aspects of human behaviour deeply at odds with liberal reason's preferred model of human nature. If that is so, certain of its characteristic responses to misconduct are likely to prove counterproductive in relation to whistleblowing. If, for example, an organization has gone awry in such a way that its staff are oppressed by a generalized sense or fear of guilt, then intensifying regulatory inspection (a perfectly normal response), so far from improving matters, could make them worse, because it could intensify that sense of guilt.

Weber's work calls the substantive reason of the Enlightenment into question (reason as, e.g., a source of truths to live by) and obliges us to reconsider whether our beliefs and ways of conducting ourselves are informed by truths underwritten by reason or are merely instrumentally rationalized. Though Weber envisages spiritual anxiety about salvation ceasing to be sociologically significant, he sees rationalization as continuing to manifest itself and expanding its empire in spiritually deadening and unaccountable bureaucracy.[39]

There is a tension between the public significance of matters that we are most likely to gain special knowledge of in our employment and our subordinate position as employees, which may deny us the freedom to use that knowledge in public debate. Where their organization retaliates against whistleblowers, it seeks to send them into a kind of exile. It is an exile not just from the organization or from their profession but also, if the retaliators have their way, from any public role or plausibility. Whistleblowers might have supposed that they were free, rights-bearing individuals, capable of shouldering responsibilities and being held accountable for their actions, and expecting others to be held accountable in their turn. But in confronting a bureaucratic administration, whistleblowers typically have to deal with a system that can be used to obscure personal responsibility and which often declines to deal with the whistleblower face to face. It is of a piece with bureaucracy's capacity to displace responsibility that accusations against Duffy are said to have circulated *covertly* within the Trust. As Arendt noted, bureaucracy can be a peculiarly tyrannical form of governance, precisely because it is 'the rule of nobody' so there is no one to hold to account.[40]

Whistleblowers may have to confront bureaucracy twice over. Most of them work within bureaucratic organizations, within bureaucratic states and, even though it is the state that the whistleblower may need to appeal to for protection, there is some sense in which the state and the whistleblower's organization are likely to be structurally akin to each other so that the state's legal prescription for whistleblowing is likely to be couched in *forms* that, almost as a matter of course, are in greater harmony with the organization of which the whistleblower complains than with whistleblowers themselves, even though in its *content* it aims to help whistleblowers.

Whistleblowers may look to the law for protection and vindication of their attempt to draw attention to real ills, but what they often find is procedural complexity and a set of complex obligations and preferences that threaten to disqualify them from such remedy as the law affords. Sir Robert Francis argues that PIDA does not really provide protection against detriment, so much as give whistleblowers a limited way of securing remedy after they have suffered detriment.[41] Though plainly not intended in this way, PIDA could even be seen as giving retaliatory employers a map showing on what grounds whistleblowers can best be attacked. A PID defence cannot be used in cases where the whistleblower has committed a crime in making the disclosure, so an organization may try to taint a whistleblower with alleged criminality (Duffy, coincidentally or not, was accused of racism and fraud). In its original form there was a requirement that disclosures had to be made in good faith, though this was removed in 2013 by the Enterprise and Regulatory Reform Act. However, a qualifying disclosure still has to be made in the 'reasonable belief' on the part of the whistleblower that what they are revealing qualifies on one of several prescribed grounds as being in the public interest. This can put the reasonableness of whistleblowers themselves under scrutiny. It may be worth remembering here that UHMBT's lawyers insisted that Duffy was making claims at the tribunal with no *reasonable* chance of success.

Even when speaking out is a professional and legal obligation, the impulse to do so may have to contend with the way one's professional identity has been formed. Professional identity, even for clinicians of the same kind, is not all of a piece. Possibly one of the difficulties Duffy ran into was that his professional identity, on his own account, was attached most powerfully to the practice of medicine as such at however humble a level (he speaks fondly of his days as a theatre orderly) rather than to his achieved status as a consultant surgeon. Deborah Gill, in a study of the formation of professional identity among junior doctors, notes that they arrive at different degrees of identification with their professional role, some being unshakably convinced that they are now 'a doctor for life' while others nurse doubts.[42] In this context, Duffy's account of his own formation as a doctor is striking for the way his lifelong identification with medical work *preceded* his becoming a doctor. His vocation was for life, and he seems never to have been overly preoccupied with his own advancement. What he recalls he wanted from the first time he witnessed an operation (once he'd recovered from having fainted) was to be part of a surgical team.[43]

This identification with medicine as such may be seen in his willingness to do mundane tasks whenever the need arises. This was attested in his citation as Doctor of the Year in 2016 at Morecambe Bay and more recently in the reasons for his being awarded an MBE for his going beyond the call of duty in fighting Covid on the Isle of Man.[44] However proud he is of his profession, he is a humble man.

In medicine and, as it happens, in academia, the formation of one's professional identity on the basis of a vocational commitment that in the last analysis trumps commitment to self-advancement often sits most happily with commitment to collegial self-organization at the departmental level. The integration of such collegial, self-organized units with a larger line-managed system is notoriously difficult, especially when resources are scarce. An obvious alternative model of formation emphasizes instead personal prestige and promotion. The existence of this broad division between the collegially and the hierarchically oriented in groups of otherwise similarly qualified professionals can give rise to friction. The value of a model of professionalism in which individual prestige and career advancement loom large is that it often goes along with a certain daring and ambition and looks likely to make one responsive to managerial imperatives. This is normal, and any organization in which people were immune to the incentives offered by promotion and recognition would be in trouble, because it would be unbiddable; but then so, too, would an organization that had no space for vocational commitment such that one's primary loyalty is to one's profession or to one's patients, rather than to one's employer.

These alternatives are not absolute: most people strike a balance between them in their professional lives. However, in cases of contested whistleblowing these differences can become battlelines. It seems possible that in Duffy's case certain features of his personality and possibly also of his medical condition were misread as weakness by those whom his outspokenness threatened, and they attacked accordingly, probably expecting, as Duffy puts it, that 'he'll just disappear', which is what he fears happens to many whistleblowers.[45]

Citizens in liberal democracies, in principle, enjoy political rights. But this is not the same as possessing the kind of public personality that will enable one fully to exercise them. That is something one has to *achieve*. Whistleblowers commonly start in private life, in relation to which their employment may be what connects them most with the world at large, even if, as employees, their roles are formally subordinate. For clinicians the formation of their professional identity usually will not have prompted them to cultivate this kind of public capacity. For those who suffer retaliation, at the moment at which it starts they are neither protected by the state and nor are they likely to have the resources or capacities to protect themselves. Their position as private individuals, whose status and freedoms many liberal democratic rights seek to uphold, is exactly what makes them vulnerable. One of the few ways in which a whistleblower who suffers retaliation and is not willing or able to back down can reconstitute themselves, having been sent into a kind of exile, is by accepting the need to move fully into the public sphere by becoming an activist for reforms of the sector in which they previously worked.

However, a commitment to activism and reform is likely to entail interminable struggle. As Julie Bailey's 2019 epilogue to her account of the misconduct she witnessed at Mid-Staffs indicates, though the situation in which the whistleblower intervenes can sometimes get better, there is seldom much sense of arriving at a definitive conclusion after which all is well. In Bailey's view the leadership of the Mid-Staffs NHS Trust continued to be flawed until 2009 when Antony Sumara became CEO. Bailey writes warmly of her support for Sumara. But his appointment did not mean she could consider her task done. She still had to struggle to secure a public inquiry (there had already been an independent inquiry, which Cure the NHS argued was inadequate). Having secured such an inquiry, Bailey attended it every day that it heard evidence, except one, when she was giving evidence to the Health Select Committee on Complaints and

Litigation. The public inquiry resulted in the *Report of the Mid Staffordshire NHS Foundation Trust Public Inquiry* (2013). Nor was that the end of the struggle. For Julie Bailey, the battle she fought at Mid-Staffs has emerged as merely one in a continuing campaign, in which her energies have increasingly been directed to larger, more systemic problems. For example, she now seeks reform of PIDA. Similarly, Eileen Chubb now campaigns for PIDA's replacement.[46]

Becoming participants in public debates resolves an inner tension for Bailey and Chubb, though it commits them to continue to struggle in the world at large. Bailey concludes the revised edition of her book with the warning that certain of the problems she identified at Mid-Staffs look set to recur. If there is anything in the case presented here about the historical roots of the problems whistleblowers encounter, such recurrent problems are symptomatic of how counterproductive normal policy responses can be when applied to the guilt-ridden dynamics of whistleblowing and retaliation. Indeed, Peter Duffy's difficulties at Morecambe came to a head in the immediate *aftermath* of the publications of the Francis reports into Mid-Staffs (2010 and 2013) and of *Freedom to Speak Up* in the NHS in general (2015) and of a report (also in 2015) into the avoidable deaths of babies and other failings in midwifery at UHMBT.[47]

Not every whistleblower feels able to follow the example set by Chubb and Bailey by engaging in public campaigns. Many of the emotions associated with whistleblowing are an obstacle to the assertion of public personality and the fulfilment of public duty. Among the emotions that might play this role are the fear and shame that can assail the whistleblower and (if this counts as an emotion) the guilt that I have suggested might play a role in motivating those who retaliate against the whistleblower. There is an affinity between *some* influential hypotheses in the history of emotions and the idea of modernity as cultivating an intense, affective and largely *private* life. To that extent, it is hardly surprising if there exists a tension between the intense emotions to which whistleblowing can give rise and a capacity to act in the public interest in a way that in law is deemed to justify whistleblowing. Though the move to appeal for judgement to the public at large and thus (in some cases) to sustained activism is one way of addressing some of the dilemmas that whistleblowers face, it is fraught with difficulty. Unsurprisingly, many whistleblowers lapse, instead, into silence.

Duffy's position appears more ambiguous than Chubb's and Bailey's for at least two reasons. His vocation is in medicine, and professionally not just his living but his identity is at stake. That vocation seems always to have taken a form that led him away from playing a public role. Duffy notes that when he was engaged in medical research he found speaking at academic conferences nerve-wracking and was glad to get back to clinical work, and, though determined to deliver the eulogy at his father's funeral, part of him would sooner have been in an operating theatre.[48] Eileen Chubb's account of her discovery of her public voice starts by explaining that, before becoming a whistleblower, she was the last person one would expect to make a fuss about anything. So she was surprised when she heard herself speak at Bromley Social Services as she handed over the signed statements of herself and six of her fellow workers at Isard House 'in a loud determined voice' that it took her a moment to recognize as her own.[49] That moment is a point at which her story and Peter Duffy's diverge. Notwithstanding his book, it is not clear that Duffy wants the kind of public role Bailey and Chubb have shouldered. He chose to go to the Isle of Man to continue to practise medicine. Only having been there for some time did he start to write an account of his experiences for publication. Three years after his constructive dismissal and more than eight years after the apparent onset of serious retaliation against him, he put his case before the public. Only at this point did Duffy step clear of the stipulations of PIDA. And, though it is too soon to know how this will work out, the publication of his book marked some seeming shift in the position of UHMBT. In September 2019, spurred on by representations from four local MPs, UHMBT's CEO Aaron Cummins acknowledged that he had 'no doubt there are ongoing issues' and appeared to be ready for there to be a proper external inquiry into the concerns raised by Duffy and others, and the Trust expressed willingness to discuss these with Duffy.[50]

To the extent that Duffy's book is an intervention in a public debate about a public institution, this reaction to it looks hopeful; and yet the book is also, arguably, an attempt to make personal sense of what he has gone through. Running through it is a yearning to return to private, family life. In working at UHMBT Duffy was working not merely in the place where his wife and himself were bringing up a family but also in the region in which he had been brought up. His loss for most of the year of access to a place that is home to him in a way that nowhere else could ever be cuts deep, and this somewhat qualifies the terms on which he engages in public argument. Eileen Chubb's book, by comparison, though full of personal experiences, is an account of the formation of an activist and of the discovery of a vocation as an activist. In a webinar on 12 September 2020, I put to Duffy the view of Eileen Chubb that PIDA is useless and the only thing that does any good is taking one's story directly to the media. Though taken aback by what he called the bluntness of the question, after thinking for a moment, ruefully he concurred.

However, one should be cautious. If there's anything in the case I have presented here, the plight of whistleblowers who suffer retaliation may have proximate causes, but it also has deep historical roots. Those roots are likely to be difficult to shift. If I am right about their existence, they point to one reason why stories of retaliated whistleblowing in different sectors and even different countries resemble one another in key respects, almost irrespective of legislation. Indeed, one reason for focusing on Peter Duffy's case in this essay is precisely that it came to a head *after* the publication of the *Freedom to Speak Up* report, with its key argument for cultural change. I concur with that argument but suspect that the cultures in question will prove resistant to change. For the time being, we live in a world in which the whistleblower's moral courage appears to be essential and yet acting on it is often at an impossibly high price for whistleblowers themselves.[51] In Bertolt Brecht's play *Leben des Galilei* (*The Life of Galileo*), Galileo publishes his finding that the earth revolves around the sun and is then intimidated by the Church and silenced to the dismay of his follower, Andrea Sarti, who rebukes Galileo with the remark that it's an unhappy land that lacks heroes. Galileo replies, '*Unglücklich das Land, das Helden nötig hat*' (It's an unhappy land that needs heroes).[52] Unless we can get at the deep roots of the problems that whistleblowing encounters, we may be glad of the heroism of whistleblowers, but we should rue the need for it.

Acknowledgements

I am grateful to Sam Ashenden, with whom this chapter was planned, though pressure of Covid-related work obliged her to leave its writing to me. We are grateful to the Birkbeck Institute for Social Research for supporting our work on guilt. The chapter is deeply indebted to Peter Duffy and to participants in the Birkbeck Guilt Group's whistleblowing colloquium on 10 June 2017, especially to our speakers: Julie Bailey, Eileen Chubb, Christine England, Marianna Fotaki, Lauren Kierans, Joe Kosow, John Meek, Wim Vanderkerckhove and Karis Winton.

Notes

1 Hart, 'Nurse Heroes'.
2 Hilton, 'Whistle-blowing in the National Health Service'.

3   See, for example, 'Teenager has testicle removed', *The Daily Mail*.
4   Duffy, *Whistle in the Wind*, 54.
5   Duffy, *Whistle in the Wind*, 82, 125.
6   Duffy, *Whistle in the Wind*, 58–9.
7   Duffy, *Whistle in the Wind*, 87.
8   Duffy, *Whistle in the Wind*, 93.
9   Duffy, *Whistle in the Wind*, 149.
10 Duffy, *Whistle in the Wind*, 145.
11 Duffy, *Whistle in the Wind*, 113.
12 Duffy, *Whistle in the Wind*, 108.
13 Alford, *Whistleblowers: Broken Lives*, 20.
14 See 'Public Interest Disclosure Act 1998'.
15 Vandekerckhove and Rumyantseva, *Freedom to Speak Up*.
16 Arnold-Forster, 'Emotional Landscape'.
17 Arnold-Forster, 'Emotional Landscape'.
18 Duffy, *Whistle in the Wind*, 136–7.
19 Duffy, *Whistle in the Wind*, 137, 152.
20 All Party Parliamentary Group on Whistleblowing, *Whistleblowing: the personal cost*, 21.
21 Other cases that follow this broad pattern include Olivia Greene at the Irish Nationwide Building Society (Kenny, *Whistleblowing: Toward a New Theory*, 106–10); Elin Baklid-Kunz at the Halifax Hospital in Florida (Mueller, *Crisis of Conscience*, 160–2); and Franz Gayl in the US Marine Corps (Mueller, *Crisis of Conscience*, 55–6).
22 See Employment Tribunal, 'Mr P Duffy v University Hospitals Morecambe Bay NHS Foundation Trust'.
23 Duffy, *Whistle in the Wind*, 187.
24 Employment Tribunal, 'Mr P Duffy v University Hospitals Morecambe Bay NHS Foundation Trust', Costs Judgment, para. 47 (c) and (f).
25 Alford, *Whistleblowers: Broken Lives*, 20.
26 Alford, *Whistleblowers: Broken Lives*, 100–2.
27 See Kenny, *Whistleblowing: Toward a New Theory*, which draws on Judith Butler's work to explore the experience of whistleblowers in the financial sector, especially in relation to subjectivity and discourse as such.
28 Examples of feature films based on real whistleblowers include *Serpico* (dir. Sidney Lumet, 1973), *Silkwood* (dir. Mike Nichols, 1983), *Erin Brockovich* (dir. Steven Soderbergh, 2000), *Official Secrets* (dir. Gavin Hood, 2019).
29 Duffy, *Whistle in the Wind*, 195.
30 Mueller, *Crisis of Conscience*, 123–31; Alford, *Whistleblowers: Broken Lives*, 117–19.
31 Chubb, *Beyond the Façade*, loc. 577.
32 Duffy, *Whistle in the Wind*, 29.

33 Mueller, *Crisis of Conscience*, 88–9.
34 Bailey, *From Ward to Whitehall*, loc. 2393.
35 See Coates, 'Personal Reflections'.
36 Telephone conversation on 8 December 2020.
37 The idea that mimicry might play a key role in escalating aggression is explored in Girard, *Violence and the Sacred*. It also presents a theory of scapegoating that has been applied (e.g. by Alford in *Whistleblowers: Broken Lives*, 124–30) to whistleblowing.
38 Weber, *The Protestant Ethic*, 123.
39 For Weber's view of bureaucracy as inescapable and expansionist, see, e.g. 'Parliament and Government in Germany'.
40 Arendt, *Responsibility and Judgment*, 31.
41 Francis, *Freedom to Speak Up*, 40, sect. 2.2.9.
42 *Becoming Doctors*, 96–7.
43 Duffy, *Whistle in the Wind*, 3–4.
44 'Birthday Honours 2020'.
45 Telephone conversation on 8 December 2020.
46 Bailey, *From Ward to Whitehall*, epilogue. loc. 2953; Compassion in Care, 'Edna's Law'.
47 Bunyan, 'Morecambe Bay report'. See also Kirkup, *The Report of the Morecambe Bay Investigation*.
48 Duffy, *Whistle in the Wind*, 21, 53.
49 Chubb, *Beyond the Façade*, loc. 952.
50 'Morecambe Bay NHS Trust'.
51 Ceva and Bocchiola in *Is Whistleblowing a Duty?* note the excessive price paid by the heroic whistleblower and propose instead a model of whistleblowing as an 'organizational duty'. In this model whistleblowing would have to be in some sense normal. But how to achieve that normality?
52 Brecht, *Gesammelte Werke*. 5: 274.

Bibliography

Alford, C. Fred. *Whistleblowers: Broken Lives and Organizational Power*. Ithaca, NY: Cornell University Press, 2001.

All Party Parliamentary Group on Whistleblowing. *Whistleblowing: the personal cost of doing the right thing and the cost to society of ignoring it*. [n.p.]: 2019.

Arendt, Hannah. *Responsibility and Judgment*, edited by Jerome Kohn. New York: Schocken Books, 2003.

Arnold-Forster, Agnes. 'The Emotional Landscape of the Hospital Residence in Post-war Britain'. In *Feelings and Work*, edited by Agnes Arnold-Forster and Alison Moulds, 58–75. London: Bloomsbury, 2022.

Bailey, Julie. *From Ward to Whitehall*, 2nd edn. [n.p.]: Cure the NHS/Amazon, 2019. Kindle EBook.

'Birthday Honours 2020: Surgeon who comforted dying patients becomes MBE'. *BBC News*, 10 October 2020. https://www.bbc.co.uk/news/world-europe-isle-of-man-544 84391.

Brecht, Bertolt. *Gesammelte Werke*. 20 Vols. Frankfurt am Main: Suhrkamp, 1967.

Bunyan, Nigel. 'Morecambe Bay report exposes "lethal mix" of failures that led to baby deaths'. *The Guardian*, 3 March 2015. https://www.theguardian.com/society/2015/mar/03/morecambe-bay-report-lethal-mix-problems-baby-deaths-cumbria.

Ceva, Emanuela, and Michele Bocchiola. *Is Whistleblowing a Duty?* Cambridge: Polity, 2019.

Chubb, Eileen. *Beyond the Façade*. Brentwood: Chipmunka Publishing, 2008. Kindle EBook.

Coates, Tracy. 'Personal Reflections on the Courage to Speak Up'. AfPP online seminar. 26 September 2020. https://www.youtube.com/watch?v=YqTlxiZQDmA.

Compassion in Care. 'Edna's Law'. https://compassionincare.com/ednas-law-0.

Duffy, Peter. 'NHS whistleblowing. The good, the bad and the ugly'. AfPP online seminar. 12 September 2020. https://www.youtube.com/watch?v=-dSfLmn2iPc.

Duffy, Peter. Telephone conversation on 8 December 2020.

Duffy, Peter. *Whistle in the Wind: Life, Death, Detriment and Dismissal in the NHS* ([n.p]: Independently published via Amazon, 2019).

Employment Tribunal. 'Mr P Duffy v University Hospitals Morecambe Bay NHS Foundation Trust: 2404382/2016 and 2406078/2016'. 28 November 2017. https://www.gov.uk/employment-tribunal-decisions/mr-p-duffy-v-university-hospitals-morecambe-bay-nhs-foundation-trust-2404382-2016-and-2406078-2016.

Francis, Sir Robert. *Freedom to Speak Up: An Independent Review Into Creating an Open and Honest Culture in the NHS*. [n.p.]: 2015. http://freedomtospeakup.org.uk/wp-content/uploads/2014/07/F2SU_web.pdf.

Gill, Deborah. *Becoming Doctors: The formation of professional identity in newly qualified doctors*. Doctoral thesis, Institute of Education, April 2013. https://core.ac.uk/download/pdf/33679204.pdf.

Girard, René. *Violence and the Sacred*. Translated by Patrick Gregory. London: The Athlone Press, 1988.

Hart, Chris. 'Nurse Heroes: A History of Blowing the Whistle'. Paper presented at *A Natural History of Raising Concerns*, Royal College of Nursing, 4 March 2020.

Hilton, Claire. 'Whistle-blowing in the National Health Service since the 1960s'. Policy Papers, *History and Policy*, 26 August 2016. http://www.historyandpolicy.org/policy-papers/papers/whistle-blowing-in-the-national-health-service-since-the-1960s.

Hood, Gavin, dir. *Official Secrets*. 2019.

Kenny, Kate. *Whistleblowing: Toward a New Theory*. Cambridge, MA: Harvard University Press, 2019.

Kirkup, Bill. *The Report of the Morecambe Bay Investigation*. London: The Stationery Office, 2015. https://assets.publishing.service.gov.uk/government/uploads/system/uploads/attachment_data/file/408480/47487_MBI_Accessible_v0.1.pdf.

Lumet, Sidney. dir. *Serpico*. 1973.

'Morecambe Bay NHS Trust: Hospital to meet whistleblower'. *BBC News*, 5 September 2019. https://www.bbc.co.uk/news/uk-england-lancashire-49598577.

Mueller, Tom. *Crisis of Conscience: Whistleblowing in an Age of Fraud*. London: Atlantic Books, 2019.

Nichols, Mike, dir. *Silkwood*. 1983.

'Public Interest Disclosure Act 1998'. https://www.legislation.gov.uk/ukpga/1998/23/contents.

Soderbergh, Steven, dir. *Erin Brockovich*. 2000.

'Teenager has testicle removed after diagnosed with cancer... then he is told "it was just a cyst"'. *The Daily Mail*, 20 January 2011. https://www.dailymail.co.uk/health/article-1348586/Teenager-testicle-removed-told-cancer--finds-just-cyst.html.

Vandekerckhove, Wim, and Nataliya Rumyantseva. *Freedom to Speak Up – Qualitative Research*, Report. University of Greenwich, 19 November 2014. https://www.academia.edu/10701006/Freedom_to_Speak_Up_in_the_NHS.

Weber, Max. 'Parliament and Government in Germany [1918]'. In *Political Writings*, edited by Peter Lassman and Ronald Speirs, 156–60. Cambridge: Cambridge University Press, 1994.

Weber, Max. *The Protestant Ethic and the Spirit of Capitalism*. Translated by Stephen Kalberg. Oxford: Blackwell, 2002.

'Whistleblower Lancaster surgeon wins £102,000 after unfair dismissal case'. *Lancaster Guardian*, 6 August 2018, https://www.lancasterguardian.co.uk/news/whistleblower-lancaster-surgeon-wins-aps102000-after-unfair-dismissal-case-849020.

12

The 'system' of service
Emotional labour and the theatrical metaphor
Jaswinder Blackwell-Pal

Since the publication of Arlie Russell Hochschild's *The Managed Heart* in 1983, the concept of 'emotional labour' which she introduced in her study, defined as 'the management of feeling to create a publicly observable facial and bodily display', has gained traction among sociologists, labour relations scholars and others interested in the changing landscape of work under neoliberal capitalism.[1] Despite its publication almost forty years ago, the work remains foundational and continues to offer the most thorough and compelling analysis of emotional labour and the toll it takes on employees forced to contend with the resultant emotional dissonance, burnout and alienation which Hochschild identifies. The text also remains key for the advancement of the theatrical metaphor and analogy within scholarship on contemporary work. Throughout her study, Hochschild draws comparisons between emotional labourers and the figure of the actor, in particular utilizing the work of Russian director Constantin Stanislavski to advance her theories of 'deep' and 'surface' acting, writing, 'Any functioning society makes effective use of its members' emotional labor. We do not think twice about the use of feeling in the theatre, or in psychotherapy, or in forms of group life that we admire.'[2]

Hochschild is not alone in drawing on the actor for her analysis. Other theorists of the changing conditions of work under neoliberal capitalism have taken the figure of the professionalized performer both as a reference point and symbol. In these accounts, the performer is understood as historically working under conditions to which other categories of workers now increasingly find themselves subject, in terms of a labour process which involves emotional and affective capabilities and conditions of employment often marked by precarity and short-term project-led work. For Paulo Virno, for example, the virtuoso, also known as the performing artist, is emblematic of wider changes under capitalism: 'the affinity between a pianist and a waiter, which Marx had foreseen, finds an unexpected confirmation in the epoch in which all wage labour has something in common with the "performing artist."'[3] Richard Sennett, in his now widely cited study of modern character, turns to the figure of Diderot's actor both as a model for understanding repetition in the labour process and to examine the demands of teamwork, characterized as 'the actor's mask of cooperation'.[4] Carl Cederström and Peter Fleming, referring to the category of artists in general, describe structural conditions defined by 'constant stress, self-employment, flexible working hours, no regulating contract and income, no pension scheme and low pay. In other words conditions almost identical to those now spreading through the post-industrial landscape.'[5]

Yet even as they attend to the incorporation of the worker's subjectivity into the labour process, comparisons such as these tend to overlook the actor as a worker themselves. While drawing heavily from Stanislavski's system of training and approach to acting, Hochschild frequently intervenes to remind her reader that this theatrical labour is qualitatively different from the forms of commercial emotional labour with which her study is concerned. By distinguishing the 'art' of acting from the 'work' of emotional labour, she also suggests that acting averts the particular dangers she identifies with emotional labour, namely emotional burnout, dissonance and detachment. On stage, she writes, 'we know who is acting' and 'the illusion leaves as it came, with the curtain'.[6] Hochschild's analysis casts actors as exempt from the exploitation and alienation identified elsewhere by virtue of theatre's status as 'art'. Sennett, similarly, argues that the comparison between factory workers and actors is false because 'the worker does not control his or her work', unlike the actor.[7] A recent increase in focus on the question of labour within the fields of theatre and performance studies allows us to trouble this formulation. Patrick McKelvey, for example, argues that 'Hochschild invokes theatre workers only to exclude them'.[8] In his exploration of performance and value in Marx's work, Shane Boyle goes further, arguing that theatrical production in fact 'exemplifies the capitalist production process'.[9] This growing body of scholarship around theatrical labour challenges us to think more carefully about actors, arguably the archetypal emotional labourers, as workers whose own labour process and conditions of employment have much to teach those of us interested in the study of emotional labour and work more broadly.

While scholarly comparisons with actors can be applied more concretely, then, there are also problems with how Hochschild's analysis deploys them as it stands and how her approach has informed the work of others who have built on her framework. Sharon Bolton and Carol Boyd, authors of one of the most direct critiques of Hochschild's analysis, retain her theatrical framing even while disregarding key elements of her political and economic analysis. Hochschild, they argue, offers an overly pessimistic focus on how emotions come under employer control through a process of transmutation and does not take account of voluntary displays of emotional labour that employees may perform, as well as the 'satisfaction, enjoyment and reward that can be gained from various forms of emotion work'.[10] Employees working in contemporary conditions requiring emotional labour are distinct from factory workers, they claim, because 'they own the means of production', that is, their own bodies, and thus 'the capacity to present a "sincere" or "cynical" performance lies within the emotional labourer'.[11] This mischaracterization of the means of production has been addressed by Paul Brook, and Bolton and Boyd's broader approach has also been discussed by other scholars.[12] However, it is notable that even in an attempt to break from Hochschild's broader analysis critics still adopt the lens of deep and surface acting and still position emotional labourers in relation to actors. Bolton and Boyd go so far as referring to the employees in Hochschild's work as 'crippled actors'.[13] That Hochschild's critics can so readily retain this element of her framework is at least in part due to the way that the theatrical lens, as established, aids an analysis with an almost exclusive focus on the experiences of individual workers, their capacities and strategies for coping with the demands of the job. As Brook has argued, Hochschild understands emotional labour 'principally through the individualized, conceptual lens of her distinction between individuals' surface and deep acting, and "transmutation of feelings"', outlining this as a weakness in her approach.[14] This tendency in turn creates problems within her analysis as it both neglects the broader and social implications of the ascendence of emotional labour, while also painting a pessimistic picture about the potential for tension or resistance within the workplace which might be organized around the demands presented by emotional labour and its attendant practices.

Hochschild's use of Stanislavski and the theatrical lens is not incidental, but rather foundational, to this individualizing mode of analysis. She introduces his approach as a way of understanding the individual emotional transmutation process of the worker, which is a limited and limiting understanding of Stanislavski's work. Hochschild writes that 'in everyday life, we are all to some degree students of Stanislavski; we are only poorer or better at deep acting, closer or more remote from incentives to do it well'.[15] But it is also the case that consideration of his legacy of systematized performer training might offer us perspectives on the collective experience of such work. As I will argue, this application of Stanislavski's work has a number of implications for how we conceive of the potential for employee organization or resistance in workplaces that are dependent on this type of labour, and the emergence of what Ben Trott has argued can be understood as 'emotional class struggle'.[16] Thinking more historically and concretely about the development of the Stanislavskian tradition can offer us new routes into thinking about how emotional labour is managed and collectivized. On this basis, this chapter will probe the theatrical analogy that informs Hochschild's work and suggest how a more nuanced consideration of the actor's profession might lend itself to studies of emotional labour beyond that profession. I will argue that there are three key problems with Hochschild's invocation of the actor. Firstly, it naturalizes culturally and historically specific notions of 'authenticity' which are in fact shaped by performance itself, both on and offstage. Secondly, her misattribution of the 'Method' school of acting to Stanislavski is a historical inaccuracy which obscures the nature of his contribution to acting, and finally her deployment of the 'deep' vs. 'surface' theory contributes to the individualization of what is actually a more collective process of shaping emotions in an institutional context. I will finish by suggesting ways in which Stanislavski might be more usefully understood in relation to emotional labour, specifically via insights into its management and direction.

The naturalization of emotional 'realism'

The question of the 'real' emotional self and its performative constitution is key to any analysis of emotional labour, which rests on making public an emotional expression underscored by the notion of authenticity. Hochschild addresses this through her use of the descriptors 'deep' and 'surface' acting – techniques available to workers who have to negotiate the professional expectation to present emotional reactions corresponding to a prescribed appropriate and authentic emotional state. Where deep acting, she writes, is 'a natural result of working on feeling' and involves 'spontaneous' expressions of 'self-induced feelings', surface acting involves feigning or 'putting on' the bodily or facial display.[17] Thus, for Hochschild, surface acting involves deceiving others about our emotional state, while deep acting also involves deceiving ourselves.[18] This self-deception (such as suppressing anger towards an insulting passenger) is achieved, Hochschild writes, 'by taking over the levers of feeling production, by pretending deeply, she [the worker] alters herself'.[19] Thus, deep acting is achieved via a fundamental change in one's own emotional self which comes about through repeat performance. The attachment an 'actor' might develop to their professional role – for example, flight attendant, security guard or barista – is determined by how much of their 'real' feeling has been 'self-induced' in the performance: deep acting is the spontaneous expression of such feeling, whereas surface acting involves a greater degree of separation between performer and role, in which expressions are actively 'put on' or the performer pretends to the emotions being enacted.[20] Where Hochschild acknowledges that she takes surface acting directly from sociologist Erving Goffman, her definition of deep acting is, she claims, adopted from the work of Stanislavski, specifically his book *An Actor Prepares*, first published in 1936.

In an article preceding the publication of *The Managed Heart*, Hochschild offers a more expansive and detailed take on the theoretical model of emotions she favours:

> Goffman suggests that we spend a good deal of effort managing impressions – that is, acting. He posits only one sort of acting – the direct management of behavioural expression. His illustrations, though, actually point to two types of acting – the direct management of behavioural expression (e.g., the given-off sigh, the shoulder shrug), and the management of feeling from which expression can follow (e.g., the thought of some hopeless project). An actor playing the part of King Lear might go about his task in two ways. One actor, following the English school of acting, might focus on outward demeanour, the constellation of minute expressions that correspond to Lear's sense of fear and impotent outrage. This is the sort of acting Goffman theorizes about. Another actor, adhering to the American or Stanislavsky school of acting, might guide his memories and feelings in such a way as to elicit the corresponding expressions. The first technique we might call 'surface acting', the second 'deep acting'. Goffman fails to distinguish the first from the second, and he obscures the importance of 'deep acting'. Obscuring this, we are left with the impression that social factors pervade only the 'social skin', the tried-for outer appearances of the individual. We are left under-estimating the power of the social.[21]

This passage is revealing in relation to the use of 'deep' and 'surface' acting and their resultant implications, to which I will return in a moment. The passage is also key, however, for demonstrating how Hochschild understands and utilizes Stanislavski within her work. By contrasting Stanislavski, whom she associated with the 'American school', to the surface acting of a supposed English school, we can see that her application of the theatrical metaphor begins with a substantial mischaracterization of his work. I will now briefly contextualize Stanislavski's work and its historical importance, before examining what the consequences of Hochschild's particular reading of him are.

Born to an industrialist family in Moscow in 1863, Stanislavski described himself as being born 'on the border between two eras', having witnessed both serfdom and Bolshevism, growing up in a successful manufacturing family but living through the Russian Revolution.[22] Beginning his career as a successful character actor, he went on to become a director and co-founder of the Moscow Art Theatre (MAT), which became notable for its landmark productions of Anton Chekhov's work. Kathy Dacre argues that Chekhov's plays, part of the emerging development of European realism and Naturalism in the late nineteenth and early twentieth centuries, forced Stanislavski to look at how the actor 'might approach roles that could not be copied from "master actors", that were not recognisable stereotypes and that depended upon ensemble playing'.[23] Rather than driven by outward action, Stanislavski considered Chekhov's characters to be defined according to what is 'hidden' behind the words, 'in the pauses, or the way the actors look at each other or in the way they radiate inner feeling.'[24] These plays, he wrote, are full of inward rather than outward action. Crucially, they were emblematized by their portrayal of characters defined by their projection of emotional interiority. The 'fundamental theme' of Chekhov's work, Stanislavski wrote, is 'Man with a capital M'.[25] Such characters demanded a new mode of performance from actors: Stanislavski lamented that theatres across Europe tried and failed to perform Chekhov's plays because they were wedded to an old style of acting that could not meet the demands of his writing. Through his work with the MAT, particularly his studio work, Stanislavski developed what was known as 'the system' – an organized approach to the training of actors which focuses on the development of a technique which aids them in reaching their own subconscious creative state. According to Peta Tait, the development of this particular form of acting 'materialised an aesthetic of acting inner emotions socially', and the control exerted over these displays in turn confirmed a broader social value system in which 'an uncontrolled expression of emotion could disrupt the stability of the social and moral order'.[26] As a result, 'realist theatre is implicated in the emotional beliefs of Western culture and therefore observable in everyday social interaction and behaviour'.[27]

A vocabulary of the 'authentic', 'real' and 'genuine' is thus fundamental to Stanislavskian acting, and equally fundamental is the conception of these notions as both individual and interior, accessible only to the actor themselves. 'Inner truth', he wrote in *My Life in Art*, 'is the basis of all acting.'[28] In opposition to the forms of mechanical and 'superficial' acting which he saw his practice as a departure from, Stanislavski argued that the creative process must be given over 'to intuition and feeling, which become the helmsman', writing that actors 'have to fill the role with inner content as you load a ship with passengers and cargo'.[29] Stanislavski's system thus privileges 'real' emotions and feelings in both the rehearsal and acting process: utilizing the actors' own lived experience in order to drive them towards presenting emotional states on stage which, in order to appear genuine to the audience, must also be experienced as genuine by the performer. The actor becomes the bearer of truth and authenticity on stage, and the willing use of their emotional interiority as material towards this goal becomes the central objective of their work, which is characterized by the search for dramatic truth through the emotional engagement of the performer, and where characterization can only be shaped 'from an actor's own inner elements'.[30]

Colin Counsell provides the most lucid account of the ideological ramifications of Stanislavskian realism. For Counsell, the hallmarks of the system are 'behavioural detail, "plausibility", a sense of profound psychological depth, a marked linearity or smoothness to the performance as a whole' and a commitment to 'internal realism'.[31] Counsell reminds us that the actor is also a social subject, but one who is trained to view themselves as a 'coherency' skilled enough to express their own psyche through the 'available codes' they are equipped with.[32] Stanislavskian acting is thus reliant on the notion that behaviour is 'innately understandable' and a 'transcultural communicative form regardless of language'.[33] David Shirley, similarly, describes the system as a form of training 'heavily dependent on coherence and unity for its effect', meaning practices which 'challenge stable and knowable concepts of selfhood' pose innate challenges to it.[34] For Counsell, such a system must by its nature avoid any 'discord and disjuncture' by offering 'the image of the illusory coherent self no matter what character is being portrayed or which text staged'.[35] In the system, humans are understood as 'desiring machines, constantly in pursuit of their own aims, their actions dictated by forces within their psyches, so that the sole author of human action, consciously or subconsciously, is the individual self'.[36] Although the MAT did present work of varying styles, this type of psychological realism remained at the heart of their approach. Describing their early efforts at producing Ibsen's symbolist work, for example, Stanislavski puts their failure down to their 'inability to live the inner life of the play realistically', elaborating that these early efforts at symbolism sprang 'not from feeling but from thought. It was artificial, not natural'.[37] Symbolism, impressionism and 'all the other subtle isms' can only be performed successfully when an actor's behaviour is both 'spontaneous' and 'normal according to the laws of nature'.[38]

This tradition is thereby marked by a form of naturalization consistent with the development of realism, which is often treated as a 'style without a style'.[39] This tendency to essentialize and naturalize authentic emotional interiority also marks the demands made on employees who are expected to provide genuine, authentic and real customer service at work. Remembering that the development of Stanislavski's system also had ideological ramifications in terms of the construction of selfhood on stage, and its relationship to wider socio-economic transformations, troubles the binary that Hochschild draws between acting as an artistic endeavour and acting within the service industries. The dramatic trends that were driven by Stanislavski are arguably foundational to the conception of performed authentic self that is now such a central part of demands for emotional labour and must equally make up a key part of any critical analysis of it. Employers who demand emotional labour deliberately cultivate specific notions of subjective authenticity as innate, natural and somehow immune to corruption in the workplace. Colluding with such a formulation can prevent attention being drawn to the ideological construct of such notions in themselves, which would in turn puncture the kind of 'capitalist realism' that they perpetuate.[40] If the emotional capabilities of employees are often framed as innate and therefore untrainable then they do not have to be treated as skills for which training and compensation must be appropriately considered. Therefore, a critical approach to emotional labour means that the underlying assumptions about the interior, authentic emotional 'self' have to be interrogated and scrutinized. Yet Hochschild not only ignores the historical and literary context of Stanislavski's innovations. She also uncritically mobilizes a partial understanding of his work in service of her own analysis, neglecting to consider how his own contributions to psychological realism have in turn shaped the very concepts of selfhood and performance that are now taken up by the businesses of which she is so critical.

The 'Method' and the 'system'

I will return to this question of essentialism and its relationship to emotional labour later in this chapter. I wish to turn now, however, to the immediate historical error in Hochschild's reading, that is, her misattribution of the American 'Method' school to Stanislavski himself. Hochschild describes Stanislavski as 'the originator of a different type of acting – called Method acting', later alluding to 'true' Method acting as espoused by him.[41] Method acting, however, is not a term used by Stanislavski but is rather associated with the teaching of Lee Strasberg, Harold Clurman, Stella Adler and their peers, at the Group Theatre in New York founded in the 1930s. The Method is an approach inspired by Stanislavski but which places primary emphasis on the personal experience of the actors and privileges certain elements of his 'system' above others. In particular, the Method is notable for its focus on the actor's own psychological material and lived experience, and the relative lack of attention it gave to the importance of physical cues, which became of far greater importance to Stanislavski later in his career. The most well-known example of Method acting is affective memory (also known as emotion memory), where the actor is asked to relive a traumatic or difficult episode from their life in order to generate the required performance. Sharon Carnicke, in her book recontextualizing Stanislavski's work, outlines the Method approach in which 'emotion took precedence' above other considerations, and 'affective memory' became a far more important technique than it ever was for Stanislavski, who himself often cautioned against an overreliance on primary feeling, as a matter of 'mental hygiene'.[42] Carnicke explains that, for Stanislavski, 'memory safely filters and controls emotion, maintaining artistic distance between the actor and the event portrayed'.[43] Affective memory, as an exercise, became, according to Carnicke, the 'cornerstone' of the Method, where emotion and the subconscious became more important to the training than other considerations such as action.[44]

Apart from the historical inaccuracy of Hochschild's account then, it also leads to an emphasis on the elements of Stanislavski's work most associated with the Method, at the expense of others. The different emphasis placed on the actor's personal emotional memory is exemplified in an example laid out by David Jackson in an article on the future of actor training within a British context. Jackson argues that Stanislavski in fact had 'little interest in the raw emotion of an actual traumatic event' and highlights a passage where one of his fictional students recounts witnessing a car accident.[45] Stanislavski compares the first impression of the event to the 'transformed image' that emerged through memory. While the 'raw' experience of the event, as recounted, is 'crudely naturalistic' and thus unsuitable for use in rehearsal, the 'symbolic quality' of the memory after it has been 'transformed by a process of distillation, elevation and association' makes it more appropriate for the actor to draw upon.[46] Jackson concludes that Stanislavski's conception of acted emotion is that it is one 'governed by specific principles, distinct from those that condition emotional response in life', namely that emotion memory becomes useful only after it has been 'processed to the point of being controllable'.[47] Jackson argues for an understanding of this kind of 'scenic emotion' as an important, and underexplored, principle of Stanislavski's work.[48] This distinction between the raw, 'real' emotion that the individual actor has access to and the theatrical or scenic reinterpretation of this emotion is missing in Hochschild's account of a Method approach.

This framing of Stanislavski via the Method is not, however, only an issue of historical inaccuracy. Rather, by taking this particular iteration of actor training as the basis for deep acting, Hochschild runs the risk of adhering to the same binaries that the businesses that demand emotional labour also subscribe to and rely upon. In particular, the dichotomy drawn between the private and professional self that is implied in *The Managed Heart* can be, and has been, critiqued for its essentializing tendencies, as it suggests that there is an integral and identifiable 'real self' which exists as separate from and outside of the workplace environment. Such a notion sits in contradiction to much of Hochschild's otherwise materialist analysis. In calling for a critical defence of Hochschild's emotional labour thesis, Brook argues that by confining alienation to the workplace Hochschild ends up with an overly individualistic analysis which fails to grapple with the broader condition of alienation across social life and which 'effectively localises the existence of alienation to workplace social relations'.[49] And Hochschild's misattribution of Stanislavski's work to the Method offshoot bolsters the weaknesses in her analysis. In drawing on Stanislavski, for instance, Hochschild makes appeals to the actor and the audience's soul: 'the body, not the soul, is the main tool of the trade', again distinguishing the actor's labour from the emotional labourer who used both their body and the 'margins of the soul' to do their work.[50] But what is the soul that Hochschild refers to, and how does someone's 'soul' or essence exist outside of the capitalist relations that shape their experiences of the world, and thus the production of their own subjectivity?

Performance and the self

These concerns lead scholars such as Kathi Weeks to identify a tension in Hochschild's analysis whereby 'she insists on the social construction and malleability of the emotions while also positing them as fundamental to the self such that their alienation is a problem'.[51] Weeks goes on to write that Hochschild's argument is animated by an ideal of the 'unmanaged heart' – associated either with a separate private world of emotional practice and contact or with what one may experience as one's 'true' self – the possibility of which it simultaneously disavows.[52]

Guerrier and Adib, similarly, in their article on emotional labour and tour reps argue that 'any notion of an "authentic self" is (merely) a part of late modern, Western, social discourses'.[53] Crucially, as Weeks reminds us, Hochschild's analysis is about the emotional labourer not only 'seeming to be but also about his or her coming to be; the work requires not just the use but the production of subjectivity'.[54] This critique, of course, mirrors the very debates that preoccupy those concerned with Stanislavskian actor training. Philip Auslander, for example, points to what he sees as the implicit assumption in Stanislavski's work that the actor's 'self' (fragmented though it may be) 'precedes and grounds her performance' and that the presence of this self in performance is what provides 'the audience with access to human truths'.[55] He argues instead for a deconstructive reading which reveals instead that 'the actorly self is, in fact, produced by the performance it supposedly grounds'.[56]

If we return to the extract at the outset of this chapter in which Hochschild critiques Goffman's model of selfhood, we see that the issue identified with this model is that Goffman offers his reader an actor who, Hochschild argues,

> does not seem to feel much, is not attuned to, does not monitor closely or assess, does not actively evoke, inhibit, shape – in a word, work on feelings in a way an actor would have to do to accomplish what Goffman says is, in fact, accomplished in one encounter after another.[57]

Instead, Hochschild aims to build a model of emotions which accounts for 'some theory of the self', one which she identifies as absent in Goffman's work.[58] Goffman's work, in this reading, does not presuppose a self that exists prior to its social performance, and Stanislavski is introduced to address this gap. Writing less than a decade after Hochschild's article, Judith Butler also addressed the question of performativity in Goffman's model, in her article *Performative Acts and Gender Constitution*. Butler draws a different conclusion from Hochschild, arguing that Goffman's theory does indeed include a pre-existing sense of self. Goffman's view, she writes, 'posits a self which assumes and exchanges various "roles" within the complex social expectations of the "game" of modern life'.[59] In contrast, Butler argues that the self 'is not only irretrievably "outside", constituted in social discourse, but that the ascription of interiority is itself a publicly regulated and sanctioned form of essence fabrication'.[60] Butler takes aim at this formulation, pursuing her theory of gender performativity on the basis of the argument that the self (at least in regards to gender identity) is only ever constituted through the process of repeat performance itself. Performance, here, is key to the formulation of what is socially understood as 'authentic' behaviour, an understanding which is lacking in Hochschild's account, which suggests that the authentic self precedes its social performance. However, where Hochschild elides this point, her account does rest on the interrogation of the institution rules and pressures which coerce employees to perform in certain ways. In contrast, the impact of employment, the workplace and similar forms of power are missing in Butler's account. I would advocate an approach that bridges Hochschild and Butler in relation to the self and performativity – taking Butler's insistence on the constitutive nature of the performative act itself and combining this with Hochschild's close attention to the impact of specifically economic capitalist forces on these performances. This helps us to retain the strongest parts of Hochschild's analysis, while taking a critical approach to the notion of the 'self' which allows us to challenge the signifiers of authenticity that are adopted in the service sector, rather than being complicit in reproducing them.

Rather than thinking of someone's emotional interiority as existing as a fixed resource to be either corrupted or protected in the workplace, a valuable insight into emotional labour might come from moving away from the question of individualized consequences of emotional labour. Like Brook, who writes that we should both defend and strengthen Hochschild's analysis, in the same spirit I would argue that an analytical reorientation to the ways in which emotional labour is *directed*, rather than just individually *performed*, can be a more useful way to apply theatrical methods and comparisons to its study than the way in which the essentialism of the Method school of acting offers. Furthermore, invoking the actor only in relation to their individual performance ignores the role of the director. Despite the problems I have outlined, there remains great utility in Hochschild's adoption of Stanislavski but only if his work is historicized and contextualized appropriately. I will now consider some of the broader structural implications of Stanislavski's work and how they might be applied to a critique of emotional labour.

The organization of theatrical labour

The 'system', and its international dissemination, remains the single biggest innovation in Western acting, marking the development of a systematized approach towards performer training which has been described as both the first attempt to organize technique into 'a coherent, usable system' and as 'the closest existing language for a vocabulary of acting in the West in the 20th and 21st centuries'.[61] As such assessments suggest, it is the *organizational* aspects of Stanislavski's work which, alongside his innovative approaches to character, are most responsible for his ongoing influence, despite the different interpretations and applications of his specific methods. What was most remarkable and crucial about his work was not necessarily the originality of his insight (many of his teachings were based on existing oral and practical traditions of acting developed long before him) but his attempt to codify and organize these techniques and philosophies into a teachable system that could be passed on. In understanding that Stanislavski's biggest contribution may have been in the *form* of training and knowledge, rather than its specific components, we can also see a clear link between the development of his approach and the broader industrialization of theatrical production which was emerging in the same historical context.

The introduction of the system in the British and American context coincided with transformations in how theatre was owned and managed and, as part of this, the actors' specific role within the production process and hierarchy. Stanislavski's work cannot, therefore, be understood as merely an isolated series of innovations in the art of acting but rather must be contextualized within the broader ruptures taking place on stage in the early twentieth century: his system offered not just a novel approach to the acting process but a way of organizing theatre on a newly industrial basis. The way in which skills in emotional management are taught to aspiring actors becomes inextricably bound with the forms of employment they then find themselves entering. Stanislavski's major contribution is twofold: acting is taken from the realm of a craft mostly passed on through an apprentice-based model and professionalized, and, in the process, cultivates new notions of subjectivity in relation to both the actor's position towards themselves and the characters they portray.

This structural element of Stanislavski's influence is missing in Hochschild's application, and thus she also overlooks the managerial implications of his 'system'. Jonathan Pitches has carefully detailed the links between Stanislavski's scientific and systematic approach to acting and the 'Scientific Management' that was firmly rooted in American industry in the early twentieth century. Like Frederick Winslow Taylor and Henry Ford who, Pitches writes, 'were striving for the most efficient and systematic, task-based approach in industry', Stanislavski, he claims, was 'proposing an organised system for the actor based on the same foundations'.[62] As recorded by the literary head of Stanislavski's theatre, he was dedicated to discovering 'the right selection of tasks, their composition, the right pattern, the execution of every task'.[63] This approach focuses on a line of work which is principally concerned with the skills of emotional management and performance. Pitches thus draws attention to what he calls the 'interplay between Taylor's industrial efficiency drives and Stanislavski's practice'.[64] Ysabel Claire has also pointed to the similarity between the 'systematizing' tendency of manufacturing at the time and Stanislavski's quest to develop his own system.[65]

What I am proposing is that Stanislavski's significance as a theatrical practitioner deeply concerned with how to generate authentic emotional performances from his actors lies less in the individual tools with which he equipped actors but rather in how his system led to the reorganization and management of theatrical labour on a wider scale, integrating elements of task management and largely moving theatre away from its previously craft-based model into a newly industrialized mode of rehearsal and production. Stanislavski's project was not just one of equipping the actor with a toolkit from which to generate their performances but was also a managerial project aiming to systematize the rehearsal process and make it more efficient from the director and producer's perspective, which is very clearly not the same as the actor's. If we were to consider how these changes impacted the coordinated emotional management of performers, we may well garner more insights both into managerial approaches to emotional labour and its place within the wider economic landscape. When we look at companies and workplaces today which demand and dictate emotional labour from their workers, it is worth thinking about how the organization of actors as exemplary emotional labourers might contribute to our understanding of managerial attempts to elicit or 'direct' such performances, rather than simply how the worker's choices under these conditions can be compared to those of the individual actor on stage.

Conclusion

In this chapter I have sought not to discredit the application of Stanislavski specifically, and theatre and performance more generally, to the study of emotional labour but rather to extend and strengthen it by thinking more historically about the development and utilization of theatrical practices. Our understanding of emotional labour could benefit by paying more detailed attention to the particular historical trajectory of the actor as the exemplary emotional labourer with much to teach us. Crucially it is important to remember that emotional labour is not solely the result of employees' individual strategies and techniques for emotion work but is also the result of the deliberate imposition and management of directorial techniques that cultivate and encourage the types of acting and emotional labour required. Stanislavski's work can offer us a new way of thinking about these techniques that can greatly improve our understanding of emotional labour as it exists off the theatrical stage. However, situating the development of these techniques within an approach that is equally responsible for setting the standards of emotional realism which are now played out in the workplace is an important precursor to any application of the theatrical analogy and metaphor. Theatre does not exist in a space completely separate from the world of commercial work, as is all too often implied.

We can see this also in how much crossover exists between professionally trained actors and other industries. Since the widespread adoption of his methods in the 1960s, Stanislavski's work has remained the cornerstone of British training, reflecting the continued demand for psychologically real characters on stage and screen. If the fundamental offering of British actor training has remained relatively unchanged since the mid-1960s, however, the application of these skills within the acting profession and other sectors besides once students graduate has been transformed. As we have seen, those who do pursue acting careers find themselves more and more likely to take on-screen roles, demanding both a different technical approach and an acceptance of very different working conditions. Away from both stage and screen, the skills of professionally trained actors are also finding themselves in demand. From the 1970s onwards, British and American capitalism has been characterized by the uneven spread of neoliberalism and the decline of manufacturing and the corresponding growth of the service sector. The skills of professional actors have become increasingly relevant in an economy heavily reliant on workers equipped with interpersonal, emotional management and communicative skills but which also places ideological emphasis on individuality, a concept which has also been identified as underpinning Stanislavski's methods.[66]

That the actor's skills, however, have found themselves in ever-greater demand in the wider economy is now beginning to have tangible effects on the provision and direction of actor training. Frank Camilleri writes that we are now witnessing 'a paradigm shift', in which performer training is becoming increasingly commercialized, packaged and split into smaller components isolated from the holistic approach of Stanislavski.[67] He argues that when these components are 'transposed into the wider context of commodities, technique takes on a different dimension and marketability informs and structures its logic', with the result being a form of training 'geared towards technical placement meant as subject formation'.[68] For Camilleri this 'subject formation' in an institutional context 'occurs in the image of the dominant socio-economic conditions'.[69] This new packaging of training, he argues, is 'ultimately, at the service of the industries that surround the phenomenon of performer training today'.[70] Although Camilleri points to academia, publishing and creative industries as key examples, we might broaden our view by considering the service sector industries that today have an interest in access to trained performers, such as call centres, hospitality and leisure establishments. As such a line of thought suggests, there is an imperative for scholars to pay more careful and sustained attention to the connections between stage and shop floor, as these forms of theatricalized and performative labour become increasingly widespread.

Notes

1. Hochschild, *The Managed Heart*, 7.
2. Hochschild, *The Managed Heart*, 12.
3. Virno, *A Grammar of the Multitude*, 68.
4. Sennett, *The Corrosion of Character*, 111.
5. Cederström and Fleming, *Dead Man Working*, 124.
6. Hochschild, *The Managed Heart*, 47.
7. Sennett, *The Corrosion of Character*, 73.
8. McKelvey, 'A Disabled Actor Prepares', 86.
9. Boyle, 'Performance and Value', 19.
10. Bolton and Boyd, 'Trolley Dolly or Skilled Emotion Manager?', 304.
11. Bolton and Boyd, 'Trolley Dolly or Skilled Emotion Manager?', 294.
12. Vincent, 'The Emotional Labour Process'.
13. Bolton and Boyd, 'Trolley Dolly or Skilled Emotion Manager?', 290.
14. Brook, 'The Alienated Heart', 98.
15. Hochschild, *The Managed Heart*, 194.
16. Trott, 'Affective Labour and Alienation', 3.
17. Hochschild, *The Managed Heart*, 35.
18. Hochschild, *The Managed Heart*, 33.
19. Hochschild, *The Managed Heart*, 33.
20. Hochschild, *The Managed Heart*, 35vi.
21. Hochschild, 'Emotion Work, Feeling Rules, and Social Structure', 558.
22. Stanislavsky and Benedetti, *My Life in Art*, 3.

23 Dacre and Boston, 'Teaching Stanislavski', 4.
24 Stanislavsky and Benedetti, *My Life in Art*, 192.
25 Stanislavsky and Benedetti, *My Life in Art*, 193.
26 Tait, *Performing Emotions*, 135.
27 Tait, *Performing Emotions*, 169.
28 Stanislavsky and Benedetti, *My Life in Art*, 184.
29 Stanislavsky and Benedetti, *My Life in Art*, 110.
30 Stanislavski, *An Actor's Handbook*, 33.
31 Counsell, *Signs of Performance*, 25.
32 Counsell, *Signs of Performance*, 31.
33 Counsell, *Signs of Performance*, 31.
34 Shirley, 'Stanislavsky's Passage into the British Conservatoire', 59.
35 Counsell, *Signs of Performance*, 32.
36 Counsell, *Signs of Performance*, 39.
37 Stanislavsky and Benedetti, *My Life in Art*, 191.
38 Stanislavsky and Benedetti, *My Life in Art*, 191.
39 Counsell, *Signs of Performance*, 24.
40 Fisher, *Capitalist Realism*.
41 Hochschild, *The Managed Heart*, 37–8.
42 Carnicke, *Stanislavsky in Focus*, 148, 158.
43 Carnicke, *Stanislavsky in Focus*, 158.
44 Carnicke, *Stanislavsky in Focus*, 64.
45 Jackson, 'Stanislavski, Emotion and the Future', 78.
46 Jackson, 'Stanislavski, Emotion and the Future', 78.
47 Jackson, 'Stanislavski, Emotion and the Future', 79.
48 Jackson, 'Stanislavski, Emotion and the Future', 81.
49 Brook, 'The Alienated Heart', 9.
50 Hochschild, *The Managed Heart*, 37.
51 Weeks, 'Life Within and Against Work', 244.
52 Weeks, 'Life Within and Against Work', 244.
53 Guerrier and Adib, 'Work at Leisure', 1401.
54 Weeks, 'Life Within and Against Work', 241.
55 Auslander, *From Acting to Performance*, 30.
56 Auslander, *From Acting to Performance*, 30.
57 Hochschild, 'Emotion Work, Feeling Rules, and Social Structure', 557.
58 Hochschild, 'Emotion Work, Feeling Rules, and Social Structure', 558.
59 Butler, 'Performative Acts and Gender Constitution', 528.
60 Butler, 'Performative Acts and Gender Constitution', 528.
61 Counsell, *Signs of Performance*, 24; Rawlins, 'Studying Acting', 17.
62 Pitches, *Science and the Stanislavsky Tradition of Acting*, 29.
63 Pitches, *Science and the Stanislavsky Tradition of Acting*, 29.

64 Pitches, *Science and the Stanislavsky Tradition of Acting*, 29.
65 Clare, 'Stanislavsky's Quest', 149.
66 Shepherd, 8.
67 Camilleri, 'Of Pounds of Flesh', 26.
68 Camilleri, 'Of Pounds of Flesh', 28.
69 Camilleri, 'Of Pounds of Flesh', 28.
70 Camilleri, 'Of Pounds of Flesh', 28.

Bibliography

Auslander, Philip. *From Acting to Performance: Essays in Modernism and Postmodernism*. London and New York: Routledge, 1997.

Bolton, Sharon C., and Carol Boyd. 'Trolley Dolly or Skilled Emotion Manager? Moving on from Hochschild's Managed Heart'. *Work, Employment and Society* 17, no. 2 (2003): 289–308.

Boyle, Michael Shane. 'Performance and Value: The Work of Theatre in Karl Marx's Critique of Political Economy'. *Theatre Survey* 58, no. 1 (2017): 3–23.

Brook, Paul. 'The Alienated Heart: Hochschild's "Emotional Labour" Thesis and the Anticapitalist Politics of Alienation'. *Capital & Class* 33, no. 2 (2009): 7–31.

Butler, Judith. 'Performative Acts and Gender Constitution: An Essay in Phenomenology and Feminist Theory'. *Theatre Journal* 40, no. 4 (December 1988): 519–31.

Camilleri, Frank. 'Of Pounds of Flesh and Trojan Horses: Performer Training in the Twenty-First Century'. *Performance Research* 14, no. 2 (2009): 26–34.

Carnicke, Sharon Marie. *Stanislavsky in Focus: An Acting Master for the Twenty-First Century*. Routledge Theatre Classics, 2nd ed. London and New York: Routledge, 2009.

Cederström, Carl, and Peter Fleming. *Dead Man Working*. Winchester, UK: Zero Books, 2012.

Clare, Ysabel. 'Stanislavsky's Quest for the Ideal Actor: The System as Socratic Encounter'. *Theatre, Dance and Performance Training* 7, no. 2 (2016): 148–64.

Counsell, Colin. *Signs of Performance: An Introduction to Twentieth-Century Theatre*. London and New York: Routledge, 1996.

Dacre, Kathy, and Jane Boston. 'Teaching Stanislavski' (Palatine, 2009) https://www.heacademy.ac.uk/system/files/teaching-stanislavski.pdf (accessed 28 June 2017).

Fisher, Mark. *Capitalist Realism: Is There No Alternative?* Zero Books. Winchester: O Books, 2009.

Guerrier, Yvonne, and Amel Adib. 'Work at Leisure and Leisure at Work: A Study of the Emotional Labour of Tour Reps'. *Human Relations* 56, no. 11 (2003): 1399–1417.

Hochschild, Arlie Russell. 'Emotion Work, Feeling Rules, and Social Structure'. *American Journal of Sociology* 85, no. 3 (November 1979): 551–75.

Hochschild, Arlie Russell. *The Managed Heart: Commercialization of Human Feeling*. Berkeley, Los Angeles and London: University of California Press, 1983.

Ikeler, Peter. 'Deskilling Emotional Labour: Evidence from Department Store Retail'. *Work, Employment and Society* 30, no. 6 (2016): 966–83.

Jackson, David. 'Stanislavski, Emotion and the Future of the UK Conservatoire'. *Stanislavski Studies* 5, no. 1 (2017): 75–83. https://doi.org/10.1080/20567790.2017.1298195.

McKelvey, Patrick. 'A Disabled Actor Prepares: Stanislavsky, Disability, and Work at the National Theatre Workshop of the Handicapped'. *Theatre Journal* 71, no. 1 (2019): 69–89. https://doi.org/10.1353/tj.2019.0004.

Pitches, Jonathan. *Science and the Stanislavsky Tradition of Acting*. London: Routledge, 2009.

Rawlins, Trevor. 'Studying Acting: An Investigation into Contemporary Approaches to Professional Actor Training in the UK'. Unpublished doctoral thesis, University of Reading, 2012.

Sennett, Richard. *The Corrosion of Character: The Personal Consequences of Work in the New Capitalism*, 1. publ. as a Norton paperback. New York: Norton, 1999.

Shepherd, Simon. 'The Institution of Training'. *Performance Research: A Journal of the Performing Arts* 14.2 (2009): 5–15.

Shirley, David. 'Stanislavsky's Passage into the British Conservatoire'. In *Russians in Britain: British Theatre and the Russian Tradition of Actor Training*, edited by Jonathan Pitches. London and New York: Routledge, 2012.

Stanislavski, Constantin. *An Actor's Handbook*. New York: Routledge, 1963.

Stanislavsky, Konstantin, and Jean Benedetti. *My Life in Art*. London and New York: Routledge, 2008.

Tait, Peta. *Performing Emotions: Gender, Bodies, Spaces, in Chekhov's Drama and Stanislavski's Theatre*. Aldershot, Burlington Vt: Ashgate, 2002.

Trott, Ben. 'Affective Labour and Alienation: Spinoza's Materialism and the Sad Passions of Post-Fordist Work'. *Emotion, Space and Society* 25 (2017): 119–26.

Vincent, Steve. 'The Emotional Labour Process: An Essay on the Economy of Feelings'. *Human Relations* 64, no. 10 (2011): 1369–92.

Virno, Paolo. *A Grammar of the Multitude*. Cambridge, MA and London: Semiotext(e), 2004.

Weeks, Kathi. 'Life Within and Against Work: Affective Labor, Feminist Critique, and Post-Fordist Politics'. *Ephemera* 7, no. 1 (2007): 233–49.

13

Emotional labour and the childcare crisis in neoliberal Britain

Claire English

The unstable situation for childcare workers, parents and carers and young children in the Covid-19 era in the UK has been one of rapid changes and 'making do' childcare options alongside seemingly unending and unpredictable policy shifts for care providers and parents and grandparents alike.[1] It has been an incredibly difficult time for those with caring responsibilities at a point in history when parents, and mothers in particular, were already feeling overstretched and overburdened.[2] The (neo)liberal feminist response to the women who feel overwhelmed with the tasks associated with childcare and general 'life work', referred to by Marxist-feminists as social reproduction, is to posit that perhaps they are doing too much 'emotional labour' – but what does this term mean in neoliberal times?[3] The unsettling transference of the term 'emotional labour' from workplace setting to that of interpersonal relationships in the home has been disputed by Hochschild, the term's originator, but the concept now has a life of its own,[4] encompassing the examples of marginalized individuals catering to the needs of more privileged others in the workplace to neoliberal feminist solutions in which couples rebalance household task division – often relying on the labour of poorer, racialized women.[5]

This chapter seeks to argue that the state has actively reduced the welfare that carers need to such a level that individual women and carers feel they are responsible for all aspects of domestic reproductive labour with little or no state support, and – for many women – no community support either. This lends itself to the middle-class, individualizing, often racialized discourses of 'emotional labour' that assume you can remedy your problems by 'training your partner to notice when the washing up basket is full' or 'hiring a cleaner',[6] or strategies of individualist 'self-care' like putting Epsom salts in your bubble bath so that you can 'finally relax'.[7]

The individualist responses to social problems, that can be understood in Marxist terms as structural or systemic, are part of an ongoing pattern of ways of thinking and being that emerged as part of the sustained project of economic neoliberalism. Following Milburn and Russell, beyond popular understandings of neoliberalism that focus on the 'rolling back' of public ownership, this chapter will focus on the social implications, the

> more nuanced processes of . . . constructing and embedding a fundamentally different vision of society and of what it means to be a successful and well-functioning human . . . neoliberalism being understood in this case as a wider ideological 'agenda of cultural and institutional change, extending – at least in potential – through every arena of social life'.[8]

This connection between the financial and social aspects of neoliberalism as a project was made explicit by Margaret Thatcher in the *Sunday Times* on 3 May 1981 in the following way: 'whilst economics are the method; the object is to change the heart and soul.'[9] This chapter will argue that the feminist mobilization of the term emotional labour is a distraction from the collectivizing processes that carers actually need to enjoy their participation in social reproduction to its fullest extent, to enjoy it with a fullness of heart and soul.

This chapter will situate the experience of caring, care work and social reproduction in the neoliberal context where the private–public divide has largely dissolved, leaving primary carers – especially mothers – describing many aspects of social reproduction as 'work' or, in the case of many, 'emotional labour'.[10] When understood in this way, the term 'emotional labour' functions differently to the way that childcare workers and nannies mobilize the term – and there are important discussions to be had about the differences between feeling alienated from the work you do in your own home with your own children and the alienation experienced as part of the wage relation. This chapter will attempt to understand some of these divisions and the overlaps between them.

These problems have not gone unnoticed, and collective organizing, comprised of those who need childcare and those who provide it, is commencing (or rather, recommencing) to forge a new path for childcare in the UK. In June 2020, a collective campaign currently known as 'Fight for Childcare' (FFC) was launched. The group has a Facebook page and has set up separate meetings for those who are parents and carers to share their experiences, with links to the union campaign led by the grassroots trade unions, United Voice of the World, who seek to organize those working in private nurseries, and the International

Workers of Great Britain's newly formed Nannies branch, for childcare workers that operate from private homes. While this chapter is very much written from the perspective of a parent or carer, rather than a nursery worker, I hope that some of the reflections in this chapter on the neo-liberalization of care and the way this produces tensions between workers and parents will be useful, and that the difficulties and rewards of forming collective projects of this kind will be recognizable to parents and workers, who also feel emotionally exhausted by the labour they have been undertaking in recent times.

This chapter is largely based on autoethnography, and participatory observation of my time with FFC and the Women's Strike Assembly UK, as both organizations seek to centre the importance of care in their political work and to plan for a world that values (and redistributes) this kind of labour differently. Following Gatrell, the chapter also draws upon a database of qualitative netnographic (or internet-based) research.[11] It analyses netnographic narratives that mothers write about their own lives, hosted by sites often referred to as 'mummyblogs' or the 'mamasphere',[12] to map the lineage of the individualizing patterns of family life[13] that have continued or newly emerged in the post-industrial period when the concept of emotional labour was popularized.[14]

As these collective projects and indeed the outcomes of the Covid-19 pandemic are still very much in motion, many of the findings and reflections around care and organizing across differentially distributed vulnerabilities are also in their infancy. The chapter maps some of the important feminist insights[15] into what can be gained via collective consciousness-raising (CR)[16] projects as a way of understanding the work of care in its social context and mobilizing these understandings to transform the shared conditions of those performing the (sometimes emotional) labour of care.[17] My hope is that these ideas will go on to shape a meaningful project that transforms neoliberal notions of care into collectivized models of care that will benefit all those who provide care and all those who need it.

Covid as a social crisis

Without a resilient childcare sector, progress towards gender equality within households and in the workplace will falter. It is critical to understand how we can support this sector during and beyond Covid-19 for children, families and gender equality.[18]

Over the past six months, academics, workers and childcare activists have been drawing attention to the oncoming likelihood that the provision of childcare in the UK may not be the same, or even comparable to what it was like before Covid-19.[19] According to a survey of more than 6,200 registered childminders, carried out by the Professional Association of Childcare and Early Years, nearly half of childminders expect to stay closed for up to a year following the pandemic, and nearly a third think it is unlikely they will reopen at all.[20] According to a survey of more than 3,000 nurseries, preschools and childminders by the Early Years Alliance, one in four say they will have to close permanently within the next twelve months due to financial problems.[21] There is increasingly little job security for those who work with children. This can be understood as an accelerated process of what was already happening in British childcare. The latest data from Ofsted indicates that over 500 nurseries, preschools and childminders have closed each month between April 2018 and March 2019,[22] due in part to an untenable model of childcare relying on thirty 'free' hours of childcare being subsidized at a pittance by the government to the point where remaining open became unfeasible for many providers – requiring what some childcare workers have been referring to as magically providing 'Champagne Nurseries on Lemonade Budgets'.[23]

In 2019, there were 24,000 nurseries and preschools providing 1 million childcare places and 35,000 childminders delivering 231,000 early years places.[24] Society relies on and functions as a result of childcare provision (both in institutional settings and in the home). The main institutional alternative to using a registered childminder to take care of your preschool children in the UK tends to be places in private nurseries, as state-funded provisions (through the nurseries attached to local schools) are only open until 3.30 pm, making them an unfeasible option for many working parents. These private nurseries operate in an environment of sporadic funding models that rely on paying minimum wage and requiring their staff (very often poorer, racialized women) to work long hours with increasing numbers of children to care for per waged adult.[25] The Social Mobility Commission found that one in eight childcare workers in the UK earns less than £5 an hour, and that the average hourly wage in the sector is £7.42. The national living wage is £8.72 an hour.[26] The national funding under the '30 free hours' model is so limited that nurseries now very often charge extra for what used to be considered the basics of care – food and nappies.

Early years provision in the UK is among the most expensive in the world. Parents pay an average of 27 per cent of their wages on childcare costs,[27] while childcare staff – overwhelmingly working-class women – are some of the lowest-paid workers in society. Eighty-four per cent of childcare is now run by private providers[28] as successive British governments (perhaps most prominently under Tony Blair's 'professionalisation' of childcare in the late 1990s)[29] have deliberately promoted the marketization of childcare as part of a narrow regulatory framework and funding model that leaves workers particularly vulnerable to market declines of the kind we are presently seeing. In addition to this, 13 per cent of private nurseries in the UK are internationally owned, and with global markets in flux it may not be possible to guarantee funding for nurseries from international avenues in the same way as before the pandemic. On top of this, at present, childcare providers are not entitled to small business grants if they are based in premises that don't attract rates relief – such as community centres.[30]

As workers and parents adapt to changing childcare provision in a pandemic, it is important to notice the growing industry of digital platforms such as Care .com, Handy, TaskRabbit and Helpling, designed to mediate the care 'gaps' presented by working parents, in the lead up to the pandemic. These app workers were increasingly emerging as the neoliberal solution to the childcare crisis in recent years as those seeking carers could pay by the hour, at the last minute, at the lowest rate.[31] The privatization of childcare is a booming market; Forbes estimates that the market size of this 'new mom economy' and its associated products and services in the United States alone stands at $46 billion today.[32]

Stronger together

In June 2020, activists from the Women's Strike Assembly along with other key groups organizing around the issue of childcare, including the New Economics Foundation and the Nanny Solidarity Campaign, formed a steering group and helped to launch a collective campaign known as 'Fight for Childcare' (FFC). The group, comprised of parents and carers, nursery workers and nannies, teachers, union organizers, researchers and people involved in running cooperative and parent-run nurseries, all came together to understand the problems with childcare, as it currently stands, and to imagine solutions to these shared (though differentially experienced) problems. Inspired by the growing self-organization of childcare workers, including the newly founded Childcare workers branch at United Voices of the World, the Nannies branch at the International Workers of Great Britain and the Nanny Solidarity Network, there was a real effort across different subjectivities to begin to understand exactly why care has been ignored, undervalued and relegated as a 'private problem' or 'a choice' for carers and workers alike rather than these struggles being seen as a sign of systemic failings by the state.

Many of these groups were already long active in advocating for the rights of carers, workers and parents. The Nanny Solidarity Network is a group of nannies who noticed that when Covid broke out, the most marginalized women were the ones who suffered. Migrant nannies, often without access to regularized ways of working, were sacked on the spot, with no recourse to public funds. A crowd funder was started, stating,

> The money donated to the childcare workers solidarity fund will provide immediate financial support for the most vulnerable childcare workers, and enable them to stay home and healthy – protecting themselves, their families and their communities while slowing the spread of coronavirus.[33]

This kind of solidarity can be seen as the basis for exploring how the problems inherent in the racialized and gendered world of childcare might be transformed.

The FFC campaign was cohered to explore the good, the bad and the ugly of the childcare provider and childcare 'service user' relationship. It is only then that those who participate in this sometimes warm, often ambivalent, sometimes outright conflictual set of relations can work together to imagine new ways of caring.[34] Many of us are overworked, and if equality has come so far, then we want to know why. The answer posed by neoliberal and individualist forms of feminism is to mediate this overwork, by changing interpersonal dynamics in the home and the workplace (I am reminded of neoliberal feminist Gemma Hartley's suggestion that women resolve these feelings of inequality and burnout by asking their husbands to hire an hourly paid cleaner), of course what this means is outsourcing tasks considered 'domestic drudgery' to women of colour.[35] Hartley's opinion piece and subsequent book, *Fed Up: Emotional Labor, Women, and the Way Forward*, popularized the term, defining emotional labour as the 'unpaid, often unnoticed work that goes into keeping those around you comfortable and happy'. Her writing mostly relates to relationships with male partners within the domestic sphere, rather than a set of labour relations. What scholars of social reproduction[36] offer us instead is the possibility of collectivizing the work that makes women feel so isolated and overburdened.[37]

As unpacked elsewhere in this collection, the original definition of emotional labour comes from Hochschild's 1983 workplace ethnography that claims that certain kinds of work colonize an individual's personal feelings and expressions while insisting it is simply 'part of the job'. She uses this to explain the pressure on frontline service workers like waitresses and receptionists to be 'nicer than necessary' or 'nastier than necessary' in order to do their jobs.[38] Macdonald and Siranni refer to those who find the majority of their work relies on this kind of emotional performance as the 'emotional proletariat' as they are very frequently in low-paid and under-recognized professions.[39] In Labour Process Theory this term relates to the management of human feelings during social interaction within the labour process,[40] as shaped by the dictates of capital accumulation – in short, that capital accumulates wealth through the curated emoting of employees.[41] Emotional labour within the workplace also differs in individualist and collectivist cultures, according to Mastracci and Adams, who argue that collectivity makes emotional labour less fraught.[42] They define emotional labour as the effort to suppress inappropriate emotions or express appropriate emotions within oneself or towards another person, where 'appropriate' and 'inappropriate' are dictated by the demands of the job, alongside cultural factors. Thus, in line with the changing conditions of neoliberal rationality and the marketization of society, where every 'field of activity . . . and entity (whether public or private, whether person, business, or state) is understood as a market and governed as a firm',[43] emotional labour and the associated gendered expectations may begin to 'feel like' work, and this is felt in a specific way by those carrying out care work, warranting the need for further academic investigation.

My wider research also traces the use of the term 'emotional labour' within and in relation to accounts of mothering and parenting in 'mummyblogs', including *Motherly*, *Scary Mommy* and *Good Housekeeping*, and those written by mothers in *Mel Magazine*, *Slate*, *Buzzfeed* and *Medium*, and compares this to any usage of the term in describing and analysing the work of childcare providers as in the 'Champagne Nurseries on Lemonade Budgets' Facebook group, the Pregnant then Screwed campaign and the Nanny Solidarity Network. By coding these netnographic insights around themes related to work, individualism and care, I hope to be able to pinpoint the varied uses of the term 'emotional labour' and make sense of it within a broader feminist critique of neoliberalism. This may help to make sense of why carers are claiming emotional labour as a term to describe their relationships in the private sphere and what it is that makes the tasks associated with socially reproductive activities and familial 'love', in fact, feel like a 'job'.

Attempting to make a space to discuss the nuances of the care relations present in FFC, the Women's Strike Assembly (a feminist collective that organizes around striking from all labour on 8 March each year) is working towards running a combination of workers' enquiries and CR discussions early in 2021 so that we can make sense of the way that care work is currently organized, express how we feel about it and attempt to situate the inadequacies we are facing in a systemic context so that we can work out how to transform them. This means changing both how we all conceive of work, but also imagining better set-ups; community-run childcare provision that parents contribute their time and energy to, demanding a liveable wage for nannies and childminders and making the grey economy – that drives down migrant wages through the use of apps like Care.com – accountable.

Neoliberalism and care in a post-industrial economy

This chapter builds upon a structural critique of why mothering continues to be so arduous in spite of the increasing social equality across society according to many measures. Wilson and Chivers Yochim's book on mothering and precarity, published in 2017, argues that safety nets, social security and public infrastructures that historically have propped up nuclear family life have been continuously eroded, resulting in mothers coming to inhabit the 'precarious ordinary' at work and at home.[44] The shift away from work that relied on 'male breadwinners' and 'stable jobs' gave way to new conditions of precarity in both employment and reproduction.[45] This arguably shifts concerns about economic security (previously guaranteed by permanent, reasonably paid work – at least for some members of the working and middle classes) to a precariousness that permeates all areas of life, to precarity as a 'structure of feeling'.[46]

This precarity is of course gendered, raced and classed. According to Dalia Gabriel, it is 'neither a secret, nor an accident that the "gigification" of care disproportionately impacts migrants and those from migrant backgrounds, making them more easily exploitable'. Gabriel claims, 'Governments and companies can get away with poorer treatment of the socially marginalised, because the rest of society is less likely to vote or act in solidarity with them'.[47] Alongside racialized impoverishment in casualized employment and draconian immigration policies, migrants and people of colour have 'fewer employment options than ever, forcing them into working conditions abhorred by workers of other subjectivities'. This economic exploitation is made easier by increasing political and social disenfranchisement of minority groups across the Western world that comes from having work opportunities and a feeling of power systemically withdrawn or attacked, if either were ever present in the British employment market to start with.[48]

This feeling of precarity is connected to the increasing individualization of responsibility, leading carers or those participating in mothering work to understand unequal and exploitative aspects of gendered labour in the home as simply the 'emotional labour' that goes along with the job. Mummybloggers see that having to 'balance' part-time and precarious work with reproductive tasks is emotional labour because it *feels* emotional, and it *feels like* work.[49] This potentially poses an interesting conjuncture, or opportunity for organizing, for the feminist movement and makes space to organize for more collective forms of reproduction.

As argued by Laura Briggs, the privatization of care has meant a growing wage gap produced by fewer benefits, attacks on the power of trade unions, regressive tax policies and the concentration of wealth and adequate care provision in the hands of those who can afford it.[50] Nancy Fraser has similarly argued that post-industrial labour relations caused not only the kind of gendered poverty that emerges when families cannot survive on a single wage, but that this was indicative of the trend away from public assistance, collectively paid for, as a right of all, towards punitive ideas of dependency that rendered all those reliant on welfare as having 'problems' be they biological, to do with their upbringing or even their neighbourhood.[51]

Social reproduction and collectivizing care

The problem with both mothering work and childcare is not that it is never enjoyable, it often is; the trouble is who it is we find always doing this labour and the conditions/labour relations in which it is done. In short, the problem is not care; it is its distribution.[52] Social reproduction, also known as 'life work', relates to 'activities and attitudes, behaviours and emotions, responsibilities and relationships directly involved in the maintenance of life on a daily basis, and intergenerationally'.[53] Rottenberg reminds us that in many ways the idea of work–life balance is a myth that relies upon certain women, usually poorer racialized women, taking on white, richer women's socially reproductive tasks, so those with better access to structural power can work more, get paid better and therefore feel that work is 'fairer' without the workplace changing at all.[54] It is on this basis that a kind of imbalanced 'balance' is met allowing the 'super mums' to 'lean in' or get ahead.[55] By exploring the social context which produces a culture of 'leaning in' and corporate feminism alongside a sustained distaste for 'stay-at-home mothers', 'working mothers' and care providers alike, it is possible to see how this shapes the way that carers, especially women, feel about the care they give, and how care work is denigrated as a result.

While the labour of care and those who provide it are undervalued, it is worth noting the concerns of queer feminists, such as Sophie Lewis, that care as it is currently mobilized is also a relation of domination, rather that collectivism or collaboration in many cases. The statement released by the Women's Strike Assembly on the International Day of Violence Against Women in 2020 (called 'A red thread of resistance and care') reminds us that the spaces of 'care' such as the home are also places of violence just as much as they are spaces of unwaged work, or indeed love. There is not space here to give arguments of this sort the justice they deserve, but care in its most collaborative state is a relation that needs to be celebrated but never completely uncritically.

In order to understand the current conditions of those doing the social reproduction of child rearing in both a paid and unpaid capacity, my developing research makes strategic use of a combination of qualitative methods that draw on the tradition of critical ethnographic research,[56] including the reflexive elements[57] of critical autoethnography,[58] sometimes called activist ethnography.[59] Following Gatrell,[60] the chapter also analyses netnographic narratives that mothers write about their own lives, the purpose of which is to form a community around motherhood and increasingly to create space to make sense of why mothers are feeling overwhelmed.[61] I also use netnographic means to understand the current conversations between parents and childcare workers taking place on social media (mostly Instagram and Facebook), such as the aforementioned 'Champagne Nurseries on Lemonade Budgets' group,[62] the Pregnant then Screwed 'save our nurseries' campaign[63] and the Nanny Solidarity Network.[64]

Following other activist ethnographies of motherhood and the labour of care, this research follows the work of anti-prison activist Ruth Wilson Gilmore, who examines the collective organizing of the mothers of prisoners and local people opposing prison expansion.[65] The strength of this work is the focus on the ways in which collectivizing aspects of social reproduction (the mothers' groups would do each other's washing and cooking and care for each other's children while others visited their children in prison or advocated for them at police stations) became a powerful part of their organizing strategy. Similarly, beginning to imagine shared and collectivized processes of social reproduction is the basis upon which this research is carried out, in sharp contradiction to the individualized strategies of neoliberal feminist mothering's focus on individual responsibility.

Activism, consciousness raising and the meanings of care

My project is in its early stages, as is some of the activism described here, and thus any outcomes at this juncture are a work in progress. In recent months the activity, energy and discussion within the FFC campaign have declined as individuals and collectives involved with the project remain confused about the best ways to proceed with fighting to better both the conditions of reproduction in the home and those who work in the increasingly erratic funding environment that is the childcare sector. As pointed out by the Women's Budget Group, the November 2020 Spending Review did little to improve the situation of childcare workers: 'There was some additional spending on childcare and social care, but neither received the investment and reform so desperately needed after ten years of austerity, exacerbated by the pandemic.'[66] Without being able to organize a demonstration or meet in person, campaign groups like FFC are seemingly struggling to know what to do beyond awareness-raising techniques.

Those FFC participants involved with the NGO sector, such as the New Economics Foundation, have focused on hosting public meetings and discussions entitled 'Childcare Under Lockdown',[67] while those involved with the Women's Strike have hosted meetings where the meaning and context of the home were scrutinized: 'A red thread of care and resistance on International Day of Violence Against Women'.[68] In terms of more general trends in changing the environment of childcare, the United Voices of the World trade union has recruited two full-time organizers to undertake unionization work in the childcare sector.[69] While all these activities continue despite the pandemic, as a participant it certainly feels like there is never enough being done to deal with this incredible gap in care infrastructure that leaves women trapped in their home or working in someone else's with very little choice, mobility or chance of a pay rise.

In early 2021, the Women's Strike Assembly is set to launch a CR project about care, centring the subjectivities of those who provide it. The idea is that by inviting those who work as care providers and those who provide care in the home, we may begin to work out the barriers to syncretic organizing,[70] or 'organizing across difference', when it comes to reproductive labour. The rationale for using CR is creating space where carers can voice their discontents – at each other, at systemic injustices and at societal attitudes more broadly.

It is reasonable to ask why forming CR groups is the right next step for a group that wants a total reimagining of care and care labour in 2020. The callout posits,

> This project comes from a desire to change the way we're thinking about the world and about activism – to start from our experience and emotional states, to foreground issues like anxiety and stress, to make those things a key part of and starting place for our strategy, and to have that inform our actions. The best way

to understand 'care' both in the ways it makes worlds and the ways it traps us in space, is to think about it together. (Women's Strike Assembly, forthcoming)

This means changing both how gendered work is made sense of under neoliberal conditions and also imagining better set-ups that could include community, parent and worker-run childcare provision. This is a method of politics that originated in the CR groups of the Women's Liberation Groups of the 1970s. The idea was that by creating a culture of shared vulnerability and reflection, conditions could be better understood and then changed in activist communities and society more generally.[71] These groups of no more than twelve women met up regularly to discuss their lives. Shulamith Firestone describes them as the backbone of second-wave feminism.[72]

According to feminist activist group Plan C, 'CR groups provide a wide and thoughtful base of supporters and militants who examine their lives, take hold of their experiences, politicise them, develop theory based on them, and take action relevant to them'.[73] CR groups were seen as key to the feminist movement and were mobilized by many different feminists, according to Gail Lewis of the Brixton Black Women's Group.[74] These ideas inspired a text by the Institute for Precarious Consciousness that had tens of thousands of shares in 2014 called 'We are all very Anxious' that advocated for a reinvigoration of CR groups in the UK.[75] This was in order to make sense of the particular affects associated with the neoliberal condition. CR in the 1970s was not so much a

> pedagogical method of disseminating already-constructed theory, but an intervention stating that women were actually the best ones to make sense of their own material conditions, and to work out how to challenge the structural powers that shaped them. Through a collective and sustained examination of the lives and experiences of those most affected, new worlds were forged. Mark Fisher famously referred to this as 'consciousness inflation'.[76]

The Institute for Precarious Consciousness and the CR groups connected to it argue that emotions such as vulnerability need to be transformed into a sense of injustice, a type of anger which is less resentful and more focused, a move towards self-expression and a reactivation of resistance. An organization's strategy 'must always be based on collective discussions of the experience of life'. For the Institute of Precarious Consciousness, creating spaces where these discussions can take place is known as 'creating a dis-alienated space'. This is what FFC is intending to provide in the groups commencing in early 2021.

What we know is that the meaning of care is changing, as it always has done, in connection with the material conditions of those experiencing it. Interestingly, what I have understood from my netnography and my time involved with the FFC campaign is that the 'gigification' of childcare, via the use of apps, for example, completely changes the way that carers and recipients of that care understand what care can be. For those who work on an app, especially if that work is a one-off 'gig', according to a member of the Care Collective in their Manifesto the Politics of Interdependence,[77] the priority is getting a good review, specifically a Five-Star rating. The Care Collective goes on to explain that the systems in place are not currently complex enough to 'rate' what caring for a child really looks like, which leads to unexpected consequences. In one instance getting a good rating meant never telling a child off for dangerous or unkind behaviour and giving them as much ice cream as they wanted.[78] It is questionable whether this is a recipe for a high level of care, which feminist scholars tell us depends on strong boundaries, building respect and (presumably) attempting to provide nutrition – even if one would prefer ice cream. Essentially, by further eroding the conditions of workers, we also rob children and their parents of high-quality care.

Conclusion

Briggs argues that women are worn out, lonely and emotionally exhausted because what is needed is a feminist vision of care where multiple kinds of households and communities collectivize their lives.[79] She suggests following the organizational strategies of collectives of single parents, like The Single Parents Liberation Movement that operated across the UK in the 1970s,[80] the Black Panthers Party Free Breakfast Program 1969–80[81] and the collective households of the gay liberation front.[82] But what is needed is a way to collectivize the situation of people who have been systemically isolated from each other through the neoliberal process of bettering individuals at the cost of the many.

The next stage in my research will be to understand better the interventions being made in care provision at the current time, including such examples as Ireland's migrant-founded and led, worker-owned social care business called the Great Care Co-op.[83] Maria Jikijela and other carers came together through the Migrant Rights Centre of Ireland because they felt they could provide social care more efficiently and oriented around the needs of those who require care and also those who work in care. According to Jikijela, those who work in the organization have equal stake and there are no shareholders. Unlike in their previous roles they have sick pay, holiday pay and pensions – challenging the for-profit model of professional 'care'.

The neo-liberalization of care has historically produced tensions between carers and parents, eliding structural problems. Propping up private providers that many parents couldn't afford before the economic downturn is not an answer on its own. Systemic solutions are needed. Organizing in the pandemic has understandably been uneven and logistically challenging, but grassroots CR can crucially inform a bolder, more ambitious vision for the future. Now is the time to guarantee free universal childcare, to stimulate the economy, save parents' jobs and ensure that all children are able to catch up on the crucial early years support they missed during lockdown. It is time for overworked and under-recognized mothers, parents and carers to receive the dignity in work they deserve. Collectivism must be prioritized over individualism, because offloading 'emotional labour' on to those with fewer opportunities needs to be seen as a strategy of neoliberal feminism that cannot deliver the world we all deserve.

Notes

1. Berry, 'If We Need Childcare to Reopen the UK Economy, Why Is It so Undervalued?'; Crook, 'Parenting during the Covid-19 Pandemic of 2020', 1226–38; Hill, 'Early Years and Childcare Sector at Risk of Collapse in England'.
2. English and Campbell, 'Striking from the Second Shift', 151–60; López et al., 'The Quarantine Archives', 195–213.
3. Hartley, *Fed Up – Women, Work and the Way Forward*.
4. Beck, 'Arlie Hochschild: Housework Isn't "Emotional Labor"'.
5. Olufemi, *Feminism, Interrupted: Disrupting Power*.
6. Hartley, *Fed Up – Women, Work and the Way Forward*.
7. Costa, 'Women's Emotional Labor in Higher Ed and the COVID-19 Crisis'.
8. Milburn and Russell, 'What can an Institution do?'
9. Butt, 'Mrs Thatcher: The First Two Years'.
10. Toler, 'Settling In to the Emotional Labor of Motherhood'.
11. Gatrell, 'Monstrous Motherhood versus Magical Maternity?', 633–47.
12. Wilson and Chivers Yochim, *Mothering through Precarity*.
13. Fraser, *Fortunes of Feminism*.
14. Brown, *States of Injury*.
15. Baumgardner and Richards, *Manifesta*.
16. Carden, *The New Feminist Movement*.
17. Fisher, *Capitalist Realism*.
18. Hardy, 'How Covid-19 Is Reshaping Early Years Childcare'.
19. Penn et al., 'COVID-19 and Childcare'.

20　Gaunt, 'Childminders Left Confused'.
21　Gaunt, 'Childminders Left Confused'.
22　Hall and Stephens, 'Quality Childcare for All'.
23　Marcus, 'Nursery Owners Create "Champagne Nurseries, Lemonade Funding" Video'.
24　Thomas, 'Coronavirus: "The Nursery I Run May Not Survive"'.
25　Reid, 'Our Childcare System Was Broken Long Before Covid'.
26　McBain, 'Why Britain's Childcare System Is on the Brink of Collapse'.
27　Harding and Cottell, 'Childcare Survey 2018'.
28　Penn et al., 'COVID-19 and Childcare'.
29　Faulkner, 'Early Childhood Policy and Practice in England'.
30　Hill, 'Early Years and Childcare Sector at Risk of Collapse in England'.
31　Hall, 'The Crisis of Care.Com'.
32　Klich, 'The New Mom Economy'.
33　Nanny Solidarity Network, 'Childcare Worker's Solidarity Fund'.
34　Bhattacharya, *Social Reproduction Theory*.
35　Olufemi, *Feminism, Interrupted*.
36　Bhattacharya, *Social Reproduction Theory*.
37　Hester, 'Care under Capitalism', 343–52.
38　Beck, 'Arlie Hochschild: Housework Isn't "Emotional Labor"'.
39　MacDonald and Sirianni, *Working In the Service Society*.
40　Taylor and Bain, 'An Assembly Line in the Head'.
41　Brook, 'In Critical Defence of Emotional Labour', 531–48.
42　Mastracci and Adams, 'Is Emotional Labor Easier in Collectivist or Individualist Cultures?', 325–44.
43　Shenk, 'What Exactly Is Neoliberalism?'
44　Stewart, *Ordinary Affects*.
45　Fraser, *Fortunes of Feminism*.
46　Orgad, 'Mothering through Precarity', 278–80.
47　Gebrial, 'If You Don't Care'.
48　Gebrial, 'If You Don't Care'.
49　I am drawing specifically on the following mummybloggers – Broadbent 2018; Hartley 2018; Marcoux 2019; Toler 2018.
50　Briggs, *How All Politics Became Reproductive Politics*.
51　Fraser, *Fortunes of Feminism*.
52　English and Campbell, 'Striking from the Second Shift', 151–60.
53　Farris, 'Social Reproduction, Surplus Populations and the Role of Migrant Women'.
54　Rottenberg, *The Rise of Neoliberal Feminism*.
55　Sandberg, *Lean In: Women, Work and the Will to Lead*.
56　Madison, *Critical Ethnography*.

57 English, 'Safe Cracking'.
58 Graeber, *Direct Action*.
59 Smith, *Decolonizing Methodologies*.
60 Gatrell, 'Monstrous Motherhood versus Magical Maternity?', 633–47.
61 Wilson and Chivers Yochim, *Mothering through Precarity*.
62 Champagne Nurseries on Lemonade Funding Facebook Group (2021).
63 Brearley, 'Save Our Nurseries'.
64 Nanny Solidarity Network, 'Childcare Worker's Solidarity Fund'.
65 Gilmore, *Golden Gulag*.
66 Women's Budget Group, 'Response to the Spending Review 2020'.
67 New Economics Foundation, 'Weekly Economics Briefing 4'.
68 Women's Strike Assembly, 'A Red Thread of Feminist Resistance and Care'.
69 United Voices of the World, 'UVW Is Hiring Two Full Time Organisers in the Childcare Sector'.
70 Gilmore, *Golden Gulag*.
71 English, 'Safe Cracking'.
72 Firestone, *The Dialectic of Sex*.
73 Plan C, 'C Is for Consciousness Raising!'.
74 Lewis, 'Consciousness-Raising'.
75 Institute of Precarious Consciousness, 'We Are All Very Anxious'.
76 Fisher, *Capitalist Realism*.
77 Verso Books, *Ann Pettifor and The Care Collective*.
78 Verso Books, *Ann Pettifor and The Care Collective*.
79 Briggs, *How All Politics Became Reproductive Politics*.
80 Ryan, 'Transforming Motherhood'.
81 Pien, 'Black Panther Party's Free Breakfast Program'.
82 Briggs, *How All Politics Became Reproductive Politics*.
83 Holland, 'Migrant Women Create Ireland's First Carers' Co-Operative'.

Bibliography

Barbagallo, Camille, and Silvia Federici. 'Introduction - Care Work and the Commons'. *The Commoner Journal* 15 (2012): 1–22.

Baumgardner, Jennifer, and Amy Richards. *Manifesta: Young Women, Feminism, and the Future*. Farrar: Straus and Giroux, 2000.

Beck, Julie. 'Arlie Hochschild: Housework Isn't "Emotional Labor" - The Atlantic'. *The Atlantic*. https://www.theatlantic.com/family/archive/2018/11/arlie-hochschild-housework-isnt-emotional-labor/576637/ (accessed 26 January 2021).

Berry, Christine. 'If We Need Childcare to Reopen the UK Economy, Why Is It so Undervalued? | Christine Berry'. *The Guardian*, 23 May 2020. http://www.theguardi

an.com/commentisfree/2020/may/23/childcare-reopen-economy-children-school-c oronavirus.

Bhattacharya, Tithi. *Social Reproduction Theory*. London: Pluto Books, 2018. https://www.plutobooks.com/9780745399881/social-reproduction-theory.

Brearley, Joeli. 'Save Our Nurseries'. 1 December 2020. *Pregnant Then Screwed* (blog). https://pregnantthenscrewed.com/save-our-nurseries/ (accessed 26 January 2021).

Briggs, Laura. *How All Politics Became Reproductive Politics: From Welfare Reform to Foreclosure to Trump*. 1st edn. Oakland, California: University of California Press, 2017. https://www.jstor.org/stable/10.1525/j.ctv1wxqbv.

Broadbent, Elizabeth. 'The Bulk Of The Emotional Labor Falls On Moms, And It's Destroying Us'. Scary Mommy, 14 September 2020. https://www.scarymommy.com/women-do-most-emotional-labor-family/.

Brook, Paul. 'In Critical Defence of "Emotional Labour": Refuting Bolton's Critique of Hochschild's Concept'. *Work, Employment and Society* 23, no. 3 (1 September 2009): 531–48. https://doi.org/10.1177/0950017009337071.

Brown, Wendy. *States of Injury: Power and Freedom in Late Modernity*. Princeton: Princeton University Press, 2020.

Butt, Ronald. 'Mrs Thatcher: The First Two Years'. *The Sunday Times*, 3 May 1981. The Margaret Thatcher Foundation. https://www.margaretthatcher.org/document/104475.

Carden, Maren Lockwood. *The New Feminist Movement*. Russell Sage Foundation, 1974. https://www.jstor.org/stable/10.7758/9781610441063.

Connell, Raewyn, Barbara Fawcett, and Gabrielle Meagher. 'Neoliberalism, New Public Management and the Human Service Professions: Introduction to the Special Issue'. *Journal of Sociology* 45, no. 4 (24 November 2009): 331–8. https://doi.org/10.1177/1440783309346472.

Costa, Karen. 'Women's Emotional Labor in Higher Ed and the COVID-19 Crisis'. WIHE, 30 April 2020. https://www.wihe.com/article-details/147/women-s-emotional-labor-in-higher-ed-and-the-covid-19-crisis/.

Crook, Sarah. 'Parenting during the Covid-19 Pandemic of 2020: Academia, Labour and Care Work'. *Women's History Review* 29, no. 7 (n.d.): 1226–38.

English, Claire, and Rosa Campbell. 'Opinion: This Is How a Strike Sparked International Women's Day – and Why We're Planning to Do It All Again'. *The Independent*, 8 March 2019. https://www.independent.co.uk/voices/international-womens-day-strike-theresa-malkiel-a8812546.html.

English, Claire, and Rosa Campbell. 'Striking from the "Second Shift": Lessons from the "My Mum Is on Strike" Events on International Women's Day 2019'. *Feminist Review* 126, no. 1 (1 November 2020): 151–60. https://doi.org/10.1177/0141778920942747.

English, Claire Louise. 'Safe Cracking : From Safe(r) Spaces to Collectivising Vulnerability in Migrant Solidarity Organising'. Ph.D., University of Leicester, 2017. https://figshare.com/articles/Safe_Cracking_From_Safe_r_Spaces_to_Collectivising_Vulnerability_in_Migrant_Solidarity_Organising/10214081.

Farris, Sara. 'Social Reproduction, Surplus Populations and the Role of Migrant Women'. *Viewpoint Magazine*, 1 November 2015. https://www.viewpointmag.com/2015/11/01/social-reproduction-and-surplus-populations/.

Faulkner, Dorothy. 'Early Childhood Policy and Practice in England: Twenty Years of Change'. *International Journal of Early Years Education* 21 (9 September 2013). https://doi.org/10.1080/09669760.2013.832945.

Federici, Silvia. *Wages against Housework*. Bristol: Falling Wall Press [for] the Power of Women Collective, 1975.

Firestone, Shulamith. *The Dialectic of Sex*. London: Verso, 2015.

Fisher, Mark. *Capitalist Realism: Is There No Alternative?* London: Zero Books, 2009.

Fraser, Nancy. *Fortunes of Feminism: From State-Managed Capitalism to Neoliberal Crisis*. 1st edition. Brooklyn, NY: Verso, 2013.

Gatrell, Caroline. 'Boundary Creatures? Employed, Breastfeeding Mothers and "Abjection as Practice"'. *Organization Studies* 40, no. 3 (1 March 2019): 421–42. https://doi.org/10.1177/0170840617736932.

Gatrell, Caroline. 'Monstrous Motherhood versus Magical Maternity? An Exploration of Conflicting Attitudes to Maternity within Health Discourses and Organizational Settings'. *Equality, Diversity and Inclusion: An International Journal* 33 (15 September 2014): 633–47. https://doi.org/10.1108/EDI-07-2012-0056.

Gaunt, Catherine. 'Childminders Left Confused by Mixed Messaging from Government over Work Return'. *Nursery World*, 12 May 2020. https://www.nurseryworld.co.uk/news/article/childminders-left-confused-by-mixed-messaging-from-government-over-work-return.

Gebrial, Dalia. 'If You Don't Care What Happens to Gig Workers during Coronavirus, You Should – You're next'. *The Independent*, 27 March 2020. https://www.independent.co.uk/voices/coronavirus-deliveroo-uber-self-employed-gig-workers-sick-pay-a9430336.html.

Graeber, David. *Direct Action: An Ethnography*. New York: AK Press, 2009.

Hall, Miranda. 'The Crisis of Care.Com'. *Open Democracy* (blog), 11 February 2020. https://www.opendemocracy.net/en/oureconomy/crisis-carecom/.

Hall, Miranda, and Lucie Stephens. 'Quality Childcare for All'. New Economics Foundation, 15 January 2020. https://neweconomics.org/2020/01/quality-childcare-for-all.

Harding, Claire, and Josh Cottell. 'Childcare Survey 2018'. Family and Childcare Trust, 31 December 2018. https://www.familyandchildcaretrust.org/childcare-survey-2018.

Hardy, Kate. 'How Covid-19 Is Reshaping Early Years Childcare', 24 November 2020. https://business.leeds.ac.uk/divisions/news/article/503/how-covid-19-is-reshaping-early-years-childcare.

Hartley, Gemma. *Fed Up – Women, Work and the Way Forward*. New York: Harper Collins, 2019. https://www.harpercollins.ca/9780062855985/fed-up/.

Hartley, Gemma. *What Is Emotional Labour? In Conversation with Cassie McCollough.* All About Women 2019, 2019. https://www.youtube.com/watch?app=desktop&v=mQ8ZpU-V7JE.

Hartley, Gemma. 'Women Aren't Nags – We're Just Fed Up'. *Harper's Bazaar*, 27 September 2017. https://www.harpersbazaar.com/culture/features/a12063822/emotional-labor-gender-equality/.

Hester, Helen. 'Care under Capitalism: The Crisis of "Women's Work"'. *IPPR Progressive Review* 24, no. 4 (2018): 343–52. https://doi.org/10.1111/newe.12074.

Hill, Amelia. 'Early Years and Childcare Sector at Risk of Collapse in England'. *The Guardian*, 31 May 2020, sec. Education. https://www.theguardian.com/education/2020/jun/01/early-years-childcare-sector-at-risk-collapse-england.

Holland, Kitty. 'Migrant Women Create Ireland's First Carers' Co-Operative'. *The Irish Times*, 23 June 2020. https://www.irishtimes.com/news/social-affairs/migrant-women-create-ireland-s-first-carers-co-operative-1.4310938.

Institute of Precarious Consciousness. 'We Are All Very Anxious'. *We are Plan C* (blog), 16 April 2014. https://www.weareplanc.org/we-are-all-very-anxious/.

Klich, Tanya. 'The New Mom Economy: Meet The Startups Disrupting The $46 Billion Millennial Parenting Market'. *Forbes*. Accessed 26 January 2021. https://www.forbes.com/sites/tanyaklich/2019/05/10/the-new-mom-economy-meet-the-startups-disrupting-the-46-billion-millennial-parenting-market/.

Land, Christopher, and Daniel King. 'Organizing Otherwise: Translating Anarchism in a Voluntary Sector Organization'. *Ephemera* 14 (1 January 2014): 923–50.

Lewis, Gail. 'Consciousness-Raising: Sisterhood and After Research Team'. The British Library. 8 March 2013. https://www.bl.uk/sisterhood/articles/consciousness-raising.

Lewis, Sophie. *Full Surrogacy Now: Feminism Against Family*. London: Verso, 2019.

López, Ligia (Licho), Christopher T. McCaw, Rhonda Di Biase, Amy McKernan, Sophie Rudolph, Aristidis Galatis, Nicky Dulfer, et al. 'The Quarantine Archives: Educators in "Social Isolation"'. *History of Education Review* 49, no. 2 (1 January 2020): 195–213. https://doi.org/10.1108/HER-05-2020-0028.

MacDonald, Cameron, and Carmen Sirianni. *Working In Service Society*. Philadelphia: Temple University Press, 1996. https://www.bookdepository.com/Working-Service-Society-Cameron-MacDonald/9781566394802 (accessed 26 January 2021).

Madison, D. Soyini. *Critical Ethnography: Method, Ethics, and Performance*. 3rd edn. Los Angeles: SAGE Publications, Inc, 2019.

Marcoux, Heather. 'Burnout Is Real, Says the World Health Organization (and Mothers Everywhere)'. *Motherly*, 29 May 2019. https://www.mother.ly/news/the-world-health-organization-says-burnout-is-real.

Marcus, Laura. 'Nursery Owners Create "Champagne Nurseries, Lemonade Funding" Video'. *Nursery World*, 31 March 2016. https://www.nurseryworld.co.uk/news/article/nursery-owners-create-champagne-nurseries-lemonade-funding-video.

Mastracci, Sharon, and Ian Adams. 'Is Emotional Labor Easier in Collectivist or Individualist Cultures? An East–West Comparison'. *Public Personnel Management* 48, no. 3 (6 December 2018): 325–44. https://doi.org/10.1177/0091026018814569.

McBain, Sophie. 'Why Britain's Childcare System Is on the Brink of Collapse'. *The New Statesman*, 22 September 2020. https://www.newstatesman.com/politics/education/2020/09/why-britains-childcare-system-brink-collapse.

Milburn, K., and B. T. Russell. 'What Can an Institution Do? Towards Public-Common Partnerships and a New Common-Sense'. *Renewal: A Journal of Social Democracy* 26, no. 4 (1 May 2018): 45–55.

Milburn, Keir. *Generation Left*. Radical Futures. Bristol: Polity Books, n.d. (accessed 26 January 2021).

Nanny Solidarity Network. 'Childcare Worker's Solidarity Fund: Love Won't Pay the Bills'. *Nanny Solidarity Network*, 4 July 2020. https://www.nannysolidarirynetwork.co.uk.

New Economics Foundation. 'Weekly Economics Briefing 4: Childcare Under Lockdown'. *New Economics Foundation*, 30 April 2020. https://neweconomics.org/2020/04/weekly-economics-briefing-4-childcare-under-lockdown.

Olufemi, Lola. *Feminism, Interrupted: Disrupting Power*. London: Pluto Press, 2020.

Orgad, Shani. 'Mothering through Precarity: Women's Work and Digital Media'. *Journal of Communication Inquiry* 32, no. 2 (1 April 2018): 278–80.

Perrier, Maud. 'Childcare Strikes on the Rise: Love Doesn't Pay the Bills'. *Discover Society*, 1 May 2019. https://discoversociety.org/2019/05/01/childcare-strikes-on-the-rise-love-doesnt-pay-the-bills/.

Pien, Diane. 'Black Panther Party's Free Breakfast Program (1969–1980)'. *Black Past* (blog), 11 February 2010. https://www.blackpast.org/african-american-history/black-panther-partys-free-breakfast-program-1969-1980/.

Plan C. 'C Is for Consciousness Raising!'. *We Are Plan C* (blog), 1 August 2015. https://www.weareplanc.org/blog/c-is-for-consciousness-raising/.

Reedy, Patrick, Daniel King, and Christine Coupland. 'Organizing for Individuation: Alternative Organizing, Politics and New Identities'. *Organization Studies* 37, no. 11 (13 May 2016): 1553–73. https://doi.org/10.1177/0170840616641983.

Reid, Mandu. 'Our Childcare System Was Broken Long Before Covid'. *Huffington Post* (blog), 24 July 2020. https://www.huffingtonpost.co.uk/entry/childcare-inequality_uk_5f1ac8f4c5b6f2f6c9f4f11b.

Robinson, Emily, Camilla Schofield, Florence Sutcliffe-Braithwaite, and Natalie Thomlinson. 'Telling Stories about Post-War Britain: Popular Individualism and the "Crisis" of the 1970s'. *Twentieth Century British History* 28, no. 2 (1 June 2017): 268–304. https://doi.org/10.1093/tcbh/hwx006.

Rottenberg, Catherine. *The Rise of Neoliberal Feminism*. Heretical Thought. Oxford and New York: Oxford University Press, 2018.

Russell Hochschild, Arlie. 'Emotions and Society'. *Emotions and Society* 1, no. 1 (29 March 2019): 9–13. https://doi.org/10.1332/263168919X15580836411805.

Ryan, Elizabeth. *Transforming Motherhood: Single Parents' Liberation in the 1970s.* Detroit: Wayne State University, 2015.

Sandberg, Sheryl. *Lean In: Women, Work and the Will to Lead.* New York: Penguin Random House, 2013. https://www.penguinrandomhouse.com/books/227762/lean-in-by-sheryl-sandberg/.

Shenk, Timothy. 'What Exactly Is Neoliberalism?' *Dissent Magazine* (blog), 2 April 2015. https://www.dissentmagazine.org/blog/booked-3-what-exactly-is-neoliberalism-wendy-brown-undoing-the-demos.

Smith, Linda Tuhiwai. *Decolonizing Methodologies: Research and Indigenous Peoples.* London: Zed Books, 1999.

Stewart, Kathleen. *Ordinary Affects.* Durham: Duke University Press, 2007. https://read.dukeupress.edu/books/book/1243/Ordinary-Affects.

Taylor, Phil, and Peter Bain. '"An Assembly Line in the Head": Work and Employee Relations in the Call Centre'. *Industrial Relations Journal.* John Wiley & Sons, Ltd, 1 June 1999. https://onlinelibrary.wiley.com/doi/abs/10.1111/1468-2338.00113.

Thomas, Daniel. 'Coronavirus: "The Nursery I Run May Not Survive"'. *BBC News,* 4 May 2020, sec. Business. https://www.bbc.com/news/business-52506919.

Toler, Sarah. 'Settling In to the Emotional Labor of Motherhood'. *Medium,* 22 March 2019. https://medium.com/@sarahannetoler/settling-in-to-the-emotional-labor-of-motherhood-26cc7a531ce2.

United Voices of the World. 'UVW Is Hiring Two Full Time Organisers in the Childcare Sector'. *United Voices of the World* (blog). https://www.uvwunion.org.uk/en/news/2020/09/uvw-is-hiring-two-full-time-organisers/ (accessed 26 January 2021).

Verso Books. *Verso Live: Ann Pettifor and The Care Collective,* 2020. https://www.youtube.com/watch?app=desktop&v=o_jPptWDOgQ.

Wilson, Julie A., and Emily Chivers Yochim. *Mothering Through Precarity: Women's Work and Digital Media.* Illustrated edition. Durham: Duke University Press Books, 2017.

Wilson Gilmore, Ruth. *Golden Gulag: Prisons, Surplus, Crisis, and Opposition in Globalizing California.* California: University of California Press, 2007. https://www.ucpress.edu/book/9780520242012/golden-gulag.

Women's Budget Group. 'Response to the Spending Review 2020'. Policy Briefing. *Austerity in Place of Ambition* (blog), 2 December 2020. https://wbg.org.uk/analysis/uk-budget-assessments/response-to-the-spending-review-2020/.

Women's Strike Assembly. 'A Red Thread of Feminist Resistance and Care'. The Women's Strike Assembly, 25 November 2020. https://womenstrike.org.uk/2020/11/25/red-threads-of-resistance-and-care/.

Zeno, Elissa, and Allison J. Pugh. 'Book Review: Mothering through Precarity: Women's Work and Digital Media by Julie A. Wilson and Emily Chivers Yochim'. *Gender & Society* 32, no. 2 (14 September 2017): 278–80. https://doi.org/10.1177/0891243217732012.

Afterword[1]

Claire Langhamer

Work is one of the defining features of human existence and a connection with it usually dominates adult life. Though there are obvious complexities of definition – thinking about work as employment ignores unremunerated domestic labour, for example – few individuals avoid having a relationship with work at some point in their lives.

Like all types of relationships, that which exists between people and their work can be deeply emotional, influencing well-being and affecting mood. The spaces, things, people and processes that are encountered through work are steeped in feeling and can have an intensity surpassing that of more ostensibly 'personal' relationships. The kinds of resentments and attachments experienced in paid employments can mirror those that develop in homes and families. How people feel about their job can frame their sense of self, other people and life. How people experience emotion at work can also determine their health and happiness. And yet we still know too little about feelings at work in past and present times. This collection of chapters extends our understanding considerably, offering a distinctively and avowedly interdisciplinary reimagining of the field.

It is an apt time to be thinking about emotions and work. Within our contemporary world, the emotional dimensions of employment are widely referenced, if not always rigorously analysed. As this book actively demonstrates, the topic has transnational and transoccupational purchase, speaking to issues of pressing significance. These include questions around skill and training, performance and burden, management and impact. And of course the Covid-19 pandemic has further reshaped the interplay between emotion and work, accelerating some of the existing drivers of change – not least the elision of 'work' and 'life' – and introducing new considerations and problematics. The essays presented here address both this recent transformative context and past historical moments, adopting diverse methodologies and disciplinary standpoints to explore the relationship between emotion and work across time, occupation and place.

Feeling seems to have been doing a lot of work, at work, in recent times. The demand for what Arlie Russell Hochschild first conceptualized as 'emotional labour' has grown significantly since the term was coined in 1983.[2] Its performance was, until Covid, as likely to be assessed by the pressing of an emoji button as by a detailed customer satisfaction survey. Workplace training programmes have actively embraced emotion as a tool for managing both the self and others, and, as Tatiane Leal shows in this volume, emotion has been positioned as a powerful, if risky, form of capital for women workers in particular. Feelings that might hitherto have been predominantly associated with non-work life – love perhaps, or happiness – are now drawn explicitly into workplace practices. 'Leading with Love' is a management strategy, kindness is a mission statement and empathy has been monetarized.[3] 'More empathetic companies are more profitable in terms of market capitalisation, growth and earnings', declares an organization dedicated to measuring empathy in business.[4]

This is not just emotion as a tool to discipline, control and encourage; it is emotion as a driver of trade and a form of self-management for those in charge. It is not now uncommon for senior managers to discuss their feelings as much as their decisions. They sometimes share these with staff, clients and customers, using the emotional 'we' to suggest a form of community. 'If the pandemic has taught us anything', wrote CEO Sean Doyle in a November 2020 email to British Airways' customers, 'it's the value of simple pleasures, the importance of kindness and [. . .] what we can achieve when we work together'.[5] Sometimes, however, the feelings are framed as apologies for past organizational behaviour because the growing visibility and use of emotion at work has also drawn attention to emotional harm, toxicity and transgression. While harassment, bullying and discrimination at work is not an invention of the twenty-first century, the #MeToo and Black Lives Matter movements have drawn attention both to its structural nature and its impact on individual lives.

And yet, as responses to the global pandemic have abundantly demonstrated, not all workplace feeling is deemed to be equal. The feelings of some workers are more highly valued, and carry greater weight, than those of others whether within organizations or across sectors. Hierarchies of workplace feeling also map on to, and exacerbate, gendered, raced and classed hierarchies. Nonetheless, all workers are encouraged to take personal responsibility for their feelings at work. The discourse of well-being promises to resolve negative workplace feeling while largely untethering it from a material context. If twentieth-century campaigns around health and safety at work tended to foreground the politics of the collective, the mindfulness industry that has emerged in recent times offers a more personalized approach to overwork, stress and anxiety.[6] Certainly twenty-first-century workers are encouraged to be selective in the feelings they bring to work. Happiness, kindness and pride may be welcome, but anger and disappointment should, generally, be left at home. Feelings must be curated and performed according to distinct spatial and relational contexts. And they must be performed according to norms that tend to re-enforce structural inequalities.

* * *

If the operation of feeling at work has responded to a changing historical context, so too has its investigation. The everyday experiences and emotional dimensions of work have long been subjected to social and psychological, if not always explicitly historical, investigation. Research in the early twentieth century focused on job satisfaction, occupational health, absenteeism, responses to automation and work-related stress.[7] Later studies have explored work–life balance, including its spatial and temporal dimensions, 'emotional labour' – the 'creep' of which Hochschild has recently critiqued – and newly emerging forms of working motherhood, explored by Sharpe in her 1984 book *Double Identity* and by McCarthy more recently in *Double Lives*.[8] Sociologists such as Illouz have also increasingly pointed to the rise of an explicitly and aggressively 'emotional' capitalism.[9]

There is a more immediate historiographical context for those working on feelings and work in the past. Some of this has strong ties to the history of medicine and includes research into the history of stress by Hayes, Jackson and Kirby, among others;[10] into occupational health by Haywood, Long, McIvor and Johnson, and Palmer;[11] and into the social psychology and emotional economy of unemployment by McKibbin and Elliott and Lawrence.[12] There is important research on work and identity by Kirk and Wall and by McIvor[13] – and on workplace politics by Moss and Saunders.[14] This research sits alongside a growing body of publications that illuminates the role of emotions within particular occupations and sectors, such as Delap's work on domestic service and Boddice's study of Victorian science.[15] There is a particularly rich seam of scholarship on the gendered dimensions of feelings at work within particular locations (e.g. Berebitsky's book on sex and the US office), among particular workers (Pringle's analysis of the experience of being a secretary is a good example) and on particular echelons – seen in Roper's oral history of middle-class managers, *Masculinity and the British Organization Man since 1945* published back in 1994.[16]

It is a broader scholarship on emotion, as much as that on work and employment, that underpins this book, however. Emotion Studies provides a framework for drawing together the glimpses of feeling evident within existing histories of work and suggests new research questions and methodologies. The early work of Peter and Carol Stearns on emotional codes and standards ('emotionology') provides a starting point, but the authors within this collection have engaged with William Reddy's delineation of the 'emotional regimes' that shape the expression and perception of emotions, with Barbara Rosenwein's model of 'emotional communities', which she defines as groups 'in which people adhere to the same norms of expression and value – or devalue – the same or related emotions', and with Benno Gammerl's attention to the spatial dynamics of 'emotional styles', that is, the ways in which emotions are framed by '*where* they occur'.[17] Monique Scheer's notion of 'emotional practice', also cited by some of the present authors, encourages attention to the things people do to create and maintain emotional communities or styles.[18]

These conceptual interventions, developed through research on different moments and locations, have here also been put to work within diverse contexts. The geographic reach of the collection extends from late-nineteenth-century London, New York and Paris to early-twentieth-century Soviet Union; from mid-century Buenos Aires to late-twentieth-century Ahmedabad and on to twenty-first-century Brazil. The workers considered include medics and scientists, actors and textile workers, shop assistants and waitresses and domestic servants and childcare workers.

While each chapter raises its own distinct set of questions, broader connections – both methodological and thematic – emerge, pointing to future directions and approaches. One of the most striking overarching themes concerns the interplay of supposed binaries such as waged and unwaged work, work space and living space and ultimately 'work' and 'life'. While the global pandemic heralded a dramatic collapse of the temporal and spatial distinctions that have previously shaped the work–life relationship of some people, the chapters presented here show that this blurring of categories has a longer history – one that defies linear narratives. For example, Arnold-Forster shows that the conflation of professional space and domestic space was a live issue within mid-twentieth-century UK hospital employment; Leal demonstrates the ways in which women's paid employment was represented as an extension of the private world in the Brazilian media of the 2010s; and Moulds explains how debates around the 'living-in' practices of late-nineteenth- and early-twentieth-century shop work were framed around the relative emotional benefits of sociability and solitude. In Chapter 7 by Pérez, the intersection between personal and labour relations is illuminated through the case study of court cases around the non-payment of remuneration for domestic service. Each of these chapters demonstrates that the relationship between work and life, including for Moulds and Arnold-Forster its implication for emotional health, was a complex formulation even before the expansion of precarious zero-hours contracts and the Zoom home-working revolution.

Nor, of course, is the political use of emotion, within and beyond the workplace, new. While Brown shows the personal cost as well as wider emotional framing of the politics of whistleblowing, Chapter 6 by Parker on women's letters to the Soviet authorities connects individual feelings about work to attempts to create a national community cohered in part by emotion. In contrast, the emotional communities that Pearson traces are transnational in nature, built around different understandings of, and emotional responses to, vivisection.

The collection offers methodological and conceptual interventions too. The utility and implications of the concept of 'emotional labour' are interrogated by three of the authors. For Blackwell-Pal, the key problem is its tendency to individualize – something that might be addressed through attention to its direction as well as its performance. The individualization and domestication of notions of emotional labour raise conceptual problems for English too, who points out 'differences between feeling alienated from the work you do in your own home with your own children, and the alienation experienced as part of the wage relation'. Whorrall-Campbell shows that not all emotional labour is conceived of as a burden. For the Lyons Corner House 'Nippies' she discusses, emotional labour was as likely to be a source of pride and satisfaction as it was a cause of suffering. Elsewhere the authors interrogate the interplay of emotion, working lives and memory, and this includes Horrocks's and Merchant's consideration of the temporal complexity of narratives of workplace emotion in academia and Barua's exploration of subjectivity and structure in the retelling of past emotional landscapes in Ahmedabad.

While the chapters presented here attend to work as a key aspect of everyday life, they also problematize an individualizing perspective, looking to illuminate the collective and the structural as much as the personalized and biographical. This is a key challenge for emotions scholars – how to point up the importance of complexity without jettisoning overarching interpretation; how, essentially, to consider the ways in which work is shaped by feeling as well as the ways in which feeling bends to the discipline of work.[19] The work of these authors suggests that a focus on emotions and work *can* deliver overarching interpretation and that it is in the movement between emotional intimacy and emotional abstraction that we see the forces of history at play.

Feeling was a powerful driver of working lives long before it became articulated as such. This book will help us to better understand the past and present of feelings at work and suggests important new lines of thinking for the future.

Notes

1. Some of these ideas will be further developed in Langhamer, *Feelings at Work in Modern Britain* (forthcoming, Oxford University Press).
2. Hochschild, *The Managed Heart*.
3. See for example, Blakeley and Blakeley, *Leading with Love*.
4. *The Empathy Business*.
5. 'A message from our new CEO, Sean Doyle', 24 November 2020.
6. Kirby, *Feeling the Strain*.
7. On the range of debates around work, see Pahl, ed. *On Work*.
8. https://www.theatlantic.com/family/archive/2018/11/arlie-hochschild-housework-isnt-emotional-labor/576637/(accessed 26 April 2021); Sharpe, *Double Identity*; McCarthy, *Double Lives*.
9. Illouz, *Cold Intimacies*.
10. Hayes, 'Industrial Automation and Stress, c. 1945-79', in Jackson, *Stress in Postwar Britain*, 75–93; Jackson, *The Age of Stress*; Kirby, *Feeling the Strain*.
11. Haywood, 'Busman's Stomach and the Embodiment of Modernity', 1–23; Long, *The Rise and Fall of the Healthy Factory*; McIvor and Johnston, *Miner's Lung*; Palmer, *Who Cared for the Carers*.
12. McKibbin, *The Ideologies of Class*; Elliott and Lawrence, 'The Emotional Economy of Unemployment'.
13. Kirk and Wall, *Work and Identity*; McIvor, *Working Lives*.
14. Moss, *Women, Workplace Protest and Political Identity in England*; Saunders, *Assembling Cultures*.
15. Delap, *Knowing Their Place*; Boddice, *The Science of Sympathy*.
16. Berebitsky, *Sex and the Office*; Pringle, *Secretaries Talk*; Roper, *Masculinity and the British Organization Man since 1945*.
17. Reddy, *The Navigation of Feeling*; Rosenwein, *Emotional Communities in the Early Middle Ages*, 2; Gammerl, 'Emotional Styles', 164.
18. Scheer, 'Are Emotions a Kind of Practice', 193–220.
19. Frank Biess argues, 'Rather than reflecting larger cultural and social transformations, emotions function as historical forces in their own right that also affect change.' Biess, 'Everybody has a Chance', 218.

Bibliography

'A message from our new CEO, Sean Doyle'. 24 November 2020.

Berebitsky, Julie. *Sex and the Office: A History of Gender, Power and Desire*. New Haven, CT: Yale University Press, 2006.

Biess, Frank. '"Everybody has a Chance": Nuclear Angst, Civil Defence, and the History of Emotions in Post-War West Germany'. *German History* 27 (2009): 215–43.

Blakeley, Karen, and Chris Blakeley. *Leading with Love: Rehumanising the Workplace*. London: Routledge, 2021.

Boddice, Rob. *The Science of Sympathy: Morality, Evolution and Victorian Civilisation*. Springfield, IL: University of Illinois Press, 2016.

Delap, Lucy. *Knowing Their Place: Domestic Service in Twentieth-Century Britain*. Oxford: Oxford University Press, 2011.

Elliott, Jane, and Jon Lawrence. 'The Emotional Economy of Unemployment: A Re-analysis of Testimony from a Sheppey Family, 1978–1983'. *Sage Open* 6 (2016): 1–11.

The Empathy Business (2020). https://theempathybusiness.com/ (accessed 26 April 2021).

Gammerl, Benno. 'Emotional Styles: Concepts and Challenges'. *Rethinking History: The Journal of Theory and Practice* 16 (2012): 161–75.

Hayes, Sarah. 'Industrial Automation and Stress, c. 1945–79'. In *Stress in Postwar Britain*, edited by Mark Jackson, 75–94. Abingdon, Oxford: Routledge, 2015.

Haywood, Rhodri. 'Busman's Stomach and the Embodiment of Modernity'. *Contemporary British History* 31 (2017): 1–23.

Hochschild, Arlie Russell. *The Managed Heart: Commercialization of Human Feeling*. California: University of California Press, 2003 [1983].

Illouz, Eva. *Cold Intimacies: The Making of Emotional Capitalism*. Cambridge: Polity Press, 2007.

Jackson, Mark. *The Age of Stress: Science and the Search for Stability*. Oxford: Oxford University Press, 2013.

Kirby, Jill. *Feeling the Strain: A Cultural History of Stress in Twentieth-Century Britain*. Manchester: Manchester University Press, 2019.

Kirk, John, and Christine Wall. *Work and Identity: Historical and Cultural Contexts*. Basingstoke: Palgrave Macmillan, 2011.

Long, Vicky. *The Rise and Fall of the Healthy Factory: The Politics of Industrial Health in Britain, 1914-1960*. Basingstoke: Palgrave, 2011.

McCarthy, Helen. *Double Lives: A History of Working Motherhood*. London: Bloomsbury, 2020.

McIvor, Arthur, and Ronald Johnston. *Miner's Lung: A History of Coal Dust Disease in Britain*. Abingdon, Oxford: Routledge, 2007.

McIvor, Arthur. *Working Lives: Work in Britain since 1945*. Basingstoke: Palgrave Macmillan, 2013.

McKibbin, Ross. *The Ideologies of Class: Social Relations in Britain, 1880–1950*. Oxford: Oxford University Press, 1990.

Moss, Jonathan. *Women, Workplace Protest and Political Identity in England, 1968–1985*. Manchester: Manchester University Press, 2019.

Pahl, Raymond Edward, ed. *On Work. Historical, Comparative and Theoretical Approaches*. New York, NY: Basil Blackwell, 1988.

Palmer, Deborah. *Who Cared for the Carers?: A History of the Occupational Health of Nurses, 1880–1948*. Manchester: Manchester University Press, 2014.

Pringle, Rosemary. *Secretaries Talk: Sexuality, Power and Work*. London: Verso, 1988.

Reddy, William. *The Navigation of Feeling: A Framework for the History of Emotions*. Cambridge: Cambridge University Press, 2001.

Roper, Michael. *Masculinity and the British Organization Man since 1945*. Oxford: Oxford University Press, 1994.

Rosenwein, Barbara H. *Emotional Communities in the Early Middle Ages*. Ithaca, NY: Cornell University Press, 2006.

Saunders, Jack. *Assembling Cultures: Workplace Activism, Labour Militancy and Cultural Change in Britain's Car Factories, 1945–82*. Manchester: Manchester University Press, 2019.

Scheer, Monique. 'Are Emotions a Kind of Practice (and is that what makes them have a history?) A Bourdieuian Approach to Understanding Emotion'. *History and Theory* 51 (2012): 193–220.

Sharpe, Sue. *Double Identity: The Lives of Working Mothers*. London: Penguin Books, 1984.

Index

academia 1, 4, 7, 133, 135–7, 139, 206, 230, 237, 259
activism 12, 40, 82, 179, 208, 243–5
 activists 4, 10, 40, 82, 207, 209, 243, 245
 animal rights 7, 186
 childcare 237, 238
 political 7, 105
age 21, 43, 44, 53, 63, 155
 infantilizing 23, 39, 43
Ahmedabad 7, 8, 76–95, 258–9
anti-vivisection 173–93
Argentina 8, 11, 117, 121, 123
authenticity 109, 218, 221, 222, 226

Brazil 151–69
Buenos Aires 117–32, 258
business 9, 28, 42, 45, 47, 154, 156, 160, 199, 203, 222, 246
 retail 41, 45
 small 238
Butler, Judith 225, 226

Cambridge 133–50, 178
canine suffering 183, 184, 186
capitalism 10, 101, 107, 110, 203, 204, 216
 affective 158
 capitalist realism 222–6
 emotional 160, 257
 neoliberal 215, 229, see also neoliberalism
careers 70, 133, 145, 158, 159, 162, 163, 229
 career advancement 64, 70, 140, 206
career women 151–69
carers 4, 234–5, 238–47
children 42, 47, 59, 64, 84, 103, 105, 120, 122, 125, 144, 155, 163, 184, 234–7, 259
 childcare 4, 9, 159, 234–54, 258
 childminders 237, 241
 child rearing 243
China 8

Christianity 88, 179, 203
class 4, 9, 21, 23, 29, 37, 39, 41, 43, 49, 53, 60, 77, 79, 100, 104–5, 110, 120–6, 155, 159, 164, 180, 218, 234, 237, 241, 256, 257
 middle class 21, 37, 41, 49, 53, 84–6, 121–3, 126, 155, 234, 237, 241, 257
 working class 20, 23, 29, 37, 49, 60, 78, 86–90, 123, 180, 237
consumer 22, 30
consumer society 19
consumption 20, 38, 49

deindustrialization 7, 76–8, 84, 86, 88, 90
distress 99, 107, 108, 110, 184, 185
doctors 5, 39, 178–81, 197, 206
domesticity 9, 11, 80, 84, 153
domestic labour 7, 102, 118, 255
domestic service 7–9, 26, 30, 39, 117, 119, 121, 123, 126, 127, 257, 259

early career researchers 1
education 6, 60, 65–7, 69, 70, 84, 99–110, 136
efficiency 22, 24, 27, 60, 79, 204, 227, 228
emotional communities 8, 11, 12, 49, 58, 101, 102, 126, 134, 174, 175, 177–9, 180, 181, 183–6, 258, 259
emotional health 3, 5, 10, 37, 38, 45, 47, 52, 53, 59, 69, 259
emotional labour 3–4, 9, 12, 19, 22, 23, 29, 30, 42, 127, 133, 175, 215–18, 222, 224, 226, 228, 229, 234–6, 239, 240, 242, 247, 256, 257, 259
emotional liberty 3, 20
emotional regimes 1, 3, 5, 20, 40, 42, 258
emotional suffering 3, 20, 175
eroticism 20, 26
ethnicity 9, 27, 80
ethnography 239
 activist 243

family   11, 42, 43, 45, 64, 78, 82, 84, 99, 107, 117–20, 125, 135, 136, 146, 151, 153, 179, 209, 236, 241
femininity   3, 19, 21, 23, 25–8, 30, 39, 80, 84, 126, 151, 152, 155–63
feminism   59, 151, 153, 155–7, 160, 164, 173, 175, 179, 234–6, 239, 240, 242, 243, 245–7
Ford, Henry   227
France   11, 176, 177, 179, 187
friendship   7, 8, 39, 42, 47–50, 53, 62, 67, 68, 89, 107, 158, 185

gender   3, 4, 6, 8–10, 19, 21, 23, 26, 29, 30, 39, 43, 53, 59, 63, 71, 101, 109, 110, 120, 121, 124, 126, 135, 136, 139, 141, 152–6, 159, 160, 163, 164, 175, 181, 225, 226, 236, 239–42, 245, 256, 257
geodesy   133–50
glamour   6, 21, 24–7
Goffman, Erving   219, 225

harmony   77, 78, 82, 87–90, 205
health care   1, 58–61, 63, 69, 70, 72, 196
Hinduism   76, 86–90
Hindu nationalism   76, 90
Hochschild, Arlie   3, 4, 20, 30, 135, 139, 215–19, 222, 224–6, 256, 257
holiday   48, 106, 140, 246, see also vacation
home   4, 8, 11, 40–2, 44, 49, 58–64, 72, 79, 80, 83, 84, 120, 122, 124, 125, 127, 153, 179, 209, 234–7, 239, 241–4, 247, 259
homosexuality   20, 21, 153
hospitals   11, 39, 40, 58–75, 186, 195, 197, 200–2, 258
housework   117, see also domestic labour
humanitarianism   173, 175, 178, 180–2, 184

imposter syndrome   110, 111, 145
India   7, 11, 76, 77, 81, 87, 90
individualism   4, 9, 10, 240, 247
industrial   20, 21, 59, 76–8, 82, 85, 86, 90, 106, 227, 228
industrial action, see strikes
industrialization   101, 227
insecurity   7, 9, 102, 133, 134, 136, 142, 146

instability   10
Islam   80, 81, 87–9, 112

journalism   123, 152, 157, 161
Judaism   27

laboratories   133, 174, 177, 180–2, 186
leadership   86, 151, 152, 154, 156–60, 162, 164, 207
London   6, 21, 27, 38, 41, 43, 44, 52, 60, 62, 64, 174, 176, 177, 179, 186, 258

magazines   9, 152, 154–6, 158–60, 162, 163
marriage   6, 9, 19, 25, 30, 59, 62–6, 117, 120, 151
masculinity   3, 9, 39, 48, 63, 84, 90, 135, 153, 158, 162, 178, 257
media   23, 151, 152, 154, 155, 158, 163, 164, 196, 209, 243, 258
memory   22, 23, 26, 29, 77, 87–8, 135, 146, 223, 259
migrants   88, 239, 241, 246
militancy   78, 82, 90

nannies   4, 159, 235, 236, 238–41, 243
National Health Service   6, 60, 62, 68–72, 194–7, 199–202, 207, 208
Naturalism   220, 223
neoliberalism   133, 160, 164, 215, 234–6, 239, 240, 243, 245–7
New York   6, 174, 177, 179–82, 184–6, 223, 258
non-violence   79, 87, 89
nostalgia   7, 8, 19, 29, 49, 52, 53, 72, 77, 79, 84, 87–90
nursery workers   4, 236, 238
nurses   39, 58–62, 68–70, 126, 194

older people   84, 85, 107
oral history   7, 58, 61, 77, 82, 84, 118, 134–6, 142, 144–6, 257

parasexuality   25
parents   4, 43, 136–8, 234–41, 243, 246, 247
Paris   6, 26, 174, 176, 177, 179, 180, 183, 186, 258

Index

pay   7, 10, 29, 37, 46, 58, 84, 104–6, 113, 119–22, 124–8, 197, 216, 237, 238, 244, 246, 259
pay inequality   103
pension   104, 216, 246
pleasure   1, 5, 7, 12, 20, 43, 46–9, 52, 53, 133, 256
post-feminism   151, 154, 160
post-industrial   76, 157, 216, 236, 241, 242
precarity   6, 10, 77, 84, 159, 241, 242, 245, 259
professional identity   1, 6, 10, 11, 59, 206, 207
professionalism   5, 66, 206
professionalization   60, 238
Protestantism   203

queer sexual encounters   20
queer sociability   27

race   9, 10, 27, 68, 121, 122, 152, 159, 160, 164, 173, 181, 185, 241, 242, 245, 246, 256
realism   218, 220–2, 229
Reddy, William   3, 20, 40, 258
religion   8, 9, 63, 78, 80, 81, 87, 103, 104, 109, 203
remuneration, *see* pay
resilience   5, 10, 84, 236
respectability   7, 23, 26, 27, 30, 43, 44, 46, 60, 79, 85, 87, 89, 126, 127

salary   37, 106, 108, 118, 121, 140, *see also* pay
science   133–50, 157, 173–93, 257
Scientific Management   227
seclusion   8, 51
self-care   5, 234
sex appeal   9, 25
sexuality   9, 20, 26, 63
sex work   25, 27, 32, 50, 51
shop assistants   37–57, *see also* shop workers
shops   11, 38, 43, 52
shop workers   21, 37–40, 44–6, 52, 258, *see also* shop assistants

sociability   8, 9, 20, 27, 49, 51, 53, 154, 258
social media   234–49
social science   133, 153
solitude   48, 51–3, 258
Soviet Union   7, 100–2, 107, 112, 258
Stanislavski, Constantin   4, 215–29
status shield   135, 139
stress   39, 59, 161, 216, 244, 257
strikes   78, 79, 82, 236, 238, 240, 243–5
suicide   76, 83, 108, 144

Taylor, Frederick Winslow   227
Taylorism, *see* Taylor
textile mills   8, 76–95, 258
theatre   4, 10, 47, 50, 215, 216, 220, 223, 227–9
theatre studies   10, 215–33
trade unionism   2, 38, 40, 76, 78, 83, 86–8, 90, 235, 242, 244
transnational   4, 174, 175, 177, 179, 180, 186, 255, 259

uncertainty   10
uniforms   21, 23, 26–9
United States   8, 9, 11, 136, 177, 179, 180, 238
university   11, 133–6, 139, 141, 176, 180, 181, 186

vacation   48, 120, 121, 127, 128, *see also* holiday
violence   78, 85–90, 164, 181, 243, 244
violence, domestic   152, 243
vivisection   173–93

waitress   21–5, 28
well-being   3, 5, 49, 51, 69, 72
wellness   5
whistleblowing   6, 194–214
work-life balance   11, 45, 53, 59, 72, 242, 257, 258

youth   21, 23, 28, 42–4, 47, 49, 53, 58, 60–4, 66, 86, 87, 136, 140, 155

zero-hour contracts   59, 259
Zoom   259

Printed in the USA
CPSIA information can be obtained
at www.ICGtesting.com
LVHW011525230224
772666LV00002B/126